Archbishop Sheen's Book of Sacraments

Also by Fulton J. Sheen
from Sophia Institute Press:

Victory over Vice

Fulton Sheen's Wartime Prayer Book

God's World and Our Place in It

The Cries of Jesus from the Cross

Lord, Teach Us to Pray

Archbishop Fulton J. Sheen

Archbishop Sheen's Book of Sacraments

These Are the Sacraments

and

Three to Get Married

Edited by Al Smith

SOPHIA INSTITUTE PRESS
Manchester, New Hampshire

Sophia Institute Press
Box 5284, Manchester, NH 03108
1-800-888-9344

www.SophiaInstitute.com

Sophia Institute Press® is a registered trademark of Sophia Institute.

paperback ISBN 978-1-64413-459-7
ebook ISBN 978-1-64413-460-3

First printing

To the Blessed Virgin Mary
who taught the sublime mystery of Love,
and who at Cana instructed us,
"Whatsoever he shall say to you, do ye."

—John 2:5

Contents

These Are the Sacraments

Three to Get Married

Introduction

When referring to the sacraments of the Catholic Church, a contemporary of the Venerable Fulton Sheen, Servant of God, Fr. John Hardon, S.J., wrote in these most unambiguous terms: "It is impossible to exaggerate the importance of understanding what we mean by the sacraments as channels of divine grace. We might almost say that Christianity is divided into two classes: those who believe that Christ instituted the sacraments as instruments of His grace and those who do not."

Fr. Hardon continued: "There are those who still believe that Christ instituted seven channels of His grace and those who may use the word 'sacrament' but no longer believe either in the sacraments as communicators of grace or the Church's authority over the sacraments. We may even say that the future of Christianity depends on professed Christians understanding — and I mean understanding — the necessity of the sacraments for reaching eternal life."

"When Christ told us," he added, "'without me, you can do nothing,' He meant this literally. Without the grace which He gives through the sacraments which He instituted, we cannot hope to remain Christians or Catholics or, least of all, channels of His wisdom to those whom we are instructing in the one true Faith on which depends the salvation of the world."

Archbishop Sheen's Book of Sacraments

Archbishop Fulton J. Sheen, who knew full well the necessity of the sacraments as channels of God's grace for the sanctification of souls, shared these deep sentiments of Fr. Hardon. He spent countless hours instructing souls in the rudiments of the Faith individually and in presentations to large classes of catechumens. Sheen desired to bring souls to the knowledge of the Catholic Faith and the graces that one can receive through the sacraments of the Catholic Church.

Archbishop Sheen gave three reasons why non-Catholics turn to the Church: (1) a moral crisis, especially the consciousness of sin and the desire of forgiveness, which the sacraments of the Church assure them; (2) an intellectual crisis when people who have wandered for years in the desert of agnosticism suddenly realize that in the Catholic Faith are to be found that conviction of mind and peace of soul which they had been searching for elsewhere in vain; (3) a physical crisis such as illness, an accident or the loss of a loved one by desertion or death, when they realize that only in the teachings of the Church can they find that courage and strength of will which they need to carry their cross in conformity to the will of God. Sheen, the consummate pastor of souls, was ever on the lookout for the lost sheep, not hesitating to call them on the phone or visit them personally.

Sheen's record of bringing souls to Christ is unprecedented. It has been noted that the Catholic Church doubled her numbers in the United States of America in the 1950s. Much of this growth has been attributed to Sheen's very successful television series *Life Is Worth Living*, where each week millions tuned in to hear him speak about social concerns of the day as well as matters of faith and morals.

Sheen had the attention of millions via the medium of television, while millions more were enjoying his books and his weekly syndicated column featured in newspapers for thirty years.

Of his sixty-six books, a number of them focus on the sacraments and the teachings of the Church. Books such as *The Priest Is Not His Own* (1963) and *Those Mysterious Priests* (1974) speak to the Sacrament of Holy Orders. In 1965, Sheen compiled a catechism series of fifty lessons, taking an inner look at a soul's sacred journey back to God. This

Introduction

series of talks is known as the "Life Is Worth Living" catechism and is sometimes referred to as the "Sheen Catechism." Written for people of all ages and religious backgrounds, Sheen answers life's most profound questions, while explaining how one can find spiritual contentment in the modern world by applying the Christian philosophy of life. His presentation of doctrine is both biblical and liturgical, with hundreds of scriptural references.

Aiming at bringing to today's reader the legacy of Archbishop Sheen's knowledge, this present collection of writings consists of two of Sheen's most memorable books on the sacraments and Matrimony. In the first part, the reader will find Sheen's 1962 book *These Are the Sacraments*. Here he explains the meaning of the sacraments, their power, and their application. Each sacrament is clearly and eloquently explained in Archbishop Sheen's impressive commentary.

The depth of meaning of each sacrament and its significance in the life of the Church and of the individual are compellingly evoked in the well-chosen prayers. Archbishop Sheen writes in his inimitable style, with immediacy, yet conveying joy and comfort in the subject matter.

In the second part of this collection of writings, the reader will find a book that has touched the lives of hundreds of thousands of souls: Sheen's *Three to Get Married*. Here, Archbishop Sheen eloquently speaks of the indispensable place of God in the union of a husband and his wife for a happy and fruitful marriage.

First published in 1951, this book illustrates why Archbishop Fulton Sheen is considered by many to be a modern-day prophet. Some may hesitate to call the book easy reading, largely because with every other sentence, one needs to pause to let the content sink in. Here, Sheen's insights are both quotable and timeless.

Although many will agree with other reviewers that this book should be required reading for every engaged couple, it also serves as a great resource in understanding the meaning of marriage. It is likewise a great read for couples as they begin this new and exciting phase of their life together, providing them with great insights and tried-and-true spiritual strategies.

Archbishop Sheen's Book of Sacraments

As a pastor of souls for over sixty years, Archbishop Sheen would undoubtedly concur with Fr. John Hardon's sentiment: "Without Christ, we can do nothing." This present volume will impress upon the reader our Lord's desire to "give Himself away" in the seven sacraments of the Catholic Church and why they are indispensable channels of divine grace for the salvation of one's soul.

The Sacraments: Divine Channels of Grace

by Fr. John A. Hardon, S.J.

It is impossible to exaggerate the importance of understanding what we mean by the sacraments as channels of divine grace. We might almost say that Christianity is divided into two classes: those who believe that Christ instituted the sacraments as instruments of His grace and those who do not. In the sixteenth century, six whole nations separated from Catholic unity because their leaders no longer believed in what we Catholics call the seven sacraments.

This is also part of the crisis in the Christian world today. There are those who still believe that Christ instituted seven channels of His grace and those who may use the word "sacrament" but no longer believe either in the sacraments as communicators of grace or the Church's authority over the sacraments. We may even say that the future of Christianity depends on professed Christians understanding—and I mean understanding—the necessity of the sacraments for reaching eternal life.

Our focus in this article will be on one word, "understanding." We ask ourselves three questions: Why did Christ institute seven sacramental channels of grace? How are these channels of grace being undermined in some professedly Catholic circles today? What is our consequent duty as teachers of the true Faith?

Why the Sacraments

God became man in order to bring the human race to join the Holy Trinity in a heavenly eternity. Our destiny is to return to the God from whom we came to share in His own perfect happiness that He enjoys. But this same God gave us a free will that we are to use, according to His will, in order to reach the celestial home where He is waiting for us.

The most fundamental condition that we are to fulfill is to be in His friendship when He calls us from time into eternity. Another name for this divine friendship is the possession of sanctifying grace. Having destined us for heavenly beatitude, in sheer justice, He provided us with the means of attaining what we call the Beatific Vision.

On these terms, the sacraments are the principal ways that we can obtain the supernatural life, without which no one can be saved.[1] It is also through the sacraments that we grow in this life of grace, as it is also the sacraments that provide us with a means of restoring the life of God's friendship that we may have lost through grave sin. We see immediately that Christ instituted the sacraments to give us the grace we need to reach Heaven, to grow in His grace and thus earn a greater happiness in eternity, and regain His friendship if we have lost it through our disobedience to His will.

The moment we say that the sacraments are channels of divine grace, we assume that we come into this world without the grace needed to reach Heaven. It is not our purpose here to explore the mysterious providence of God in allowing so many people not to receive the sacraments which Christ instituted. There is such a thing as not receiving the sacraments actually but only in desire. Nevertheless, the basic principle remains: the sacraments are the means which Christ provided for the salvation of the human family. Immediately certain conclusions follow. Each of the seven sacraments has its own divinely intended purpose.

---

[1] The Church teaches, "*God has bound salvation to the sacrament of Baptism, but he himself is not bound by his sacraments*" (CCC 1257, emphasis in original). For more on salvation, including the possible salvation of non-Catholics, please see CCC 846–848; 1257–1261.

The Sacraments: Divine Channels of Grace

Baptism

We need, first of all, to receive a share in the divine life. Christ instituted the Sacrament of Baptism in order to provide us with a share in His own divinity. When Christ told Nicodemus that he must be reborn of water and the Holy Spirit, He meant this literally. He presumed that we have a principle of natural life for the body, which is the human soul. What He revealed to the wondering Nicodemus, however, was that we are also to have an above-natural principle of life for the soul. St. Augustine called it the soul of the soul. But whatever name you give the source of life for the human spirit, we dare not question that Christ provided the means of obtaining this life. The basic means is the Sacrament of Baptism. The Savior could not have been clearer. When Nicodemus pressed Him on what all of this means, Jesus used the strongest language at His command. He said, "Unless you are reborn of water and the Holy Spirit, you shall not reach the kingdom of heaven" (John 3:5).

The Holy Eucharist and Penance

Once He told us that we need Baptism to receive the life of grace in our souls, Christ made sure that we also know how to preserve this life to the dawn of eternity. Three chapters later, in St. John's Gospel, the Savior told His startled listeners that they needed to receive His Flesh and Blood to keep spiritually alive. No less than we need food and drink to sustain our natural lives do we need the food and drink of the Holy Eucharist to stay alive in His grace. Again, He used the strongest language possible: "Unless you eat the flesh of the Son of Man and drink His blood, you shall not have life in you" (John 6:54 [53]).[2] Baptism is necessary to obtain a share in the life of God. The Eucharist is equally necessary to remain spiritually alive. Christ foresaw that His followers would sin and even lose the divine life. He, therefore, provided the means for restoring this life in the Sacrament of Penance, which He instituted on Easter Sunday night.

---

[2] Verse numbers given in brackets indicate the numbering used in other translations.

Holy Orders

The Church which Christ founded is a visible reality. It is no mere abstraction or a poetic society of believers or the predestined. During His visible stay on earth, He was Himself the channel of the graces that He gave those who believed in His name. But Christ's mission of communicating grace was to continue after His return to heavenly glory. That is why He made sure that the Church He founded would continue the work He had begun. That is why at the Last Supper, He instituted two sacraments, the Holy Eucharist and the priesthood, which would ensure His continued bodily presence on earth and His communication of the fruits of Calvary through the Sacrifice of the Mass.

Holy Matrimony

Most of Christ's followers would be married. As He told the startled Pharisees, those who believed in Him would be expected to remain "two in one flesh" for the rest of their lives (Matt. 19:4–6). No more polygamy or a writ of divorce with the right to remarry. Lifelong monogamy would be an imperative for those who called themselves Christians. Clearly, Christ had to give His married followers the superhuman grace they would need to remain faithful to His teaching. Matrimony, therefore, had to become a sacrament if Christians were to live an impossibly human life in the married state.

Confirmation

Throughout the Gospels, Jesus made no secret of the strength His followers would need to remain firm in their faith. That is why He gave them the Sacrament of Confirmation. Over the centuries, it has been called the sacrament of spiritual strengthening. In our day, it is being seen as the sacrament of martyrdom. As He told the disciples, on the day of His Ascension, we are to witness to Him, literally be His "martyrs" (from the Greek word for "witnesses") even to the ends of the earth (Acts 1:8).

The Sacraments: Divine Channels of Grace

Anointing of the Sick

As our bodies approach the end of their days, our souls need the help that only Christ can give to enter eternity with peaceful confidence in God's mercy. That is why we have the Sacrament of the Anointing of the Sick. As only priests would know, people who are facing bodily death need extraordinary assistance from the Savior. This sacrament, we may say, completes the work that Christ began when we were baptized.

Catholic Sacraments Undermined

Over the centuries of the Church's history, the sacraments have been one of the principal targets of what we now call dissenters but what more accurately are heretics who deny one or more of the cardinal mysteries of the Catholic Faith. Already in the time of Christ, many of His disciples left the Master because they would not accept His teaching on the Real Presence of the living Christ in the Blessed Sacrament. For the next fifteen centuries, one after another of the sacraments instituted by Christ was either openly denied or so re-interpreted as to leave nothing but the name. Finally in the sixteenth century, an avalanche of anti-sacramentalism broke loose in one formerly Catholic country after another.

It was only logical, therefore, that the Council of Trent issued the following condemnation: "If anyone says that the sacraments of the New Law are more or less than seven, namely: Baptism, Confirmation, the Eucharist, Penance, Extreme Unction, Order, and Matrimony; or even that any of these seven is not truly and properly a sacrament, let him be anathema."

Needless to say, the followers of Luther, Calvin, Zwingli, and Cranmer did not change their minds. Their underlying reason for rejecting the sacraments was the more fundamental premise of absolute predestination. Those will reach Heaven who have been predetermined to be saved. The very meaning of "grace" was changed. Instead of being a free gift of God's mercy that we are to accept and cooperate with, grace was redefined as the selective mercy of God which those receive who are destined to be saved.

Even more basic than the theory of absolute predestination was the denial of a supernatural life. Man was never elevated to a share in the divine life. On these terms, there could be no question of receiving the supernatural life through Baptism, or restoring this life through Penance, or nourishing this life through the Holy Eucharist. Even when the word "sacrament" might be used, a large part of world Christianity, outside of Roman Catholicism, no longer believes either that Christ instituted the sacraments or that we need them for our salvation.

However, a new phenomenon has entered Christian history in our day. A growing number of still-professed-Catholic writers are reinterpreting the Church's teaching on the sacraments with a license and a devastating consequence that has no counterpart in the last half-millennium. I will never forget the conference of the Midwestern Theological Society I attended. The keynote speaker was Fr. Richard McBrien. Through one hour of learned discourse, he gave the audience one reason after another why the Catholic priesthood was not a sacrament instituted by our Lord at the Last Supper. It was a later-second-century innovation. A logical consequence of this position is to question whether Christ had instituted any of the sacraments.

One of the most prestigious universities on the east coast is currently teaching a course which identifies the supernatural with mythology. In fact, more than one dictionary describes the supernatural as the unreal or the fanciful.

We cannot overstate the widespread elimination of faith in the sacraments as channels of divine grace in some still nominally Catholic circles. The widespread desecration of the Holy Eucharist as the sacrament of Christ's physical presence now on earth through the Sacrament of the Eucharist; the massive departure from the priesthood of so many men who had received the Sacrament of Holy Orders; the nationwide, in our country, and the worldwide international drop in Confession; the closing of over one hundred parishes in just two dioceses in a few years; the epidemic of annulments of persons who putatively received the Sacrament of Matrimony: all of these are symptomatic of a plague of sacramental error that threatens to undermine the Catholic Church in one so-called developed country after another.

The Sacraments: Divine Channels of Grace

We are now reading books and magazines and hearing of classes and lectures that threaten the very essence of our sacramental faith. As we read these publications and listen to these talks, one thing becomes clear: there is a massive loss of faith not only in the sacraments but in the supernatural life which the sacraments are to confer and strengthen in our lives. We are being told that the sacraments were not instituted by Christ but invented by Christians over a period of several centuries. What we call the sacraments, it is said, goes back to the ancient religions of pre-Christian times. The rituals that we call sacraments today are simply a continuation of what all the religions celebrated long before Christianity was born. Every sacrament of Catholic Christianity is being traced to its pre-Christian history. Washing with water, the breaking and sharing of bread, the pouring and drinking of wine, anointing with oil, laying on of hands to bless and ordain, calling down divine power, pronouncing words of forgiveness: all of these are as ancient as religious history and were practiced long before the word sacrament was even used in religious discourse.

On these grounds, it would be not only mistaken but deceptive to associate and, much less, identify the sacraments with the ritual of the Catholic Church. To speak of the Church founded by Christ as the universal sacrament of salvation is at best a misnomer and at worst a blasphemy. Christ had no claim, we are told, on our human destiny. Nor does the Church He is said to have founded have any monopoly on the goodness of God.

Those who deny the divine origin of the Christian sacraments appeal to such geniuses as Fr. Karl Rahner. Building on his premises, they claim it is impossible to say that God's grace depends on the Church which Christ founded. The Church, people are told, has no rules or regulations, no imperatives, no prohibitions. It is emphatically not the clergy, nor the sacramental ritual, nor the worship by the people in sacramental celebration. All of these are adjuncts or, if you wish, superfluous additions to what Christianity really is. It is the living event of God's presence. It is people, no matter what their religious beliefs or practices may be, who constitute "The People of God." They have been touched by God, are

11

loved by Him and belong to Him, regardless of what religion they profess or even if they have no religion at all.

On these terms the "sacraments" are not channels of divine grace. Bread and wine, oil and water, sex and prayer are themselves the expressions of authentic Christianity.

Behind this reassessment of the sacraments, the new theologians are appealing to what they call "the spirit of the Second Vatican Council." They are heartened by the use of names like "liturgy" and "eucharist" and "eucharistic celebration" as substitutes for the supposedly outdated word, "Mass." They do not hesitate to accuse Catholics of seeing a magical significance in the number of sacraments. They take comfort in the widespread practice of "general absolution" instead of making a private confession of one's sins to the priest.

Our Responsibility

Pope John Paul II introduces the *Catechism of the Catholic Church* by declaring, "Guarding the deposit of faith is the mission which the Lord entrusted to His Church and which she fulfills in every age."

As believing Christians, loyal to the Vicar of Christ, our first responsibility is to guard the deposit of faith in the sacraments for which Christ became man to give us the grace we need to reach eternal life. This guarding of the sacramental faith carries with it a number of grave obligations.

We cannot begin to guard our faith unless we understand what we believe. In Christ's parable of the good seed which fell on different kinds of ground, the first infertile soil was the pathway. The seed fell on the hard ground and the birds of the air came along and picked up the seed. This, we are told, is what happens to those who have been given the true Faith but fail to understand what they believe. The result is tragedy. The devil comes along and steals the Faith from the hearts of once-professed believers.

Ours is the most academically educated age of human history. The five million Americans on college campuses every year are only a symbol of the widespread growth in knowledge in our day. But this growth in secular knowledge will not only do no good. It will destroy the faith of once-believing Catholics if they have not used their minds to grow in grasping what they believe. They must grow in understanding the meaning of their faith. They must grow in the clarity of mind in seeing the subtle distinctions hidden behind their faith. They must grow in the certitude of what they profess to believe. They must grow in knowing how to defend this faith in the face of opposition that is sweeping across the Catholic world like a demonic hurricane.

But understanding the Faith is not enough. The sacraments will become for them what they have become for so many others, unless they put their faith into daily practice. We believe that the Sacrament of the Eucharist, as sacrifice, communion, and presence is nothing less than Jesus Christ alive and active on earth to provide us with the light and strength we need, especially to practice that charity by which we are recognized as His disciples. To remain faithful Catholics in today's self-intoxicated world we must expect to practice heroic generosity and heroic patience, which are impossible without the superhuman strength that only Jesus Christ in the Holy Eucharist can give us.

We asked what is our duty as teachers of the true Faith in an atmosphere that is clouded to the point of blindness on the meaning of the sacraments. We shall be as faithful teachers of the true Faith as we are courageous in explaining this Faith, without compromise and without fear of the consequences. To teach the Catholic Faith on the sacraments can literally mean living a martyr's life.

In Pope John Paul II's masterful encyclical, *The Splendor of Truth*, we are told to understand the Faith, as it has been entrusted by Christ to His Church, and proclaim this faith with heroic courage even at the cost of martyrdom.

When Christ told us, "Without me you can do nothing," He meant this literally. Without the grace which He gives through the sacraments which He instituted, we cannot hope to remain Christians or Catholics or, least of all, channels of His wisdom to those whom we are instructing in the one true Faith on which depends the salvation of the world.

These Are the Sacraments

Introduction

The Sacraments

A Divine Sense of Humor

No one can ever understand the sacraments unless he has what might be called a "divine sense of humor." A person is said to have a sense of humor if he can "see through" things; one lacks a sense of humor if he cannot "see through" things. No one has ever laughed at a pun who did not see in the one word a twofold meaning. To materialists this world is opaque like a curtain; nothing can be seen through it. A mountain is just a mountain, a sunset just a sunset; but to poets, artists, and saints, the world is transparent like a windowpane; it tells of something beyond; for example, a mountain tells of the power of God, the sunset of His Beauty, and the snowflake of His Purity.

When the Lord Incarnate walked this earth, He brought to it what might be called a "divine sense of humor." There is only one thing that He took seriously, and that was the soul. He said: "What exchange shall a man give for his soul?" Everything else was a tell-tale of something else. Sheep and goats, wine bottles and patches on clothing, camels and eyes of needles, the lightning flash and the red of the sunset sky, the fisherman's nets and Caesar's coin, chalices and rich men's gates—all of these were turned into parables and made to tell the story of the Kingdom of God.

Our Lord had a divine sense of humor, because He revealed that the universe was sacramental. A sacrament, in a very broad sense of the term, combines two elements: one visible, the other invisible — one that can be seen, or tasted, or touched, or heard; the other unseen to the eyes of the flesh. There is, however, some kind of relation or significance between the two. A spoken word is a kind of sacrament, because there is something material or audible about it; there is also something spiritual about it, namely, its meaning. A horse can hear a funny story just as well as a man. It is conceivable that the horse may hear the words better than the man and at the end of the story the man may laugh, but the horse will never give a horse laugh. The reason is that the horse gets only the material side of the "sacrament," namely, the sound; but the man gets the invisible or the spiritual side, namely, the meaning.

A handshake is a kind of sacrament, because there is something seen and felt, namely, the clasping of hands; but there is something mysterious and unseen, namely, the communication of friendship. A kiss is a kind of sacrament: the physical side of it is present if one kisses one's own hand, but the spiritual side of it is missing because there is no sign of affection for another. One of the reasons why a stolen kiss is often resented is that it is not sacramental; it has the carnal side without a spiritual side; that is, the willingness to exchange a mark of esteem or affection.

This book on the sacraments is written because men live in a world that has become entirely too serious. Gold is gold, nuclear warfare is nuclear warfare, dust is dust, money is money. No significance or meaning is seen in the things that make a sound to the ear, or a sight to the eye. In a world without a divine sense of humor, architecture loses decoration and people lose courtesy in their relationships with one another.

When civilization was permeated with a happier philosophy, when things were seen as signs of outward expression of the unseen, architecture was enhanced with a thousand decorations: a pelican feeding her young from her own veins symbolized the sacrifice of Christ; the gargoyle peering from behind a pillar in a cathedral reminded us that temptations are to be found even in the most holy places. Our Lord, on the occasion of His planned entrance into Jerusalem, said that if men withheld their praise of Him, "the very stones would cry out" (Luke 19:40), which they did as, later, they burst into Gothic cathedrals.

The Sacraments

Now the stones are silent, for modern man no longer believes in another world; they have no story to tell, no meaning to convey, no truth to illustrate. When faith in the spiritual is lost, architecture has nothing to symbolize; similarly, when men lose the conviction of the immortal soul, there is a decline in the respect for the human. Man without a soul is a thing; something to be used, not something to be reverenced. He becomes "functional" like a building, or a monkey wrench, or a wheel. The courtesies, the amenities, the urbanities, the gentility that one mortal ought to have for another are neglected once man is no longer seen as bearing within himself the divine image. Courtesy is not a condescension of a superior to an inferior, or a patronizing interest in another's affairs; it is the homage of the heart to the sacredness of human worth. Courtesy is born of holiness, as ornamentation is born of the sense of the holy. Let us see if ornamentation returns to architecture, if courtesy also returns to human manners; for by one and the same stroke, men will have lost their dull seriousness, and will begin to live in a sacramental universe with a divine sense of humor.

Life is a vertical dimension expressed in the soaring spire, or in the leaping fountain, both of which suggest that earth, history, and nature must be left behind to seek union with the Eternal. Opposite to this is an error which substitutes the horizontal for the vertical, the prostrate form of death for the upright stature of life. It is the disease of secularity and of naturalism. It insists on the ultimacy of the seen and the temporal, and the meaninglessness of the spiritual and the invisible.

Two errors can mar our understanding of the natural world: one is to cut off entirely from Almighty God; the other is to confound it substantially with Him. In the first instance, we have the clock without the clock maker, the painting without the artist, the verse without the poet. In the second instance, we have the forger and the forged rolled into one, the melting and the fusing of the murderer and the victim, the boiling of the cook and his dinner. Atheism cuts off creation from its Creator; pantheism identifies nature with God. The true notion is that the material universe is a sign or an indication of what God is. We look at the purity of the snowflake and we see something of the goodness of God. The world is full of poetry: it is sin which turns it into prose.

The Bible Is a Sacramental

Coming closer to the meaning of sacrament, the Bible is a sacramental in the sense that it has a foreground and a background. In the foreground are the actors, the cult, the Temple, the wars, the sufferings, and the glories of men. In the background, however, is the all-pervading presence of God as the Chief Actor, who subjects nations to judgment according to their obedience or disobedience to the moral law, and who uses incidents or historical facts as types, or symbols, of something else that will happen. For example, take the brazen serpent in the desert. When the Jewish people were bitten by poisonous serpents, God commanded Moses to make a brazen serpent, and to hang it over the crotch of a tree; all who would look upon that serpent of brass would be healed of the serpent's sting. This apparently was a rather ridiculous remedy for poison and not everyone looked on it. If one could divine or guess their reason, it would probably be because they concentrated on only one side of the symbol; namely, the lifeless, shiny, brass thing hanging on a tree. But it proved to be a symbol of faith: God used that material thing as a symbol of trust or faith in Him.

The symbolism goes still further. The Old Testament is fulfilled in Christ, who reveals the full mystery of the brazen serpent. Our Lord told Nicodemus that the brass serpent was lifted up in the desert, so that He would have to be lifted up on a Cross. The meaning now became clear: the brass serpent in the desert *looked* like the serpent that bit the people; but though it *seemed* to be the same, it was actually *without* any poison. Our Blessed Lord now says that He is like that brazen serpent. He, too, would be lifted up on the crotch of a tree, a Cross. He would look as if He Himself was filled with the poison of sin, for His body would bear the marks, and the stings, and the piercing of sin; and yet as the brass serpent was without poison so He would be without sin. As those who looked upon that brass serpent in the desert in faith were healed of the bite of the serpent, so all who would look upon Him on His Cross bearing the sins and poisons of the world would also be healed of the poison of the serpent, Satan.

The Sacraments

The word "sacrament" in Greek means "mystery," and Christ has been called by St. Paul "the mystery hidden from the ages." In Him is something divine, something human; something eternal, something temporal; something invisible, something visible. The mystery of Bethlehem was the Son of God taking upon Himself a human nature to unite human nature and divine nature in one Person. He who, in the language of Scripture, could stop the turning about of the Arcturus, had the prophecy of His birthplace determined, however unconsciously, by a Caesar ordering an imperial census. He who clothed the fields with grass, Himself was clothed with swaddling bands. He from whose hands came planets and worlds had tiny arms that were not quite long enough to touch the huge heads of the cattle. He who trod the everlasting hills was too weak to walk. The Eternal Word was dumb. The Bird that built the nest of the world was hatched therein.

The human nature of our Blessed Lord had no power to sanctify of and by itself; that is to say, apart from its union with divinity. But because of that union, the humanity of Christ became the efficient cause of our justification and sanctification and will be until the end of the world. Herein is hidden a hint of the sacraments. The humanity of Christ was the bearer of divine life and the means of making men holy; the sacraments were also to become the effective signs of the sanctification purchased by His death. As our Blessed Lord was the sensible sign of God, so the sacraments were to become the sensible signs of the grace which our Lord had won for us.

If men were angels or pure spirits, there would have been no need of Christ using human natures or material things for the communication of the divine; but because man is composed of matter and spirit, body and soul, man functions best when he sees the material as the revealer of the spiritual. From the very beginning of man's life, his mother's fondling is not merely to leave an impress upon his infant body, but rather to communicate the sublimely beautiful and invisible love of the mother. It is not the material thing which a man values, but rather what is *signified* by the material thing. As Thomas à Kempis said, "regard not so much the gift of the lover as the love of the giver." We tear price tags from gifts so that there will be no material relationship existing between the love that gave the thing and the thing itself. If man had no soul or spiritual destiny, then communism would satisfy. If man were only a biological organism, then he would be content to eat and to sleep and to die like a cow.

What the Sacraments Bring to Man

The sacraments bring divine life or grace. Christ's reason for taking upon Himself a human nature was to pay for sin by death on the Cross and to bring us a higher life: "I have come so that they may have life, and have it more abundantly" (John 10:10). But, it may be said, that man already has life. Indeed he does; he has a biological, physiological life. He once had a higher divine life which he lost. Christ came to bring that life back to man. This higher life which is divine, distinct from the human, is called grace, because it is *gratis* or a free gift of God.

Two tadpoles at the bottom of a pond were one day discussing the problem of existence. One said to the other, "I think I will stick my head out to see if there is anything else in the world." The other tadpole said, "Don't be silly. Do you think there is anything else in this world besides water?" So those who live the natural life ignore the beauty of the higher life of grace.

Man may live at three different levels: the sensate, the intellectual, and the divine. These may be likened to a three-story house. The *sensate* level, or the first floor, represents those who deny any other reality except the pleasures that come from the flesh. Their house is rather poorly furnished and is capable of giving intermittent thrills which quickly dry up. The occupant of this first floor is not interested in being told of higher levels of existence; in fact, he may even deny their existence.

On the second floor, there is the *intellectual* level of existence, that of the scientist, the historian, the journalist, the humanist; the man who has brought to a peak all of the powers of human reason and human will. This is a much more comfortable kind of existence, and far more satisfying to the human spirit. Those on the second floor may think their floor is "a closed universe," regarding as superstitious those who desire a higher form of life.

But there is actually a third floor which is the floor of *grace* by which the human heart is illumined by truths which reason cannot know; by which the will is strengthened by a power quite beyond all psychological aids, and the heart is entranced with the love which never fails; which gives a peace that cannot be found on the two lower levels.

There is light outside the window, but it is up to man to open the blinds. The opening of the blinds does not constitute light; it is rather the condition of its entrance. When God made us, He gave us *ourselves*. When He gives us grace, He gives us *Himself*. When He created us, He gave Himself to us in a way which makes us one with Him.

One often sees signs painted on roadways, "Jesus Saves." Now this indeed is true, but the important question is how does He save? What relation have we in the twentieth century to Christ in the first? Do we establish contact with Him only by reading about Him? If that be all, our relationship is not much closer than that which we can have with Plato. If Christ is only a memory of someone who lived centuries ago, then it is rather difficult to see that His influence will be any different than that of Socrates or Buddha.

The answer to the question of how Christ saves is to be found in the sacraments. The divine life of Christ is communicated through His Church or His Mystical Body in exactly the same way that His divine life was communicated when He walked on earth. As He then used His human nature as the instrument of divinity, and used material things as signs and symbols of the conferring of His pardon, so He now uses other human natures and material things as the instruments for the communication of that same divine life.

In the earthly life of our Lord, we read that there were two kinds of contact. There was the *visible* contact with humanity by which His power was communicated to the palsied man and to the blind, both of whom He touched. But there was also the *invisible* contact, in which our Blessed Lord showed His power by working miracles at a distance, such as the curing of the servant of the centurion of Nazareth. The second kind of contact is an anticipation of the way that Christ, who is now in Heaven, extends and communicates His power through the sacraments.

Seven Conditions of Life

The physical or the natural life requires seven conditions, five of which refer to the person as an individual, and the other two as a member of society. The five conditions of leading an individual life are: (1) In order to live, one must obviously be born; (2) He must nourish himself, for he who does not eat shall not live; (3) He must grow to maturity, throwing away the things of the child, and assume the responsibilities of adult life; (4) In case he is wounded, he must have his wounds bound and healed; and (5) In case he has disease (for a disease is very different from a wound), the traces of the disease must be driven out. As a member of society two further conditions are required: (1) He must live under government and justice in human relationships, and (2) He is called to propagate the human species.

Over and above this human life, there is the divine Christ-life. The seven conditions of leading a personal Christ-life are the following: (1) We must be spiritually born to it, and that is the Sacrament of Baptism; (2) We must nourish the divine life in the soul, which is the Eucharist; (3) We must grow to spiritual maturity and assume full responsibilities as members of the spiritual army of the Church, which is Confirmation; (4) We must heal the wounds of sin, which is Penance; (5) We must drive out the traces of the diseases of sin, which is the Anointing of the Sick; (6) We must live under the spiritual government of the Church, which is Holy Orders; (7) We must prolong and propagate the Kingdom of God on earth, which is Matrimony.

Every sacrament has an outward or visible sign; for example, in Baptism it is water, in the Eucharist it is bread and wine. But the sacrament also has a *form* or *formula*, or words of spiritual significance given to the *matter* when it is conferred. Three things then are absolutely required for a sacrament: (1) Its institution by Christ; (2) An outward sign; and (3) The power of conferring the grace or divine life purchased for us by the Passion, Death, and Resurrection of Christ.

The Sacraments

The Power and Efficacy of the Sacraments

The sacraments derive their power and efficacy from the Passion, Death, and Resurrection of our Lord. Why was a blood sacrifice required to bring us the seven-fold sanctification? For several reasons: life is in the blood, but so also is sin. The sins of the alcoholic, the libertine, and the pervert are often written on their faces; their excesses are recorded in every cell of their body and every drop of their blood. If, therefore, sin is to be done away with, there should be some shedding of blood, as if to symbolize the emptying of sin. It is often the death of soldiers that brings freedom to a nation; it is the giving of one's blood to another which heals him of anemia. The blood bank from which others may draw healing is hint of another blood bank from which souls may be healed of the ravages of sin.

Furthermore, blood is the best symbol of sacrifice, because blood is the life of man: when man gives up his blood, he gives up his life. Hence, St. Peter writes:

> What was the ransom that freed you from the vain observances of ancestral tradition? You know well enough that it was not paid in earthly currency, silver or gold; it was paid in the precious Blood of Christ; no lamb was ever so pure, so spotless a victim. (1 Pet. 1:18–19)

The blood of Christ had infinite value because He is a divine person. The life of a lamb is more precious than that of a fly, and the life of a man is more precious than the life of a beast, and the life of the God-Man is more precious than the life of any human being.

Our mind, our will, and our conscience become completely sanctified through the application of the merits of Christ:

> Shall not the Blood of Christ, who offered Himself, through the Holy Spirit, as a victim unblemished in God's sight, purify our consciences, and set them free from lifeless observances, to serve the Living God? (Heb. 9:14)

The Application to the Sacraments

Calvary is like a reservoir of divine life or grace. From it, there flow seven different kinds of sanctification for man in different stages of his spiritual existence. Each of these seven channels is a sacrament by which the power of the Risen Christ is bestowed on souls by a spiritual and effective contact. This divine life pours into the soul when we receive the sacraments, unless we put an obstacle in the way, just as water will not flow out of a faucet if we put our hand in front of the faucet. But a faucet in a house has no power to quench thirst unless there is a reservoir and a pipeline. So the sacraments do not confer grace as magical signs; they communicate it only because they are in contact with the Risen Christ.

What makes the difference between the sacraments is how each is applied to us. The Christ-life affects us in a different way when we are born than when we are about to die; in a different way when we reach the age of responsibility than when we enter into marriage; in a different way when we wound ourselves than when we exercise government. The sunlight is the same whether it shines on mud to harden it or on wax to soften it. It shines on some flowers and makes them grow; it shines on a wound and heals it. So too, the blood of Christ applied at different moments of life results in a different kind of power.

A principle of philosophy states: "Whatever is received is received according to the mode of the one receiving it." If you pour water into a blue glass, it looks blue; if you pour it into a red glass, it looks red. If you pour water into the parched earth, it is quite different than water poured onto a carpet or into oil. So too, when the blood of Christ and its merits flood in upon the soul, it depends upon the one receiving it. Does the soul come for strengthening? For nourishment? For healing? For a long journey? For induction into the spiritual army? The effects will differ as to whether a person is spiritually dead or spiritually living. If a member of the Church is spiritually dead, then it will revive him as does the Sacrament of Penance, or the Sacrament of Baptism.

1

The Sacrament of Baptism

The sunshine, the carbons, and the rain could never share the life of the plant unless they died to their lower existence and were assumed or taken up into plant life. Plants could never share the sensitive and locomotive power of animals, unless they died to their lower existence and were taken up by the animal. None of the things in lower creation could live in man, and share his arts, his sciences, his thinking and his loves unless they ceased to be what they were, submitting to the death of knife and fire.

Now, since there is a life above the human, the Christ-life, man, or the old Adam, cannot share in it unless he dies to himself. But here there is no confiscation or violent appropriation as there is when the cow eats grass. Christ will not take us up to Himself unless we freely give ourselves to Him. This death to the life of sin, this sharing of the divine life, is Baptism.

Water: The Material Sign of Baptism

Water is used for cleansing from dust and dirt; therefore, it may be the symbol of a *spiritual washing* from Original Sin. But it can also symbolize both death and life. One can plunge into water and be submerged by it; then it is a symbol of *death*. After the plunge, one may rise from the water; then it is a token of *resurrection*. A descent into water has always been a description of penetration into deep and mysterious fecundities; the Greeks believed that the whole living universe came from water.

From another point of view, water is an excellent symbol of Baptism, because it is an open sign of *separation*. Water very often is the natural boundary between city and city, state and state, nation and nation, continent and continent, tribe and tribe. Those who live on one side of water are "separated" from those who live on the other. In the early days, before rapid communication, it was a dramatic experience to pass from one territory to another. This symbolism, therefore, was well-fitted for the Divine Master to indicate the separation of the Christian from the world, as the water which was divided in the Red Sea was a symbol of the separation of Israel from the slavery of Egypt.

Once the Jews had crossed the Red Sea, another symbol was used to "separate" them as the people of God, and that was circumcision. Not only was it a token of their covenant or testament with God, but it was required of all Israelites who partook of the Passover. In the New Testament, the same order is followed. Baptism, or incorporation into the Church, is the condition of reception of the New Passover, the Eucharist.

As ranchers brand their cattle, as ancient Romans branded their slaves, so God branded His own, both in the Old Testament and in the New; with circumcision of the flesh in the Old and circumcision of the spirit, or Baptism, in the New.

It may be objected, what good does a little water do when poured upon the head of a child? One might just as well ask what does a little water do when poured into the boiler. The water in the boiler can do nothing of and by itself, nor can the water on the head of a child. But when the water in the boiler is united to the mind of an engineer, it can drive an engine across a continent or a ship across the sea. So too, when water is united to the power of God, it can do more than change a crystal into life. It can take a creature and convert him into a child of God.

Naaman in the Old Testament was something like those today who think of the power of Baptism coming from water rather than from the Passion of Christ. Naaman was the general of the king of Syria. A maid who came from Samaria said that she wished that he had known the great prophet of Israel, for he could have cured him. The king then bade Naaman to go to Israel where he met the prophet, Eliseus. Eliseus said to him: "Go and wash seven times in the Jordan, and thy flesh shalt recover health and thou shalt be clean" (2 Kings 5:10).[3] Naaman was insulted because he was told to go to that insignificant river Jordan to bathe:

> "Why," he said angrily, "I thought he would come out to meet me, and stand here invoking the name of his God; that he would touch the sore with his hand and cure me. Has not Damascus its rivers, Abana and Pharphar, such water as is not found in Israel?" (2 Kings 5:11–12)

His servants, however, bade him go wash and be made clean, and he went down and washed seven times according to the word of the man of God, and his flesh was restored and was made like the flesh of a little child when he was made clean. Then he confessed that it was done by the power of God: "I have learned, he said, past doubt, that there is no God to be found in all the world, save here in Israel" (2 Kings 5:15).

Baptism and the Life of Christ

Under the Old Law people believed in, or yearned for, a Messiah who was to come. Abraham believed and his faith was accounted to him as justice, and he received circumcision as a sign of faith.

What was the faith, therefore, that justified Abraham, who was the father of the Jews? It was the faith in the Messiah, or the Christ who was to come. There is no salutary faith except in Christ. The Jews believed in the Christ who *was to come*; we believe in Christ who *has come*. The times have changed, but the reality of faith has not changed. There is only one faith. The faith that saves all men, making them pass from carnal generation to spiritual birth.

The reason our Lord was baptized was because it was part of the whole process of emptying, of humiliation, of the Incarnation. How could He

---

[3] 2 Kings is called 4 Kings in some editions of the Bible.

be poor with us, if He did not in some way conform to our poverty? How could He come among sinful men to redeem them, if He did not also reveal the necessity of being purged from sin? There was no need of our Blessed Mother to submit to the rite of purification, as there was no need of our Lord to submit to the rite of baptism by John. He had no need personally of having sins remitted, but He assumed a nature which was related to sinful humanity. Though He was without sin, He appeared to all men as a sinner, as He did on the Cross. That was why He walked into the Jordan with all the rest of the sinners to demand the baptism of penance "in remission of sins."

In a very special way, Baptism is related to the Death and Resurrection of Christ. In order to be saved, we have to recapitulate in our own lives the Death and the Resurrection of Christ. What He went through, we have to go through. He is the pattern, and we have to be modeled after Him. He is the die, and we are the coins that have to be stamped with His image. In all of the sacraments, the virtue of the Passion and Resurrection of Christ is in some way applied to us. In Baptism, there is a very close relationship between the burial and the resurrection. The catechumen is plunged into the water as Christ was plunged into death. We say plunged into death because of the words of our Lord: "There is a baptism I must be baptized with, and how impatient am I for its accomplishment" (Luke 12:50). Baptism not only incorporates us into the death of that which is evil in us, but also to the Resurrection of Christ, and therefore, to a new life.

There was recently found an inscription on a baptistry erected in the time of Constantine in the beginning of the fourth century, and it reads: "The waters received an old man, but brought forth a new man." St. Paul speaks of this: "It follows, in fact, that when a man becomes a new creature in Christ, his old life has disappeared, everything has become new about him (2 Cor. 5:17).

The Blessing of Baptismal Water

The water used in Baptism is blessed on Holy Saturday after the Litany of Saints, whose intercession is invoked on all those who will receive the sacrament. Then follows a prayer asking God to send forth "the Spirit of adoption" on those who are to be baptized. God has one Son who exhausts the fullness of His glory, but Baptism gives Him millions of adopted sons because it makes them partakers of His divine nature. The baptismal water is blessed by a prayer which recalls beautifully all the events of salvation which were in any way connected with water, from the beginning of the world when God's Spirit hovered over the water, down to the commandment of Christ to baptize.

Throughout the Old Testament water is represented as a sinister element, and is supposed to be the abode of demons. To confirm this idea, the Apocalypse[4] affirms that there will be no sea in the new earth after the resurrection of the just. Water, because of its unholy association, is exorcised on Holy Saturday that it may become "holy and innocent." The priest then takes the water, divides it into four quarters of the globe to symbolize the four waters that branched out of paradise and covered the earth. Next, he breathes upon the water three times, symbolizing the Holy Spirit, then dips the Paschal Candle (the symbol of the risen Christ) into it three times. Here the Consecration formula uses the symbolism of human generation: "May the power of the Holy Spirit descend into this brimming font, and make the whole substance of this water fruitful in regenerative power." And again, "Just as the Holy Spirit came down upon Mary and wrought in her the birth of Christ, so may He descend upon the Church, and bring about in her maternal womb (the font), the rebirth of God's children."

The baptismal font in a church is now generally placed as far from the altar as possible. It often is a corner to the left of the entrance. In the early Church, the baptistry was sometimes placed outside the Church. The reason is that the person about to be baptized was not yet a member of the Church and, therefore, was not allowed to participate in its mysteries.

The baptismal font, if properly erected, has steps going down into it, to indicate that it is a pool. Its shape was octagonal, because the

---

[4]   The Apocalypse is called the book of Revelation in some editions of the Bible.

Resurrection took place on the eighth day, or the day after the Jewish Sabbath.

In the Old Testament, circumcision was always performed on the eighth day. The son that David had through his sin with Bethsabee died on the seventh day. The first seven days were symbols of the bonds of sin; hence, the eighth day represented the breaking of those bonds and the liberation from them. In the New Testament, Easter is the eighth day *par excellence*, and that was the reason why Baptism was administered on Easter.

Baptism in the Early Church

Baptism was usually given the night before Easter Sunday, but the baptismal ceremonies began with the opening of Lent. At that time all of the candidates, converts, or catechumens had their names inscribed by a priest in the Church. They were then brought before a bishop who examined the candidates concerning their moral life. Generally, the bishop would bring out the fact that the candidate for Baptism had lived under Satan, but now he must abandon him. This meant a conflict and a battle. That is why we still have in the Church the Gospel of the temptation of Christ for the First Sunday of Lent, because it was the theme of the bishop to the catechumens at the beginning of their instructions.

The ceremony of Baptism took place then in three places and in like manner today: (1) Before the entrance to the church, which in the early Church was at the beginning of Lent; (2) Inside the church and before one comes to the baptistry, which happened in the middle of Lent in the early Church; and (3) Finally, the baptistry itself on Holy Saturday night, or Easter morning.

In the baptismal ritual, the stole of the priest at the beginning of the Baptism is violet in color; this is because in the early Church, the first part of the ceremony of Baptism was during Lent. Toward the end of the ceremony, the priest changes his stole to white, following again the tradition of the early Church, when Baptism was administered on Easter Sunday.

The Sacrament of Baptism

Outside the Church

The Dialogue

The Baptism begins with a dialogue. The ceremony begins with: "What do you ask of the Church of God?" The answer is: "Faith." The priest asks: "What does faith offer you?" The candidate or his sponsors answer: "Eternal life." Note the close connection between faith and Baptism. After His Resurrection, our Lord said to His Apostles: "Go out all over the world and preach the gospel to the whole of creation; he who believes and is baptized will be saved; he who refuses belief will be condemned" (Mark 16:15–16).

Our Blessed Lord first put belief before being baptized. In order to be saved, one must believe *and* be baptized. One can be saved by faith without the sacramental sign of Baptism; that is, through desire or by martyrdom, but he who refuses to believe will be condemned: "For the man who believes in him, there is no rejection; the man who does not believe is already rejected; he has not found faith in the name of God's only-begotten Son" (John 3:18).

The dialogue begins with "What do you ask of the Church of God?" Why the Church? Because the Church precedes the individual, not the individual the Church. When a person is baptized, he is not to be thought of as another brick that is added to an edifice, but rather as another cell united to the Christ-life. The Church expands from the inside out, not from the outside in. The foundation cell of the Church is Christ, and through Baptism, there is a multiplication of the cells of His body until there is a differentiation of functions and the building up of the whole Church. As a child is formed in the womb of the mother, so the Church, as a spiritual mother, forms and gives birth to the children of God. The Christian life resulting from Baptism is not an individual and solitary experience. It is a life in the Church and by the Church. As St. Paul expresses it: "Through faith in Christ Jesus you are all now God's sons" (Gal. 3:26).

Baptism does not first of all establish an individual relationship with Christ, and then accidentally make one a member of His body, the

Church. It is the other way around. The baptized person is first made a member of the Church, and thus he is incorporated into Christ. Baptism is social by nature. We are made members of Christ's body before being established in our individual relationship with Christ:

> We, too, all of us have been baptized into a single body by the power of a single Spirit, Jews and Greeks, slaves and free men alike; we have all been given drink at a single source, the one Spirit. (1 Cor. 12:13)

Sponsors

In Baptism, infants are incorporated into Christ, not through an act of their own will, but through an act of the sponsor who represents the Church and assumes responsibility for the spiritual education of the infant. The parents, of course, must consent to the Baptism; the Church refuses to baptize anyone against his or her will, or even to baptize an infant unless there is some guarantee that the child will be raised in the Faith. The sponsors are representatives of the Church, not representatives of the parents. They witness the incorporation of the infant into the fellowship of Christ.

It may be asked why should a child be baptized when he has nothing to say about it? Well, why should a child be fed? Is he asked his advice before he is given the family name? If he receives the name of the family, the fortune of the family, the rank of the family, the inheritance of the family, why should he not also receive the religion of the family? In our own country we do not wait until children are twenty-one and then allow them to decide whether or not they want to become American citizens, or whether they want to speak the English language. They are born Americans; so we in Baptism are born members of the Mystical Body of Christ. If one waits until he is twenty-one before learning something about his relation to the Lord who redeemed him, he will have already learned another catechism, the catechism of his passions, his concupiscences, and his lusts.

The Sacrament of Baptism

Exorcisms

Though the Hebrews had passed through the Red Sea, they were, nevertheless, followed by the Egyptians; so too, though a person is baptized, he is still followed by Satan throughout his life. That is why the baptized person is asked to renounce Satan and all of his seductions. This renouncing of Satan has as its parallel the attachment to Christ or the transfer from one master to another. In Baptism today, the ceremonies of exorcism follow rapidly upon one another, and thereby have lost the significance which they had in the early Church when they were separated by several weeks. This evil that the baptized are invited to combat, is not just a moral force or a vague kind of paganism; it is a cosmic reality, for the devil is, as our Lord said, the prince of this world. That is why even before the Church begins the Baptism of a person, it blesses water, oil, and salt, in some instances even with exorcisms, in order to snatch them out of the power of Satan.

There is a triple renouncing of Satan which corresponds to the threefold profession of faith:

Question: *Do you renounce Satan?*

Answer: I do renounce him.

Question: *And all his works?*

Answer: I do renounce them.

Question: *And all his allurements?*

Answer: I do renounce them.

This question has reference to the words of St. Paul to the Romans: "Let us abandon the ways of darkness, and put on the armor of light" (Rom. 13:12).

Thus the triple profession of faith accompanies the triple renouncing of Satan, and is bound to a gesture; namely, the anointing with the oil of catechumens. The one who baptizes dips his thumb in oil, and then traces a cross on the breast and between the shoulders of the one to be baptized. Formerly the oil was rubbed all over the body. This was also done on athletes who were engaging in some sport in the arena, but here the signification is spiritual, for it is the beginning of a spiritual competition (1 Cor. 9:24–27).

The exorcisms look both to the future, as well as to the past, to remind the catechumen that the struggle against the forces of Satan is a confrontation of God and the devil, the devil seeking to dispute the souls which our Lord won, as he tempted our Lord in the desert.

In the early Church, the renouncing of Satan was done facing the west. This is because the west is where the light of the sun disappears; therefore, it was regarded even by the ancient Greeks as the place of the gates of Hades; also, because Christ on the Last Day said He would come from the east to the west: "When the Son of Man comes, it will be like the lightning that springs up from the east and flashes across to the west" (Matt. 24:27). The baptismal liturgy of Milan reads: "Ye were turned to the east for he who renounced the demon turns himself to Christ. He sees Him face to face."

In the exorcism, the priest says: "I exorcise you, unclean spirit, in the name of the Father, of the Son, and of the Holy Spirit. Come forth, from this servant of God [name] for He commands you, spirit accursed and damned, He who walked upon the sea and extended His right hand to Peter as he was sinking. Therefore, cursed devil, acknowledge your condemnation and pay homage to the true and living God; pay homage to Jesus Christ, His Son, and to the Holy Spirit, and depart from the servant of God [name], for Jesus Christ, our Lord and our God, has called him [her] to His holy grace and blessing, and to the font of Baptism."

When the priest signs the forehead with his thumb in the form of a cross, he says: "Then never dare, cursed devil, to violate the Sign of the Cross which we are making upon his [her] forehead through Christ our Lord."

The various exorcisms, the laying on of hands, breathings, and Sign of the Cross are done in the vestibule of the Church. The second act of the ceremonies takes place at the entrance of the baptistry. The evil spirit has no authority in the holy place; that is why the final exorcism of the devil is at the entrance.

The Body in Baptism

Because the body is to become by Baptism the temple of God, because God dwells in it, it is fitting that it have an important role in the sacrament.

Each of the senses are spiritualized in the sacraments: hearing, taste, touch, smell, and sight.

The ears of the baptized person are touched with the words, "Be thou opened." The Hebrew word our Lord used in opening the ears of the deaf man was *ephpheta*. The assumption is that the person up to this moment has been deaf to the hearing of the word of God. Now his ears are opened, so that he can understand the word of God, and the confidences which God exchanges with him about the Kingdom of Heaven.

Tasting is testing. Before food goes into the stomach, it passes through the laboratory of the mouth for either approval or disapproval. In the spiritual order, the taste is not for body-food, but soul-food; the material element here used as a symbol for tasting Divine Wisdom and the Eucharist is salt. Placing salt on the tongue of the candidate for Baptism, the Church says: "Satisfy him [her] with the Bread of Heaven that he [she] may be forever fervent in spirit, joyful in hope, zealous in your service." Scripture bids us: "How gracious the Lord is. Taste and prove it" (Ps. 33:9 [34:8]).

The symbolism is that the truths of faith infused at Baptism will be preserved from error; that the person may reflect the savor of Christ in his life, and this taste of salt may be converted into a yearning for the Bread of Life, the Eucharist, which is the end of all the sacraments. When the faith is gone, everything is gone, as our Lord warned:

> You are the salt of the earth; if salt loses its taste, what is there left to give taste to it? There is no more to be done with it, but throw it out of doors for men to tread it under foot. (Matt. 5:13)

The body, during the ceremony, is touched in three places with oil: on the breast, between the shoulders, and on the head. The first two anointings are with the oil of catechumens, the last with chrism. The Sign of the Cross is made on the breast with oil to indicate that the heart must love God; between the shoulders to remind us that we are to carry the Cross of Christ; on the head, as a sign of eternal election in Christ our Lord.

The Apocalypse, describing the end of the world, says the destroying angel was "to attack men, such as did not bear God's mark on their foreheads" (Rev. 9:4). The elect will be known, because they have already been signed and have lived up to all the Cross commits them to in this life.

The last anointing with chrism, which takes place after Baptism, is the symbol of the Holy Spirit. In the Old Testament, oil was poured upon the head of the priest (Exod. 29:7), and upon kings (1 Sam. 10:1), to render them holy unto the Lord. Pulled out of the powers of darkness by Baptism, the Christian is now transported into the light of God and into His kingdom; that is why he becomes royal. St. Leo bade the faithful: "Recognize, O Christian, thy dignity."

We associate goodness with sweet odors and badness with foul odors. We have a "nose" for detecting the healthy and the unhealthy. This sense of smell is spiritualized in Baptism, and is made to symbolize sanctity or holiness.

The Church speaks of saints as dying in "the odor of sanctity." Sometimes their bodies after death give forth a sweet odor. The saintly Curé of Ars would walk along a line of several hundred persons waiting to go to Confession. He would pick out one here and there and put them first in line. When asked how he could do it, he answered: "I can smell sin." As the Church signs the nostrils of the catechumen, she says: "I sign you on the nostrils that you may perceive the sweet fragrance of Christ."

The eyes of the candidate are anointed, as the Church says: "I sign you on the eyes that you may see God's glory." By this is symbolized a new kind of vision: the things of God in addition to the things of earth: "Fix (your) eyes on what is unseen, not on what we can see. What we can see lasts but for a moment; what is unseen is eternal" (2 Cor. 4:18). Our Blessed Lord spoke of some who had eyes and yet were blind, because they had no faith: "Have you eyes that cannot see?" (Mark 8:18).

As a further example of the role of vision, a lighted candle is given to the one baptized. He is bidden to receive this burning light, and keep the grace of his Baptism without blame. This refers to the words of our Lord: "Your light must shine so brightly before men that they can see your good works, and glorify your Father who is in Heaven" (Matt 5:16).

We have the same eyes at night as during the daytime, but we cannot see at night because we lack the light of the sun. So there is a difference in persons looking upon the same reality, such as life, birth, death, the world. The baptized person has a light which the others do not have. Sometimes the person with the light of faith will regard the other person as ignorant or stupid, but actually he is only blind. On the other hand, the one who is baptized must not believe that his superior insights are due to his own reason, or his own merits. They are solely due to the light that has come to him through Christ.

There are various lights in the world: the light of the sun, which illumines our senses; the light of reason, which illumines science and culture; and the light of faith, which illumines Christ and eternal verities.

The Baptism Itself

The actual moment of Baptism comes when the priest pours water on the head of a person, saying: "I baptize thee, in the name of the Father, the Son, and the Holy Spirit." The personal pronoun "I" refers not only to the priest, but to Christ who speaks through the tongue given Him by the Church as He spoke through the tongue given Him by Mary. As the portals of the flesh once opened to the life of the human, now the womb of the Church opens and exults: "A child is born."

St. Augustine said this is a greater act than the creation of the world, for it blots out our debt of sin to God, Original Sin if it be an infant, original and personal sins if it be an adult. The full effects of this act will be mentioned later.

The Lighted Candle and Baptism
Because the Sacrament of Baptism opened the eyes of the soul to see, it was called the sacrament of illumination: "Remember those early days, when the light first came to you" (Heb. 10:32). Once asleep to the wonders of Redemption, eyes are now awake to receive Christ, the light of the world (John 1:9; 8:12) and to become sons of light (1 Thess. 5:5).

Because Baptism is the sacrament of faith, it is the sacrament of light. This baptismal candle in the early Church was always kept by the person baptized, and was lighted on the anniversary of one's Baptism and on feast days, and brought to the church for the Easter Vigil and the renewal of baptismal vows. Then later, if the person was married, the candle was lighted at his wedding. If he was ordained, it was lighted at his ordination, and when he died, it was lighted again as he went to his Judge.

The White Robe of Baptism

That the body is now the temple of God is further indicated by putting on a white robe after the Baptism itself. Today this is often only a small white cloth, but its symbolism still remains: "The body is for the Lord."

In the Transfiguration, our Blessed Lord's garment was white (Matt. 17:2) as a symbol of holiness and purity. White was the color of the vestments in the Old Testament. It was the color of the veil which divided the sanctuary. It was the attire of the high priest. It was the color of festivity (Eccles. 9:8), and of triumph (Rev. 6:2), and a symbol of glory and majesty (Matt. 28:3). The prayer that is said at Baptism is a petition that this garment be kept without stain: "Receive this white garment. Never let it become stained, so that when you stand before the judgment seat of our Lord you may have life everlasting." Dante, in his practical knowledge of human nature, knowing that many do not keep it sinless, described Purgatory as a "place where we go to wash our baptismal robes."

The white robe further symbolizes the recovery of the vestment of light which was man's before the Fall. As Gregory of Nyssa said: "Thou hast driven us out of paradise and called us back; Thou hast taken away the fig leaves, that garment of our misery, and clothed us once more with the robe of glory."

Because Baptism in the early Church was by immersion, there was an additional symbolism attached to the new garment that was put on, namely, to signify the entirely new life that came to one after one was "buried with Christ in his death " (Rom. 6:4). The neophyte did not resume the clothing he had taken off. He put on a new white garment, which he wore at all services during the entire Easter Octave. A week later, in the early Church, there was "the sabbath of the removal of white robes." These were solemnly taken off and deposited in the treasury of the baptismal Church.

The Sacrament of Baptism

Effects of Baptism

The first effect of Baptism is the restoration to friendship with God which was lost by Original Sin. The baptized person is made a partaker of the divine nature and, therefore, a sharer in divine life. There is more difference between a soul in the state of grace which begins in Baptism and a soul not in the state of grace than there is between a baptized person in the state of grace on this earth and a soul in glory in Heaven. The relation of the first two is the relationship between a crystal and an elephant: one cannot beget the other. The second relationship is that of an acorn and an oak. The acorn has the potential of becoming an oak; the baptized person in grace has the potential to enjoy the glory of God. That is why Baptism is said to make the person a new creature: "In fact, when a man becomes a new creature in Christ, his old life has disappeared, everything has become new about him" (2 Cor. 5:17).

This sharing of the divine nature makes us the adopted sons of the eternal Father. Just as Christ is the Divine Son incarnate; so we become adopted children, as distinct from the natural Son:

> But all those who did welcome him, He empowered to become the children of God. (John 1:12)

> Those who follow the leading of God's Spirit are all God's sons. (Rom. 8:14)

The dauphin, the father of Louis XVI, gave a lesson on the effect of Baptism to his two sons. They had been baptized as infants but in emergency. It was only years later, when they had reached the age of reason, that the related ceremonies were performed. Immediately after Baptism, it was noted that the names of the two children were registered after a common laborer about the palace. The royal father later said:

> See, my children, in the eyes of God, men of all conditions are equal. In His sight, faith and virtue are all that matters. One day you will be greater than this child in the eyes of the world; but if he is more virtuous than you, then he will be greater than you in the sight of God.

This likeness to God or the unlikeness will be the determinant of our future state. A mother knows her daughter is her own because that child shares her nature; a mother also knows the child next door is not her own because of the diversity of nature and parentage. So it will be with Christ on the last day. He will look into a soul and see His divine resemblance and say: "Come, ye blessed of my Father" (Matt. 25:34). "I am the Natural Son and you are the adopted children"; but to those who have not that likeness, Christ will say: "I know you not" (Matt. 25:12)—and it is a terrible thing not to be known by God.

Another effect is incorporation in the Mystical Body of Christ. Baptism is not just a bond existing between the person and Christ: to be united to Christ is to be united with the Church, for the Church is His body. The Church is not an organization, but an organism. As circumcision was an incorporation into the spiritual body of Israel, so Baptism is incorporation into the spiritual Body of the Church. A physical body is made up of millions of cells, and all of these coordinate and cooperate into a unity, thanks to the soul which organizes them, the invisible mind which guides them, and the visible head which directs them. So too, all the baptized are incorporated into the Mystical Body, thanks to the Holy Spirit which vivifies it; thanks to the invisible head, Christ, who rules the organism of the Church; and thanks to the visible head, its Vicar of Christ, who directs it on earth.

The two most common errors concerning the Church are these: (1) the belief that Christians came first and then the Church; and (2) that to justify the Church one must go to the New Testament—which antedated the Church.

In regard to the first error, the Christians did not come before the Church. The physical body of Christ was the beginning of the Church, and the Apostles constituted its first prolongation. The Church, or the Body of Christ, was not composed of the will of individual Christians; the latter were not first brought to our Lord and then inducted in some way into the Church. The Church has its origin not in the will of man, nor in the flesh of man, but in the will of Christ, our Lord. The Apostles were the ministers of the Lord Himself. The world is called into the Church, but the world does not make the Church by sending men into it.

Regarding the second error, the Church was in existence throughout the entire Roman Empire, before a single book of the New Testament was written. Long before St. Paul wrote any of his epistles, he said that he had "persecuted the Church." The Church was in existence before he wrote about it so beautifully. The Gospel came out of the Church; the Church did not come out of the Gospel.

Because Baptism makes us a cell in the Body of Christ, it is called the door of the Church. Each new generation of baptized Christians is taken up into that already existing unity. St. Peter, changing the analogy, describes those who are inducted into the Church as living stones:

> Draw near to Him; He is the living antitype of that stone which men rejected, which God has chosen and prized; you too must be built up on Him, stones that live and breathe, into a spiritual fabric. (1 Pet. 2:4–5)

The very fact that the ceremony of Baptism begins outside of the church, or at the door of the church, and that the adult to be baptized is led in by a stole, confirms the fact that the unbaptized is not yet a member of the Church.

The Infusion of Virtues

Another effect is the infusion of virtues. A virtue is something like a habit. There are two kinds of habits: infused habits, such as the infused habit of swimming which a duck has when it is born; and acquired habits, such as playing the violin or speaking a foreign language.

Baptism *infuses* seven virtues into the soul, the first three of which relate to God Himself, namely, faith, hope, and charity. We are thus enabled to believe in Him, hope in Him, and love Him. But four other virtues, called moral virtues, are related to the means of attaining God; these are prudence, justice, fortitude, and temperance. By the right use of things for God's sake, by paying our debts to God, by being brave about witnessing our faith and temperate about even the legitimate pleasures of life, we reach God more quickly.

One of the reasons there is little difficulty in convincing children of the existence of God and the divinity of the Church is that they already have the gift of faith infused in their souls at the moment of Baptism. This faith, however, requires practice and intellectual fortification. If one woke up suddenly and became endowed with the gift of playing the organ, he would still have to practice to retain the gift. So, even though the gift of faith is infused, it nevertheless requires practice. In the adult, Baptism demands faith, but faith supposes that one has already received the word of God:

> Only, how are they to call upon him until they have learned to believe in him? And how are they to believe in him, until they listen to him? (Rom. 10:14)

It may be asked why adults who already have the Faith are said to need Baptism. If the adult is already justified by faith, Baptism is necessary in order that he may be incorporated visibly and sacramentally to Christ in His Church. Furthermore, they receive, in virtue of Baptism, a *fuller grace*. In the case of children, the habit of virtue becomes a conscious act later on. The faith is not just a profession of doctrine, but is the commitment to our Lord and Savior.

Another effect, which is closely bound up with grace, is the indwelling of the Trinity in our souls, from which arises a triple relationship with the Godhead. First is the relationship with *God the Father*. The baptized may now say "Our Father." By nature, we are only creatures of God; by Baptism, we are sons:

> The spirit you have now received is not, as of old, a spirit of slavery, to govern you by fear; it is the spirit of adoption, which makes us cry out, Abba, Father. (Rom. 8:15)

We also have relationship with the Son of God, who is "the firstborn of many brethren" (Rom. 8:29). The baptized person will, therefore, try to reproduce in his soul the image of Christ. As it is put in *Imitation of Christ*:

The Sacrament of Baptism

Who will give me, Lord, to find You and You alone, and to offer You my whole heart… You in me, and I in You, and therefore together, evermore to dwell.

Finally, there is union with the Holy Spirit. At the moment of Baptism the priest says, "Depart, unclean spirit, and give place to the Holy Spirit." St. John writes: "This is our proof that we are dwelling in Him and He in us; He has given us a share of His own Spirit" (1 John 4:13). The Spirit within us is a moving Spirit, illumining the mind and strengthening the will to sanctify ourselves and others:

Nor does this hope delude us; the love of God has been poured out in our hearts by the Holy Spirit, whom we have received. (Rom. 5:5)

The world, therefore, is divided into the "once born" and the "twice born": between the sons of the old Adam, and the sons of the New Adam, Christ; between the unregenerate and the regenerate. There is a real inequality in the world. There are "superior" and "inferior" peoples, but the basis of distinction is not color, race, nationality, or wealth. The superior people of the earth are the supermen, the Godmen; the inferior people are those who have been called to that superior state but, as yet, have not embraced it. But the reborn must follow the laws of divine life, for which the Lord has prepared other sacraments.

2

The Sacrament of Confirmation

In the biological order, a creature must first be born, then it must grow. In the supernatural order of grace, divine life is born in the soul by Baptism; then it must grow "in age and grace and wisdom before God and men." The soul who receives the Sacraments of Baptism and Confirmation is born spiritually and matures spiritually. It receives citizenship in the Kingdom of God and is inducted into God's spiritual army and the lay priesthood of believers. This soul is "born of the Virgin Mary" — the Church — and begins its apostolate as our Lord began His preaching after the descent of the Holy Spirit at His baptism in the Jordan.

Confirmation, like every other sacrament, is modeled upon Christ, and reaffirms some aid or gesture in His life. It is bound up with our Lord's baptism in the Jordan when the Holy Spirit descended upon Him in the form of a dove.

Our Lord had a double priestly anointing corresponding to two aspects of His life: the first, the Incarnation, made Him capable of becoming a victim for our sins, because He then had a body with which He could suffer. As God He could not suffer; as man He could. This first aspect culminated in the Passion and Resurrection, which one participates in by Baptism.

But the Sacrament of Confirmation is particularly a participation in the second anointing of our Lord, that of the coming of the Spirit in the Jordan, which ordained Him to the mission of preaching the apostolate. This reached its culmination on Pentecost, when He filled His Church—His Mystical Body—with His Spirit. Pentecost is to the New Testament what the gift of the law is to the Old Testament, only it is more perfect.

The descent of the Holy Spirit on Christ in the Jordan had a double effect on our Lord. It prepared Him for combat:

> Jesus returned from the Jordan full of the Holy Spirit, and by the Spirit He was led on into the wilderness, where He remained forty days, tempted by the devil. (Luke 4:1)

It prepared Him for preaching the Kingdom of God:

> The Spirit of the Lord is upon me; He has anointed me, and sent me out to preach the gospel to the poor, to restore the broken-hearted; to bid the prisoners go free, and the blind to have sight; to set the oppressed at liberty, to proclaim a year when men may find acceptance with the Lord. (Luke 4:18–19)

About three years later, at the Last Supper, our Blessed Lord promised to send the Spirit to His Apostles, disciples, and followers, which He did fifty days after the Resurrection on Pentecost. It would seem better if our Lord had remained on earth, so that all ages might have heard His voice and thrilled to the majesty of His person; but He said it was better that He leave, otherwise the Spirit would not come. If He remained on earth, He would have been only an example to be copied, but if He sent the Holy Spirit, He would be a life to be lived.

Though our Lord knew on Holy Thursday that His Apostles were distressed because He spoke of His approaching death, He consoled them with the advantages of His leaving this earth and yet remaining in it, in another way:

> So full are your hearts with sorrow at my telling you this. And yet I can say truly that it is better for you I should go away; he who is to befriend you will not come to you unless I do go, but if only I make my way there, I will send him to you. (John 16:6–7)

The Sacrament of Confirmation

His perpetual presence, even in His glorified state, would have limited His moral and spiritual influence. He might have become to man the type of Christ that Hollywood presents—a celebrity. Instead of being in our hearts, He would only have been in our senses.

Would men ever have thought of spiritual fellowship with Christ, when physical fellowship might be had; when good and bad would have had equal perception of Him; when He would be external to the soul of man, not internal? Where would faith be, if we saw? And would not the world have tried to re-crucify Him, though that would have been impossible after His Resurrection?

These questions are in vain; Divine Wisdom said it was better that He depart from the globe for, once in glory, He would send His Spirit, "the Truth-giving Spirit to guide you in all Truth" (John 16:13). Great men influence the earth only from their funeral urns; but He, who gave the earth the only serious wound it ever received—the empty tomb—would rule it at the right hand of the Father through His Spirit.

This Spirit He sent upon the Church on Pentecost, like a soul entering a fetus; chemicals which are disparate and disconnected became a living thing. So the Apostles, with their individual whims and ignorances, were, under the fires of Pentecost, fused into the visible, living, Mystical Body of Christ. It is not to the point in a book on the sacraments to describe this; but it is to the point to say that Confirmation is a kind of Pentecost to a baptized soul. Christ dwelling in the flesh would normally be in one place only at one time, but His Spirit, unbound by fleshy bonds, could cover the earth, working on a million hearts at once. Nor would such hearts be without comfort at His physical absence, for the Spirit He called "another Comforter."

It is the Son, Christ our Lord, who reveals the Heavenly Father. We would never know the mercy and love of the Father, if He had not sent His Son to walk this earth and pay our debt for sin. But who reveals the Son? It is the Holy Spirit.

We know what goes on in other minds because we, too, have minds or souls; we know what goes on in the mind of Christ because we are given His Spirit. The natural or unbaptized man cannot perceive the things of God, for they are spiritually discerned. As the scientist knows nature, so the Christian, thanks to the Spirit, knows Christ:

> He will not utter a message of His own; he will utter the message that has been given to Him; and He will make plain to you what is still to come. And He will bring honor to me, because it is from me that He will derive what He makes plain to you. I say that He will derive from me what He makes plain to you, because all that belongs to the Father belongs to me. (John 16:13–15)

It is through the Spirit received in Confirmation that Christ walks the earth again in each obedient Christian; it is through the Spirit that we are sanctified, comforted, and taught to pray.

These and other words of our Lord about sending the Spirit of Truth who will enlarge our knowledge of Him, prove that the whole truth is not available to us in written records. Pentecost was not the descent of a book, but of living tongues of fire. Confirmation gives the lie to those who say that "the sermon on the mount is enough for them." Our Lord's teaching, as recorded in the Gospels, was implemented, complemented, and revealed in its deeper meaning through the Spirit of Truth He gave to His Church. We indeed know Christ by reading the Gospels, but we see the deeper meaning of the words, and we know Christ more completely when we have His Spirit. It is only through the Spirit that we know He is the divine Son of God and Redeemer of humanity:

> Those who live the life of nature cannot be acceptable to God; but you live the life of the spirit, not the life of nature; that is, if the Spirit of God dwells in you. A man cannot belong to Christ unless he has the Spirit of Christ. (Rom. 8:8–9)

Because an added measure of the Spirit is given in Confirmation, it was administered, even in the early Church, not by disciples but by Apostles or by the bishops who had the fullness of the priesthood.

The deacon Philip went to a city of Samaria and preached Christ to them. He converted and baptized many. But, in order to "lay hands on

The Sacrament of Confirmation

them" or confirm them, it was necessary for the Church in Jerusalem to send Peter and John (Acts 8:14–17). Later on we read about Confirmation at Ephesus by the Apostle Paul: "When Paul laid his hands on them, the Holy Spirit came upon them" (Acts 19:6).

Administration of the Sacrament

The candidates kneel with hands joined before the bishop, who, extending his hands over the ones to be confirmed, says:

> Almighty, everlasting God, who has deigned to beget new life in these Thy servants by water and the Holy Spirit, and has granted them remission of all their sins, send forth from Heaven upon them Thy Holy Spirit, with His sevenfold gifts: The spirit of wisdom and understanding. Amen. The spirit of counsel and fortitude. Amen. The spirit of knowledge and piety. Amen. Fill them with the spirit of fear of the Lord, and seal them with the sign of Christ's Cross, plenteous in mercy unto life everlasting. Through the selfsame Jesus Christ, Thy Son, our Lord, who liveth and reigneth with Thee in the unity of the Holy Spirit, God eternally. Amen.

Dipping his thumb in holy chrism, he confirms the person, saying:

> [Name,] I confirm thee with the chrism of salvation. In the name of the Father [making the Sign of the Cross] and of the Son [making the Sign of the Cross] and of the Holy Spirit [making the Sign of the Cross].

Then he gives the one confirmed a slight blow on the cheek, saying, "Peace be to you."

Other prayers and a penance follow, all of which are destined to make the Christian a witness, a teacher to an unbelieving world, and even a martyr, if need be, for the Church. Two of the effects and obligations of the Church deserve special consideration, and this follows.

The Sacrament of Combat

Every sacrament is related to the death of Christ, but Confirmation intensifies that resemblance. Baptism gives the Christian a treasure; Confirmation urges him to fight to preserve it against the three great enemies: the world, the flesh, and the devil.

The military character of the sacrament is evidenced in the following four symbols or acts:

1. *The forehead is anointed with chrism in the Sign of the Cross.* The cross, by its nature, evokes opposition. The more one crucifies his passions and rejects the false teachings of the world, the more he is slandered and attacked. Calvary united not only the friends of our Lord; it also united His enemies. Those who were opposed to one another merged their lesser conflicts for the sake of the greater hate. Judas and the Sanhedrin, Pharisees and publicans, religious courts and Roman overlords—though they despised one another, nevertheless they rained common blows of hammer and nails on the hands and feet of Christ:

> It is because you do not belong to the world, because I have singled you out from the midst of the world, that the world hates you. (John 15:19)

When the Little Flower, St. Thérèse, prepared herself for Confirmation, she saw that it implied crucifixion:

> I went into retreat for Confirmation. I carefully prepared myself for the coming of the Holy Spirit. I cannot understand why so little attention is paid to the sacrament of love. Like the Apostles, I happily awaited the promised Comforter. I rejoiced that soon I should be a perfect Christian, and have eternally marked upon my forehead the mysterious Cross of this ineffable sacrament. On that day I received the strength to suffer, a strength which I much needed, for the martyrdom of my soul was about to begin.

2. *The interior grace of the sacrament gives fortitude and other gifts destined for the battle of the Spirit.* The Apostles on Pentecost were made witnesses

to the Resurrection of Christ, and the word "witness" in Greek means "martyr." So, in Confirmation, the Christian is marked with power and boldness on the forehead, so that neither fear nor false modesty will deter him from the public confession of Christ. Cattle are often branded with the owner's name; and slaves or soldiers in the emperor's service were tattooed so that they could be easily recognized if they ever deserted the service. Plutarch states it was a custom to brand cattle that were destined for sacrifice, as a sign that they were set apart for something sacred. Herodotus tells of a temple in Egypt in which a fugitive might take the right of sanctuary: once he did so, he was stamped, marked, or tattooed as an indication that he was the property of God and, therefore, was inviolable and sacrosanct.

The spiritual significance of marking is anticipated: "All alike destroy till none is left, save only where you see the cross marked upon them" (Ezek. 9:6 [5–6]). On the last day, the elect will be sealed on their foreheads in the name of the Lamb and of His Father, to protect them from destruction (Rev. 7:3). Confirmation, then, is the sealing of a person in the army of the Lord. St. Paul says: "Do not distress God's Holy Spirit, whose seal you bear until the day of your redemption comes" (Eph. 4:30).

3. *A slight blow on the cheek is given the person confirmed to remind him that, as a soldier of Christ, he must be prepared to suffer all things for His sake.* To deny one's faith for a passing carnal pleasure, or to surrender it under ridicule, is far more serious in the eyes of God than a soldier deserting his duty. Péguy, bemoaning a want of spiritual bravery, writes:

> Shame upon those who are ashamed. It is not a question of believing or not believing; it is a question of knowing what is the most frequent cause of loss of faith. No cause can be more shameful than shame—and fear. And of all the fears the most shameful is certainly the fear of ridicule; the fear of being taken for a fool. One may believe, or one may not believe. But shame upon him who would deny his God to avoid being made a mark for witticisms. I have in mind the poor, timorous wretch who looks fearfully on every side to be sure that there is not some high personage who has

Archbishop Sheen's Book of Sacraments

laughed at him, at his faith, at his God. Shame upon the ashamed. Shame implies a cowardice that has nothing to fall back upon. Shame upon those who are ashamed.

4. *The combative character of Confirmation is further shown by the fact that its ordinary minister is the bishop, who is, as it were, a general in the military of the Church.* Because Confirmation gives an increase of the Holy Spirit over Baptism, it is fittingly administered by the one who has the fullness of the priesthood. When the bishop extends his arms over those confirmed, as a successor of the Apostles, he imitates Peter and John who laid hands on new converts of Samaria, so that "they received the Holy Spirit" (Acts 8:17). He also imitates Paul at Ephesus: "When Paul laid his hands on them, the Holy Spirit came upon them" (Acts 19:6). The bishop is not a hoarder of his authority; he is a dispenser of it, as was our Blessed Lord who told His Apostles that they were to make disciples of all nations (Matt. 18:19–20).

The bishop, as the authority in the Church, incorporates the one confirmed into *adult* responsibilities. From now on, the one confirmed does not lead an individual Christian life: he becomes commissioned in the army. Confirmation is, therefore, the first great manifestation of the relation established between the authority of the Church and Christian personality.

Confirmation Both Personal and Social

Every sacrament has been set as a kind of balance between the individual and the community. The individual is baptized, but his Baptism incorporates him into the community of believers—the Church. The grace descends into the soul of the individual, but the grace is for the perfection of the Mystical Body. This is true also of the Sacrament of Confirmation for, even more than Baptism, it orients us toward the community or fellowship of believers. Love is a union by which one escapes from egotism. When one reaches spiritual adulthood, one is open for a wider love. Children live for themselves; adults cease to live exclusively for themselves, particularly those who reach the "perfect age" in the spirit. The combat of Baptism was, we said, a *personal* combat: in Confirmation, the combat is *ex officio* military, and under the orders of the chief. Baptism is principally the battle against invisible enemies: in Confirmation, it is the battle against social enemies, such as the persecutors of the Church.

The mystical death one undergoes in Baptism is individual: in Confirmation, the mystical death is communal. We are prepared to die, to be a martyr, or a witness to Christ for the sake of the "body which is the Church" (Col. 1:24). Confirmation then relates us to the community; that is why the Spirit was given on Pentecost when all the Apostles were assembled together with Mary in their midst.

Confirmation makes us soldiers of Christ. Soldiers do not come together of and by themselves to constitute an army. Rather, it is the political authority of government which summons the soldiers and constitutes them as an army. So it is in Confirmation. The Church does not have a spiritual military because her members volunteer for service. It is rather that the Church makes them grow spiritually to a point where they can carry spiritual arms and be authorized as her combatants bearing the "breastplate of justice fitted on ... the shield of faith ... the helmet of salvation ... and the sword of the spirit" (Eph. 6:14, 16, 17).

The Sacrament of the Lay Apostolate

The laity are summoned by Confirmation to share in the apostolate of the Church, to be witnesses to Christ before those who know Him not, to be prophets or teachers in an unbelieving world and, together with the priesthood, to offer their bodies as a reasonable sacrifice to the Heavenly Father:

> You are a chosen race, a royal priesthood, a consecrated nation, a people God means to have for Himself; it is yours to proclaim the exploits of the God who has called you out of darkness into His marvelous light. (1 Pet. 2:9)

The laity share in the general priesthood of the Church because all are members of Jesus the priest; but they do not share in the ministerial or hierarchical priesthood which comes with Holy Orders, in which there is a *personal* representation of Christ, such as offering the eucharistic sacrifice and absolving sins.

The laity have a double consecration through Baptism and Confirmation, which gives them a certain participation in the priesthood of Christ. The ministerial or hierarchical priesthood, however, has the third and specific consecration from Holy Orders. There are thus two sorts of priesthood: the first is *external* and reserved for the hierarchical priesthood; the second is *internal* and common to all the faithful.

The person who is confirmed always has a personal and, in some instances, a canonical mission. He has a personal mission inasmuch as, through his own personal contact, he must help bring other souls to Christ—just as Andrew brought Peter, Philip brought Nathaniel, the Samaritan woman brought her townspeople, and Philip converted the eunuch of the Ethiopian court. But the mission given by Confirmation requires a wider outlook than the personal work of witnessing and converting. It is not only individual souls, but also the milieu, the environment—the whole social order in all its political, scientific, journalistic, medical, legal, recreational, and economic structures—which also has to be Christianized.

This canonical mission of spiritualizing the world in an organized way is dependent on the hierarchy and the teaching authority of the Church. There is some communication of this teaching office in the ceremony of the imposition of hands. The laity do not participate in the hierarchy, but they participate in the apostolate of the hierarchy. The Apostles and their successors have a divine mission to teach; the laity receives from the hierarchy a canonical mission to teach.

What makes Catholic Action[5] is not the fact that Catholics are organized, but that they have received a mission to bear witness to Christ

---

[5] Catholic Action is the organized work of the laity performed under a bishop's mandate or direction. See "Catholic Action," Britannica, https://www.britannica.com/topic/Catholic-Action.

The Sacrament of Confirmation

over and above their own personal witnessing to Christ in the holiness of their lives. The laity are not just the Church taught; they participate in the Church teaching. As Leo XIII said, the laity cannot arrogate to themselves this authority, but when circumstances demand it, they have the right to communicate to others, as echoes of the magisterium of the Church, that which they themselves have learned. And Pope Pius XII addressed a new group of cardinals as follows:

> The laity must have an ever clearer consciousness, not only of belonging to the Church, but of being the Church; that is, of being the community of the faithful on earth under the guidance of their common leader, the Pope, and the bishops in communion with him. *They are the Church.*

The Acts of the Apostles twice shows that when the disciples were scattered by persecution, the laity immediately began to preach God's word and increase the Church (Acts 8:4; 9:31), something that is happening today in persecuted lands. Aquila and his wife, Priscilla, completed the instructions of Apollos (Acts 18:26), and later on became the trusted helpers of St. Paul (Rom. 16:3). Apollos, who never seems to have received any ministerial consecration, was a vigorous preacher of Christ (Acts 18:27–28).

There have even been laymen who taught theology. For example, John d'Andrea was professor of canon law at Bologna from 1302 to 1348. Wilfred G. Ward was professor of dogmatic theology at St. Edmund's Seminary of London, England, from 1851 to 1858.

More and more, the Church is emphasizing the teaching mission conferred by Confirmation. In mission lands, catechists number tens of thousands. Abroad and at home, the canonical mission of teaching is conferred implicitly on teachers when the bishops appoint them to parochial schools.

3

The Sacrament of the Eucharist

A young wife, who had been taking instructions for a year, told the writer she could believe everything in the Faith except the Eucharist. Upon inquiring about her husband, it was learned that he was in the Pacific on military duty. In answer to further questions, she admitted that she corresponded with him every two days and that she had his photograph before her in the house.

We argued there was nothing wanting for perfect happiness. What more could she want than the constant memory of him through the photograph and a written communication in which heart poured out to heart. But she protested that she could never be truly happy except through union with her husband.

But, it was retorted, if human love craves oneness, shall not Divine Love? If husband and wife seek to be one in the flesh, shall not the Christian and Christ crave for that oneness with one another? The memory of the Christ who lived twenty centuries ago, the recalling of His mercy and miracles through memory, the correspondence with Him by reading the Scriptures—all these are satisfying, but they do not satisfy love. There must be, on the level of grace, something unitive with Divine Love. Every heart seeks a happiness outside it, and since perfect love is God, then the heart of man and the heart of Christ must, in some way, fuse. In human friendship the other person is loved as another self, or the other half of one's soul. Divine friendship must have its mutual "indwelling": "He who dwells in love dwells in God and God in him" (1 John 4:16). This aspiration of the soul for its ecstasy is fulfilled in the Sacrament of the Eucharist.

The Eucharist: Sacrifice and Sacrament

The Sacrament of the Eucharist has two sides: it is both a *sacrifice* and a *sacrament*. Inasmuch as biological life is nothing but a reflection, a dim echo, and a shadow of the divine life, one can find analogies in the natural order for the beauties of the divine. Does not nature itself have a double aspect: a sacrifice and a sacrament? The vegetables which are served at table, the meat which is presented on the platter, are the natural sacraments of the body of man. By them he lives. If they were endowed with speech, they would say: "Unless you have communion with me, you will not live."

But if one inquires as to how the lower creation of chemicals, vegetables, or meats came to be the sacrament or the communion of man, one is immediately introduced to the idea of sacrifice. Did not the vegetables have to be pulled up by their roots from the earth, submitted to the law of death, and then pass through the ordeal of fire before they could become the sacrament of physical life, or have communion with the body? Was not the meat on the platter once a living thing, and was it not submitted to the knife, its blood shed on the soil of a natural Gethsemane and Calvary before it was fit to be presented to man?

Nature, therefore, suggests that a *sacrifice* must precede a *sacrament*; death is the prelude to a communion. In some way, unless the thing dies, it does not begin to live in a higher kingdom. To have, for example, a Communion service without a sacrifice would be, in the natural order, like eating our vegetables uncooked, and our meat in the raw. When we come face to face with the realities of life, we see that *we live by what we slay*. Elevating this to the supernatural order, we still live by what we slay. It was our sins that slew Christ on Calvary, and yet by the power of God risen from the dead and reigning gloriously in Heaven, He now becomes our life and has communion with us and we with Him. In the divine order, there must be the Sacrifice or the Consecration of the Mass before there can be the sacrament or the Communion of the soul and God.

Relation of Baptism and the Eucharist

Baptism is the initiation to the Christian life, and corresponds in the biological order to the beginning of life. But the birth to divine life comes only through a death; that is to say, an immersion under water which mystically symbolizes dying and being buried with Christ. The Eucharist is a sacrifice; it also incorporates us to the death of Christ. Baptism, however, is a more passive representation of that death, particularly in an infant, where the will of the infant does not submit to it, except through the sponsors. The Eucharist is a much more *active* representation of the death of Christ because the Mass is an unbloody presentation of the sacrificial death of Christ outside the walls of Jerusalem.

The Fathers of the Church were constantly struck by the relationship between Baptism and the Eucharist; the blood and the water which flowed from the side of Christ on the Cross had deep significance. Water was the symbol of our regeneration and, therefore, betokened Baptism; blood, the price of our Redemption, was the sign of the Eucharist.

This brings up the question, if there is a relationship to the death of Christ in both sacraments, what is the difference between them? One of the differences is that in Baptism and the other sacraments, except the Eucharist, we are united to Christ simply by a participation of His grace, but in the Eucharist, Christ exists substantially, and is really and truly present — Body, Blood, Soul and Divinity. In the Eucharist, man realizes more fully his incorporation to the Death and Resurrection of Christ than in Baptism. In the physical order, birth always gives resemblance to parents; but when a mother nourishes her child, there is a new bond established between the child and the mother. So in Baptism, there is a resemblance to the divine nature created, inasmuch as we are made "other Christs"; but in the Eucharist, we receive the very substance of Christ Himself. Because of the close relationship between the two sacraments, the Council of Mayence in 1549 directed pastors to administer Baptism in the morning during the course of the Mass, or at least as soon after Mass as possible.

There is somewhat the same relationship existing between Baptism and the Eucharist as there is between faith and charity or perfect love. Baptism is the sacrament of faith, because it is the foundation of the spiritual life. The Eucharist is the sacrament of charity or love because it is the re-enactment of the perfect act of love of Christ; namely, His death on the Cross and the giving of Himself to us in Holy Communion.

The Old Testament and the Eucharist

It would take pages to reveal the prefiguration of the Sacrament of the Eucharist in the Old Testament. Melchisedech offering bread and wine was a figure of Christ Himself, who chose bread and wine the night of the Last Supper as the elements for both the sacrifice and the sacrament. The manna that fell in the desert was also a symbol of the Eucharist, which our Blessed Lord said was Himself: "I myself am the living bread that has come down from heaven" (John 5:51). St. Paul, picking up the analogy, said that what the Jews ate in the desert was a figure of our spiritual food: "They all ate the same prophetic food.... It is we that were foreshadowed in these events (1 Cor. 10:3, 6).

The blood of the paschal lamb, sprinkled on doorposts to preserve the Jews from destruction, was a sign not yet of a reality, but a figure of the blood of Christ sprinkled on our souls, which would save us from evil. Because the paschal lamb was a figure of Christ, it was on the feast of the Passover that our Blessed Lord gave to His Church the Eucharist which He had promised over a year before at Capharnaum.

The Eucharist as a Sacrifice, or the Mass

The Mass has three important parts: the Offertory, the Consecration, and the Communion. In the order of human love, these correspond to engagement, the marriage ceremony, and the consummation of the marriage.

The Sacrament of the Eucharist

When a man becomes engaged to a woman, he generally brings her the gift of a precious ring; it is not of tin or straw, because these represent no sacrifice. Regardless of how much he might pay for the ring, he would still tear off the price tag, in order that his beloved might never establish any correspondence between the price of the gift and his love. No matter how much he gave her, the gift to him would seem inadequate. The ring is round in order to express the eternity of his love which has neither beginning nor end; it is precious, because it is a symbol of the total readiness to give his whole personality to the beloved.

The Mass, too, has an engagement which corresponds to the Offertory of the Mass, in which the faithful bring gifts of bread and wine, or its equivalent, that which buys bread and wine. As the ring is a symbol of the lover offering himself to the beloved, so too, the bread and wine are the symbols of a person offering himself to Christ. This is apparent in several ways: first, since bread and wine have traditionally nourished man and given him life, in bringing that which was the substance of his life, he is equivalently giving himself. Second, the readiness to sacrifice himself for the beloved is revealed in the bread and wine; no two substances have to undergo more to become what they are than do wheat and grapes. One passes through the Gethsemane of a mill, the other through the Calvary of the winepress before they can be presented to the Beloved on the altar. In the Offertory, therefore, under the appearance of bread and wine, the faithful are offering themselves to Christ.

After the engagement comes the marriage ceremony in which the lover sacrifices himself for the beloved, and the beloved surrenders devotedly to the lover. The groom practically says, "My greatest freedom is to be your slave. I give up my individuality in order to serve you." The joining of hands in the marriage ceremony is a symbol of the transfer of self to another self: "I am yours and you are mine. I want to die to myself, in order to live in you, my beloved. I cannot live unto you, unless I give up myself. So I say to you, 'This is my body; this is my blood.'"

In the Mass, the faithful are already present on the altar under the appearance of bread and wine. At the moment of the Consecration of the Mass, when the priest as Christ pronounces the words "This is my

Body" and "This is my Blood," the substance of the bread becomes the substance of the Body of Christ, and the substance of the wine becomes the substance of the Blood of Christ. At that moment, the faithful are saying in a secondary sense with the priest: "This is my body; this is my blood. Take it! I no longer want it for myself. The very substance of my being, my intellect, and my will—change! Transubstantiate!—so that my ego is lost in Thee, so that my intellect is one with Thy Truth, and my will is one with Thy desires! I care not if the species or appearances of my life remain; that is to say, my duties, my avocation, my appointments in time and space. But what I am substantially, I give to Thee."

In the human order, after the engagement and the marriage is the consummation of the marriage. All love craves unity. Correspondence by letter, or by speech, cannot satisfy that instinctive yearning of two hearts to be lost in one another. There must, therefore, come some great ecstatic moment in which love becomes too deep for words; this is the communion of body and blood with Body and Blood in the oneness which lasts not long, but is a foretaste of Heaven.

The marital act is nothing but a fragile and shadowy image of Communion in which, after having offered ourselves under the appearance of bread and wine and having died to our lower self, we now begin to enjoy that ecstatic union with Christ in Holy Communion—a oneness which is, in the language of Thompson, "a passionless passion, a wild tranquility." This is the moment when the hungry heart communes with the Bread of Life; this is the rapture in which is fulfilled that "love we fall just short of in all love," and that rapture that leaves all other raptures pain.

The Sacrifice of the Mass may be presented under another analogy. Picture a house which had two large windows on opposite sides. One window looks down into a valley, the other to a towering mountain. The owner could gaze on both and somehow see that they were related: the valley is the mountain humbled; the mountain is the valley exalted.

The Sacrifice of the Mass is something like that. Every church, in a way, looks down on a valley, but the valley of death and humiliation in which we see a cross. But it also looks up to a mountain, an eternal mountain, the mountain of Heaven where Christ reigns gloriously. As the valley and the mountain are related as humiliation and exaltation, so the Sacrifice of the Mass is related to Calvary in the valley, and to Christ in Heaven and the eternal hills.

All three, Calvary, the Mass, and the glorified Christ in Heaven are different levels of the great eternal act of love. The Christ who appeared in Heaven as the lamb slain from the beginning of the world, at a certain moment in time, came to this earth and offered His Life in Redemption for the sins of men. Then He ascended into Heaven where that same eternal act of love continues, as He intercedes for humanity, showing the scars of His Love to His heavenly Father. True, agony and crucifixion are passing things, but the obedience and the love which inspired them are not. In the Father's eyes, the Son-made-Man loves always unto death. The patriot who regretted that he had only one life to give to his country would have loved to have made his sacrifice eternal. Being man, he could not do it. But Christ, being God and man, could.

The Mass, therefore, looks backward and forward. Because we live in time and can use only earthly symbols, we see successively that which is but one eternal movement of love. If a motion picture reel were endowed with consciousness, it would see and understand the story at once; but we do not grasp it until we see it unfolded upon the screen. So it is with the love by which Christ prepared for His coming in the Old Testament, offered Himself on Calvary, and now re-presents it in Sacrifice in the Mass. The Mass, therefore, is not another immolation but a new presentation of the eternal Victim and its application to us. To assist at Mass is the same as to assist at Calvary. But there are differences.

On the Cross, our Lord offered Himself for all mankind; in the Mass we make application of that death to ourselves, and unite our sacrifice with His. The disadvantage of not having lived at the time of Christ is nullified by the Mass. On the Cross, He potentially redeemed all humanity; in the Mass we actualize that Redemption. Calvary happened at a definite moment in time and on a particular hill in space. The Mass temporalizes and spatializes that eternal act of love.

The Sacrifice of Calvary was offered up in a bloody manner by the separation of His blood from His body. In the Mass, this death is mystically and sacramentally presented in an unbloody manner, by the separate Consecration of bread and wine. The two are not consecrated together by such words as "This is my Body and my Blood"; rather, following the words of our Lord: "This is my Body" is said over the bread; then, "This is my Blood" is said over the wine. The separate Consecration is a kind of mystical sword dividing Body and Blood, which is the way our Lord died on Calvary.

Suppose there was an eternal broadcasting station that sent out eternal waves of wisdom and enlightenment. People who lived in different ages would tune in to that wisdom, assimilate it, and apply it to themselves. Christ's eternal act of love is something to which we tune in, as we appear in successive ages of history through the Mass. The Mass, therefore, borrows its reality and its efficacy from Calvary and has no meaning apart from it. He who assists at Mass lifts the Cross of Christ out of the soil of Calvary and plants it in the center of his own heart.

This is the only perfect act of love, sacrifice, thanksgiving, and obedience which we can ever pay to God; namely, that which is offered by His Divine Son incarnate. Of and by ourselves, we cannot touch the ceiling because we are not tall enough. Of and by ourselves, we cannot touch God. We need a Mediator, someone who is both God and man, who is Christ. No human prayer, no human act of self-denial, no human sacrifice is sufficient to pierce Heaven. It is only the Sacrifice of the Cross that can do so, and this is done in the Mass. As we offer it, we hang, as it were, onto His robes, we tug at His feet at the Ascension, we cling to His pierced hands in offering Himself to the Heavenly Father. Being hidden in Him, our prayers and sacrifices have His value. In the Mass we are once more at Calvary, rubbing shoulders with Mary Magdalen and John, while mournfully looking over our shoulders at executioners who still shake dice for the garments of the Lord.

The priest who offers the Sacrifice merely lends to Christ his voice and his fingers. It is Christ who is the Priest; it is Christ who is the Victim. In all pagan sacrifices and in the Jewish sacrifices, the victim was always *separate* from the priest. It might have been a goat, a lamb, or a bullock. But when Christ came, He the Priest offered Himself as the Victim. In the Mass, it is Christ who still offers Himself and who is the Victim to whom we become united. The altar, therefore, is not related to the congregation as the stage to an audience in the theatre. The communion rail is not the same as footlights, which divide the drama from the onlooker. All the members of the Church have a kind of priesthood, inasmuch as they offer up with the Eternal Priest this eternal act of love. The laity participate in the life and power of Christ, for "Thou hast made us a royal race of priests to serve God" (Rev. 5:10).

The expression sometimes used by Catholics, "to hear Mass," is an indication of how little is understood of their active participation, not only with Christ, but also with all of the saints and members of the Church until the end of time. This corporate action of the Church is indicated in certain prayers of the Mass. For example, immediately before the Consecration, God is asked to receive the offering which "we Thy servants and Thy whole household make unto Thee"; and after the Consecration the faithful again say, "We Thy servants, as also Thy holy people, do offer unto Thy most excellent majesty of Thine own gifts bestowed on us." All participate, but the closer we are to the mystery, the more we become one with Christ.

No man can ever come to the real fullness of his personality by reflection or contemplation; he has to *act it out*. That is why through all ages man laid his hand on the best of the herd and destroyed it in order to indicate the offering and surrender of himself. By laying his hands on the animal, he identified himself with it. Then he consumed it, in order to gain some identification with the one to whom it was offered. In the Mass, all the ancient dim foreshadowings of the supreme sacrifice are fulfilled. Man immolates himself with Christ, bidding Him to take his body and his blood. Through this destruction of the ego, there is a void and an emptiness created, which makes it possible for the Divinity to fill up the vacuum and to make the offerer holy. Man dies to the past, in order that he may live in the future. He chooses to be united with his Divine King in some form of death, that he may share in His Resurrection and glory. Thus dying he lives; chastened he is not killed; sorrowful he always rejoices; giving up time, he finds eternity. Nothingness is exchanged for everything. Poverty turns into riches, and having nothing, he begins to possess all things.

The Eucharist as a Sacrament, or Holy Communion

Running through the universe is the law that nothing lives unless it consumes. Plant life, obedient to this law, goes down to the earth, eats and drinks from its waters, phosphates, and carbonates, and circulates them through its organism. The animal, because endowed with a higher life than that of the plant, is in still greater need of nourishment. It needs not only the nourishment of the mineral order, the air, the sunlight and the like, but also the nourishment of plant life. The instinct of the animal is to seek food. The animal roaming in the field, the fish swimming in the water, the eagle soaring in the air, all are in search of daily bread, for without knowing it, they acknowledge that life is impossible without nourishment, that life grows only by life, and that the joy of living comes from communion with another kind of life.

Because men, as well as animals, have bodies, they are under the necessity of feeding these bodies. The food for which they clamor is more delicate because the human body is more delicate. The body is not content, as the plant, to take its food from the ground, raw, uncooked, and unseasoned. It seeks the refinement that comes with a higher creature but in doing so, acknowledges the law that every living thing must nourish itself.

Man has a soul, as well as a body. The spiritual part of him demands a food which is above the material and the physical and the biological. Some would call a halt to the law, that all life must nourish itself, and assert that the soul can find its satisfying food here below without any appeal to a higher life. But the broken minds and tortured hearts testify to the fact that nothing can satisfy the soul hunger of man except a nourishment suited to his soul and its aspirations for the perfect. A canary does not consume the same kind of food as a boa constrictor, because its nature is different. Man's soul being spiritual demands a spiritual food. In the order of grace, this divine food is the Eucharist, or the communion of man with Christ and Christ with man.

This is not something contrary to the natural law, for if the chemical could speak, it would say to the plant: "Unless you eat me, you shall not have life in you." If the plant could speak, it would say to the animal: "Unless you eat me, you shall not have life in you." If the animal, plant, and air could speak, they would say to man: "Unless you eat me, you shall not have life in you." With the same logic, but speaking from above and now below, because the soul is spiritual, our Blessed Lord actually says to the soul: "Except you eat the flesh of the Son of Man and drink His blood, you shall not have life in you" (John 6:54). The law of transformation works consistently through nature and grace. The lower transforms itself into the higher, the plant transforms itself into the animal when taken as food; man is transformed by grace into Christ when he takes Christ into his soul, for it is a quality of love to transform itself into the object that is loved.

Why should we be surprised that He gives Himself to us as food? After all, if He furnishes food for the birds and the beasts in the natural order, why should He not furnish it for man in the supernatural order? If the plant nourishes its seed before it is ripe, and if the bird brings food to its young before they can fly, shall we deny to Him that which we allow to a creature? To every infant at the breast, the mother virtually says: "Take, eat and drink; this is my body and blood." The mother would be untrue to nature if she said, "This *represents* my body," knowing that it is her body. So too, the Lord would be untrue to fact if He said: "This is not my Body and Blood. It is only a representation or a symbol of it." The analogy with the mother, however, breaks completely down, because here a nourishment is on the same level, that of the human with the human. But in the Eucharist, the nourishment is on two different levels: The divine and the human.

First Effect: Union with the Life of Christ

If Christianity were only the memory of someone who lived over nineteen hundred years ago, it would not be worth preserving. If He who came to this earth is not God, as well as man, then we are dealing merely with the fallible and the human. But even granting that He is God in the flesh, how do we contact Him? Certainly, not by reading books about Him, although they are edifying and instructive; obviously not by singing hymns, though these do help us emotionally. The human heart craves contact with the beloved. If we can have contact with nature through the food we eat; if lower creation winds up somehow inside of my body, why should not means be provided in order that there might be communion of the soul? This is one of the first effects of Holy Communion: we receive from Christ what we gave to Him. We gave to him our human nature — when, in the name of all humanity, Mary gave Him manhood, like unto us in all things save sin. He divinized that human nature because it was made substantially one with His Divine Person. In Communion, He gives it back to us, purified, regenerated, ennobled, a promise and a pledge of what our nature is to be on the Last Day in the resurrection of the just. Our Blessed Lord made it so clear, it is almost difficult to understand how one misses it:

> As I live because of the Father, the Living Father who has sent me, so he who eats me will live, in his turn, because of me. (John 6:58 [57])

> ... that they may all be one; that they too may be one in us, as thou Father, art in me, and I in thee; so that the world may come to believe that it is thou who has sent me. And I have given them the privilege which thou gavest to me, that they should all be one as we are one." (John 17:21–22)

In the natural order, a living thing assimilates its food and incorporates it into its own substance. In the Eucharist, the roles are reversed. The Eucharist is food for our soul, but the power of assimilation here belongs to Christ, and it is He who, feeding us, unites us and incorporates us with His life. It is not Christ who is changed into us, as is the food we eat; it is we who are incorporated in Him. With John the Baptist we say: "He must become more and more; I must become less and less" (John 3:30).

The moment of communion is that special intimacy reserved to real lovers. There are three intimacies in life: hearing, speaking, and touching. Our first contact with anyone who loves us is to hear his voice, our second is to see him, the third — and this is reserved only for intimates — is the privilege of touch. We *hear* of Christ in the Scriptures, we *see* Him by the eyes of faith, but we *touch* Him in the Eucharist. He only asks that we should purge our consciences of sin and come to Him, ready to receive what He wants to give us, for He knows that we need Him.

Second Effect: Union with the Death of Christ

Holy Communion is incorporation not only to the life of Christ, but also to His death. This second aspect is sometimes forgotten. St. Paul mentions it: "So it is the Lord's death that you are heralding, whenever you eat this bread and drink this cup, until he comes" (1 Cor. 11:26). In another place, St. Paul tells us that we are to fill up in our own body that which is wanting to the Passion of Christ (Col. 1:24). To save our souls, the life of Christ must be duplicated in our own life. What He did in His birth, at Calvary, in His Resurrection, and Ascension, we must do. But we cannot enter into those heavenly blessings except through the touch of the Cross, namely, through penance, mortification, and self-denial, and a death to our egotism.

Hence, the Church insists that we be in the state of grace in order to receive our Lord in the Eucharist. As a corpse cannot receive nourishment, so neither may one without the divine life in his soul receive the divine nourishment. In addition to this, the Church demands a certain amount of fasting before Communion. This is to remind us that the Eucharist is not only a sacrament of life, but also the sacrament of mortification. Only when we are stamped with the sign of the Cross will we be stamped with the glory of His Resurrection. From the moment of His death on Calvary until the end of time when He comes in glory, the dying Christ is continually at work re-presenting His death on the altar, and urging us to re-present it in our detachment from the seven pallbearers of the soul — the seven capital sins.

We are the wax and He is the seal. He wants to see something of His victimhood in us; and it is up to every Christian, therefore, to lead a dying life: to be more humble when we are thwarted, more patient when things go wrong, dying a little to the world and to our selfishness, being ever happy to "herald His death in our body until He comes."

Third Effect: Communion with the Mystical Body of Christ

No one was ever so wrong as the professor who said: "Religion is what a man does with his solitariness." If man is solitary, he is like a cell that is isolated from the body. The body can live without an individual cell, but the cell cannot live without the body. No man can live the divine life without some incorporation either in fact, or in desire, with the Mystical Body of Christ which is the Church. But the Mystical Body of Christ can live without an individual member. Our Blessed Lord described our union with Himself the night He gave the Eucharist, as that of the "vine and the branches." St. Paul speaks of us, too, as being many and yet one because we all eat the one bread. There is no autonomic individualism in the Scriptures or in humanity. The whole historical existence is transformed; that is to say, both humanity and the visible creation. The first was transformed through the Incarnation; the second, through the sacraments and its symbols which animate personality.

As there is a lymph which passes through the human body, each cell drinking of that life; so too, the Eucharist is the divine lymph of the Mystical Body of Christ on which every member feeds. The members of the Church are not little spiritual islands each cherishing its own isolation. What blood plasma is to the physical body, the Eucharist is to the Mystical Body — the bond of its unity: "The one bread makes us one body, though we are many in number" (1 Cor. 10:17).

The Tabernacle

The Blessed Sacrament is present in the tabernacle day and night. There Christ dwells, Body, Blood, Soul and Divinity, under the sacramental appearances of bread. How do we know it? Because Christ told us so! Is there any other fundamental evidence? None other than that; but is there any other reason in the world as strong as the word of God

The Sacrament of the Eucharist

Himself? Hence, the Eucharist is above all other sacraments — it is the sacrament of faith.

The faithful believe that Christ is as really and truly present sacramentally in the tabernacle as you are present while you read this book. It is this that makes the church different from any other building. Not a pulpit, not an organ, not a choir, but Christ is the center. As the tabernacle was the center of worship in the Old Testament, so the tabernacle and the altar are the center of worship in the New Testament. Visitors to the church say they "feel the difference," though they know nothing about the Eucharist, as they might feel heat and know not the nature of fire.

But to the faithful members of Christ's Mystical Body, here is Christ! Before His Eucharistic Presence, the downcast eyes of sin find wealth of purging tears; here the heart wounded by betraying loves breaks its silence to the invitation of the Living Savior: "Child, give me thy heart." Here the knee is humbled in genuflection and the heart exalted in adoration; here priests make their "Holy Hour" in answer to the invitation of their Lord in the Garden. Here is the trysting place of love, for this is the "bread which is come down from heaven" (John 6:41) and will remain with us "unto the consummation of the world" (Matt. 28:20). Here Emmaus lives again as His disciples recognize Him in the breaking of the bread (Luke 24:30–31).

4

The Sacrament of Penance

The Sacrament of Penance is for spiritual wounds received after Baptism. Original sin was washed from the infant in Baptism, and in the case of the adult, personal sins as well. But the Lord is "practical." He knows that the white robe given in Baptism is not always kept immaculate; that the "just man falleth seven times a day" (Prov. 24:16), and that the offenses against us should be forgiven "seventy times seven" (Matt. 18:22). Therefore, in His mercy, He instituted a sacrament which is a tribunal of mercy for spiritual healing.

There have been those who say that there is no difference between the Sacrament of Penance and psychoanalysis because, in both, the human mind, when disturbed, seeks to throw off its burden. True it is that as the hand will go to the eye to provide relief from a speck, so the tongue will come to the aid of the heart to secure relief. As Shakespeare put it: "My tongue will tell the anger of my heart; Or else my heart, concealing it, will break." We are not here criticizing the psychoanalytic method, but only the error of saying that there is no difference between it and the Sacrament of Penance. But the differences between psychoanalysis and Confession are enormous.

Contrast of Psychoanalysis and Confession

Psychoanalysis is the avowal of an attitude of *mind*; Confession is an avowal of *guilt*. The first comes from the subconsciousness, the other from conscience. A person can be proud of his state of mind; some are proud of being atheists, or immoral, or gangsters. Many a patient will tell a psychiatrist, "Have you ever heard a case like mine, Doctor?" On the contrary, no one is ever proud of his guilt. Even in isolation, the sinner is ashamed. It takes no courage to admit that one is "mental" but guiltless; but it takes a tremendous amount of heroism, of which few are capable, to take the burden of one's own guilt to Calvary and lay one's hands at the feet of the Crucified and say: "I am responsible for this."

Psychoanalysis proceeds according to a *theory*, and not always one theory. Confession, however, is based upon conformity or non-conformity to the absolute standard of the *law of God*. Psychoanalysis does not agree on a particular theory by which a mental state is to be judged. There are three main theories: one attributes mental disturbances to sex (Freud); another to an inferiority complex (Adler); and the third to a drive toward security (Jung). The analyst, because he is guided by a theory, is *never required to have any moral fitness for his task*; his personal ethical right to receive confidences is never raised. He may be living with his sixth wife, and yet advise people how to be happy in marriage.

But in Confession, it is different. The deliverances of the penitent are always on the *moral* plane — not on the *psychological*. The penitent knows that he is before a judgment, not a theory, and that the confessor who hears his sins stands in the place of God. Because the priest is the Mediator between God and man, the Church always asks that the priest who absolves the penitent be himself in the state of grace; that is to say, a participant in divine life. The avowal of guilt, therefore, on the part of the penitent is not subject to the individual whims, theories, idiosyncrasies, and kinks of the one who hears it, but to the divine law, and to the order and the moral standards of Christ, who taught that one must be holy to make holy.

A third difference is that in psychoanalysis, there is the probing by an alien or *outside* mind; in Confession, it is the *penitent himself* who is his own prosecuting attorney and even his own judge. In analysis, there is often a seeking out of attitudes to bolster up a theory; but in a spontaneous confession, the penitent analyzes his own faults and confesses them without having them wander and riot in "free association" and then be submitted to "private interpretation of the subconscious" which took the place of private interpretation of the Bible. Man naturally accords pardon to others who have done injury by a simple avowal of faults, without someone else dragging them out. One indispensable condition of receiving pardon in the sacrament is this *open* avowal of guilt, such as the prodigal son made when he returned again to the father's house.

Another difference is that what is told in the confessional is absolutely secret, and may never be divulged, or made part of a book, or turned into a case history, such as is often done with the material that is brought out in a psychoanalytic examination. The offenses man commits against God *do not belong to any man*; hence, he may not make use of them. The material of Confession belongs to God, and sins may never be revealed by the confessor until God does so on the Day of Judgment. The confessor's ears are God's ears, and his tongue may never speak what God has heard through his ears.

Another difference is in the attitude that a person assumes in Confession and psychoanalysis. In one instance, the mentally disturbed person is on a *couch*; in Confession, he is on his *knees*. There is a passivity about the admission of a mental state on a *couch*; but there is a humble activity on the part of one who admits moral guilt while on his knees. In the psychological examination, there is never any such thing as contrition or satisfaction. In Confession, sorrow and the making up for our sins are integral parts of the sacrament. When one sees a string of confessional boxes in a large church, with feet protruding from under the curtains like wiggling worms, one realizes that man has reduced himself almost to the humble state of the worm, in order that he might rise again, restored to the glorious friendship of the Christ who died for him.

A final and important difference between psychoanalysis and Confession is this: in psychoanalysis, the admission of mental states comes from ourselves; in Confession, the impetus or the desire to confess our sins is from the *Holy Spirit*. The night of the Last Supper, our Blessed Lord said that He would send His Spirit to convict the world of sin (John 16:8). It is only through the Spirit of Christ that we know we are sinners, as we see our lives in relationship to the Cross. The Holy Spirit summons the soul to find its way back to the shelter of the Father's arms. When a person is in sin, he is in exile from home, a dweller in a foreign land who looks forward to the joy of return. It is an urge to share in the joy of the Good Shepherd as He carries back the lost sheep and the straying lamb to the sheepfold of the Church.

The reason this summons must come from God is that we are captives of sin. Just as a prisoner cannot release himself from the chafing bars or chains, so neither can the sinner without the power of the Spirit. To God alone belongs the initiative in this sacrament. It is His voice which calls us to repentance. We may make our confessions because our conscience urges us to do so, but the voice that speaks to us is the voice of the Holy Spirit telling us of God's mercy and love, and righteousness. Under the impetus of the Holy Spirit, the soul feels like Lazarus risen from the dead.

Two Basic Requirements for the Sacrament

In order that there might be a Sacrament of Penance, two things are required, both of which are, from a human point of view, almost impossible to find. First, one must create the penitent and, secondly, one must create a confessor. To create a penitent, one must take a man in his pride, enveloped in a glacial silence, which refuses to unburden its guilt, and say to him: "Thou shalt come to a man and kneel before him—a man who is perhaps no better than you are—and you shall tell him what you hide from yourself and your children. You shall tell him that which makes you blush; and you shall do all of this on your knees."

However difficult it may be to create a penitent who will confess everything with a firm purpose of amendment, it is even more difficult to create the confessor. Where find one empowered by God with authority to forgive sins? How train the human heart to heal the wounds of others, and then seal his lips forever that what he has learned as God's representative be never revealed to men?

Only God could bring these two creations together, for outside of His power and mercy, we would say: "Humanity is too proud, you will never have penitents"; "Humanity is too indiscreet, you will never have confessors." And yet the sacrament exists. There are penitents because there are confessors, and there are penitents and confessors because Christ is God.

The Sacrament Deals with Sins

When a baby is born, it is generally healthy; but as time goes on, it becomes subject to diseases and organic troubles which oppress and torment life. In the spiritual order, too, though the soul is made clean and free from all sin by Baptism, it nevertheless contracts stains and spiritual diseases during life. These are known as sins. If the sin is serious enough to rupture the divine life within, then it is called "mortal" because it brings death to the life of Christ in the soul. If the wrong done does not destroy the divine life, but only injures it, it is called "venial."

A serious sin always produces in the soul a three-fold effect. The first is self-estrangement. A sinner feels in his inmost being like a battlefield where a civil war rages. He no longer is a unit but a duality in which two forces within him struggle for mastery.

Serious sin estranges the sinner from his fellow man, because a man who is not at peace with himself will not be at peace with his neighbor. World wars are nothing but the projection, into great areas of the earth's surface, of the psychic wars waging inside of muddled souls. If there were no battles going on inside of hearts, there would be no battlefields in the world. It was after Cain's murder of Abel that he asked the anti-social question, "Am I my brother's keeper?"

The most serious effect of sin is not alienation from self and from fellow man; it is the estrangement from God. Inasmuch as grace is the divine life within the soul, it follows that a serious sin is the destruction of that divine life. That is why the Epistle to the Hebrews asks: "Would they crucify the Son of God a second time, hold Him up to mockery a second time, for their own ends?" (6:6). Sin, therefore, is a second death. The merits we gained are lost; but those merits can be regained, thanks to the mercy of God, in the Sacrament of Penance.

Instituted by Christ

The Sacrament of Penance was instituted by Christ in the form of a judgment, for the remission, through sacramental absolution, of sins committed after Baptism and granted to a contrite person confessing his sins.

All through the Old Testament there was a preparation for this sacrament, inasmuch as God strove to induce men to acknowledge their sins before Him. To elicit a confession, God said to Adam: "Hast thou eaten of the tree?" (Gen. 3:11). God said to the first murderer: "Where is thy brother?" (Gen. 4:9). In Mosaic legislation, a sinner brought a sin offering, which was burned in a public place, to show that the sinner was not afraid to admit his guilt. The prophet, Nathan, heard David's confession after his sin with Bethsabee, and assigned to him a penance. John the Baptist heard the confession of those who came to hear him preach. These were only types and figures of the sacrament that was to come, because forgiveness became possible only through the merits of our Lord's Passion.

No one questions the fact that our Blessed Lord had the power to forgive sins. The Gospels record the miraculous cure of the paralytic at Capharnaum. Our Lord first told the paralytic that his sins were forgiven him, whereupon those round about laughed at Him. In response the Savior told them that it was just as easy to cure the man as it was to forgive his sins; so He cured the paralytic: "To convince you that the Son of Man has authority to forgive sins while He is on earth" (Mark 2:10).

Our Blessed Lord was saying that God in the form of man had the power to forgive sins; that is to say, through the instrumentality of the human nature, which He received from Mary, He was forgiving sins. Here is an anticipation of the fact that it is through humanity that He will continue to forgive sins; i.e., through those who are endowed with sacramental power to do so. Man cannot forgive sins, but God can forgive sins through man.

Our Lord promised to confer this power of forgiveness, first of all, to Peter whom He made the rock of the Church. He told Peter that

The Sacrament of Penance

He would ratify in Heaven the decisions which Peter took on earth. These decisions were explained in two metaphors of "binding" and "loosing." The power of jurisdiction was given to the one who had the keys of the kingdom. This promise made to Peter was followed up a little later on by one made to the Apostles. The second promise did not bestow the primacy, for that was reserved to Peter. Our Lord told the Apostles:

> I came upon an errand from my Father, and now I am sending you out in my turn. With that, he breathed on them, and said to them, Receive the Holy Spirit; when you forgive men's sins, they are forgiven, when you hold them bound, they are held bound. (John 20:21–23)

Our Divine Redeemer here says that He was sent by the Father; now He sends them with the power to forgive or not forgive. These words imply "hearing confessions," because how would the priests of the Church know which sins to forgive and which sins not to forgive if they did not hear them?

One can be very sure that this sacrament is not of human institution, for if the Church had invented any of the sacraments, there is one that it certainly would have done away with, and that is the Sacrament of Penance. This because of the trials that it imposes upon those who have to hear confessions, sitting in the confessional box for long hours while listening to the terrific monotony of fallen human nature. Because it is a divine institution—what a beautiful opportunity it is to restore peace to sinners and to make them saints!

It may be asked, why did our Lord demand a telling of sins? Why not bury one's head in one's handkerchief, and tell God that one is sorry? Well, if this method of being sorry is not effective when we are caught by a traffic policeman, why should it be effective with God? Shedding tears in one's handkerchief is no test of sorrow, because we are then the judges. Who would ever be sentenced to prison, if every man were his own judge? How easy it would be for murderers and thieves to escape justice and judgment simply by having a handkerchief ready!

Because sin is pride, it demands a humiliation, and there is no greater humiliation than unburdening one's soul to a fellow man. Such self-revelation cures us of many a moral illness. Hurtful things often hurt more if they are shut up. A boil can be cured, if lanced to release the pus; so too is a soul on the pathway to the Father's House when it admits to its own sin and seeks forgiveness. All nature suggests an unburdening of oneself. If the stomach takes a foreign substance into it which it cannot assimilate, it throws it off; so it is with the soul. It seeks deliverance from that which troubles it, namely the unbearable repartee within.

Furthermore, when a sin is avowed and admitted, it loses its tenacity. Sin is seen in all its horror when viewed in relationship to the Crucifixion. Suppress a sin, and it becomes buried, and later on will come out in complexes. It is very much like keeping the cap on a tube of toothpaste. If one submits it to great pressure, the toothpaste will come out somewhere; one does not know where. The normal place for it to come out is through the top. So too, if we suppress our guilt or deny it, we put our mind under pressure and it creates abnormalities. The guilt does not come out where it ought to be, namely, in the sacrament. Thus it was that Lady Macbeth's guilt came out in the washing of hands. It should have been her soul that was washed, and not her hands.

Confession to a Priest

It may be asked, why confess one's sins to a priest? Maybe he is not as holy as the penitent. That indeed could be. But though he is not holier in his *person*, he is holier in his *powers*, because Christ gave this power to His Church — only the Church claims it, and only the Church exercises it. The mayor of a town may not be as good as some of the citizens, but he has the power which the citizens do not; so it is with the priest.

Furthermore, it is not the priest who absolves: he is only the instrument of Christ. Can man of and by himself forgive sins? No! Can man united to God forgive sins? Yes! That is the way Christ the Son of God forgave sins through His human nature. That is the way He forgave the sins of Magdalen; that is the way He forgave the sins of the paralytic;

that is the way He forgave the sins of the thief on the right. That power
He gave to His Church.

Because the priest acts in Christ's name, he is bound by the seal of
Confession. Not even under the penalty of death may he reveal sins that
are confided to him in Confession. As a person, he has not heard any sins.
They are not a part of his knowledge. It was Christ who heard the sin
and He alone has knowledge of it. Suppose a murderer came into a rectory and confessed to a priest. On leaving the priest, the murderer shook
hands with him. After the murderer left, the police entered, found blood
on the priest's hands and accused him of the murder. The priest could
not say: "It was the man who just went out. I did not do it." He may not
make any defense of himself, nor may a priest outside the confessional
ever speak to that person about his sins. For example, he may not say to
a penitent whom he meets on the street, "Oh, did you ever pay back the
hundred dollars you stole?" If someone stole money from a drawer in my
desk, and then came and confessed the stealing of money; I could order
the money returned, but I would not be permitted to lock the drawer,
because that was information which I gained in God's sacrament.

Another reason for confessing sins to a priest is that no one sin is individual. We are members of the Mystical Body of Christ. If one member
is unhealthy, the whole body is unhealthy. If we have an earache, the
whole body suffers. Now, every personal sin has a social effect: all the
other cells of the body of the Church are affected because of the defect in
this one cell. Every sinner is blameworthy, not only in regard to himself,
but also in regard to the Church, and first and foremost to God. If he is
ever to recover, it can only be by the intervention of the Church, and
by an intervention of God.

No medicine will act on a member of the body, unless the body coop-
erates in some way with the medicine. Because every sin is against God
and the Church, it follows that a representative of God and His Mystical
Body must restore the sinner again to fellowship. The priest, acting as
the representative of the Church, welcomes back the penitent to the
community of believers. When our Blessed Lord found the lost sheep,
He immediately integrated them again into His flock:

Jesus was to die for the sake of the nation; and not only for that nation's sake, but so as to bring together into one all God's children, scattered far and wide. (John 11:51–52)

The priest reestablishes the sinner in grace; he restores the sinner to his rights as a son of the Eternal Father; he reconciles him not only to God, but also to God's society of the Church.

The social nature of Penance is seen further in the fact that the penitent recognizes the right of the Mystical Body to judge him, since it is through the Mystical Body he is in relation with God. Forgiveness of sin, then, is not just a matter between God and our individual souls. It is the Church which has been injured by transgressions. Therefore, our sins are not just our concern, they are the concern of the whole Church — the Church Militant on earth and the Church Triumphant in Heaven.

The Examination of Conscience

Before the penitent goes into the confessional box, there is the examination of conscience. This used to be a daily practice of Christians, and still is among many. It was not even unknown to the pagans. The Stoics, for example, recommended it. The examination of conscience centers not only on the wrong we have done, but also on the motivations. Our Blessed Lord, examining the conscience of the Pharisees, called them "whited sepulchres, clean on the outside, but on the inside full of dead men's bones" (Matt. 23:27). He pierced beneath the pretensions and hypocrisies of their prayers, their almsgivings, and their philanthropies, saying they did these things to be seen by men and to have a human reward — and that is the only reward they will ever receive. So in the examination of conscience, all the thoughts, words, and deeds of the soul are brought to the surface, examined, and considered in conformity with the law of God.

One of the differences between psychoanalytic examination and examination of conscience is that in the former one stands in one's own light; in the examination of conscience, one stands in the light of God.

The Sacrament of Penance

That is why Scripture says, "Search my soul, O my God" (Ps. 139:23). The divine light looks into the mind, takes the mind off itself and its own false judgments, and makes things appear as they really are; at the end, one does not say, "Oh, what a fool I've been," but rather, "God, be merciful to me, a sinner" (Luke 18:13).

A day comes when the abused conscience will turn with fury and harass its victim, tormenting his waking life and making his dreams a poison and his darkness a nightmare. When night gives inner vision scope, the guilty conscience lies awake, fearful of being known in its ugliness. There is nothing that so much arouses an unhealthy fear as a hidden guilt. As the cock crowed when Peter denied our Lord, so our nature rises in revolt against us when we have denied the Lord of conscience. Sins have a way of finding us out. Just as a refusal to study in childhood begets an ignorance in mature life, so too, sins which we rationalize away are thrust down into unconsciousness, but somehow they make themselves felt in our health, our mental attitudes, and our general outlook on life.

Alongside every human being there are three pools, each of which gives a different reflection. We look into one pool and we are pleased with ourselves, because in that pool we see ourselves as we think we are. In the second pool, we see ourselves as our neighbor sees us, or as our press clippings reveal us. In the third pool, we see ourselves as God sees us, and as we *really* are. It is into this third pool that examination of conscience takes us, bringing to the surface the hidden faults of the day, discovering the weeds that are choking the growth of God's grace, our sins of omission and commission, the good deeds left undone, the failure to aid a needy neighbor, the refusal to offer a word of consolation to one burdened with sorrow, and malicious remarks, lies, acts of dishonesty, and the seven sins which are the enemy of peace: self-love, inordinate love of money, illicit sex, hate, over-indulgence, jealousy, and laziness.

Examination of conscience also embraces what is called our predominant passion. Every person has one sin which he commits more than another. Examination of conscience roots out all our self-deception, for every person has a little corner in his heart he never wants anyone to venture into, even with a candle. We say we are following our consciences, when actually what we mean is that we are making our consciences, and then following what we made. It is this kind of deceit that is unveiled in the examination and, by curing us of self-deception, it cures us of depression. Depression comes not from having faults, but from refusing to face them. What else is self-pity but a total unconcern with the interests of others?

It must not be thought that in the examination of conscience one concentrates on his own wounds; rather he concentrates on the mercy of God. A sick person thinks less of his own sickness than the physician who will heal him. The examination of conscience develops no complex, because it is done in the light of God's justice. The self is not the standard, nor is it the source of hope. All human frailty and human weakness are seen in the light of God's infinite goodness. Sorrow is aroused, not because a code has been violated, but because love has been wounded. As an empty pantry drives the housewife to the bakery, so the empty soul is driven to the bread of life. Examination of conscience, instead of inducing morbidity, becomes an occasion of joy.

There are two ways of knowing how good God is: one is never to lose Him through the preservation of innocence; the other is to find Him again after He has been lost. There is no self-loathing, there is only a God-loving character about the examination of conscience. We put ourselves in God's hand as we would put a broken watch in the hand of a watchmaker, certain that he will not ruin it, but will make it function well.

The closer we get to God, the more we see our defects. A painting reveals few defects under candlelight, but the sunlight may reveal it as a daub. It is true that we do find ourselves quite unlovable in the examination of conscience, but it is this that makes us want to love God because He is the only One who loves the unlovable.

When one has finished the examination of conscience, there may be a load to drag into the confessional, which is sometimes called the "box." If it is a "box," it is not Pandora's, for at the bottom of it is hope. Then we realize that we are bringing it to Christ Himself. It is wonderful to know that there is one place where we can taste the freedom of Heaven, where a man can be spared the hypocrisy of maintaining a pose. There comes the joy of knowing that neither the penitent nor the priest ever recalls the sin confessed. A shutter drops. Something is put into a well, and a cover is laid on it forever.

In the early Church, sins which were committed publicly were confessed publicly. This survives in the *Roman Pontifical*, in a ceremony called "The Expulsion of Public Penitents on Ash Wednesday"; another ceremony is called, "The Reconciliation of Penitents on Maundy Thursday"; and still another special rite is used for the absolution of those who have been publicly excommunicated. Though public sins in the early Church were confessed publicly, secret sins were confessed secretly and under the seal.

Sorrow for Sin: Contrition

The other sacraments demand that the subject has proper dispositions, but they do not constitute the *matter* of the sacrament. In Penance, sorrow is not only a condition; it is the *matter* itself; for without the sorrow for sin, forgiveness is not granted.

The priest gives absolution from sins in the sacrament provided there is sufficient sorrow of mind, or contrition, which is a hatred of the sin committed with the resolution not to sin again. The word contrition is taken from the Latin word which means to *grind* or *pulverize*; in an applied sense, it means being bruised in heart. Contrition is a sorrow of mind, not an emotional outburst or psychological remorse.

The prodigal son had gone through many emotional stages of remorse, particularly when he was feeding the swine, or realizing how much better the servants in his father's house were. But the real sorrow did not come until it penetrated his soul with the resolution: "I will arise and go to my father" (Luke 15:18).

Sometimes it is said that all a Catholic has to do is go to Confession and admit his sins, and he will come out white as snow and then continue committing the same sins. This is a libel upon the sacrament for, where there is no purpose of amendment, there is no sorrow. The sins of such a penitent are not forgiven. The sorrow for sin necessarily includes a resolution not to sin again; this is not merely a wish which has no relationship to practice. Part of the Act of Contrition contains this amendment: "And I firmly resolve with the help of Thy grace to confess my sins, to do penance, and amend my life. Amen." It means that here and now we take the resolution not to sin; we resolve to take all the means necessary for avoiding sin in the future, such as prayer and staying away from the occasions of sin. The absolution will not be efficacious if there is not in the sorrow this essential element, a purpose of amendment.

This does not imply an absolute certitude that no one will ever sin again, for that would be presumption. There are two ways to verify a firm purpose: one is to make up for the sin as soon as possible; for example, if one is guilty of sarcastic remarks against a neighbor, to seek the neighbor's pardon or, if one has stolen, to return what has been stolen. The second is to avoid the occasions of sin, such as bad reading, evil companions, drinking parties, or any act that previously led us into sin.

There are two kinds of contrition: perfect and imperfect. Both are implied in the Act of Contrition which the penitent says in the confessional:

> And I detest all my sins because I dread the loss of Heaven and the pains of Hell [imperfect sorrow], but most of all because they offend Thee, my God, who art all good and deserving of all my love [perfect sorrow].

Two kinds of fear serve as the basis of distinction between the two kinds of contrition or sorrow: one is a *servile* fear, the other is a *filial* fear. A *servile* fear is a fear of punishment, which we justly deserve from a master whom we disobeyed. *Filial* fear is the fear that a devoted son might have for a loving father; namely, the fear of injuring him. Applying this to contrition, servile fear draws us toward God because of the dread of a punishment for sin, namely, Hell. *Filial* fear is a dread of being separated from God, or of offending Him whom we love.

Imagine twins who had disobeyed a mother in exactly the same way. One of the twins runs to the mother and says: "Oh, Mommy, I am sorry I disobeyed. Now I can't go to the picnic, can I?" The other one throws her arms around the mother's neck and weeps: "I'll never hurt you again." The first has imperfect contrition, the second perfect contrition.

The Sacrament of Penance

Which kind of contrition, perfect or imperfect, is sufficient in sacramental Confession? Imperfect contrition is sufficient, though it is our belief that most penitents are sorry not because of the punishment their sins deserve from God, but rather because they heartily are sorry for having re-crucified Christ in their hearts.

Suppose, however, that a person is in a state of mortal sin and is unable to go to Confession; for example, a soldier who is ordered into battle. Would imperfect contrition then suffice for the forgiveness of sins? No, but perfect contrition would, if he had the resolution to receive sacramental Confession at the earliest opportunity.

That makes a word about perfect contrition more imperative. The usual attitude of penitents is to make a personal equation between their own sins and the Crucifixion. Each one says in his heart as he receives the sacrament: "If I had been less proud, the crown of thorns would have been less piercing. If I had been less avaricious and greedy, His hands would have been dug less by the steel. If I had been less sensual, His flesh would not be hanging from Him like purple rags. If I had not wandered away like a lost sheep, in the perversity of my egotism, His feet would have been less driven with nails. I am sorry, not just because I broke a law: I am sorry because I wounded Him who died out of love for me."

Our Lord had to die on the Cross before the abysmal dimensions of sin could be appreciated. We do not see the horror of sin in the crimes paraded in the press, nor in the great crises of history, nor in the wholesale violence of persecutors. We see what evil is only when we see *Goodness nailed to the Cross.* If any of us says in our heart, "I am not as bad as those who crucified Him," we are forgetting that *they* did not crucify our Lord; sin did. They were our representatives, our ambassadors, that day at the court of Satan. We empowered them with the right to crucify.

One look at the crucifix, therefore, is a double revelation! A revelation of the horror of sin and the love of God. The worst thing that sin can do is not to kill children or bomb cities in nuclear warfare; the worst thing that sin can do is to crucify Divine Love. And the most beautiful thing that Love can do, at the moment of Crucifixion, is to extend to us forgiveness in the priestly prayer to His heavenly Father: "Forgive them, for they know not what they do" (Luke 23:34).

In perfect contrition, we become tremendously impressed with the infinite endurance of our Lord to suffer the worst that evil can inflict, and then pardon His enemies. He certainly did not teach us to be indifferent to sin, because He took its full consequences upon Himself. He paid for it, but on the other hand, there was mercy with that justice. He offered forgiveness in the hope that we would repent out of gratitude for His payment of the debt which our sins created.

Satisfaction

Satisfaction for sins, or what is sometimes called "penance," is distinct from sorrow. Few dwell sufficiently on the difference between being forgiven and atoning for the sin which was forgiven.

Suppose I stole your purse in the course of a conversation, and then I said to myself: "What a scandal I am to this person. I am supposed to bring justice and the love of God, and here I violate God's law of justice, impugn His mercy, and nail Him to the Cross by stealing the purse." So I say to you, "Will you forgive me?" In your kindness, you would certainly say: "I forgive you." But you would also say something else, would you not? Would you not say, "Give me back my purse?" Could I really say that I was sorry unless I returned the purse?

There is a story told, which is sheer imagination with no basis in fact, about a man who came to Confession to a priest. During the course of the Confession, he stole the priest's watch. At the end of the Confession, he said to the priest: "Oh, Father, I forgot to tell you. I stole a watch." The priest, emphasizing the necessity of satisfaction, said: "You must return the watch to the owner." The penitent said: "I'll give it to you, Father." The priest said: "No, I don't want it. Return it to the owner." The penitent said: "The owner doesn't want it." The priest said to him: "Well, in that case, you can keep it."

Immediately one can see some of the fallacies. First, there was no real sorrow in Confession; otherwise, he would not have added a sin while confessing others. Second, there was deceit in his satisfaction. There must always be satisfaction for sin, because every sin disturbs the order of God. Sin upsets a balance. It is to no purpose to say, "Don't cry over spilled milk," just because we happen to have spilled someone else's milk. If we cannot gather up the spilled milk, we can at least pay for the bottle, or buy some more milk.

At the end of the Confession, the priest gives to the penitent what is called a "penance," a certain number of prayers to say, or fasting, or the giving of alms, or acts of mortification, or a way of the Cross, or a Rosary. All of these are to "make up" for the sin, and to prove that the sorrow was sincere. This is what Catholics call "saying my penance" or "doing my penance."

God does not ask us to make an exact reparation for our sins, but rather to do it in a proportional manner. This is because the Sacrament of Penance is less a tribunal of strict justice than a reconciliation between friends. The priest, representing Christ, is not a judge sentencing a criminal to prison. The penitent is not an enemy. He is a reconciled friend, and the reparation, penance, or satisfaction is the work of friendship between members of Christ's Mystical Body. The penance also has a medicinal value, that of healing the wounds of the soul, which is why it has to be performed in a state of grace. Our Lord forgave our sins on the Cross, but He paid for them in justice. Our Lord forgave the thief on the right, but He did not stop his crucifixion. The pain the thief endured was a reparation for his evil life. Penance is a sign that we are applying Christ's death on Calvary to ourselves.

Here the Sacrament of Penance differs from the Sacrament of Baptism. In Baptism, the merits of Christ's Passion are applied to ourselves without any action on our part; but in the Sacrament of Penance, we make some satisfaction. Power and efficacy are given to our acts, because they are united with the Passion of Christ. There are two debts to be paid for sin. One is the eternal debt, which is Hell; and the other is the temporal debt, or atoning in our lifetime for our imperfections and our want of charity, after our sin has been forgiven. The *eternal* debt of Hell is completely remitted in the sacrament. The *temporal* debt for sin remains.

In Scripture, we find records of people being forgiven, for whom a temporal punishment remains. Adam and Eve were restored to grace, but they were made subject to death. Miriam, the sister of Moses, gained forgiveness for her sin, but she was shut out from the camp for seven days and afflicted with leprosy. Moses was forgiven, but was punished for his lack of trust in God by being excluded from the Land of Promise. David's sin with Bethsabee was forgiven, but he had to suffer misfortunes for it, and the child died as a punishment.

That is why St. Paul urges us to take on voluntary penances that we may "help to pay off the debt which the afflictions of Christ still leave to be paid, for the sake of his body, the Church" (Col. 1:24). Daniel consoled Nabuchodonosor with the words: "Deign my lord king, to be advised by me; with almsgiving, with mercy to the poor, for fault and wrong-doing of thine, make amends; it may be that he will condone thy guilt" (Dan. 4:24). And Joel writes: "Time now, the Lord says, to turn the whole bent of your hearts back to me, with fasting and mourners' tears" (Joel 2:12). Did not our Lord say of certain cities that they would be condemned because in them "were done most of His miracles, but for that they had not done penance (Matt. 11:20).

Penances given after Confession are generally light. Some say they are too light. But we must not forget indulgences. To understand them, we should recall that we are members of Christ's Mystical Body. When we do evil, or commit sin, we affect every member of the Church in some way. This is even done in our most secret sins. It is evident that we do it in stealing, murder, and adultery; but we do it even in our solitary sins, even in our evil thoughts. How? By diminishing in some way the content of charity and love within the whole Mystical Body. Just as a pain in the eye affects the whole organism and makes us hurt all over so, if I love Christ less, do I impair the spiritual well-being of the Church.

But because I can harm the Church by my sin, so can I be helped by the Church when I am in debt. St. Paul applied to the Mystical Body the lesson of the physical body: "All the different parts of it [the body] were to make each other's welfare their common care" (1 Cor. 12:25).

The Sacrament of Penance

Religion is not individual, it is *social*; it is organic. Look to the natural order, and see how many benefits I receive from my fellow man. There are a million ways in which they are indulgent to me. I did not raise the cow that furnished the leather that went into my shoes. I did not raise the chicken I eat at dinner—but that is a bad example; I do not like chicken! So let us say, the chicken you eat. Somebody's work or labor allowed you to indulge in this luxury. We might almost say that we are surrounded by social "indulgences," because we share in the merits, talents, arts, crafts, sciences, techniques, needlework, and genius of society.

Now, in the society of Christ's people, His Mystical Body, it is possible to share in the merits and the good works, the prayers, the sacrifices, the self-denials, and the martyrdoms of others. If there be an economic "indulgence," so that I can ride in a plane someone else built, why should there not also be a spiritual indulgence, so that I can be carried to Christ more quickly through the bounty of some members of the Mystical Body.

Go back now to the distinction between forgiveness of guilt and satisfaction for guilt. Every sin has both an eternal and a temporal punishment. Even though our sins were forgiven, there still remained some satisfaction to be made in time; or else in Purgatory after death, provided we die in the state of grace. An indulgence refers not to sin, but to the temporal punishment. Before the indulgences can apply, there must have been forgiveness of the guilt.

Actually, there are several ways of making up for the punishment due after the guilt of sin has been forgiven. Three are personal, one is social: (1) The saying or doing of the penance given in the confessional box at the end of Confession; (2) Any works of mortification which are freely undertaken during life, such as helping the poor and the missions, fasting, and other acts of self-denial; (3) The patient imitation of our Lord's sufferings on the Cross by enduring the trials of life; and (4) The social remedy of applying the superabundant merits of the Mystical Body to our souls. As we depend on intellectual society to make up for our ignorance, so we depend on a spiritual society to make up for our spiritual bankruptcy.

It may be asked where the Church gets power to remit temporal pun-ishment due to sin? Well, the Church happens to be very rich *spiritually*, just as some men are very rich financially. In a village there lived a rich banker who set up a trust fund in a bank; he bade all of the sick, infirm, and unemployed to draw from that reserve. The banker told them: "Have no fears that this fund will ever run out, for I am rich enough to care for all of you." If the banker paid part of the hospital bills, that would be a *partial indulgence* of the debts of the sick; if he paid all of their bills, that would be a *plenary indulgence* of their expenses and costs.

The Church is a spiritual banker. It has all the merits of the Passion of our Lord and the Blessed Mother, the merits of the martyrs, saints, and confessors, and the patient endurance of persecution in the present time; all of these merits are far greater than those needed for salvation of these saintly and good people. The Church takes that surplus, puts it into her treasury, and bids all her weak and wounded, who cannot pay all the debts they owe for their sins, to draw on those reserves. The Church lays down certain conditions for making use of this treasure, just as the banker did. The users have to be deserving, they have to be in the state of grace, they have to fulfill certain conditions; e.g., a prayer, a pilgrim-age, or any one of a thousand little things.

When the debt of temporal punishment due to sin is liquidated only in part by an indulgence, it is called a partial indulgence. But if all the debts of temporal punishment are paid for by fulfilling the conditions, it is called a *plenary indulgence*.

Suppose I am standing in the center of the room, that you have a right to command me, and that I am bound in conscience to obey you. You order me to take three steps to my right. I disobey, and take three steps to my left. When I take the three steps to my left, I say to you, "I am very sorry. I have disobeyed you. Will you forgive me?" You say: "Yes, I will forgive you." But look where I am! I am actually six steps from where I ought to be, and I am three steps from being in neutral ground. Since I have taken three steps in disobedience, I must put my foot down three times humbly and in penance, in order to get back to "neutral" before I can begin doing right. Those three steps, taken penitentially, represent the payment of the temporal punishment due to sin.

Now suppose that I just took two steps and someone carried me the other one, I would then have an indulgence of one step. If someone carried me two steps, I would then have the indulgence of two steps. If someone carried me the three steps, that would be a plenary indulgence.

That brings up the question of "days." One often hears of the indulgence of "forty days," "one hundred days," or "forty years." The Church has to have some standard of measurement, and "days" and "years" are merely approximations. In the first several centuries of the Church, penances were very severe for certain public sins. One might have to dress himself in sackcloth and ashes and beg at a church door for forty days, or three years, or seven years, or sometimes ten years in the case of atrocious crimes. Because these sins gave grave scandal to the public, the penitent would be permitted to assist at the Mass at the door or in a special part of the Church.

Later on, there began to be intercessions of persons of high merit, that they be given more or less extended remission of the temporal punishment due to their sins; these became known as indulgences. The Church then took, as a standard of measurement, the severe penances of the early days and applies them today to indulgences. For example, for saying certain prayers, one receives an indulgence which is the equivalent of "forty days" penance in the early Church, or the equivalent of "one hundred days" penance in the early Church, or a "year," as the case may be.

There is no exact statistical relation between the sin and its expiation, as there is none between the money you pay for a suit of clothes, and the cooperation of the sheep herder, the wool-gatherers, and the suit manufacturer.

What a beautiful doctrine and how consoling is this sacrament! See how it combines the poor sinner who is in debt, the Mystical Body to which he is restored by absolution in the confessional, and the mercy of Christ, the Head of His Mystical Body who gave this power to His Church: "Whatsoever thou shalt loose on earth is loosed also in Heaven" (Matt. 18:18).

My prayer is only a drop but, when it is joined to the other cells of the Mystical Body, when it becomes a bead in a rosary which unites the Church Militant on earth with the Church Triumphant in Heaven and Church Suffering in Purgatory, when it fuses into the tears of Christ on the Cross and with the sword in Mary's heart at the foot of the Cross, then it makes its way to the sea which is God where we all meet. Thus, thanks to my little drop of a prayer, I have the right to say, "I, too, am the ocean."

One feels like singing for joy, for here is a greater thrill than the bath that cleanses the body. Regular Confession prevents sins, worries, and anxieties from seeping down into the unconscious and degenerating into melancholy fears and neuroses. The boil is lanced before the pus can spread into unconsciousness. Our Lord knew what was in man so He instituted this sacrament, not for His needs but for ours. It was His way of giving man a happy heart. It is not easy, indeed, for a man to make his way to the Cross and to admit that he has been wrong. It is very hard; but the penitent knows that it was harder to hang on that Cross! We are never made worse by admitting we are brokenhearted, for unless our hearts are broken, how can God get in?

5

The Sacrament of the Anointing of the Sick

There are two sacraments of healing: one for spiritual illness, which is the Sacrament of Penance; the other for physical illness, which is the Sacrament of the Anointing of the Sick. An older term for it was "Extreme Unction," which some interpreted as meaning that it was administered only when death was inevitable. For that reason, the sacrament was sometimes postponed until there was no hope of recovery, so as not to frighten the recipient or unduly sadden the relatives and friends.

This is a misinterpretation of the sacrament which is directed to the uncertainty which sickness implies; the sacrament looks to sickness as such. Two extremes are to be avoided, one which would say it was destined only for death; the other, that it is solely a grace of healing. It is rather a sacrament for the time of serious sickness; that is why it may not be given to those who are facing death for any reason other than illness. If it were a sacrament destined solely for those who are about to die, it would be given to a criminal on a scaffold. But the sacrament may not be given in such a case. In those under sentence of death there is no hope of recovery, which this sacrament implies.

It is not a sacrament exclusively for those at the point of death. In the liturgy of the sacrament, the priest does not mention death, but prays for a return to health of body and soul:

Heal, O Redeemer, the infirmities of the sick person; heal his wounds and forgive him his sins. Make all the infirmities of his body and soul disappear, and by Thy Mercy, give him full spiritual and corporal health, that re-established by the effect of Your goodness, he can resume the fulfillment of his duties.... Grant that Thy servant, freed from sickness and restored to health, may be re-established by Thy Name and given back to Thy Holy Church.

Two other prayers follow in which the restoration to health is emphasized:

We implore Thee, O Lord, look with kindness on Thy servant [name] who is growing weak as his [her] body fails. Cherish and revive the soul which Thou didst create, so that, purified and made whole by his [her] sufferings, he [she] may find himself [herself] restored by Thy healing through Christ our Lord. Amen.

O Lord, Father Almighty,... free Thy servant from sickness. Restore to him [her] his [her] health. Raise him [her] up by Thy right hand, strengthen him [her] by Thy power, protect him [her] by Thy might, and give him [her] back to Thy Holy Church with all that is needed for his [her] welfare through Christ our Lord. Amen.

The oil of the sick, which is consecrated at the Pontifical Mass on Holy Thursday, contains no allusions to death or the dying. The words of the bishop are:

Pray that this oil may serve to give renewed strength to God's temple... that all who are anointed with the heavenly remedy of this oil may find it a medicine for body and soul, quick to remove all suffering and to drive away all sickness and infirmity of soul and body.

The official teaching of the Church condemns those who deny that it is a sacrament of healing. The Council of Trent stated:

If anyone says that the anointing of the sick neither confers any grace nor remits sins, nor comforts the sick, but that it has already ceased, as if it had been a healing grace only in the olden days, let him be anathema.

When the salvation of the person, under providence, calls for the postponement of death, the sacrament will bring about this recovery. The writer recalls giving the Sacrament of the Anointing of the Sick to a woman who was given to a life of sin. She had been poisoned. As the poison infected the brain, she had the impression of losing each of the external senses. She would reach for her eye and say to her mother: "Mother, here is my eye. You keep it when I am gone." She would reach for her ear and say to me, "Here, you keep this when I am gone." The Sacrament of the Anointing of the Sick was administered and immediately she was restored to health. The next day she came to the rectory and began leading an apostolic life which continued for many years, until her death. The anointing was for her death, but it happened to be for a postponed death.

St. James, in describing the Sacrament of the Anointing of the Sick, puts the emphasis on the healing:

Is one of you sick? Let him send for the presbyters of the church, and let them pray over him, anointing him with oil and the Lord's name. Prayer offered in faith will restore the sick man, and the Lord will give him relief; if he is guilty of sins, they will be pardoned. (5:14–15)

Here it is to be noted that the people who are to benefit are not necessarily those at death's door, but the sick. The sick man is described as one able to call in the priests of the Church. St. James says also that the prayer of faith shall save the sick man, which is the physical side of the sacrament; the forgiveness of sins being the spiritual side.

The purpose of the sacrament is clear from the fact that the person is sick—not the body alone, nor the soul alone. All the sacraments are aimed at a single whole, made up of matter and spirit. Even the Eucharist pertains to the body, as well as the soul, for our Lord said that He would "raise up on the last day" those who would receive it (John 6:55 [54]).

Sickness has spiritual repercussions: no person can be sick in body without having his soul disturbed. The Anointing of the Sick, therefore, is to some extent *psychosomatic*.

Sickness and the Soul

A serious illness cuts us off from the occasion of sin. The will to sin is weakened by the physical inability to sin. It is true that many a man believes he has left the passions behind, when it is really that the passions have left him behind. This moment of enforced detachment from the allurements of the world is always an opportunity for the reception of grace.

The approach to death emphasizes the uniqueness of personality. During life we lose ourselves in the mob, in the anonymous "they," in the masses, in "togetherness." But the nearness of death confronts self with self: "I am I — unique — responsible for every thought, word, and deed of life." The soul begins to see itself as it really is, and God in His mercy prepares a sacrament for this dread moment when personality is confronted with its load of sin.

Sickness breaks the spell that pleasure is everything, or that we ought to go on building bigger and bigger barns, or that life is worthless unless it has a thrill. Sickness enables us to adjust our sense of values, as an actual grace illumines the futility and emptiness of many ambitions: "What does it profit a man if he gain the whole world and lose his soul?" (Matt. 16:26).

There is a world of difference between the Christian in serious illness and the pagan. As Franz Werfel wrote:

> The skeptic believes in nothing more than death; the believer believes in nothing less. Since the world to him is a creation of
> . spirit and love, he cannot be threatened by eternal destruction in his essential being, as a creature of the world.

A man who in life never prepares for death, uses every means to conceal it, to render it unobtrusive, to disguise it, even feels awkward in the presence of death and knows not how to console those who are bereaved.

The Sacrament of the Anointing of the Sick

The pagan fears the loss of the body; the Christian fears the loss of the soul, knowing that the destiny of the body will be the destiny of the soul. To a pagan, this world is everything and death deprives him of all there is; to the Christian, this world is only a scaffolding through which souls climb to the Kingdom of God. When the last soul shall have climbed up through the scaffolding, then it shall be torn down and burned with fervent fire, not because it is base, but simply because it has done its work — it has brought us back again to God. Hence, to the Christian, his whole being is never threatened by death. All during life, the pagan is moving toward death; but the Christian is moving backward. He starts with the fact that he must die and render an account of his stewardship; knowing that he will die, he plans his life accordingly.

The Christian, having been signed with the sign of death, the Sign of the Cross at Baptism, is committed to leading a life of mortification, which means a dying to the ego, in order that the Christ-life may be more manifest.

The Church is, therefore, constantly recommending a daily rehearsal for the great event, or tiny little deaths in preparation for the final one. No masterpiece is ever created in a day, and death itself is a masterpiece. The sculptor who wishes to carve a figure out of a block of marble uses his chisel; first cutting away great chunks of marble, then smaller pieces; finally he reaches a point where only a brush of the hand is needed to reveal the figure. In the same way, the soul at first has to undergo tremendous mortifications, then more refined detachments and little deaths until finally the divine image is revealed. Because mortification is recognized as a practice of death, it was fittingly described on the tomb of Duns Scotus: *Bis mortuus; semel sepultus* — He died twice, but was buried only once.

As evidence of how seriously the Church takes grace or divine life in the soul, in contrast to physical life, its liturgy calls the day on which saints die, their "birthday," or *natalitia*. The world celebrates a birthday on the day a person was born to physical life; the Church celebrates it when a person is born to eternal life. There are three exceptions to this in the liturgy of the Church, and for very good reasons. The only physical birthdays in the liturgy are those of our Divine Lord (December 25th), the Blessed Mother (September 8th), and John the Baptist (June 24th). This is because each of these births marked a special infusion of divine life into the world: our *Lord is Eternal Life*; the Blessed Mother, through her Immaculate Conception, participated in that eternal life from the first moment of her conception; and St. John the Baptist was sanctified in his mother's womb, when he was visited by his Lord, still tabernacled within the Blessed Mother.

This does not mean, even for the Christian, that death has no terrors. There is still something very frightening about it. If death were merely a physical *must*, we would not fear it; our fear comes from the moral fact that we know we ought not to die. We fear death because we realize it was not part of the original plan. The dying Christian knows that the personal judgment at the moment of his death will be a revelation of the meaning of his personal life, just as the cosmic judgment at the end of time will be a revelation of how he lived in society.

Death is not just a mere emancipation of the soul from the limitations and burdens of the body, and a passage into a purely spiritual state, such as Plato conceived. This would completely forget the resurrection of the body. The body has had a share in the virtues or the vices of the soul; therefore, it will take on a quality after death corresponding to the quality of the soul. If a green liquid is poured into a glass, the glass looks green. If the liquid poured in is red, the glass looks red. So too, when evil is poured into the soul, the body takes on the quality of evil, and is in a state of incorruptible "corruption," whereas the body of the person who dies in the state of grace shares in the glory of the soul.

What this glorified body will be like we do not know, except that it will correspond with the "new heaven" and the "new earth" of which the Apocalypse speaks. When the soul leaves the body at death, it does not leave the body's sphere altogether. The soul still has a tendency to be reunited with the body. We put our hand on warm wax and we leave the imprint of the hand. So too, the imprint of the soul is in some way in the body, and the soul to some extent bears the body within itself. In the resurrection of the dead, God will give the soul its body-forming power, and the opportunity to build up the body will be entrusted to it, as it was meant to be.

The Sacrament of the Anointing of the Sick

To understand the sacrament, one must never lose hold of the fact that there is a double life: biological and spiritual. So there is a double death, death of body and death of the soul. St. John states: "Thou dost pass for a living man, and all the while art a corpse" (Rev. 3:1). A body may be physically alive but the soul spiritually dead. Such would be a person in the state of serious sin and alienation from God. We see corpses walking on the street every day; biological life is in them, but not spiritual life.

The real reason man dies in his flesh is because his soul, having turned away from God, has lost the dominion it once exercised over the body. One of the penalties of Original Sin was that the body should die. When the sinful soul is restored to the state of grace, it has its power returned *potentially* to effect the quickening of the flesh and the restoration of the body, but the actual rejuvenation is deferred until the last day.

In its present state, the body often depresses the soul; it restrains it in its upward flight. It is almost a cage which prevents the soul, as a dove, from flying to God. A sickness accentuates this weight, producing sometimes a lethargy in the soul. Herein is the purpose of the Anointing of the Sick: to enable the soul to be free in this life, either through the healing of the body, or else to be eventually free from the body in death, with all the traces of sin blotted out.

How the Sacrament Is Administered

In speaking of the sacrament, St. James said that the priests of the Church were to be called in — not merely the priest. Though it is one person who is sick and one organism that is disordered, nevertheless, sickness is not considered a private affair any more than sin is a private affair. Just as one sin in a soul diminishes the sum or the content of charity in the Mystical Body, so the sickness of any one of the members of the Church grieves in some way the fellowship of the saints. The Church, representing our Lord, responds to this sickness in any one of her members, by sharing her own corporate wealth with the one who is ill. Her prayer is that the sick person be cured of his weakness, and if it be God's will, be restored to the life of the Mystical Body.

The unction of the sick is a kind of a prolongation both of Baptism and of Penance, in the sense that it is a remedy for sin. It is not to be thought that the sacrament operates in the sick in the nature of a miracle, or takes the place of medical science, any more than Baptism takes the place of birth, or Holy Communion takes the place of eating. The Council of Trent said that the Anointing of the Sick was a consummation not only of Penance, but of the whole Christian life which ought to be a continual penance. The Anointing of the Sick is a sacrament of the living and, therefore, normally presupposes the state of grace, just as medicine is given only to the living, and holy oil is a medicine.

As was pointed out above, physical life may have either wounds or diseases. There is a difference between having a finger cut by a knife and a body suffering from smallpox or cancer. Penance looks more to the wounds of the soul; Anointing of the Sick more to the sickness of the body, but never apart from the soul.

The administration of the sacrament starts with the basic psychological fact that we cannot think of a single sin that ever got into our soul that did not come through our body. The sin of envy, for example, comes through the eyes; we may have seen how much more the Joneses have. The sin of pride, in like manner, often comes from the eyes, as one makes a comparison between how much richer, smarter, or more beautiful one person is than another. Drunkenness, adultery, robbery, blasphemy — we often walk into these occasions of sin. Even the nose contributes to sin and to vanity, either through the smell of good food leading to gluttony, or through perfumes which, according to advertisements, are allurements to sin.

Just as physical diseases leave certain marks on the body — tuberculosis leaves spots on the lungs, smallpox marks on the face, leprosy scars — so too, sin leaves behind some traces in the senses and in the body. The spiritual scar of every sin is evident from the fact that one feels weaker after the sin than before, and less resistant to wrong. Other diseases or viruses leave little "tails" — not speaking scientifically — or traces of their existence in the body. Just as sewers become clogged and chimneys sooted and ships contract barnacles, so too, the germs of sin leave little "tails" behind, which are remnants or relics of the rebellion which ravished the soul and the body. Though an alcoholic may give up his alcohol and repent for his sin, alcoholism may remain in the body in marred and ruined organs.

The Church now comes along in a serious illness, not only to blot out the sin, which is done primarily in the Sacrament of Penance (also here if Penance cannot be received), but also to cleanse away the remains of sin. Because sin came into the soul through the eyes, ears and nostrils, mouth, hands and feet, the Church lays hold of these senses and organs which in some way cooperated with the soul in sinning. It prepares the soul either for the restoration to the Mystical Body of Christ or for a passage to God. The poor member of the Church is covered with the dust of action and the spatterings of life, with the mire and dregs of half-fought battles, with the weakness of swords half-drawn; with one eye toward the world and the other toward Christ. That is why the Church prays: "Remember not, then, his old sins, nor the excesses to which anger or the fervor of an evil will has led him. For, though he has sinned, yet he has not denied Thee, O God."

When the eyes are anointed, the priest says: "By this holy anointing and with His holy loving Mercy, may the Lord forgive you whatever wrong you may have done by the use of your sight. Amen."

When the ears are anointed, the priest says: "By this holy anointing and His most loving Mercy may the Lord forgive you whatever wrong you have done by the sense of hearing. Amen."

When the nose is anointed, the priest says: "By this holy anointing and His most loving Mercy, may the Lord forgive you whatever wrong you have done by your use of the sense of smell. Amen."

When the mouth with closed lips is anointed, the priest says: "By this holy anointing and His most loving Mercy, may the Lord forgive you whatever wrong you may have done by the use of the sense of taste and the power of speech. Amen."

When the hands are anointed, the priest says: "By this holy anointing and His most loving Mercy, may the Lord forgive you whatever wrong you may have done by the use of the sense of touch. Amen." The priest on dying is anointed on the back of his hands, his palms having been anointed in Holy Orders. The lay person is always anointed on the palms.

When the feet are anointed, the priest says: "By this holy anointing and His most loving Mercy, may the Lord forgive you whatever wrong you may have done by the use of your power of walking. Amen."

In the following prayer which the Church recites, there is no mention of death:

> Cure, we beseech Thee, our Redeemer, by the grace of the Holy Sacrament, the ailments of this sick man [woman]; heal his wounds and forgive his sins. Deliver him from all miseries of body and mind; mercifully restore him to perfect health inwardly and outwardly, that having recovered by an act of kindness, he may be able to take up his former duties. Thou, who with Father and the Holy Spirit, liveth and reigneth God world without end. Amen.

If the illness is to last for some time, the sacrament gives to the sick person the necessary grace to endure his sickness in the spirit of holiness; it also remits to some extent the temporal punishment that is due to sin. There have not been wanting some theologians in the past who have held that, if received with great faith, it remits all temporal punishment due to sin, and in case of death, prepares the soul for Heaven.

In this sacrament, sins are not remitted in virtue of an act of jurisdiction or by judicial sentence, as they are in the Sacrament of Penance. Why? Because with serious illness there is the possibility of passing into another community; that is, from the Church Militant to the Church Suffering or the Church Triumphant. The soul particularly in danger of death is about to go before the throne of the Eternal Judge and, therefore, to Him alone is reserved the jurisdiction or the judgment of the Sacrament of the Anointing of the Sick. That too is why, in the administration of this sacrament, there is more of the imprecatory form of prayer than in Penance. The priest puts the prayer in the form of a petition because he is exercising his power only as a delegate of the Church Militant. In the Sacrament of Penance, the priest said: "I absolve you from your sins"; in the Sacrament of the Anointing of the Sick, "May the Lord forgive you any sins, etc." The measure of the distribution of grace here is left entirely to the merciful Love of God.

The Sacrament of the Anointing of the Sick

Because oil is used in the sacrament, it must not be forgotten that oil has a double purpose—strengthening and illumination or enlightenment. The aspect of strengthening has already been mentioned, but enlightenment also comes with this sacrament: it sheds a new outlook on the meaning of death. Many who receive this sacrament have the fear of death taken away from them, and may even desire it, as St. Paul said: "I desire to be dissolved and be with Christ" (Phil. 1:23).

This comes from a higher wisdom of the soul, because it has been purified of the remains of sin. Just as we see what is outside a window more clearly when the window has been washed, so too, our soul more clearly sees the purpose of life once the senses and soul have been purified. Saints very often undergo in life, through a great penance, what is called a "dark night of the soul." Thanks to this dark night, they then arrive at a kind of mystical union with God, or even a mystical espousal. Thanks to the anointing of this sacrament, one may also pass through a dark night of the soul, but in a much shorter period of time, and one looks forward to mystical union with Christ. Therefore, there can take place in the soul, in a very short space of time, both the purgative and illuminative way at the last moments of life: a cleansing of the soul and a greater vision of the glory and beauty of God.

The spiritual life would be terrible if the Good Lord had not instituted this sacrament for an illness, which is a rehearsal for the final battle of life. Thanks to it, the Church takes us in her maternal arms and shows us Heaven saying:

> My children, here is your fatherland. Come with me. If it be God's will, we will cross over this arid desert of life together, and we will confide you to the angels who will carry you through to your eternal repose.

The Viaticum

The Sacrament of the Anointing of the Sick is not the sacrament of the dying or, in the strict sense of the term, the "last sacrament." In the liturgy of the Church, the Sacrament of the Anointing is given before the Eucharist; when the latter is administered to the dying it becomes the "last sacrament." This is very fitting, for the Sacrament of the Eucharist has reference to the body as well as to the soul. Our Blessed Lord said that those who received Him in the Eucharist would be assured of the resurrection of the body. Furthermore, in the Mass there is a prayer immediately before Communion, which begs that the Eucharist "may be to me a safeguard for body and soul, and a remedy."

When given to those who are dying, the Eucharist is called Viaticum, which means "going with you" on the way to eternity. The Eucharist deposits in our body "a seed of immortality." It is a provision for the journey to eternity, when one is at the door of death. The Church makes its reception at this moment a matter of grave obligation, even more strict than the Anointing of the Sick.

The Viaticum received in danger of death, just as the Eucharist received in life, is social in its implications. There is not merely the union of Christ and the soul, but there is also the union of the sick with the whole Church. The dying person, if he is in a state of grace, is leaving the Church Militant on earth for either the Church Triumphant in Heaven or the Church Suffering in Purgatory. Hence, when a priest places the Eucharist on the tongue of the recipient, he says: "Receive, brother, [or sister] the Viaticum of our Lord Jesus Christ that He may preserve thee from the malignant enemy and bring thee to everlasting life." The reference to "brother" or "sister" refers to the family and the fellowship of the Church and the saints. There should even be a solemnity about the last Communion, as there is about the First Communion. The family should gather about the one who receives the Viaticum, and its solemnity is increased when administered by the pastor himself who is the head of the parochial community.

The Catholic who is dying is never lonely because there is another rite connected with the Viaticum; namely, the commending of the soul to God. The priest gives him a crucifix to kiss while an invocation is said to the Cross: "We adore Thee, O Christ, and we bless Thee, because by Thy Holy Cross Thou has redeemed the world." As the moment of death approaches there is the official discharge to the dying:

The Sacrament of the Anointing of the Sick

Go forth, Christian soul, out of this world, in the Name of God, the Father Almighty, who created thee; in the Name of Jesus Christ, the Son of the Living God, who suffered for thee; in the Name of the Holy Spirit, who has poured forth upon thee. . . . May thy place be this day in peace and thy abode in holy Sion.

Then the Church calls on the angels and the saints:

May the Angels lead thee into Paradise. At thy coming, may the Martyrs receive thee and lead thee into the holy city, Jerusalem. May the choir of Angels receive thee, and with Lazarus, who was once poor, mayst thou have eternal rest.

Death is one of the penalties for sin but, when accepted, it becomes an atonement also for sin. Every Christian knows that it is not just a happy life that one must seek, but also a happy death. Hence, he prays that he may be fortified by the sacraments, and that he may be fully conscious when he receives the last rites, in order that he may, as it were, peer through the door of Heaven to his eternal reward.

6

The Sacrament of Holy Orders

Because man lives in a society of free men, there must be some government and order to make justice prevail. Since there is the order of grace above creature, it too must have degrees, order, hierarchy, and government; this Christ supplied in the Sacrament of Holy Orders with its three ascending levels of deaconship, priesthood, and episcopacy.

Our Blessed Lord is the Mediator between God and man, being both God and man. But in order to mediate His Redemption, He desires human instruments between Himself and the world, each of whom will be "the minister and dispenser of the Mysteries of God" (1 Cor. 4:1). And so, some men are appointed by God to deliver the sacraments to others, just as in human societies one group serves and ministers to another:

> The purpose for which any high priest is chosen from among his fellow men, and made a representative of men in their dealings with God, is to offer gifts and sacrifices in expiation of their sins. (Heb. 5:1)

The Call from God

In the fifth chapter of Hebrews, verse four, there is written: "His vocation comes from God, as Aaron's did; nobody can take on himself such a privilege as this." When a priest receives the call from God, something happens to his soul, like that which happened to Peter in his barque one dark night when Christ entered it. The young man with a vocation reacts as did Peter: "Depart from me, O Lord, for I am a sinful man" (Luke 5:8). There is a double tension: one of attraction to the divine, the other, subtraction, because of one's own unworthiness; a desire to approach the All-Holy, and a shrinking because of one's own sense of inadequacy.

Then begins a minimum of six years of difficult study and moral and spiritual discipline, as one asks himself a thousand times if he is worthy. Either with the crucifix that hangs on the wall of his simple room, or to the crucifix on his desk, he carries on a constant dialogue.

The seminarian knows how human he is, and yet, like Christ on the Cross, suspended between Heaven and earth, abandoned by one and rejected by the other, the world expects him to be more than human. Called to be as pure and as holy as an angel, he is conscious of his own weakness, bearing about as he does the rich treasure in a frail vessel. And yet he must fulfill the words of his Master: "Thou hast sent me into the world on thy errand, and I have sent them into the world on my errand" (John 17:18). From now on, he no longer takes the short breaths of the world; he must draw in strength from the world of the Spirit.

The Priest and Celibacy

Our Lord wished to have a group of men who would have the freedom to give full time to His service; hence He ordained in order that they who served the altar were to live by the altar. Celibacy in the Latin Rite stresses this quality of total dedication. The priest is a celibate in order that he might not have the cares of family and, therefore, not be afraid to minister to people in plague or to give the last rites to soldiers dying in battle. St. Paul, speaking of celibacy as a spur to undivided service, writes: "And I would have you free from concern. He who is unmarried is concerned with God's claim, asking how he is to please God" (1 Cor. 7:32).

Chastity, however, is not something cold or negative. It is, as Francis Thompson called it, "a passionless passion, a wild tranquillity." A man cannot live without love, though he can live without romantic love or the *eros*. The divine command, "increase and multiply" (Gen. 1:28) may be verified not only with reference to the body, but also to the soul. There can be increase of man in the cultural, moral, and religious spheres. The priest is called a "father," because he begets souls in Christ. As St. Paul wrote to the Galatians: "My little children, I am in travail over you afresh, until I can see Christ's image formed in you" (Gal. 4:19). The purer the mirror of his humanity is, the better he reflects the image of Christ.

Though a priest is called a father, nevertheless, he is also a "mother" of children. Our Blessed Lord used two analogies to describe His attitude toward the city that He loved, and also to all humanity. He said that He loved Jerusalem as a hen who gathers her chickens, but the city refused His love. The night of the Last Supper, He used the similitude of a mother about to bring forth a child, implying that He would be in labor in His Crucifixion, but would bring forth new life in His Resurrection.

The Ordination of the Priest

The dress of the priest takes one back to the classical days of Greece and Rome, when the Church became the spiritual Israel. The early clergy wore no distinctive dress, but rather clothed themselves in the garb of the ordinary people. Later on when the classical Roman dress began to be superseded by the dress of the barbarians, the conservativeness of religion asserted itself and, in consequence, the priest wore vestments which were no longer in secular use.

When the deacons enter the cathedral to be vested, they wear an amice, which was originally a white linen kerchief worn about the neck and the shoulders. When he put it on his head and shoulders, he said the prayer: "Place, O Lord, the helmet of salvation on my head to the defeat of diabolical invasion." Over the amice, he wears the alb, which was the original Roman tunic with long sleeves, around the waist of which he ties the cincture which is the symbol of chastity.

Over the alb is worn a maniple, which in the early days of the Greeks and Romans was a kind of handkerchief worn on the left forearm, used at meals for wiping mouth and hands. The consul during the Roman Empire used it as a sign to start the races in the circus. The Church first used it to wipe Communion vessels and hands in the celebration of the Mass. The symbolism of the maniple is to remind the priest of the bonds which once held the hands of the Savior. This is signified in the prayer which is offered when the maniple is put on, begging that the cares and sorrows of earthly life should be borne with patience in view of heavenly reward.

Now we come to two vestments which are worn by deacons when they come to the altar for ordination; namely, the stole and the chasuble. The stole originally was a loose robe worn by the ancients, and in this sense the word is still used by the English poets. Thus, Milton pictures Melancholy as having "a sable stole of cypress lawn, over her decent shoulders drawn."

In the Old Testament, the Levites were described as being clad in stoles when conducting the sacred Ark to Jerusalem. In the book of the Apocalypse, the saints are "clothed in white stoles." The stole is worn only by deacons, priests, and bishops, but each wears it in a different way, and it is associated with sacred Orders. When, however, the deacon enters the church, the stole is carried only on one shoulder, while over the left arm the deacon carries a folded chasuble. In the right hand, he bears a lighted candle, and in the cincture is a linen cloth, which will eventually be used for tying the hands, after they have been anointed with oil.

During the ceremony of ordination, the bishop draws a part of the stole which rests at the back of the candidate's neck over the breast and lays the two ends crosswise. The chasuble which he carries and which is a symbol of charity, is folded at the beginning of the ordination ceremony, as an indication that the one who wears it is not a priest. At a later point in the ceremony, the chasuble is unfolded. The symbolism of this is that, in the first part of the Mass, the deacon is made a priest and given the power of offering sacrifice to God. In the second part of the ceremony, the chasuble is then let down when he is empowered to preach and forgive sins. This indicates the more complete powers of the priest.

St. John Chrysostom explains well the reason why priests wear different vestments at the altar than on the street: "When you see a priest offering the Sacrifice, do not think of it as if it were *he* that is doing this;

it is the Hand of Christ invisibly stretched forth." The priest is really only a tool, but he is a tool in the sense that Aristotle called man a living tool. The vestments hide and submerge his own personality so that men may know it is Christ who teaches, who governs, and who sanctifies.

The Call from the Bishop

No man can be ordained unless he has been called by Christ through the bishop. When our Lord called His Apostles, He called them by name, and this ceremony is repeated in the Sacrament of Holy Orders. The Latin rite begins by the archdeacon presenting the deacons, saying that the Holy Church asks them to be elevated to the rank of priest. The bishop, reading from the *Roman Pontifical*, reminds them of the old custom of the Church, when the people were consulted concerning the life, conduct, and morals of the clergy before they were elevated to the priesthood. He then tells them that as Moses elected seventy elders from the different tribes of Israel to aid him in the government of the people of the Old Law, as our Lord chose seventy-two disciples to preach the gospel, so are they to aid the bishop in the sacred ministry of sacrificing, blessing, presiding, preaching, and baptizing.

The bishop seated on the faldstool at the middle of the altar begins the ceremony of ordination. The archdeacon summons the future priests with these words: "Let all those who are to be ordained priests come forward." As they advance, their names are read out one by one. Each answers: *Adsum* ("I am present") and then steps forward. The calling by name means that there shall be no intruders and that the priesthood is a divine vocation or calling. Our Lord "calls His sheep by name" (John 10:3) even now as He did in Galilee.

After the bishop calls out the names, there follows a very solemn warning, that they come not under false pretenses, that they are under no penalties of the Church, and that they be not illegitimate:

Most Reverend Father and Lord in Christ, [name of Bishop] by the grace of God and the Apostolic See, Bishop of [diocese] commands and charges under pain of excommunication that no one here present for the purpose of taking Orders, shall presume to come forward for ordination under any pretext, if he be irregular, excommunicate in any law or by judicial sentence, under interdict or suspension, illegitimate or infamous, or in any other way disqualified, or of any other diocese, unless he has the license of the bishop; and that none of the ordained shall depart until the Mass is over and the Bishop's blessing has been received.

The archdeacon then bids the bishop to ordain these deacons "to the burden of the priesthood." The phrase that is used is *onus* or burden. The priesthood and the episcopacy are both called burdens, not honors. This is because the terrific burden or responsibility of saving souls entrusted to them is laid upon them there. Such was the idea given to Moses when he complained to the Lord: "Must I carry a whole people like a weight on my back?" (Num. 11:11).

As if still hesitant as to whether or not the deacons should be ordained, the bishop then asks the archdeacon the question: "Do you know them to be worthy?" To which he answers: "So far as human frailty allows one to know, I do know, and I testify that they are worthy to undertake the burden of this office." The bishop then answers, *"Deo Gratias"* (Thanks be to God).

Moral certitude about the worthiness of the candidates is required like the certitude that Moses was to have when God told him to gather seventy men among the ancients of Israel whom he *knew* to be worthy. This concern for the worthiness of the candidates has always been present in the Old Testament and the New, for St. Paul tells Timothy that before he ordains any priests he should be very certain of their worthiness: "He must bear a good character, too, in the world's eyes; or he may fall into disrepute, and become a prey to the False Accuser" (1 Tim. 3:7).

The bishop, as if not satisfied with assurance of the archdeacon, asks the people if they know any reason why the deacons should not be ordained. There follows a moment of silence, in which the people are given an opportunity to protest, if need be, against any one of the candidates.

The Sacrament of Holy Orders

The Prostration

The deacons now prostrate themselves flat upon the ground and become as dead men, while over them the Church, chanting the Litany of the Saints, invokes Heaven to intercede, or pray for them, to be merciful to them, and to make them good priests.

The prostration of the deacons during the Litanies is a slightly different form of prayer than that which was used in the Old Testament, when the Jews generally stood to pray. It was only in times of great stress that they ever knelt (Acts 7:59 [60] and 9:40), such as when Stephen and Peter knelt. The Jews, however, did lay prostrate before the high priest for a solemn blessing on the Day of Atonement (Sir. 50:19–26),[6] and as our Lord did in the Agony in the Garden (Matt. 26:39). But the reason for the kneeling is somewhat related to a prayer that went before, where the *ordinandi* were told "as they celebrate the mysteries of the Lord's death, they must be earnest in mortifying their members of all vices and concupiscence." Being prostrate is a symbol of their spiritual death, in which they die to their flesh and its concupiscences at the same time, that they invoke all the saints in Heaven to let them have a resurrection worthy of being ministers of the Word.

As the body of Adam came from the slime of the earth, when God breathed into it a living soul, so each priest yielding his body to be an instrument of Christ prays fervently that it may never be a blunt instrument. Then when he rises from the ground, his hands are bound with a purificator, tied together in slavery, but that sweet slavery of love. With Paul he says "I am alive; or rather, not I; it is Christ that lives in me" (Gal. 2:20).

The Laying on of Hands

The bishop lays hands on the priests without saying anything. When a bishop is consecrated, the hands of the consecrating prelates are laid

---

[6] Sirach is called Ecclesiasticus in some editions of the Bible.

on him with the words: "Receive the Holy Spirit," but in ordination, these words are omitted. This laying on or imposition of hands is what is called the "matter" of the sacrament, and is part of the ritual of other sacraments, like Baptism, Confirmation, Penance, and the Anointing of the Sick.

There are many instances in the Old Testament of laying on of hands. Jacob put his right hand on the head of Ephraim, and his left hand on the head of Manasse and pronounced a blessing (Gen. 48:14–16). Aaron and his sons placed their hands on the heads of victims to be offered in sacrifice:

> He is to lay his hand on the head of the victim, and it is to be immolated at the entrance of the tabernacle that bears record of me, the priests who represent Aaron's family pouring its blood upon the altar. (Lev. 3:2)

God told Moses to lay his hand on Josue (Num. 27:18) and Aaron after offering sacrifice. In the Old Testament, it signified that a victim or a person was dedicated to a holy purpose, and also that there was a flowing out of power from the one who laid on the hands.

Investiture of Priesthood

The bishop chants a preface invoking the Holy Spirit upon those who are to be ordained; then follows what is known as the "form" of the sacrament:

> We beseech Thee, Almighty Father, invest these Thy servants with the dignity of the priesthood. Do Thou renew in their hearts the spirit of holiness. Help them to be steadfast in the office of second priestly rank received from Thee, O Lord, and to inspire others to strive for perfection by their example. May they become zealous fellow workers in our ministry. May they shine in all the Christian virtues, so that they will be able to give a good account of the stewardship entrusted to them, and finally attain the reward of everlasting life. Through the same Jesus Christ, Thy Son, our

The Sacrament of Holy Orders

Lord, who lives and reigns with Thee, in the unity of the Holy Spirit, God forever and ever. Amen.

The bishop arranges the stole in the form of a cross over the chest, saying: "Take the yoke of the Lord, for His yoke is sweet and His burden light." Then he invests each with the chasuble, still unfolded, saying: "Receive, the vesture of priesthood, which is the symbol of charity. God is well able to increase charity in you and make perfect your works."

After the *Veni Creator Spiritus* has been sung, in which the Holy Spirit is invoked, the bishop proceeds to anoint the hands of each in the form of a cross. The bishop's right thumb is dipped in the oil of catechumens; with the oil he traces a cross with his right thumb, a line from the thumb of the right hand to the index finger of the left, and the other from the thumb of the left to the index finger of the right. Then he anoints the hands all over, and as he does so, he says: "Be pleased, O Lord, to consecrate and hallow these hands by this anointing and our blessing. Amen." He makes a sign over each saying: "Whatsoever they bless may be blessed, and whatsoever they consecrate may be consecrated and hallowed in the Name of our Lord Jesus Christ."

In the Old Testament, the candidate was anointed with holy oil which, in the case of the high priest, was poured upon his head, but in the case of the other priests, it was merely put upon his forehead. The anointed hands of the priests are folded and tied together with a linen cloth, so as to allow the oil to penetrate into his hands. He then becomes Christ's bondsman (Eph. 3:1).

The Delivery of Instruments

The bishop now presents each of the newly ordained with a *chalice* containing wine and water, and a *paten* upon the chalice with a host. Because the anointed hands of the priest are bound, he touches with the fore and middle fingers both the paten and the cup of the chalice. During the ceremony the bishop says: "Receive the power to offer sacrifice to God and to celebrate Mass, both for the living and the dead in the name of our Lord. Amen."

Concelebration

After the Offertory, the newly ordained priests begin to celebrate Mass with the bishop saying the prayers aloud with them. They even say the words of Consecration with him. The meaning of the ceremony is that as the Apostles learned to celebrate Mass from our Blessed Lord at the Last Supper; so too, in concelebrating with the bishop, the new priests learn a ritual from a successor of the Apostles. As the newly ordained priests concelebrate with the bishop, so too, they receive Communion, drinking from the same chalice, and consuming a Host that was consecrated at the Mass.

The Commission to Absolve

Before the Communion prayer is read, the Mass is interrupted a second time to give the priests a new function in the Mystical Body of Christ. After the profession of faith, the bishop sits down and lays both hands on the head of each one kneeling before him, and says: "Receive the Holy Ghost; whose sins you shall forgive, they are forgiven them; and whose sins you shall retain, they are retained" (John 20:22–23).

The bishop does not wear gloves for this second imposition, but he does for the first.

The Mass is interrupted here, for the second time, to give the power *to forgive sins*, because this power was given by our Lord at a time distinct from that of the authority *to offer the Mass*. The night of the Last Supper our Lord ordained His priests, *after having offered* the sacrifice of bread and wine, saying: "Do this in commemoration of Me." But it was after His Resurrection that He gave them priestly power to forgive sins and the power of binding and loosing. This corresponds also to the double ceremony of the chasuble: first, the putting it on as folded for the pre-Resurrection power; and secondly, the unfolding, to indicate the giving of additional priestly powers of forgiveness. When the chasuble is unfolded, the bishop prays: "May the Lord clothe you with the robe of innocence."

The Sacrament of Holy Orders

The Promise of Obedience

The newly ordained priests now come up for what is called the *stipulatio*. There is not a clasping of hands here, for that would signify equality. The hands, being the instruments of action and service, are put *inside* the bishop's hands to signify his will to be put at the service of the bishop. It is a commitment of the young priest to his father in Christ.

The Consecration of a Bishop

The bishop too must be called by the Vicar of Christ and cannot be consecrated without his express permission. The consecration ceremony begins with the question, "Have you the mandate?"; i.e., has the Holy Father, the successor of St. Peter, given us the authority to number this priest among the Apostles? Two things hang together there: apostolic succession and the Primacy of Peter. The night of the Last Supper when our Lord consecrated His Apostles, He reminded them of how they were bound together in Peter, whom He had chosen as the rock, the leader and the first, not only in honor, but in jurisdiction.

What is very singular about the words of our Lord is that He did not pray for all of the Apostles as equals: *He prayed for them in and through Peter.* It was through their oneness with Peter that they would share in His prayer of victory over the evil of the world. This is brought out in the way our Lord addressed Peter in the second person singular in distinction to the Apostles whom He addressed in the second person plural:

> And the Lord said, Simon, Simon, behold, Satan has claimed power over you all, so that he can sift you like wheat: but I have prayed for thee, that thy faith may not fail, when, after a while, thou hast come back to me, it is for thee to be the support of thy brethren. (Luke 22:31–32)

He told Peter that he would deny Him but afterward would return and be the support of his brethren.

When the Communists in China attempted to destroy the Church, they cleverly sought to insert a division between apostolic succession and the Primacy of Peter. Brainwashing a few bishops, they succeeded in inducing them to consecrate a few priests. The priests would then, because they were consecrated by bishops, be in the line of apostolic succession; the Communists thus hoped that the faithful would accept them. But because they had not the authority or the mandate from the Holy Father to do so, the Communists thereby denied the Primacy of Peter. As it turned out, the Catholics refused to accept the bishops who may have been in the line of apostolic succession, but certainly were not embraced in the prayer of Christ for Peter.

Both apostolic succession and the recognition of the Primacy of Peter go together. It is very much like the problem of lighting a city by electricity. Suppose in this city there were a thousand houses. The wire from one house ran only a foot, another twenty feet, another five hundred feet, another fifteen hundred feet, another eighteen hundred. But suppose that the dynamo that supplied all of this power was about two thousand feet away from the houses. It would follow that none of the copper cables would be able to light a house; regardless of how close they came to the dynamo, they would not be in actual contact with power.

So it is with the transmission of priestly authority and power. Any organization which starts today, or which started fifty years ago, or five hundred years ago, or one thousand years ago, is incapable of transmitting the divine power of Christ's Passion, unless there is a contact with Christ Himself and under the conditions Christ laid down. As in biology, life comes from life, so in theology, divine life comes from divine life. An unbroken succession of authority and power is essential for the divinization of souls in the twentieth century. The bishops, who are successors of the Apostles, are one in Peter and his successors, to whom alone Christ promised that the "faith would fail not" (Luke 22:32).

During the ceremony, after the bishop-elect has been interrogated concerning his fidelity, submission, and obedience to God and the Church and all the truths of faith, the consecrating prelate accompanied by two co-consecrators tells him at the beginning of Mass: "It is the duty of a bishop to judge, interpret, consecrate, ordain, offer, baptize, and confirm." After all the saints of Heaven have been invoked in the Litany, the consecrator and his co-consecrators successively touch with both hands the head of the bishop elect saying: "Receive the Holy Spirit." These words constitute the matter of the sacrament. Then comes the prayer that is known as the form:

> Be propitious, O Lord, to our supplications, and bestowing the abundance of sacerdotal grace upon this Thy servant, pour upon him the power of Thy blessing, through our Lord Jesus Christ who liveth and reigneth with Thee in the unity of the Holy Ghost.

He anoints the head of the consecrated kneeling before him, making first the Sign of the Cross on the crown, and then anointing the whole crown of the head, saying: "May the head be anointed and consecrated by heavenly benediction in the pontifical order in the Name of the Father +, in the Name of the Son +, and of the Holy Ghost. + Amen."

After a prayer, the newly consecrated bishop has his hands anointed with chrism in the form of a cross. The consecrator draws two lines with the thumb of his right hand, one from the thumb of the right hand to the index finger of the left, the other from the thumb of the left hand to the index finger of the right; then the whole palm of the consecrated is anointed while these words are said by the consecrator:

> May these hands be anointed with the sanctified oil and the chrism of sanctification; as Samuel anointed David to be king and prophet, so may they be anointed and consecrated in the Name of the Father +, the Son +, and the Holy Spirit +. We make the Sign of the Holy Cross of our Savior, Jesus Christ, who redeemed us from death and led us to the Kingdom of Heaven.

The newly consecrated bishop concelebrates the Mass with his consecrator, even drinking of the same chalice. Passing over many other details for want of space, his newly acquired powers are symbolized in his crozier, mitre, ring, and gloves.

Because the bishop is the father of a spiritual family, or a shepherd, he is given a shepherd's staff. Our Blessed Lord called His bishops and priests to be both shepherds and fishermen. Because the bishop is the spouse of the Church, he is given a ring to indicate that espousal. Because he is to be a Mediator of the Old and the New Testament, he wears the helmet of salvation, which is the mitre. Because he hopes to receive the blessing of the Heavenly Father, as Jacob received the blessing—thanks to covered hands—he wears gloves.

After the enthronement, the consecrated bishop then gives His blessing. He goes to the Epistle corner of the altar, kneels, and sings, "For many years"; then going to the middle of the altar, he again kneels and sings in a higher voice, "For many years." As he approaches the one who consecrated him, kneeling a third time he sings in a still higher voice, "For many years." Then he receives the kiss of peace from the bishop who consecrated him and from the other bishops.

The keynote of the bishop's mission is not administration, but life —the communication of the life that Christ brought to this earth. If there is administration—and administration there must be—it is in the service of divine life. All the bishop's powers are directed to the formation of Christ in the souls of the people. Others may be instructors, but in each diocese there is only one father, the bishop. As St. Paul said: "Yes, you may have ten thousand schoolmasters in Christ, but not more than one father; it was I that begot you in Jesus Christ, when I preached the gospel to you" (1 Cor. 4:15).

Father he is, because he has the right and power to administer all the sacraments. Father he is, because his government is in the exercise of the Heavenly Fatherhood. Father he is, because his domain is universal. He is sent first to the world and then, only for jurisdictional reasons, assigned to a diocese. The reason is that the universal Church is not the sum total of all the diocese throughout the world; rather, the dioceses derive from the Church, not the other way around. The Church preceded them. It has been founded entirely on the episcopacy and its mission to make disciples of all nations (Matt. 28:18-20). The bishop is not primarily the pastor of a single flock. He is a pastor of the universal Church in union with the supreme head of the Church, Peter and his successors. Hence, one of the primary responsibilities of the bishop is to the missions of the Church.

The Sacrament of Holy Orders

The bishop is a father also because he alone has the power to generate priests, though priests have the power to generate Christians. No priest has the power to ordain another priest, though he has the power to beget the faithful.

The priest, or the bishop, in his daily round, is a minister of God, a messenger from another world, bringing upward to God prayers and adoration, and bringing down from God graces and blessings to the people. He is to lay hold of anything and anybody who wills to be ennobled curiosity, or an accountant, like Matthew at his desk, or a fellow-traveler with the enemy. His feet are scarred from thorns, where the lost sheep or the fallen-aways have become entangled; they are to be dusty from searching and sweeping for the lost coin of spiritual wanderers.

From proud tempers, he will meet ridicule and insult; from the blasphemer, blows; from the oppressed, entreaty; from the poor, a pleading. But he is one who after every contact should inspire others to say as the woman at the well: "Come and have sight of a man who has told me the whole story of my life; can this be the Christ?" (John 4:29).

No case to him is hopeless. Every soul must be to him like the drop of water in the ugly gutter which, looked at closely, reflects the deep serious blue of the far off sky. He knows that he cannot convince others that he comes from another world, unless he acts as if he had been there. The world may see his acts, but they do not know his thoughts.

When he mounts the altar, he carries with him all the woes and the wounds of the world. His feet, that walk up the altar steps, must have on them the imprint of the homeless, the refugees, and the wanderers of the earth. His face, as he kisses the altar, should bear within it the faces of those whose eyes are blasted before furnaces, darkened in salt mines, wet with the tears of grief and furrowed with the worry of sin. His vestments should be heavy with the millions of souls who know not Christ and yet who are clinging to his vestments, hoping for they know not what. As his fingers lift up the Body and Blood of Christ, he asks that all the sufferings of the world be united with Christ and that no pain go to waste.

He will feel sad, because he knows how men are bitterly losing the good in their lives, but he will be consoled knowing that God is near them even if they know it not; around them, even though they perceive it not. In his conversations, he will seek to lift flippancy into reverence, controversy into thoughtfulness, frivolity into practical life. When he mounts the pulpit, he should be a speaking crucifix.

But above all, he will not be just a priest, but a victim, for Christ was that, offering Himself for our salvation. There will be no tear shed by fellow man that does not bedew his own cheek; no mourning parent who will not pierce his heart with grief; no sheep who will be without a shepherd. And because he knows that he is too often a priest offering Christ, and too seldom a victim sharing His Cross, he will daily pray to the Mother of Christ:

> Since you formed Christ the priest and victim in thy body, form Him, I beg thee in my heart. Do this, that in addition to the words of Consecration at Mass, I may say them, as thou didst gaze on thy Son on the Cross: "This is *my* body; this is *my* blood." Then I shall, through thy help, live and die with Him.

7

The Sacrament of Matrimony

Love exists on three different levels: the sex level, the friendship-love, and the sacramental.

Sex love alone is directed toward another for the sake of pleasure which the other person gives the ego. The partner is regarded as one of the opposite sex, instead of as a person. The infatuation associated with it is nothing but the boundless desire of self-centeredness to express itself at all costs. Because it cares only for its own rapture and its own fulfillment, such love quickly turns to hate when no longer satisfied.

Over and above sex love, there is *personal* love. Personal love includes sex in marriage, but in its essence, it is based on the objective value of another person. The other person may be loved for artistic or moral excellence, or because of a common, sympathetic interest. Personal love exists wherever there is reciprocity, duality, and understanding. This kind of love can exist with carnal love in marriage, or quite apart from carnal love, for there is no direct connection between the flesh and love. It is possible to be in love without there being physical attraction, as it is possible to have physical attraction without being in love. Personal love is in the will, not in the body.

In personal love, there is no substitution of persons possible; this person is loved, and not another. But in carnal or erotic love, since there is not of necessity a love for another person, but only a love of self, it is possible to find a substitute for the one who gives pleasure. Sex love substitutes one occasion of pleasure for the other, but real love knows no substitution. No one can take the place of a mother.

Beyond each of these two is *Christian love*, which loves everyone either as a potential or actual child of God, redeemed by Christ; it is a love which loves without even a hope of return. It loves the other, not because of attractiveness, or talents, or sympathy, but because of God. To the Christian, a person is one for whom I must sacrifice myself, not one who must exist for my sake. Sex love demands carnal reciprocity; personal love finds it difficult to survive without it; but Christian love requires no reciprocity. Its inspiration is Christ, who loved us while we were sinners and, therefore, unlovable.

The sanctity of married life is not something which takes place *alongside* marriage, but *by* and *through* marriage. The vocation to marriage is a vocation to happiness which comes through holiness and sanctity. Unity of two in one flesh is not something that God tolerates, but something that He wills. Because He wills it, He sanctifies the couple through its use. Instead of diminishing in any way the union of their spirits with one another, it contributes to their ascension in love. The sacrament which sanctifies this kind of love is Matrimony.

Marriage: A Symbol of the Nuptials of Christ and the Church

Marriage as a sacrament belongs to an entirely different order than the mere union of man and woman through a civil contract. It basically regards a husband and wife as symbols of another marriage; namely, the nuptials of Christ and His Church.

The analogy of the heavenly nuptials goes back to the Old Testament, where God appears as the Bridegroom, and Israel appears as the bride. When God becomes incarnate in Christ, He called Himself, and was called, the Bridegroom; it is the new Israel, or the Church, which becomes His bride or His spouse. It is often forgotten that our Blessed Lord called Himself a Bridegroom. When our Lord was asked why the disciples of John fasted, but His own did not, He answered: "Can you expect the

The Sacrament of Matrimony

men of the bridegroom's company to go fasting, while the bridegroom is still with them? As long as they have the bridegroom with them, they cannot be expected to fast" (Mark 2:19). John the Baptist called himself "the friend of the bridegroom" (John 3:29), or what might be, in modern language, the "best man." The title of Bridegroom, which belonged to Christ, was shared by no other, as John himself said: "The bride is for the bridegroom; but the bridegroom's friend, who stands by and listens to him, rejoices too, rejoices at hearing the bridegroom's voice" (John 3:29).

On the other hand, the wife's relationship to the husband is the relationship of the Church to Christ. That is why when St. Paul speaks of marriage he says, "Those words are a high mystery... applying ... to Christ and His Church" (Eph. 5:32). The ultimate consummation of this espousal of Christ and His Church will be after the resurrection, when the Church "without spot or wrinkle" will appear "as a bride adorned for her husband" or as the "spouse of the Lamb" (Eph. 5:27; Rev. 21:2, 9; see Rev. 22:17).

The Sacrament of Matrimony is not a pious extra added to the marriage contract; it is rather the elevation of a natural marriage contract to the order of grace, in which the husband loves the wife, as Christ loves the Church, and the wife loves the husband as the Church loves Christ. The husband and wife are not just a symbol of the union of Christ and the Church; they enjoy a real participation in that union. As Christ lives in the Church and the Church in Christ, so the husband lives in the wife and the wife in the husband, and the two are in one flesh.

The role of the priest in the sacrament is to ratify, to witness, and to bestow the Church's official blessing on those whom she now empowers to furnish new members to Christ's Mystical Body. This is the one sacrament in which the contracting parties are the ministers of the sacrament to each other. In the words of one to the other and in the giving of the hand to each other, there is the mutual surrender of rights and the acceptance of duties. But to be a sacrament, a representative of the Church must be there to witness it.

Matrimony, in virtue of the mutual inherence of man and woman, is a little cameo reflecting the greater espousal of Christ and His Body, the

Church. The word "body" is used throughout Scripture to signify not only the human body, but also the Eucharistic Body or the Real Presence of Christ, and also the Mystical Body which is the Church. All three are in some way united. In the marriage ceremony the bridegroom, though he does not say so expressly, is by implication saying to the bride: "This is my body; this is my blood." The bride says the same to him. It is a kind of "consecration" on a lower level. When during the Mass they hear the words of Consecration, "This is my Body; This is my Blood," they give themselves to Christ in the same action, they give themselves to one another. The epistle of their marriage Mass reminds them of this bond to the Church:

> Wives must obey their husbands as they would obey the Lord. The man is the head to which the woman's body is united, just as Christ is the head of the Church, He, the Savior, on whom the safety of His body depends; and women must owe obedience at all points to their husbands, as the Church does to Christ. (Eph. 5:22–24)

The man is the "head" of the wife, as Christ is the Head of the Church. What did Christ do for the Church as her Head? He died for it. Hence, husbands must show love to their wives. The "headship" is not overlordship, but love unto sacrifice. The wife, in her turn, will show to the husband the devotion and love the Church does to Christ.

As further evidence of how seriously the Church takes marriage as the symbol of Christ and the Church, St. Thomas Aquinas makes a distinction between a marriage that is merely *ratified* at the altar, and a marriage that is *ratified and consummated*, when husband and wife become two in one flesh. The Church has always made this distinction in her canon law concerning marriage. A marriage that is merely ratified at the altar, but not consummated, represents the union of *Christ with the soul through grace*. A marriage ratified at the altar and consummated in the marriage act symbolizes the union of *Christ and the Church*.

The marriage that is ratified only, is a symbol of a personal union of the soul with Christ through grace. This union can be broken by sin. If,

The Sacrament of Matrimony

therefore, a husband and wife separated immediately after the marriage at the church door, and never consummated their marriage, that marriage would be breakable under certain conditions, because it is only the symbol of the union of the soul and grace. But the marriage bond of a baptized husband and wife which has been consummated is absolutely unbreakable, as the union of Christ and the Church is unbreakable.

The Administration of the Sacrament

The sacrament when administered at a nuptial Mass takes place before the Mass commences, and begins with an exhortation to the couple. A sample exhortation often appears in liturgical books, though it is not part of the sacrament; a priest may and should prepare his own sermonette to the lovers.

After the young couple have been reminded of the nature of the sacrament and its obligations, the priest asks the groom: "[Name,] will you take [Name] here present for your lawful wife, according to the rite of our Holy Mother the Church?" The bridegroom answers: "I will." Then the bride is asked: "[Name,] will you take [Name] here present for your lawful husband, according to the rite of our Holy Mother the Church?" The bride answers: "I will." The priest bids them join their right hands; then first the groom and then the bride says: "I take you [name] for my lawful wife [husband] to have and to hold, from this day forward, for better, for worse, for richer, for poorer, in sickness and in health, until death do us part."

Then follows the confirmation of the marriage bond in which the priest says: "Your marriage contract, I, by the authority of the Church, now seal and bless in the Name of the Father, and of the Son, and of the Holy Ghost." When the ring is blessed the priest says: "Bless, O Lord, this ring, which we are blessing in Thy Name so that she who wears it keeping faith with her husband in unbroken loyalty may ever remain at peace with Thee, obedient to Thy will, and may live with him always in mutual love through Christ our Lord. Amen."

Because the sacrament represents the heavenly espousals, the Church practically asks the bride and groom what guarantee they will give that they love one another until death. If they say, "We pledge our word," the Church will answer: "Words and pacts can be broken, as the history of the world too well proves." If they say, "We give the pledge of a ring," the Church will answer: "Rings can be broken and lost, and with them the memory of the promise." It is only when the ring which is given becomes a symbol of the love of Christ and His Church, does the Church unite in marriage. Eternal salvation is involved in their reception of the sacrament. Their lives become bonded at the altar, sealed with the seal of the cross, signed with the sign of the Eucharist which they both receive into their souls, as a pledge of their unity in the spirit, which is the foundation of their unity in the flesh.

The Bride in the Marriage Ceremony

In a nuptial Mass, the bride and bridegroom come to the altar immediately after the *Pater Noster*. The prayer that is said here is for the bride. There is no special prayer said for the bridegroom. Part of the prayer is as follows:

> Look in Thy mercy upon this Thy handmaid, who is to be joined in wedlock and entreats protection and strength from Thee. May the yoke of love and of peace be upon her. True and chaste may she wed in Christ; and may she ever follow the pattern of holy women; and may she be dear to her husband like Rachel; wise like Rebecca; long-lived and faithful like Sara. May the author of deceit work none of his evil deeds within her. May she ever be knit to the Faith and to the commandments. May she be true to one husband, and fly from forbidden approaches. May she fortify her weakness by strong discipline. May she be grave in demeanor and honored for her modesty. May she be well taught in heavenly lore. May she be fruitful in offspring. May her life be good and sinless. May she win the rest of the blessed and the Kingdom of Heaven.

The bridegroom is now included in the prayer for the bride: "May they both see their children's children unto the third and fourth generation, and may they reach the old age which they desire. Through the same Christ, our Lord."

The liturgy is very interesting in that it gives the emphasis to the bride. Even from a worldly point of view, the bride is the one who receives the attention in marriage. There are showers of gifts for the bride, but not always for the bridegroom. The marriage song is "Here Comes the Bride," but there is no song "Here Comes the Bridegroom." Everyone, too, is interested in what the bride wears, not in what the bridegroom wears.

In Scripture, where there is the final marriage of the Church and Christ in heavenly glory after the end of the world, all the emphasis is upon the Bridegroom, Christ, and little upon the bride. It would seem as if time, human history, or the waiting for the Second Coming of Christ is the season of the bride; but eternal glory is for the Bridegroom. In the "book of Ruth," where the final glory is typified and symbolized, there is emphasis only upon Boaz. The bride is quietly at home awaiting the coming of the groom. She does not appear in the ceremony at the gate. Though in worldly weddings and even in the liturgy of the Church, the bride steals the show, it is not so at the wedding of the Lamb in Heaven. There He becomes the center of attention. All the bride possesses is in Him, and through Him and with Him. In the book of the Apocalypse, a long description of how the Bridegroom would be dressed is given, but there is only a very simple description of the bride: "Hers it is to wear linen of shining white; the merits of the saints are her linen" (Rev. 19:8). The Apocalypse calls the final union of Christ and the Church the wedding of the Lamb, not the wedding of the bride.

An Unbreakable Bond

Because Matrimony images forth in the order of flesh the union of Christ and the Church, it follows that it is unbreakable. In the Incarnation, our Blessed Lord took human nature which was the beginning of His Mystical Body, not for three years, nor for thirty-three, but for all eternity. So man and woman, reflecting the eternal union of Christ and the Church, take one another until death do they part. The enduring character of marriage, "until death do us part," is evident even in the natural order, where there are but two words in the vocabulary of love, "you" and "always." "You" because love is unique; "always" because love is enduring. No one ever said: "I will love you for two years and six months." That is why all love songs have the ring of eternity about them. No power on earth can fragment that which is one, and husband and wife are made one in marriage. To try and make of them two single and separate individuals, as they were before marriage, is actually to make them fragments of a joint personality, like unto Solomon taking his sword and threatening to divide the babe.

Other evidence of the unbreakable character of marriage is to be found in the way Scripture speaks of marriage—never interpreting it in terms of sex, but always in terms of "knowledge": "And now Adam had knowledge of his wife, Eve, and she conceived" (Gen. 4:1). When the angel Gabriel announced to the Blessed Mother that she was to be the Mother of God, she asked: "How can that be, since I have no knowledge of man?" (Luke 1:34). St. Paul later on enjoins husbands to "possess your wives in knowledge."

Why is marriage in the Bible related to knowledge? It is in order to reveal the close union of man and wife. There is nothing in the universe that reveals a deeper union than that of the mind and that which it knows. When the mind knows a *flower* or a *tree*, it possesses these objects within itself. They are not identified with intellect: they are distinct from it, and nothing can separate them.

Because marriage is knowledge, it follows that it demands fidelity. Suppose a student, until he entered college, never knew the soliloquy of Hamlet. Once he came to *know* it, he would always be dependent on the college which had given him that knowledge. That is why he calls his college his "beloved mother" or his *alma mater*; she caused something to happen in him which was unique. He could go on enjoying the soliloquy all the days of his life, but he could never reacquire it.

So too, when a husband and wife come to know one another in marriage they may enjoy the union many times, but they can never again reacquire that knowledge. As long as time endures, it is this man who has made her a woman; it is this woman who has made him a man. A deep bond of relationship is established between the two, though not in the same order as the bond between the mother and the child.

This suggests a union between man and woman that is much more personal than carnal. Both man and woman, in the moment of knowing, receive a gift which neither ever knew before, and which can never be known again, except by repetition. The resulting psychic changes are as great as the somatic. A woman can never again return to virginity; the man can never again return to ignorance. Something has happened to make them one, and from that oneness comes fidelity so long as either has a body. Sex is never just an "experience"; it is a bond registered through eternity.

The great advantage of the marriage vow which relates husband and wife to the union of Christ and the Church is that it guards the couple against allowing the moods of a moment to override reason. There is no other way to control capricious solicitation except by a vow. Once its inviolable character is recognized, an impulse is subject to probing one's own faults and the making of new efforts to deepen love and understanding.

The Begetting of Children

The union of husband and wife also imitates the Church in its fecundity. In the union of Christ and the Church, there is spiritual fecundity (increase in conversions); in the human marriage, there is corporal fecundity. As the Church begets children out of the womb of the baptismal font, fecundated by the Holy Spirit, so husband and wife beget children. Hence, in the prayer of the Church during the sacrament, God is asked: "May they both see their children's children unto the third and fourth generation, and may they reach the old age which they desire. Through the same Christ, our Lord."

If the ultimate aim of the union of man and woman is not life, then there can be only one alternative, namely, death. The child is the physical expression of the fecundity of the Godhead, in which the Father is the source of the eternal generation of the Son. The gift of generation is not a push from below; it is a gift from above. It comes not from the animals of the field, but rather it descends from Heaven as a reflection of the Father saying to His Son: "This day have I begotten Thee."

This primary end of Matrimony brings the couple in relationship to the Divine Trinity, as the duality of husband and wife ends in the begetting of children, the third term in their love. This is in keeping with the very nature of love, which may be defined as a *mutual self-giving which ends in self-recovery*. All love must be a giving, for without a giving there is not goodness; without self-outpouring there is no love. In marriage, love is first a mutual self-giving, for love's greatest joy is to gird its loins and serve.

But if love were only mutual self-giving, it would end in self-exhaustion, or else become a flame in which both would be consumed. Mutual self-giving also implies self-recovery. The mutual self-giving of husband and wife, like the love of earth and tree, becomes fruitful in new love. There is a mutual self-surrender as they overcome their individual impotence by filling up, at the store of the other, the lacking measure. There is self-recovery as they beget not the mere sum of themselves, but a new life which makes them an earthly trinity. Love that is ever seeking to give, and is ever defeated by receiving, is the shadow of the Trinity on earth; therefore, a foretaste of Heaven.

Behind the urge to procreate is the hidden desire of every human to participate in the eternal. Since man cannot do this in himself, he compensates for it by continuing life in another. Our inability to externalize ourselves is overcome by giving, with God's help, something immortal to the human race. Thus, the parents become co-creators with God, as the angel told Tobias:

> Then, when the third night is past, take the maid to thyself with the fear of the Lord upon thee, moved rather by the hope of begetting children than by any lust of thine. So, in the true line of Abraham, thus shalt have joy of thy fatherhood. (Tob. 6:22)

Instead then of reflecting in any way upon sex, the sacrament sees generation as a reflection of the eternal generation of the Son in the bosom of the Father. As St. Thomas Aquinas puts it: "If one is led to perform the marriage act either by virtue of justice, in order to render the debt to the partner, or by virtue of religion, that children may be procreated for the worship of God, the act is meritorious."

As the sacrament sees in the father of the family the reflection of divine paternity, so there is in motherhood a relation to the Eucharist. The mother says to her child, "As I live because of Christ, so you will live because of me." As, under the species of bread, day by day Christ nourishes the Christian soul, so drop by drop the mother nourishes the child. As the Divine Eucharist gives immortality, so this human eucharist of motherhood is the guarantee of temporal life. The angel that once stood at the gate of paradise to prevent man from eating the tree of life now sheathes the sword. Life comes into its own. There is communion with human life at the breast and Communion with divine life at the altar.

When the Son of God espoused humanity and became a Child, there was a new emphasis on fecundity. It placed primacy at a point never before seen in history. Up until the Incarnation, the order had been father, mother, and child. Now it was turned backward, and became Child, Mother, and father. For centuries humans looked up to the heavens and said: "God is away up there." But when a Mother held a Child in her arms, it could truly be said that she looked *down* to Heaven. God was way down there in the dust of human lives. If it be objected that Mary had only one Child, it must be repeated that she had only one Child according to the flesh, but she had other children according to the spirit, for our Blessed Lord said to her at the foot of the Cross: "Behold, thy son" (John 19:26), referring to John. And John, being unnamed, stood for all humanity. At that moment she became by divine decree the Mother of all whom Christ redeemed and the Patroness of all mothers.

For Better or for Worse

Because of human frailty there may be, despite love's effort, a failure to achieve common union in mind and body; but this does not give the offended party the right to contract a new marriage. "What God, then, has joined, let no man put asunder" (Matt. 19:6).

When human love and sex love break down, there is always Christian love, which steps in to suggest that the other person is to be regarded as a *gift* of God. Most of God's gifts are sweet; a few of them, however, are bitter. But whether bitter or sweet, the partner is still a gift of God, for whom the other must sacrifice himself or herself. Selfish love would seek to get rid of the burden of the other person simply because he is a burden. Christian love takes on the burden in obedience to the command: "Bear the burden of one another's failings; then you will be fulfilling the law of Christ (Gal. 6:2).

What sickness is to an individual, an unhappy marriage may be to a couple; namely, a trial sent by God in order to perfect them spiritually. If a husband were suffering from pneumonia, the wife would not leave him. In like manner, if the husband is unfaithful or unkind, the wife will not leave him for another marriage. The acceptance of the trial of marriage is not a sentence to death. A soldier is not sentenced to death because he takes an oath to his country, but admits that he is ready to face death rather than lose honor. Being wounded for the country we love is noble; being wounded for the God we love is nobler still.

Just as there is a communication of vital forces between husband and wife, so too, there can be a communication of spiritual forces: "The unbelieving husband has shared in his wife's consecration, and the unbelieving wife has shared in the consecration of one who is a brother" (1 Cor. 7:14). What a blood transfusion is to the body, reparation for the sins of another is to the spirit. Instead of separating when there are trials, the Christian solution is to bear the cross for the sake of the sanctification of the other. A wife can redeem a husband, and a husband can redeem a wife, as Christ offered Himself for His spouse, the Church. As skin can be grafted from the back to the face, so merit can be applied from spouse to spouse. This spiritual communication may not have the romantic satisfaction in it of carnal communication, but its returns are eternal.

The great difference between a Christian and a pagan in such a trial is that the Christian *receives* suffering; he even speaks of it as coming from the hands of the Crucified; the unbeliever, however, finds no place for it in the universe because it negates his egotism; it cancels out his love of pleasure, and it begets an inferno within him. A cross to the Christian is outside him and therefore bearable; the double cross on the inside of the unbeliever is insoluble, unbearable.

Christian love not only can make such suffering bearable; it can even make it sweet. The Son of God voluntarily ended on a Cross; but it did not conquer Him because it came from without: "He suffered under Pontius Pilate." The Christian, in like manner, sees that if Innocence did not spurn the Cross, then somehow or other, it must fit into his life, which is far from innocent. Since marital love is the shadow cast on earth by the Love of Christ for His Church, then it must reflect Christ's redemptive quality. As Christ delivered Himself up for His spouse, so there will be some wives and some husbands who will deliver themselves up to Golgotha for the sake of their spouse.

Just as in the spiritual life there is the "dark night of the soul," so in marriage there is the dark night of the body. The ecstasy does not always endure. In the days of romance, the emphasis is on the ego's durability in love. Later on, the Christian sees that marriage is not two persons directed toward one another, but rather two going out to a common purpose beyond themselves.

When the incarnate Son of God burst the bonds of death and rose to glory, Scripture revealed that the physical universe is groaning in pain until it is destined to be transformed as a perfect instrument of the Spirit; that is, until there is a new Heaven and a new earth. In the meantime, the Church makes use of the material things of this creation and associates action and prayer with it. Water, bread, wine, oil, and other things are made the effectual signs of the spiritual gifts which God bestows upon His people through the Church as His agency. As Cardinal Newman put it:

We approach and in spite of the darkness our hands, our head, our brow, or our lips become, as it were, sensible of the contact of something more than earthly. We know not where we are, but we have been bathing in water and a voice tells us that it is blood. Or we have a mark signed upon our forehead and it speaks of Calvary. Or we recollect a hand laid upon our heads and surely it had the print of the nails upon it and resembled Him who gave sight to the blind and raised the dead. Or we have been eating or drinking, and it was not a dream surely that One fed us from His Wounded Side and renewed our nature by the heavenly meat He gave us.

It would be a false view to look on water, oil, bread, and the matter of sacraments as having any power of and by themselves. This was the mistake made by Naaman, the Syrian general, when Eliseus told him that he could be cured of his leprosy if he would bathe in the Jordan seven times. Naaman answered: "Has not Damascus its rivers, Abana and Pharphar, such water as is not to be found in Israel?" (2 Kings 5:12). Thinking that the cure would be wrought through water alone, Naaman argued that the dirty water of the Jordan could not compare with the purer waters of his own land. Finally, at the urging of a servant, Naaman was healed and immediately saw that it was due to the power of God, not to the power of the waters. So it is in the sacraments. God uses men and matter; the power is not in them, but in God.

Postlude

Once God became a Babe and was laid in a manger, men could say: THIS IS GOD WITH US. So real was this union between God and man in Him, that all of His acts and words, all of His agonies and tears, all of His thoughts and feelings, resolves and emotions, while being properly human were, at the same time, the acts, the words, the agonies, the tears, the thoughts, and the feelings of the Eternal Son of God.

This is a mystery of a sacrament on an infinitely higher level than man himself. What does man have but a kind of union, on an immeasurable lower level, of two different substances: one material and the other spiritual, one the body and the other soul, both united in a human personality? What is more remote from the emotions of the flesh than the reasonings of the spirit? Antecedent to their unity, how difficult would it be ever to conceive a moment when body and soul would be united in a single personality? And yet they are so united in an experience clear to every mortal. We cease to marvel at it because of its familiarity. The God who brings body and soul together and one human personality, notwithstanding the difference of their nature, now brings human nature from Mary and His divine nature under the control of His Eternal Personality.

Human nature, which our Blessed Lord assumed from His Virgin Mother, was used as the *instrument* for communication of the Truth, the Life, and the power of His divinity. No miracle was ever worked, no body ever healed, no mind ever illumined, no apostle ever taught, no disciple assigned to preach except by and through the instrumentality of His human nature. Men heard words falling from Galilean lips, but the Speaker was the Word of God: eyes saw hands lifted in absolution of a palsied man, but the forgiveness came from God in the form of man. St. John tells us that if all He had done had been written down, the world would not be large enough to contain the books thereof.

The Role of Nature in the Incarnation

The book of Genesis reveals that after the fall of man thistles grew, beasts became wild, women brought forth children in sorrow, and man was obliged to earn his bread by the sweat of his brow. In other words, all nature seemed to share in the rebellion against God. When the big cog in an intricate machine breaks, all the lesser cogs fail to function. It is inconceivable that the exceptions one often finds in nature, such as plants sweeping out of their course, are, as Milton said, the repercussion of that original rebellion.

Since nature rebelled against God, and since, as St. Paul said, "all creation groans for redemption" (Rom. 8:23), why did God only become man? If the trees and the flowers and the earth "fell" from their due order, why should we not have had pantheism instead of an Incarnation? Why should not God have mixed His substance with oil and bread in the material universe, as the animists believe, and many of the Oriental religions still believe?

The answer is that creation did not fall *directly* but indirectly, that is, through man. It is, therefore, through man that creation is to be revived. When God took upon Himself a human nature and, through Calvary and the Resurrection, regenerated and re-created it, then it was up to men, who share in that Redemption, to regenerate nature and bring it back again to God. Because man has a spiritual soul, he can know all things and contain all things within himself. He is bigger than the world because he can get the world into his head. The stars may be above him, but he knows that the stars *are* above him, but the stars do not know it. He is, therefore, like a little microcosm, the spokesman of the minerals and the plants and the animals, and it is his mission, or his natural priesthood, to lead them all back again to God.

The mineral cannot thank God for its creation, but man can do so in the name of the mineral. Plants have no other language than their flower, and animals no other speech than their cry or moan. Their dumb gaspings would fall mute before the doors of the Heavenly Father were there not someone to gather them up, to articulate them, to give them voice and speech and meaning. This is the role of man in relationship to lower creation. He is the pontiff or the bridge-builder, standing midway between earth and Heaven, destined by God to be the mouthpiece of creation, and to chant with the three youths in the fiery furnace a *Benedicite* to the Creator. In the Incarnation, Christ said to His Apostles: "Preach the gospel to every *creature*" (Mark 16:15). He did not say preach the gospel to "every man." By this He meant that the material universe is to *have a part in worship*. St. Paul said: "All are yours, you are Christ's and Christ is God's" (1 Cor. 3:22–23).

In the building of a cathedral, man goes down to the bowels of the earth and says to its gold, silver, and marble: "Praise ye the Lord"; he then lifts them up until they become a chalice, or an arch, or a statue. He goes into the forests with their trees, so conscious of having borne a burden of the penitent thieves, and says: "Praise ye the Lord," and elevates them until they become a confessional or a pew. The wax of the bees, the wool of the sheep, the oil of the olive, the water of the stream—all these are put upon the paten of man's will and are offered to God, thus spiritualizing, sacramentalizing, and giving them a meaning and purpose which they cannot articulate of and by themselves.

Nature, in general, has a role to play in religion. Some parts of nature, namely those which Christ used in a special way, will be the material side of *sacraments*, or the chariots upon which Christ rides triumphantly into souls.

Since creation fell indirectly through man, why should not material creation be made as a channel for the spiritual and divine, as His human nature was the visible sign of His invisible goodness and love? Isolated bits of "human material" were found in this disordered world, such as Simon, Andrew, and Matthew—into them He infused His divine life force. So, just as the growing vine can take an atom of carbon and incorporate it into its living structure, He would use certain elements of the disordered material universe in order to make them the vehicles for carrying His divine life into souls.

Christ Acts through the Sacraments

When our Lord walked the earth, He used an animate instrument to convey divinity, namely, His human nature, in somewhat the same way that an artist uses his right hand to paint. After our Lord's Resurrection, when He became invisible to men, He began to use *animate* but *separate* instruments, namely, the one who ministers the sacrament and the sacrament itself. The moment that a minister of the sacrament performs a sacramental rite, he places himself under the influence of Christ by his *intention*. He makes an *act of will* to allow Christ to use him as His instrument.

The power of the sacrament *does not depend upon the holiness* of the one who ministers it, but upon his voluntary bond with the causality of Christ, and the fact that Christ has communicated to him this power. No sacrament is vitiated because the minister is unworthy. The sun shining through a dirty window does not become polluted because of the dirty window. Neither does the grace of Christ become lessened because of the want of holiness in the minister. The source from which all divine life derives is Christ Himself.

Though all this grace comes from Christ, it must not be assumed that it is given independently of the disposition of the one who receives. The Jews used to say of the manna that fell in the desert that it did not taste alike to everyone. The taste of the manna depended to some extent upon the disposition of the one who received it. Though the grace or the increase of divine life in the soul is not dependent upon our subjective belief alone, but upon the objective reality of the value of the Passion of Christ, our spiritual state is important. The Gospel words are verified:

Postlude

"The measure in which you give is the measure in which you will be repaid, and more will be given you besides" (Mark 4:24).

It cannot be too often repeated that the efficacy of the sacraments comes from Christ Himself. *It is Christ who baptizes; it is Christ who forgives sins; it is Christ who anoints; it is Christ who ordains.* If Judas had baptized, it would have been just as valid as if Peter had done it, or Paul. When a priest preaches, the effect he produces depends upon his own spirituality and the industry and preparation of his sermon. But when he administers a sacrament, as a representative of the Church of Christ, it is Christ Himself who confers it. He lends Christ his hand and his lips and his fingers. If he administers a sacrament unworthily, he is guilty of sin. But the one who receives the sacrament receives it just as validly as if the priest were holy, because the sanctification comes from Christ.

The priest, therefore, in Confession does not say Christ absolves you from your sin, but "I absolve you." He does not say Christ baptizes, but "I baptize." This does not mean that he does it personally, but for that moment he is Christ Himself. The right to administer the sacraments validly comes from Christ's Mystical Body, the Church.

The minister of the sacrament is only the *bearer*, not the cause, of the gift. The priest is only the channel; that is to say, the conduit or the pipe, which may be of gold or of clay; what is important is the water of life that passes through the channel. The priest is like a poor messenger that brings gifts to a rich king and says, "Do not look at my poor rags; look at what I bring."

The Number of the Sacraments

The sacraments are seven in number. Before enumerating them, one immediately thinks how often in Scripture the number six is used to symbolize darkness and evil, and seven is used as the symbol of perfection. The sign of the beast in the Apocalypse is 666 which, in each instance, is one short of perfection—something approximating it and yet falling short of it (see Rev. 13:18). Our Lord was crucified by His enemies on the sixth day of the week, and about the sixth hour of the day He was delivered up by Pilate. The serpent was created on the sixth day. The sixth clause of the Lord's Prayer speaks of sin. Cain's descendants are recorded only as far as the sixth generation.

Seven in Scripture is very often the symbol of perfection. That may be because it unites the four directions of earth with the Trinity of Heaven. In any case, God's Covenant with Abraham reached its fulfillment with the destruction of the seven nations; the seventh day was set aside for worship. Peace was ordered in the Old Testament by sevenths of time. God often required things to be done by seven. For example, seven priests, seven trumpets, and walking around the walls of Jerusalem seven days. The Apocalypse speaks of the seven churches, seven candlesticks, seven spirits, seven stars, seven fields, seven trumpets, seven thunders, seven vials, seven plagues, and the seven angels that pour them out upon the earth. The early Fathers of the Church used to say that the sacraments were prefigured by the seven pillars sustaining the house built by Wisdom (Prov. 9:1). They also believed the seven branch candlesticks of the Old Testament typified the seven sacraments.

There is some dim suggestion of the reason for seven in the analogy of the sun. No one can look directly at the sun. It is the one mysterious thing; everything else is seen. As Chesterton said, "We can see the moon and see things under the moon, but the moon is the mother of lunatics." We could never guess the colors that are in the sun by looking at it, but if the sunlight is shot through a prism, it will split up into the seven rays of the spectrum. So too, the Divine Mystery of Christ risen and glorified in Heaven is so rich that our human intellects cannot comprehend its power. That Divine Light shining through the prism of the Church, or His Mystical Body, splits up into the seven rays or channels of grace, called the *seven sacraments*.

Moving to more solid ground, it has been stated that man is capable of leading two lives: the human life and the Christian life; the life he receives because he is born of his parents, and the life he lives because he is born of God. The one makes him a creature of God; the other makes him a child of God. Each of these lives, the physical and the divine life of grace, are possible only on the seven conditions.

Postlude

The blood of goats, sheep, and bullocks offered in the Old Testament could not cover guilt; they were merely *types* of the true reparation that was to come. Nothing less than the blood of God's own Son, who took human nature, could effect reconciliation.

The Seven Sacraments Are the Seven Kisses of God

From another point of view, the seven sacraments represent the seven kisses of God. There seem to be seven bestowals of affection in the great crises of life. There is the first kiss the mother gives to her child; later on, the kiss as the son or daughter leaves home to begin life with its full responsibilities, such as joining the army, going to college, or beginning a career. If the child is ever wounded, there is the kiss of healing: "Let Mommy kiss the sore away." If there is a disease, there is the kiss of joy at the recovery. When one enters into the social order there is an embrace, or the kiss at the conferring of an honor or a degree. And finally, there is the kiss of the bride and groom.

God too, has His seven kisses for the soul. The kiss is often mentioned in Sacred Scripture: "greet one another with the kiss of the saints" (2 Cor. 12:13). St. Augustine in one of his Easter sermons said: "Christians give one another a holy kiss. It is the sign of peace that which the lips show outwardly in our heart." St. Cyril in Alexandria wrote, "Let us embrace one another and give the kiss of peace. Do not think that this is the kiss which friends accustomed to giving one another when they meet in the marketplace. This is not such a kiss, for it unites souls to one another and destroys all resentments. The kiss is the sign of the union of souls."

The holy kiss which was given in the early Church was a kind of symbol of the seven kisses with which God greets the soul. At the beginning of divine life, He kisses the soul when it is born in Baptism; when He feeds the soul in the Eucharist; when He forgives sins in the Sacrament of Penance; when He blots out the traces of the disease of sin in the Sacrament of the Anointing of the Sick. God kisses the soul of the priest and the bishop when He ordains and consecrates them. And, finally, God kisses the soul of the bride and groom as they symbolize the Church and Himself.

Sacraments and the Acts of Christ

Every sacrament is an act and a gesture of Christ Himself and, therefore, they are to be found not only in His words, but also in seven great moments of His Life.

Baptism He associated with His death: "There is the baptism I must need to be baptized with, and how impatient I am for its accomplishment" (Luke 12:50). It was through His death that men would receive the new life in Baptism. One cannot be born to a higher life without a death of the lower. In the very beginning of our Lord's public life, He spoke to Nicodemus concerning Baptism, and His very last words on earth were the order to baptize. The link that held both together was the baptism of His death on the Cross.

Confirmation—our Lord began His life in the womb of Mary overshadowed by the Holy Spirit, and His public life at the borders of the Jordan with the descent of the Holy Spirit, immediately after which He accepted the full responsibility of His mission of teaching and redeeming.

The Eucharist was the sacramental sign of His Passion and His Death which He enacted the night of the Last Supper, when He fulfilled the thousands of Passovers of the Jews by revealing that He was the Lamb of God who offered Himself for the sins of the world under the appearances of bread and wine.

Penance—Dead to sin upon Calvary and buried in a tomb, He showed the power over sin and death which comes in its wake by rising from the dead. Also, while on the Cross, He forgave the sins of the penitent thief; and to all who would embrace His meritorious pardon, He proclaimed: "Father, forgive them for they know not what they do" (Luke 23:34).

The Anointing of the Sick—He healed the sick, opening the eyes to the light of His sunshine, and lifting up limbs long palsied with disease. He also ordered His Apostles to anoint the sick with oil and to heal them. This sacrament, like all others, unites us to the Life of Christ and, in particular, the moment of the Last Supper which the Gospel describes: "Jesus already knew that the time had come for His passage from this world to the Father" (John 13:1).

Holy Orders — The night of the Last Supper, when our Blessed Lord instituted the Eucharist, He communicated the power of renewing sacramentally His Passion and Death in the Mass by the words, "Do this in commemoration of Me" (Luke 22:19). After He had risen from the grave, where the sins of man had put Him, He gave the Apostles the power to forgive sins: "Whose sins you shall forgive, they are forgiven" (John 20:23).

Matrimony — He began His public life by assisting at a marriage feast, which the Jews always regarded as the symbol of the union of God and Israel. Upon the Cross, He united Himself mysteriously with His Church as the Spouse and thereby proclaimed that Matrimony, or the union of husband and wife, is the symbol of the union of Himself, the Bridegroom, and His Church, the Bride.

The general principle of the sacraments in relation to the fallen humanity, our Lord describes in the parable of the Good Samaritan. The man who went down from Jerusalem to Jericho, fell among robbers, and was left half-dead, was the *type* of human nature. He who was given so many gifts when he was created in the garden of paradise, was stripped of them by the robber Satan. He was wounded in nature; his intellect was darkened, his will weakened, so that the good which he willed to do, he did not, and the evil which he willed not, he did. In the parable, the priest and the Levite saw the wounded man and passed by. These represented the Old Testament priesthood and the legal observances of the Old Law which were only foreshadowings of the one that was to come. Of and by themselves, they could not heal from sin; they could only point to the regeneration of man that was yet to come. It was not by the blood of goats or calves, but by His own blood, that the eternal ransom of wounded man would be paid. The sacraments of the Old Law were merely the anointing of the flesh; they did not heal the spirit. As Isaiah, the prophet, said: "From sole to crown, nothing but wounds, and swollen sores, that none binds up, or medicines, or anoints with oil" (Isa. 1:6).

The Good Samaritan who passed by and was moved with compassion was Christ Himself. Who, because of His love for us, descended from Heaven and became incarnate. And binding up the wounds of the sick man, and pouring in oil and wine, He used the raw elements of material creation as vehicles for spiritual healing. The wounded man is brought finally to an inn where he is well cared for; the inn being the Body of Christ, the Church. The beast on which the man was carried, St. Peter almost seems to suggest, was His own flesh which bore our sins. "So, on the Cross, His own body took the weight of our sins; we were to become dead to our sins and live for holiness; it was his wounds that healed you" (1 Pet. 2:24).

Indelible Marks

Three sacraments imprint an indelible mark upon the soul and may not be repeated, except conditionally. These three sacraments are: Baptism, Confirmation, and Holy Orders.

St. Augustine said, "Suppose a soldier deserts the Roman army and, as he does so, he looks at the tattoo or the brand that has been marked on his body. He is filled with fear, and resolves to appeal to the emperor for pardon, and is returned to his military duties." St. Augustine now asks, "Will such a soldier ever be marked again?" St. Augustine answers in the negative. So it is with the Sacraments of Baptism, Confirmation and Holy Orders.

When one is validly baptized and confirmed and ordained, there is no repetition of the sacraments. These three marks impressed on those who receive the sacrament will endure for all eternity, either for the glory of the saved, or for the shame of the lost.

Many reasons can be given why these sacraments may not be conferred again, if once validly received. First, from the natural or biological point of view, there are three moments in life that represent stages that cannot be crossed over again: we can be born physically only once; so in the spiritual order, we can be baptized or born to Christ only once. We grow to maturity only once and accept the duties of our station in life. This is paralleled in the Sacrament of Confirmation, whereby we receive our spiritual adulthood as a soldier of Christ and defender of the Faith only once. If born in a royal family, there is no subsequent rebirth needed to maintain that royalty. If we are born to the royalty of the priesthood of Christ, then no rebirth is necessary.

From another point of view, these three sacraments are related to three kinds of sacrifice mentioned in the Bible and in the Mass: the sacrifice of Abel, of Melchisedech, and of Abraham. The sacrifice of Abel was a *bloody* sacrifice of animals to God, indicating that only through the shedding of blood was there remission of sins. Cain refused to recognize the necessity of a blood sacrifice by offering the first fruits of the earth. Abraham offered a *voluntary* sacrifice inasmuch as he willed, during the three days it took him to go to the top of the mountain, to sacrifice his son, Isaac. A ram was provided in the place of his son, but the will to sacrifice endured, and was eternal, as far as Abraham was concerned. Finally, there was the *sacramental* sacrifice of Melchisedech who offered bread and wine.

These three sacrifices were prototypes of the three sacrifices of Christ: 1) His bloody sacrifice upon the Cross, which was related to Abel, slain by jealous brethren of the race of Cain; 2) the non-bloody sacramental sacrifice on the night of the Last Supper; and 3) the enduring will to sacrifice, for Christ is pictured as the "Lamb slain from the beginning of the world." His earthly life also was a continuous offering of self, from the cradle to the grave. Everyone else came to live; He came to die. It was His constant will.

Three sacraments relate us to these three kinds of death. Baptism is related to the sacrifice of Abel, pre-figuring the death of Christ on Calvary. Every baptized person participates in the Passion of Christ, as if he had just suffered and died himself. Confirmation relates us to the daily voluntary sacrifice of Abraham, in which we 'die daily' for the sake of Christ and His Church; Holy Orders, with the sacramental sacrifice of Christ on the night of the Last Supper when He gave His priests the power to continue that oblation until the end of time.

A final reason for the three indelible marks is that each of these sacraments incorporates us, in a certain manner, in one of the triple offices of

Christ. During His earthly life, He was King, He was Teacher or Prophet, and He was Priest. Everything He said or did could be reduced to one of these three functions. In fact, He bequeathed these three offices to His Mystical Body, the Church, whose role is to govern, to teach, and to sanctify.

Baptism incorporates us to Christ the King, for by this sacrament we are born into His Kingdom. Confirmation incorporates us to Christ the Teacher, for by it we become witnesses to Christ's Truth in the world. Holy Orders incorporates us to Christ the Priest, who offered the supreme Sacrifice for our salvation, and communicated that power to His Church when He said: "Do this in memory of Me" (Luke 22:19). The other sacraments do not imprint a character on the soul, for they do not empower the Christian with any public function. All three are particular participations in the priesthood of Christ.

Oil

Three kinds of oil are used as the material sign in some of the sacraments: the Oil of Catechumens; the Oil of the Infirm, or the Sick; and the Holy Chrism.

The symbolism of oil is multiple. The olive, always green, designates fecundity. After the flood, the dove returned to the ark carrying an olive branch, which became the symbol of hope and peace. Oil has been used to strengthen athletes, to remedy sickness, and to provide a source of light and illumination. Perfumed oil is abstained from on days of mourning, but used on days of feasting; hence, it is called *oleum gaudii*, or the oil of gladness. Throughout the Old Testament and the New Testament, God used oil as the material sign for conveying a spiritual power or office or refreshment.

Jacob spread oil upon the stone of Bethel (Gen. 28:18; 35:14). Oil was put on the tabernacle and the objects of cult (Exod. 30:26; 40:10). Oil was put on the altar (Exod. 29:36; Dan. 9:24; Gen. 31:13). The head of the priest was anointed with oil (Lev. 8:12); priests other than the high priest were sprinkled with oil (Lev. 8:30). Kings were also anointed, for example, Saul, David, and Solomon. Prophets were also anointed with oil.

Postlude

The title of Anointed was given by excellence to our Lord. His very name, Christ, means "Anointed," that is, His human nature which He assumed from Mary was "anointed" by His divinity: "Jesus of Nazareth, whom God anointed with the Holy Spirit" (Acts 10:38). This is a reference to the Messiah who was anointed by God. The word "Christ" in Greek means "the anointed one"; that is to say, He was anointed of God as Prophet, Priest, and King. The Hebrew word "Messiah" also means "anointed." Seven centuries before Christ was born, Isaiah, the prophet, foretold: "One shall be born, on whom the Spirit of the Lord will rest" (Isa. 11:2).

The three oils are blessed on Holy Thursday by the bishop. Seven subdeacons, seven deacons, and twelve priests in procession carry the balsam and the oil. The balsam is not exorcised, because its sweet odors presume it to be free of malign influences. The bishop calls it "the sacerdotal perfume, the sanctifying balsam, the instrument of a happy faith." The bishop mixes the balsam with oil, and as he does so, he recalls that in our Blessed Lord, humanity and divinity were inseparably united. The bishops and the twelve priests who assist breathe three times in the form of a cross upon the oil of chrism to show that the power of the Holy Spirit is communicated to this element by the merits of Christ and in the name of the three Divine Persons. As the exorcism is announced, God is asked that all diabolical power be taken away from the oil.

Next is the blessing of the oil of the catechumens. The primary use of the oil is the anointing before Baptism; its secondary use is the anointing of the hands of the priest at ordination and the anointing of kings and queens at their coronation. Like the blessing of the oil of the sick, the oil of the catechumens has only an exorcism and a prayer. Following a triple breathing on the oil, the bishop prays that by the expulsion of the spirit of evil the recipients "may be purified for the divine sacraments, for the adoption of the spirit and flesh ... and that their bodies may be sanctified for the receiving of every spiritual grace."

Later, the oil of the infirm or sick has its particular blessing after the Our Father of the Mass. The prayer used is practically the same as found in the liturgies of the year 200, namely that the anointing may be a remedy for soul and body, putting to flight all sorrow, sickness, and suffering, both physical and moral.

Conclusion

When the incarnate Son of God burst the bonds of death and rose to glory, it was revealed that the physical universe would now groan in pain until it is destined to be transformed as a perfect instrument of the Spirit, that is, until there is a new Heaven and a new earth. In the meantime, the Church makes use of material things out of this creation and associated action and prayer with it. Water, bread, wine, oil, and other things are made effectual signs of the spiritual gifts which God bestows upon His people through the Church as agency.

As Cardinal Newman put it:

We approach and in spite of the darkness our hands, our head, our brow, or our lips become, as it were, sensible of the contact of something more than earthly. We know not where we are, but we have been bathing in water and a voice tells us that it is blood. Or we have a mark signed upon our forehead and it speaks of Calvary. Or we recollect a hand laid upon our heads and surely it had the print of the nails upon it and resembled Him who gave sight to the blind and raised the dead. Or we have been eating or drinking; and it was not a dream surely that One fed us from His Wounded Side and renewed our nature by the heavenly meat He gave us.

Upon what conditions can I receive this gift of a higher life? What are the normal ways in which this divine life is given? What effect will it have on me? How can one contact this divine life which Christ merited for all? In somewhat the same way that everything in nature received a higher life than that which it naturally possesses: (1) by something higher coming down to that which is lower, and (2) by the lower surrendering its imperfect nature in order to be incorporated into something higher.

How poor and tawdry would be our sanctification if it came only through the actions and the words of men! A pulpit can provoke man to greater moral efforts, but it cannot give the power for betterment. This must come from Christ, and it ought to come to us now the way Christ gave it to us, namely, through a human nature and natural things, or signs. Man cannot forgive sins, but God can forgive sins through man; that is the way our Lord forgave sins during His earthly Life, namely through the human nature He assumed for that purpose. That is the way He still does it: through other human natures whom He has officially incorporated to Himself who trace their authority back to Him.

Then, since nature rebelled when man rebelled, that too is used by God to sanctify men, in the form of water, wheat, grapes, oil, and even human gestures. Thanks to visible signs we now are receiving invisible grace. Water helps us know we are being washed; an uplifted hand making a Sign of the Cross and pronouncing words of absolution makes us see the forgiveness of the Cross applied to our souls; the appearance of bread helps us know we are being fed by the true Bread of Life. These and others are not arbitrary signs nor allegories; they are very natural and related to the grace which is imparted when the words are pronounced. As our Lord said: "You, through the message I have preached to you, are clean already" (John 15:3).

Christ as God is the Author of the sacraments; He alone sanctifies. As Head of the Church, He suffered and merited on the Cross, and now He diffuses His grace and merits, through the Body and its members. Each sacrament is given for the well-being of the Mystical Body; they are not only individual but also social in their effects. Though all give grace, one sacrament surpasses all others that look to it: that is the Eucharist. The other sacraments give grace, the Eucharist gives us the Author of grace. The other sacraments are rivers of grace; the Eucharist is the Source.

Three to Get Married

1

The Differences between Sex and Love

Love is primarily in the will, not in the emotions or the glands. The will is like the voice; the emotions are like the echo. The *pleasure* associated with love, or what is today called "sex," is the frosting on the cake; its purpose is to make us love the cake, not ignore it. The greatest illusion of lovers is to believe that the intensity of their sexual attraction is the guarantee of the perpetuity of their love. It is because of this failure to distinguish between the glandular and spiritual — or between sex which we have in common with animals, and love which we have in common with God — that marriages are so full of deception. What some people love is not a person, but the experience of being in love. The first is irreplaceable; the second is not. As soon as the glands cease to react with their pristine force, couples who identified emotionalism and love claim they no longer love one another. If such is the case they never loved the other person in the first place; they only loved being loved, which is the highest form of egotism. Marriage founded on sex passion alone lasts only as long as the animal passion lasts. Within two years the animal attraction for the other may die, and when it does, law comes to its rescue to justify the divorce with the meaningless words "incompatibility," or "mental torture." Animals never have recourse to law courts, because they have no will to love; but man, having reason, feels the need of justifying his irrational behavior when he does wrong.

There are two reasons for the primacy of sex over love in a decadent civilization. One is the decline of reason. As humans give up reason, they resort to their imaginations. That is why motion pictures and picture magazines enjoy such popularity. As thinking fades, unrestrained desires come to the fore. Since physical and erotic desires are among the easiest to dwell upon, because they require no effort and because they are powerfully aided by bodily passions, sex begins to be all-important. It is by no historical accident that an age of anti-intellectualism and irrationalism, such as our own, is also an age of carnal license.

The second factor is egotism. As belief in a Divine Judgment, a future life, Heaven and Hell, a moral order, is increasingly rejected, the ego becomes more and more firmly enthroned as the source of its morality. Each person becomes a judge in his own case. With this increase of selfishness, the demands for self-satisfaction become more and more imperious, and the interests of the community and the rights of others have less and less appeal. All sin is self-centeredness, as love is otherness and relatedness. Sin is the infidelity of man to the image of what he ought to be in his eternal vocation as an adopted son of God: the image God sees in Himself when He contemplates His Word.

There are two extremes to be avoided in discussing married love: one is the refusal to recognize sexual love, the other is the giving of primacy to sexual attraction. The first error was Victorian; the second is Freudian. To the Christian, sex is inseparable from the person, and to reduce the person to sex is as silly as to reduce personality to lungs or a thorax. Certain Victorians in their education practically denied sex as a function of personality; certain sexophiles of modern times deny personality and make a god of sex. The male animal is attracted to the female animal, but a human personality is attracted to another human personality. The attraction of beast to beast is physiological; the attraction of human to human is physiological, psychological, and spiritual. The human spirit has a thirst for the infinite which the quadruped has not. This infinite is really God. But man can pervert that thirst, which the animal cannot because it has no concept of the infinite. Infidelity in married life is basically the substitution for an infinite of a succession of finite carnal experiences.

The Differences between Sex and Love

The false infinity of succession takes the place of the Infinity of Destiny, which is God. The beast is promiscuous for an entirely different reason than man. The false pleasure given by new conquests in the realm of sex is the ersatz for the conquest of the Spirit in the Sacrament! The sense of emptiness, melancholy, and frustration is a consequence of the failure to find infinite satisfaction in what is carnal and limited. Despair is disappointed hedonism. The most depressed spirits are those who seek God in a false god!

If love does not climb, it falls. If, like the flame, it does not burn upward to the sun, it burns downward to destroy. If sex does not mount to Heaven, it descends into Hell. There is no such thing as giving the body without giving the soul. Those who think they can be faithful in soul to one another, but unfaithful in body, forget that the two are inseparable. Sex in isolation from personality does not exist! An arm living and gesticulating apart from the living organism is an impossibility. Man has no organic functions isolated from his soul. There is involvement of the whole personality. Nothing is more psychosomatic than the union of two in one flesh; nothing so much alters a mind, a will, for better or for worse. The separation of soul and body is death. Those who separate sex and spirit are rehearsing for death. The enjoyment of the other's personality through one's own personality, is love. The pleasure of animal function through another's animal function is sex separated from love.

Sex is one of the means God has instituted for the enrichment of personality. It is a basic principle of philosophy that there is nothing in the mind which was not previously in the senses. All our knowledge comes from the body. We have a body, St. Thomas tells us, because of the weakness of our intellect. Just as the enrichment of the mind comes from the body and its senses, so the enrichment of love comes through the body and its sex. As one can see a universe mirrored in a tear on a cheek, so in sex can be seen mirrored that wider world of love. Love in monogamous marriage includes sex; but sex, in the contemporary use of the term, does not imply either marriage or monogamy.

Every woman instinctively realizes the difference between the two, but man comes to understand it more slowly through reason and prayer.

Man is driven by pleasure; woman by the meaning of pleasure. She sees pleasure more as a means to an end, namely, the prolongation of love both in herself and in her child. Like Mary at the Annunciation, she accepts the love which is presented to her by another. In Mary, it came directly from God through an angel; in marriage, it comes indirectly from God through a man. But in both instances, there is an acceptance, a surrender, a *Fiat*: "Let it be unto me according to thy word" (Luke 1:38). The pagan woman who has not consciously thought of God is actually half woman and half dream; the woman who sees love as a reflection of the Trinity is half woman and half Spirit, and she waits upon the creative work of God within her body. Patience thus becomes bound up with her acceptance. Woman accepts the exigencies of love, as the farmer accepts the exigencies of nature, and waits, after the sowing of the seed, the harvest of autumn.

But when sex is divorced from love there is a feeling that one has been stopped at the vestibule of the castle of pleasure; that the heart has been denied the city after crossing the bridge. Sadness and melancholy result from such a frustration of destiny, for it is the nature of man to be sad when he is pulled outside himself, or exteriorized without getting any nearer his goal. There is a closer correlation between mental instability and the animal view of sex than many suspect. Happiness consists in interiority of the spirit, namely, the development of personality in relationship to a heavenly destiny. He who has no purpose in life is unhappy; he who exteriorizes his life and is dominated, or subjugated, by what is outside himself, or spends his energy on the external without understanding its mystery, is unhappy to the point of melancholy. There is the feeling of being hungry after having eaten, or of being disgusted with food, because it has nourished not the body, in the case of an individual, or another body, in the case of marriage. In the woman, this sadness is due to the humiliation of realizing that where marriage is only sex, her role could be fulfilled by any other woman; there is nothing personal, incommunicable, and therefore nothing dignified. Summoned by her God-implanted nature to be ushered into the mysteries of life which have their source in God, she is condemned to remain on the threshold as a tool or an instrument of pleasure alone, and not as a companion of love. Two glasses that are empty cannot fill up one another. There must be a fountain of water outside the glasses, in order that they may have communion with one another. It takes three to make love.

Every person is what he loves. Love becomes like unto that which it loves. If it loves Heaven, it becomes heavenly; if it loves the carnal as a god, it becomes corruptible. The kind of immortality we have depends on the kind of loves we have. Putting it negatively, he who tells you what he does not love, also tells what he is. *Amor pondus meum*: "Love is my gravitation," said St. Augustine. This slow conversion of a subject into an object, of a lover into the beloved, of the miser into his gold, of the saint into his God, discloses the importance of loving the right things. The nobler our loves, the nobler our character. To love what is below the human, is degradation; to love what is human for the sake of the human, is mediocrity; to love the human for the sake of the Divine, is enriching; to love the Divine for its own sake is sanctity.

Love is trinity; sex is duality. But there are many other differences between the two. Sex rationalizes; love does not. Sex has to justify itself with Kinsey Reports, "But Freud told us," or "No one believes that today"; love needs no reasons. Sex asks science to defend it; love never asks, "Why?" It says, "I love you." Love is its own reason. "God is love." Satan asked a "Why?" of God's love in the garden of paradise. Every rationalization is farfetched and never discloses the real reason. He who breaks the divine law and finds himself outside of Christ's Mystical Body in a second marriage, will often justify himself by saying: "I could not accept the doctrine of Transubstantiation." What he means is that he can no longer accept the Sixth Commandment. Milton wrote an abstract and apparently a philosophical treatise on "Doctrine and Discipline of Divorce," in which he justified the divorce on the grounds of incompatibility. But the real reason was not what he set down in the book; it was to be found in the fact that he wished to marry someone else while his wife was living. What is important is not *what* people say, but *why* they say it. Too many assume that the reason people do not come to God is because they are ignorant; it is more generally true that the reason people do not come to God is because of their behavior. Our Lord said: "Rejection lies in this, that when the light came into the world men preferred darkness to light; preferred it, because their doings were evil. Anyone who acts shamefully hates the light" (John 3:19–20). It is not always doubt that has to be overcome, but evil habits.

From another point of view, sex seeks the part; love the totality. Sex is biological and physiological and has its definite zones of satisfaction. Love, on the contrary, includes all of these but is directed to the *totality* of the person loved, i.e., as a creature composed of body and soul and made to the image and likeness of God. Love seeks the clock and its purpose; sex concentrates on the mainspring and forgets its mission to keep time. Sex eliminates from the person who is loved everything that cannot adapt itself to its carnal libido. Those who give primacy to sex for that reason are anti-religious. Love, however, does not concentrate on a function, but on personality. An organ does not include the personality, but the personality includes the organ, which is another way of repeating the theme: love includes sex, but sex does not include love.

Love concentrates on the object; sex concentrates on the subject. Love is directed to someone else for the sake of the other's perfection; sex is directed to self for the sake of self-satisfaction. Sex flatters the object not because it is praiseworthy in itself, but rather as a solicitation. It knows how to make friends and influence people. Most sound minds resent flattery because they see the egotism behind the screen of altruism. The ego in sex pleads that it loves the alter ego, but what it loves is really the possibility of its own pleasure in the other ego. The other person is necessary for the return of the egotist upon himself. The egotist finds himself constantly being encircled by non-being, purposelessness, meaninglessness; he has the feeling of being exploited. Refusing to be related to anything else, he soon sees that nothing is for him: The whole world is against him! But love, which stresses the object, finds itself in constantly enlarging relationships. Love is so strong it surpasses narrowness by devotedness and forgetfulness of self. In history, the only causes that die are those for which men refuse to die. The more love grows, the more its eyes open to the needs of others, to the miseries of men, and to compassion. The remedy for all the sufferings of the modern brain lies in the enlargement of the heart through love, which forgets itself as the subject and begins to love the neighbor as the object. But he who lives for himself will eventually find that nature, fellowman, and God are all against him. The so-called "persecution complex" is the result of egotism. The world seems against him who wants everything for himself.

Sex is moved by the desire to fill a moment between having and not having. It is an experience like looking at a sunset, or twirling one's thumbs to pass the time. It rests after one experience, because glutted for the moment, and then waits for the reappearance of a new craving or passion to be satisfied on a totally different object. Love frowns upon this notion, for it sees in this nothing but the killing of the objects loved for the sake of self-satisfaction. Sex would give birds flight, but no nests; hearts emotions but no homes; throw the whole world into the experience of voyagers at sea, but with no ports. Instead of pursuing an Infinite which is fixed, it substitutes the false infinity of never finding satisfaction. The infinite then becomes not the possession of love but the fruitless search for love, which is the basis of so many psychoses and neuroses. The infinite then becomes restlessness, a merry-go-round of the heart which spins only to spin again. Real love, on the contrary, admits the need, the thirst, the passion, the craving, but it also admits an abiding satisfaction by adhesion to a value which transcends time and space. Love unites itself to being and thus becomes perfect; sex unites itself to non-being and thus becomes irritation and anxiety. In love, poverty becomes integrated into riches; need into fulfillment; yearning into joy; chase into capture. But sex is without the joy of offering. The wolf offers nothing when he kills the lamb. The joy of oblation is missing, for the egotist by his very nature seeks inflation. Love gives to receive. Sex receives so as not to give. Love is soul contact with another for the sake of perfection; sex is body contact with another for the sake of sublimation.

A body can exhaust itself, but it cannot nourish itself. If man needed only nourishment, he could devour love as he devours food. But having a spirit which needs the Divine Love as a unitive force, he can never be satisfied by devouring the love of another person. A potato has a nature;

a man is a person. The former can be destroyed as a means to an end; the human may not. Sex would turn man into a vegetable and reduce a person to an animal. Sex makes hungry where most it satisfies, for the person needs the person, and a person is a person only when seen in an image of God.

2

Our Vital Energies

Freudianism interprets man in terms of sex; Christianity interprets sex in terms of man. The romanticist loves love; the Christian loves a person. There is a world of difference between sex loving sex and a person loving a person. Sex tries to be simultaneously both the receiver and the giver of passion; both the subject and the object. In sex the male adores the female. In love the man and woman together adore God. As a result of this dismemberment of sex from personality, sex is cerebralized, in the sense that it is made an intellectual problem. In normal human beings, sex is physical and organic. In the abnormal, it is something thought about, studied, dissected, and reduced to statistics and reports. In the older barbarism, sex was considered as physical. In the newer barbarism it is mental. Much advertising is based on sex. Instead of concupiscence arising from the body, it is now made to rise within an artificially stimulated imagination.

There is no doubt whatever that sex is an important energy in human life, but *is it the basic energy* as so many psychologists contend? Or is it, better, only one of the branches on the tree of life? Instead of being the reservoir, may it not be one of several channels through which the original Life Endowment is communicated? As water is basically H_2O and can appear as liquid, steam, and ice, so there may be in the human person a fundamental dynamism and power, which comes from the soul-body unity, and which flows out in three different directions.

Man is not a soul. As St. Thomas says: "My soul is not myself." But the soul of man is the actuating principle of the body and makes it exist as a body, unifies it, possesses it, and develops it. The parents prepare the body; God infuses the soul and makes the person. The union of the body and spirit form one being! The original source of power, energy, thought, action, love, and passion comes from the soul united to the body! This original energy, which we will call *Vita*, has three principal manifestations, because man may be considered as related (1) to himself, (2) to humanity, and (3) to the cosmos.

In relation to himself, *Vita* appears as self-preservation, a consciousness of dignity, an urge to be all that one *ought* to be. Personality feels itself, therefore, as a bearer of inalienable rights and liberties which are given by God, and which no state or dictator can take away. The right to life inspires not only needed physical development, but mental and spiritual development, as well. In brief, it implies not only a self-respect, but also a very legitimate self-love, which strives for perfection. "You are to be perfect, as your heavenly Father is perfect" (Matt. 5:48).

In relation to humanity, this *Vita* manifests itself in the generation of the human species, the begetting of a family, which in turn becomes the unit of a state and society, in which his personal rights and liberties are conditioned by the rights and liberties of others for the sake of the good of all.

In relation to the universe, the *Vita* takes another channel, which is that of compensating for the poverty of personal being through having, which becomes the ownership of private property as the economic guarantee of external liberty, as the soul is an inner and spiritual guarantee.

These three distillations of *Vita* are good because given by Divine Goodness. And all three emanations go together. No one would ever be so short-sighted as to describe man's role as self-development, leaving out his magnificent power of cooperating with God in the begetting of new areas of love. Neither would one be so narrow as to describe man in terms of the things on which he works, or which he eats, or with which he clothes himself. It would be like describing an elephant in terms of his tusk, or his tail, or his trunk alone.

Our Vital Energies

But, and here is the important fact, the right to self-preservation could become egotism, and the power of generation could become license, and ownership could be monopolistic capitalism or communism, if there ever were a basic disturbance of the *Vita* and the God-given relations of soul and body. And that is precisely what did take place in what is called the Fall of man. The fringes of this truth modern psychology has rediscovered in the conflicts and tensions and anxieties which go on inside of man. Something has happened to man to make him what he is. Whatever he is, he is not what he ought to be. All the disorder and anarchy both within himself and society possess the earmarks of being due to an abuse of freedom. Even though man now and then acts as if he lived in a jungle, one can still see in some of his actions that he once played in a Garden.

It is not our point here to describe the rebellion of man against His Creator. Every one analyzing his conscience can find examples of what happened, especially when he becomes sad and remorseful because he has hurt someone he loved. When the mainspring of a clock becomes broken, all the works are still there, but they do not function. In like manner, as a result of the rebellion against Divine Love, the *Vita*, the fundamental soul-body unity in man, lost its balance; it did not become intrinsically corrupt. A derangement took place among the three outlets of the *Vita*. In relation to himself, man became inclined not always to do what he *ought*, but to do what he *pleased*, even though he hurt others and himself. In relation to the human race, man, because he was endowed with reason, could manipulate the levers of life, which animals could not do, and could seek the pleasures of the flesh without assuming responsibilities. Finally, in relation to the cosmos, he became inclined to *want* more than he needed in the way of property, or to use illegitimate means to acquire what he did not have, or else to deprive others of what was their own.

If the pendulum denies its dependence on the clock, it is no longer free to swing. Because man denied his dependence on God, who alone is the Source of his independence, the harmony of his nature became disturbed. There sprang up in his *Vita* what is called *libido*, or concupiscence, a tending toward certain things in defiance of rational restraint.

Abnormality was introduced in all the three channels of the *Vita*. From now on legitimate self-love could become egotism and selfishness; the union of two in one flesh could become sex, in the modern sense of the term; and the right to property could become communism, monopolistic capitalism, and revolution. They need not become any of these things, for man still has human freedom, but it became harder for man to keep the lower passions tamed and under control. This concupiscence or libido is not a sin; it is more like a temptation, which becomes a sin only when the will consents to this disorder. This original catastrophe to human nature made man eccentric, that is, inclined to get off center, from which tendency has come the need of abnormal psychology.

The first of these concupiscences becomes pride or egotism, the second becomes lust, and the third, avarice or greed, and from these three flow all the sins that a human can commit. Note that there are three concupiscences or libidos, and not one of them is to be identified with the *Vita*. Pride is not the basic energy of life, nor is sex, nor greed, but all three are tendencies toward disorder in the one basic energy or *Vita*.

Most psychologists are narrow, in the sense that they take one of these to the exclusion of the others. Freud takes sex and forgets the other two equally important libidos. Adler takes pride, and Jung takes greed or security. Psychology will never give a total understanding of man until it incorporates all three and relates them to something more basic in man. Freud is right in speaking of the importance of sex in man, as a man is right in describing the importance of a trunk to an elephant. Our complaint is that it is not scientific, because not total. The libido is not sex, but sex is one of the expressions of the libido. The inferiority complex is not the basic libido of life, but it is one of them. The desire for security is not the sole explanation of man, but it is an important part of the explanation. Each of the great schools is *one-third* right. Of the three, Freud has chosen the one which is certainly the most appealing to a dis-God-ed generation. It is also very important, because the other libidos are not both personal and social. Pride involves only one individual and avarice involves things. But sex implies two persons, and through them humanity. Freud dropped one dim hint that possibly he was too narrow, for toward the end of his life he suggested widening the term sex. But it was never widened enough to include even remotely the other two eccentric tendencies and disharmonies without which no psychology is complete.

If sex were as "natural" as the sex psychologists assume it is, there should never be associated with it the sense of shame. But if anarchy was introduced into human nature by an abuse of freedom, it follows that the shame accompanying sex has some hidden relationship to man's rebellion against God.

Sacred Scripture tells us that before the Fall, Adam and Eve were "naked but not ashamed" (Gen. 2:25). They were naked and not ashamed because the passions were completely subject to reason, and there was not yet in the human body a tendency on the part of the passions to rebel against reason. The nakedness without shame was due in part to that inner spiritual perfection. It is a well-attested fact that those people who are most impoverished in their souls try to cover up this inner destitution by extreme luxury on the outside. The more naked the soul, that is, the more devoid of virtue, the greater the need of the body to give the appearance of possession through fantastic dress, display, and ostentation. The more the soul is clothed with virtue, the less is the need of outer compensation. The poor boy who wishes to be known as rich must make a display of riches. The boy who is really rich needs no such prop. We meet the reversal of this distinction of the poverty and riches of the body and soul in the ceremony known as the clothing of nuns. In many communities, the day the young lady becomes professed she dresses first as a rich bride and is adorned with many jewels. Some believe this is to express the fact that she is the Bride of Christ. That such is not the case is evident from the fact that after she pronounces her vows, she goes to her cell and exchanges the elaborate gown for the humble and menial habit of her community. The implication is that now that her soul is adorned with the beauty of God's grace, there is no longer need for seeming richness of the body. It is very likely that Adam and Eve, instead of being naked in our sense of the term, had reflected in their bodies an effulgence of light, which came from Original Justifying

Grace in the soul. As a result, one perceived less a body than a person bearing the divine image.

It was only after our first parents rebelled against God that they disturbed the equilibrium of their human nature. It need hardly be stated here that Catholic tradition has never taught that their sin was the marriage act. On the contrary, God told our first parents to "increase and multiply." As St. Augustine says: "He who says that there would have been neither copulation nor generation but for the sin, simply makes sin the origin of the holy number of the saints." The position of St. Thomas is that there was far greater pleasure in the marriage act before Original Sin. "There would not have been less pleasure then, as some people have asserted. Rather the same pleasure would have been all the greater, inasmuch as man's nature was then purer, and his body was therefore capable of more exquisite sensations."

No one sins against Love without hurting himself. A triple concupiscence, or tendency to excess, resulted from Adam's and Eve's turning from God. What effect did that have on the second manifestation of *Vita*, or generation? As regards the marital act, St. Thomas says we "must distinguish two features in the present state of things: One which is natural, namely, the conjunction of male and female for the purpose of generation.... The other is a certain deformity consisting in immoderate concupiscence. The latter would not have been present in the state of innocence, for then the lower powers were already subject to reason." This tendency to derationalize or irrationalize the passion of generation, along with acts associated with it, is what is embraced in the modern use of the term "sex." It includes, therefore, what is good (the passion of the flesh to generate) and what is evil (namely, its disorder and excess).

It was after the loss of grace that our first parents perceived themselves to be naked and were ashamed. To some extent, the sense of shame may be natural, but it now begins to appear as associated with guilt. Shame can be, and often is, the expression of the tension and antinomy which in its higher realms was a rebellion against God. Original Sin tore them from the union with God through grace, which is a participation in the divine nature. But the disruption of the union of man and God had an echo in the disturbance of the union of soul and body. The big cog in the machine broke, so the little cogs went out of order, too. Nothing better describes and represents this initial rebellion against God than the tendency of the body to rebel against the spirit. Shame is one of the expressions of that rent.

It must be repeated that it was not because of sex that Adam and Eve were ashamed, for they had sex, and they used it before their sin. It may very well be that the unsatisfying character of the union, in the sense that it does not fulfill the infinite longings of the soul for unity, is a reminder of how the finite was torn from the infinite and the creature from his Creator.

St. Augustine also states that in a sense shame is related to disobedience. Positively, this would mean that when there is perfect obedience to God, there is no shame. This confirms, somewhat, the spiritual truth that Catholic educators have observed, namely, that as obedience to the law of Christ increases, concupiscence or the passions actually diminish. The sex passions are not the same in all persons. They are so much under control in some, that they resist them with the same automatic reflex as the blinking of their eye when dirt gets into it. The history of mysticism reveals that temptations of the flesh become less as one gets closer to God, although the temptations to pride may increase. The Holy Eucharist, which is the Body of Christ, when worthily received, does diminish the uprisings of concupiscence. There is not the hardship imposed on a celibate priest that the sex-world would imagine, for, given power over the Physical Body of Christ, he already has the cure for the rebellion of his own physical body. In a lesser degree, parents who are married by a sacrament and live their married life in union with a love of Christ probably feel between themselves an almost complete extinguishing of a sense of shame, precisely because of their obedience to the Spirit.

There is also another reason for shame, which is more related to the natural order. Sex is rightly called a mystery. It has its matter and form. Its matter is the physical power of generation; its form is its power to share in the creative purposes of God. Because sex is related to creativity, and God is the source of all creativity, sex is seen to have an intimate bond with religion. Because it is a summons to share in creation, and because man and woman are God's coworkers in quarrying humanity, there is an awesomeness about the act. That is why all peoples have associated marriage with a religious ceremony.

But everything that is mysterious tends to be hidden and concealed. The Eastern World is much more aware of this than the Western World. That is why the Consecration in the Eastern religions takes place behind a screen, whereas in the Western rite it is more public. The very hiding of the mystery of transubstantiation is a highly developed form of the concealing of anything which has to do with God. Since, in the natural order, there are few acts more mysterious than the union of two humans in one flesh, it follows that there should be a tendency on the part of man and woman to veil and hide themselves from others when they enter into the performance of that act which, in the supernatural order, symbolizes the mystery of Christ and the Church, and which in the natural order makes them co-creators with God. Here the explanation would not be a sense of shame in the sense of guilt, but rather a sense of shame in the sense of reverence. This is what Pope Pius XII said in an address to mothers: "The sense of modesty is akin to the sense of religion."

3

What Love Is

It takes three to make love, for lover and beloved are bound together on earth by an ideal outside both. If we were absolutely perfect, we would have no need of loving anyone outside ourselves. Our self-sufficiency would prevent a hankering for what we have not. But love itself starts with the desire for something good. God is good. God is being, and therefore has no need of anything outside Himself. But we have being: creation may be described as the introduction of the verb "to have" into the universe.

What makes us creatures is the fact that we are dependent; all that we have, we have received. Because we are not perfect, we constantly strive to make up for what is lacking, or to complement our *having* by having *more*. The craving for private property, for example, is one of the natural aspirations of man, for by it man hopes to enlarge his personality and to extend himself by owning things.

Love has three causes: goodness, knowledge, and similarity.

It is possible for man to mistake what is good for him, but it is impossible for him not to desire goodness. The prodigal son was right in being hungry: he was wrong in living on husks. Man is right in trying to fill up his life, his mind, his body, his house with what is good; he may be wrong perhaps in what he chooses as a good. But without the desire for goodness, there would be no love, whether it be love of country, love of friend, or love of spouse. Through love every heart seeks to acquire a perfection or a good which it lacks, or else to express the perfection that it already has.

It follows then that all love is produced by goodness, for *goodness by its nature is lovable*. It may be difficult to understand why certain people are loved, but of this we can be sure: those who love see a goodness in them which others do not see. God loves us because He *puts* His Goodness into us and finds it there. We love certain creatures because we *find* goodness in them. Saints love those whom no one else loves, because after the manner of God, they put goodness into other people and find them lovable. If it be asked why the drunkard loves alcohol, why the libertine loves perversion, or why the criminal loves stealing, it is because each of them sees some good in what he does. What each seeks is not the highest moral good, for endowed with free will, each can always choose a partial rather than a total good, thus making a god of his appetites. Evil in order to be attractive must at least wear the guise of goodness. Hell has to be gilded with gold of paradise, or men would never want its evil. If evil were always called by its right name, it would lose much of its appeal. When the exaggerations and perversions of sex are called the "Kinsey Report," they give an air of scientific goodness to that which would have no appeal if it were called "lust." Goodness by its nature is lovable, and love finds it impossible not to pursue goodness. Goodness is perfective of our being, and thus compensates for the meagerness of our *having*.

If one is asked why he is in love with a particular person, he may, if he is a logician, put his argument into some such form as this:

It is our nature to love goodness:

But X is good:

Therefore, I love X.

As we have said, this goodness is not always moral goodness; it can be physical goodness, or utilitarian goodness. A person is then loved because of the pleasure he gives, or because he is useful, or because "he can get it for you wholesale." But good he must be, under one of his aspects, otherwise he would not be loved.

The second cause of love is knowledge. A woman cannot love a man unless she has had at least some knowledge of him. "Introduce me to him"

What Love Is

is a demand for knowledge preceding love. Even the dream girl of the bachelor has to be constructed out of fragments of knowledge. The unknown is the unloved. The love of the animal begins with the knowledge that comes through its senses, but the knowledge of man comes from his senses and his intellect. As love comes from knowledge, so hatred comes from want of knowledge. Bigotry is the fruit of ignorance.

Though at the beginning, knowledge is the condition of love, in its latter stages love can increase knowledge. A husband and wife who have lived together for many years have a new kind of knowledge of one another which is deeper than any spoken word, or any scientific investigation; it is knowledge that comes from love, a kind of intuitional perception of what is in the mind and the heart of the other. It is possible to love more than we know. A simple person in good faith may have a greater love of God than a theologian, and as a result a keener understanding of the ways of God with the heart than psychologists have. Goodness alone in isolation from knowledge could not prompt love; it must first be proposed to the mind and understood as good.

Knowledge can be either abstract or emotional. Geometry is abstract knowledge, but knowledge about sex is emotional knowledge. An isosceles triangle arouses no passions, but sex knowledge can do so! Those who advocate indiscriminate sex education to prevent sexual promiscuity forget that, because of the emotional tie-up, sex knowledge could lead to sex disorders. It is argued that if a man knew there was typhoid fever in a house, he would lose the desire to go into it. True, but the knowledge of sex is not the same as the knowledge of typhoid fever. No one has a "typhoid" passion to break down doors with quarantine warnings, but the human being does have a sex passion, which needs a control.

One of the psychological reasons why decent people shrink from vulgar sex discussion is because by its very nature it is not a communicable kind of knowledge. Its method of communication is so personal as to make the two who are involved shrink from making it general. It is too sacred to be profaned. It is a psychological fact that those whose knowledge of sex has passed to a unifying love in marriage are least inclined to bring it back from the realm of their inner mystery to that of public discussion. It is not because they are disillusioned about sex but because it has passed on to love, and only two can share its secrets. On the other hand, those whose knowledge of sex has not been sublimated into the mystery of love, and who therefore are most frustrated, are those who want to talk incessantly about sex matters. Husbands and wives whose marriages are characterized by infidelity are most loquacious on sex; fathers and mothers whose marriages are happy never speak about it. Their knowledge has become love; therefore they do not need to gossip about it. They who presume to know so much about sex actually know nothing about its mystery, otherwise they would not be so gabby about it.

The third cause of love, besides goodness and knowledge, is similarity. This is a denial of the oft-repeated axiom that "opposites attract." Opposites do attract, but only superficially. Tall men marry short girls; fast talkers marry good listeners; and tyrants marry milquetoasts. But in a more profound way, it is not unlikeness but likeness which attracts.

The likeness between persons can be twofold: one arises from two persons having the same quality *actually*, as, for example, a mutual love of music. This likeness causes the higher love of friendship, in which one wishes good to the other as to himself. This is what is meant when it is said that two persons are a "perfect match," or "they were made for each other." The other kind of likeness arises from one having *potentially*, or by way of desire or inclination, a quality which the other has *actually*, for example, a poor girl wanting to marry a rich man. The stingy man loves the generous man because he expects from him something he desires. The vicious man can love the virtuous man when he sees virtue in conformity with what he would like to be. This kind of likeness causes love of concupiscence, or a friendship founded on usefulness or pleasure. In this kind of love, the lover loves himself more than his friend. That is why, if the friend ever prevents him from realizing what he wants, his love turns to hate.

Because we are imperfect beings, we seek to remedy our lack by possessions. Thus people who are "naked" on the inside, in the sense that they have no virtue in their soul, try to compensate for it by excessive luxury on the outside. What one person lacks it is hoped the other will supply. Because the human heart desires beauty as its perfection, the ugly young man seeks to marry a beautiful rather than an ugly girl. On the surface, it would seem that his ugliness is the opposite of her beauty, but really it is his love of beauty (which he does not possess actually), which attracts him to that which is beautiful.

The loves of all hearts are so many mirrors revealing their characters. Weak men in high positions surround themselves with little men, in order that they may seem great by comparison. Capitalists who became rich because they struck some of God's wealth in the earth, love to build libraries to parade a learning which they do not possess. They love in appearance that which is similar to what they love in hope and desire. The woman who wishes to be a social climber will cultivate friends who are "useful," because of this similarity. They have what she wants to have: social prestige. Saints love sinners, not because they both have vice in common, but because the saint loves the possible virtue of the sinner. The Son of God became the Son of Man because He loved man.

On this subject no one has written with greater precision than St. Thomas Aquinas, who in his monumental summary of Divine Wisdom points out that there are four effects of love. Because he envisages love as something higher than sex or a biological function, his observations apply in varying degrees to both human and Divine Love. These four effects of love are: unity, mutual indwelling, ecstasy, and zeal.

All love craves unity. This is evident in marriage where there is the unity of two in one flesh. When a person loves anything, he sees it as fulfilling a need and seeks to incorporate it to himself, whether it be the wine that he loves, or the science of the stars. In friendship, the other person is loved as another self, or the other half of one's soul. One seeks to do the same favors for him as one would do for oneself, and thus intensify the bond of union between the two. Whether it be love of wisdom, spouse, or friend, love is a unifying principle of both lover and beloved. Aristotle quotes Aristophanes as saying: "Lovers would wish to be united into one, but since this would result in either one or the other being destroyed, they seek a suitable or becoming union, to live together, speak together, and share the same interests."

Because love creates unity, we have explained why some heroic souls are willing to take on the sufferings and sins of others. A loving mother faced by a child's pain would take on that pain, if she could, in order to free her child of it. She *feels* the pain as her own, because her love has made her one with the infant. Just as love in the face of pain takes on the pain because of oneness with the beloved, so love in the face of evil takes on the sins of others, because of oneness with the beloved. This sacrificial love reached its highest psychological expression in the Garden of Gethsemane, where Christ so identified Himself with sinners that He began to sweat crimson drops of blood. It reached its greatest physical expression on Calvary, when He offered His life for those whom He loved. But before Gethsemane and Calvary, the law that love tends to unify the lovers produced the Incarnation, in which God, who loved man, became man to save him from his sins.

As saints become one with our Lord through the identification of their will with God's will, so those who love unto marriage become "two in *one* flesh." The human heart would never be reaching out for unity, either socially, economically, or sexually, were there not within it a fundamental sense of incompleteness, which only God can perfectly satisfy. The sense of emptiness in a person pushes him on to overcome his deficiencies, until ultimately he becomes one with what he loves. Incidentally, since love produces unity, it follows that one must be careful about that with which he is ultimately unified. Unity with God is necessarily immortal love. A love that has no higher destiny than the flesh will share the corruption of the flesh. Our Lord made the fact of sex identification one of the reasons for His condemnation of divorce. "But I tell you that the man who puts away his wife (setting aside the matter of unfaithfulness) makes an adulteress of her, and whoever marries her after she has been put away, commits adultery" (Matt. 5:32).

Sex love creates a completeness between man and woman which goes far beyond any other unities of the social or political order! That is why the state which respects the family unity as the basis of civilization is much more unified than a civilization which ignores it. A divorce-ridden civilization is already in *cause*, a disrupted civilization. It may take a few decades for the cracks in the family to become earthquakes in the political order, but one must not conclude, because its tombstone is not yet erected, that the civilization is not already dead. "Thou dost pass for a living man, and all the while art a corpse" (Rev. 3:1). The state may break the outer bond uniting husband and wife through divorce, but it can never break the *inner bond* which unity in one flesh has created. To justify their breaking of the unity, they may say: "Love has deceived me." Rather it is they who have deceived love. And their deceit began with the day when they confused love and "sex thrill." They never loved in the first place, for love never takes back that which it gives, even in unfaithfulness. God never takes back His love, though we are sinners. We may betray Him, but He never abandons us.

Mutual indwelling, the second effect of love, literally means that in love one inheres or exists in the other. The passion of love is not satisfied with mere possession but even seeks to assimilate the other into itself. There is hardly a woman in the world who has ever held a babe, who did not say: "This child is so sweet. I would like to eat it." Hidden in these words is the mystery of assimilation which reaches its peak in Holy Communion, where the God incarnate satisfies our desire for complete inherence with His divinity and humanity, under the form and appearance of bread.

If love did not imply inherence, there would be no psychological explanation for the fact that the harm and injury which is done to our friends can be felt as done to us. This love in the supernatural order becomes an inherence which is identical with fixation. Sanctity is fixation in the love of God. Married love is fixation in human love for the love of God. "He who dwells in love dwells in God, and God in him" (1 John 4:16).

This indwelling of the thing or person loved is a fact in an intellectual as well as an affective way. The astronomer loves the stars, and he has the stars in his head, not in their material being but in a manner which is peculiar to his spiritual intellect. But if the universe were not in his head, he could not love the universe. Here the thing loved is in the lover. In affection, the lover inheres in the beloved, and the beloved in the lover. What is it that makes the lover so curious and interested in all that the beloved does? Why is every tiny gift treasured, every word recalled again and again to memory? Why is every scene colored by the vision of the beloved, if it be not that in some way there is no peace without complete inherence of the one in the other? No lover is ever satisfied with a superficial knowledge of the one loved. The lover of music can never have too much knowledge of music. The lover of God never knows the words "too much." Those who accuse others of loving God or religion too much really do not love God at all, nor do they know the meaning of love. Those who are united in love, enjoy and are pained at the same things. The Psalmist who loved God would say that his heart was cast down at the thought of those who broke the law of God.

This mutual inherence, as the second effect of love, adds something to unity in marriage. Unity of the flesh now becomes unity of the mind and heart. The intermittent carnal oneness demands another kind of unity than the flesh. St. Paul says husband and wife ought to act toward one another "as if married in the Lord" (Eph. 5:21); that is, as conscious of their vocation to be one in Christ. As Elizabeth Barrett Browning wrote: "Two human loves make one divine." Mutual inherence is much more than a sharing of interests and an exchange of properties: rather these are the *effects* of a deeper fellowship which reaches into the core of their being.

Love that is held together only by the flesh is as fragile as the flesh, but love which is held together by a spiritual oneness and based on a *love of a common destiny*, is truly "until death do us part." What makes a true mutual inherence is not the sharing of the same sensations of pleasure. Rather the "sister-soul" and "brother-soul" are formed in the daily communion with the same joys, sorrows, efforts, and sacrifices. One can yearn for another after knowing flesh unity, but it is impossible to yearn for another after soul unity. It is not enough just to share the same words and the same enjoyments; one must also share the same silences. "Mary treasured up all these sayings, and reflected on them in her heart" (Luke 2:19). Those who do not yet love one another deeply have need of words; those who deeply love, thrive on silences.

The third effect of love is ecstasy, which means being "carried out of oneself." In a broad kind of way, because love makes the lover dwell on the beloved, he is to some extent already taken out of himself. Adolescents are often surprised that their elders know they are in love. But the fumbling with tasks and the skipping of meals indicate they are in a dreamer's state. They are already lifted out of their natural way of acting. The Greeks describe a strong love as "madness," not in the sense of abnormality, but inspiration. The poet who was inspired was said to be "mad" with his love, as in romantic language today, the lover describes himself as being "mad" over his beloved. Employers are not reluctant to allow their employees to take a week or two off, knowing that they are practically useless during the time of "ecstasy." As Shakespeare wrote: "This is the very ecstasy of love." Later on they are said to be "getting down to earth," as if to imply that previously they had their heads in the heavens.

The professors who are absent-minded about their studies, to the extent that on rainy nights they put the umbrella to bed and stand in the sink all night, are proving that love makes us indifferent to our ordinary surroundings. Where there is great love, people can put up with every manner of hardship because of the quality of love which lifts them up from their environment. The hovel of the husband and wife who are in love is not nearly as boring as the rich apartment of the husband and wife who have ceased to love one another. The saint, like Vincent de Paul, has such a love of God's poor that he forgets to feed himself. The particular spiritual phenomenon of levitation, in which saints in their ecstasies are lifted bodily off the ground, is a still higher manifestation of a love in which matter seems powerless to restrain the spirit.

The difference between love of humans and love of God is that in human love, ecstasy comes at the beginning, but in the love of God it comes only at the end after one has passed through much suffering and agony of soul. The flesh first has its feast, and then the fast and sometimes the headache. The spirit has first the fast, and then the feast. The ecstatic pleasures of marriage are in the nature of a "bait," luring lovers to fulfill their mission, and they are also a divine credit extended to those who later on will have the burden of rearing a family.

No great ecstasy of flesh or spirit is ever given for permanent possession without casting out something. There is a price tag on every ecstasy! The glory of an Easter Sunday cost a Good Friday. The privilege of the

Immaculate Conception was an ecstasy given before the payment, but Mary had to pay for it at the foot of the Cross. Our Lord gave her "credit" but she later paid the debt.

Young couples who equate marriage and the thrill often refuse to reimburse nature with children and thus lose love, as the violinist with a gift for music, who does not practice, loses the gift. "Take the talent away from him" (Matt. 25:28). The first love is not necessarily the lasting love. The thrill of the young priest at his First Solemn Mass, and the near ecstasy of the nun at her clothing, are like "candy" given by God to urge them to climb spiritually. Later on the sweetness is taken away, and it takes a supreme effort of the will to be all one ought to be. So with the honeymoon of marriage. The term itself indicates that at first the love is honey, but afterward it is as changeable as the moon.

The first ecstasy is not the true ecstasy. The latter comes only after purging trial, fidelities through storm, perseverance through mediocrities, and pursuit of divine destiny through the allurements of earth. The deep ecstatic love that some Christian fathers and mothers have after passing through their Calvaries is beautiful to behold. True ecstasy is really not of youth, but of age. In the first ecstasy, one seeks to receive all that the other can give. In the second ecstasy, one seeks to give everything to God. If love is identified with the first ecstasy, it will seek its duplication in another, but if it is identified with unifying, enduring love, it will seek the deepening of its mystery.

Too many married people expect their partner to give that which only God can give, namely, an eternal ecstasy. If man or woman could give that which the heart wants, he or she would be God. Wanting the ecstasy of love is right, but expecting it in the flesh that is not on pilgrimage to God is wrong. The ecstasy is not an illusion; it is only the "travel folder" with its many pictures urging the body and soul to make the journey to eternity. If the first ecstasy reaches its climax, it is an invitation not *to love another*, but to *love in another way*. And the other way is the Christ Way.

Zeal, the fourth effect of love, is that particular passion which makes us want to spread and diffuse the love which we know, and to exclude everything which is repugnant to it. The romantic lover seeks out those companions who will listen to his praise of the beloved, and to whom he can show her picture. The saint in love with Christ becomes a missionary and travels even into lands where the name of Christ has never been heard, in order that other hearts may share the passion for the Tremendous Lover. In carnal love, St. Thomas says, "husbands are said to be jealous of their wives, lest association with others prove a hindrance to their exclusive individual right. In like manner, those who seek to excel, are moved against those who are above them, as though they were a hindrance to their own ambitions."

In the higher lover of friendship, zeal is not only positive, such as becomes apostleship in religion, but is also negative, in the sense that it seeks to repel all that is contrary to the will of God. When our Lord entered the Temple of Jerusalem and found it prostituted by the buyers and sellers, He fashioned a whip of cords and drove them out: "I am consumed with jealousy for the honour of the house" (John 2:17).

From the mother bird defending her nest of young to the martyr dying for the Faith, love pours itself out in zeal of the right kind. But the wicked can also be zealous for the evil which they love, whether it be the miser for his gold, or the adulterer for his accomplice, or the Communist for his world revolution. Those things for which we would spend our energy to defend, or die to keep, are the measures of our zeal! Love is the cause of everything we do. The subjects we talk about, the persons we hate, the ideals we pursue, the things that make us angry, these are indicators of our hearts. Few realize how much they betray their characters in revealing what their hearts love most. "Out of the abundance of the heart, the mouth speaketh" (Luke 6:45). If our loves are wrong, our lives are wrong, as well.

What zeal is to religion, fidelity and fecundity are to marriage: devotion to the person loved, and the extension of that love in the family. This fidelity is not born of habit which is akin to organic or economic necessity; rather, it is an affirmation that this person has an absolute significance for life. This kind of zeal not only crushes all alien biological desires; it also is based on the fact that the other person is the one whom God has willed for us, "for better or for worse, for richer or poorer, until death do us part." As Euripides said: "He is not a lover who does not love forever." And as Shakespeare sang:

> Let me not to the marriage of true minds
> Admit impediments. Love is not love
> Which alters when it alteration finds,
> Or bends with the remover to remove:
> O no; it is an ever-fixed mark,
> That looks on tempests, and is never shaken;
> It is the star to every wandering bark,
> Whose worth's unknown, although his height be taken.
> Love's not Time's fool, though rosy lips and cheeks
> Within his bending sickle's compass come:
> Love alters not with his brief hours and weeks,
> But bears it out even to the edge of doom.
> If this be error, and upon me prov'd,
> I never writ, nor no man ever lov'd.

Zeal also manifests itself spiritually, in bringing other souls to God, and physically, by begetting children for God. Fruitfulness is the natural effect of the love of tree and earth, of missionary and pagan, of husband and wife. Love does not thrive on moderation. Zeal is generosity. The love that measures the sacrifices it will make for others takes the edge off aspirations. Our Lord said that zealous love had two characteristics; first, it is forgiving, and second, it recognizes no limits. It is forgiving, because it knows that God's forgiveness of me is conditioned upon my forgiveness of others. Love never wears magnifying glasses in looking on the faults of others. Married life requires this zeal in the shape of forbearance, which is not a gritting of teeth in the face of annoyance, nor the cultivation of indifference; it is, rather, a positive and constructive action putting love where it is not found. One feels under an obligation more exquisite and divine than a marriage contract.

Zeal knows no limits. It never pronounces the word "enough." Our Lord said that after His followers had done all they were supposed to do, they were to consider themselves as "unprofitable servants" (Luke

17:10). Knocking the boundaries out of love, He said: "But I tell you that you should not offer resistance of injury; if a man strikes thee on the right cheek, turn the other cheek also towards him; if he is ready to go to law with thee over thy coat, let him have it and thy cloak with it; if he compels thee to attend him on a mile's journey, go two miles with him of thy own accord" (Matt. 5:39–41).

In divine service and in marriage, therefore, there should be a generosity which goes quite beyond the limits of justice. The neighbor who offers to come in for an hour to help and stays two; the doctor who in addition to a professional call "drops in just to see how you are"; the husband and wife who vie with one another in love; all have understood one of the most beautiful effects of love: its zeal, which makes them fools for one another. "We are fools for Christ's sake" (1 Cor. 4:10).

4

The Three Tensions of Love

Despite the highest idealism, there are potentials for conflict in marriage. Marriage has three basic tensions which are always inseparable from it, because they are grounded in the metaphysical nature of man.

All love craves for unity, a moment when separatedness is vanquished and there is a fusion of entities in a center outside of both. Flesh, though a means to unity when united to a soul, is in itself an obstacle, because matter is impenetrable. A block of marble cannot be made one with another block without losing the identity of either. But the spiritual is a bond of unity. Two persons learn poetry without one depriving the other of his knowledge; poetry thus becomes the bond of their unity. Matter is the basis of division; spirit the root of unity. The flesh is a means to unity because it is bound up with a soul in a living person. To the extent that love loses its soul, it loses its unity. When the spirit is gone, there is left only a mere body proximity which bores and fatigues.

This passion for a crescendo of intimacy until oneness is achieved cannot be completely satisfied in the physical order, because after the *act* of unity, there remains the *status* of two separate personalities, each with his or her individual mystery. The paradox is clear: the souls of lovers aspire to unity, but the body alone, though the momentary symbol of that unity, is nevertheless exclusive of it. The flesh is impervious to that kind of unity which alone can satisfy the spirit. No marriage is free from this tension. The tension increases as the body goes through the motions of love without the soul, and it decreases as the soul loves through the body. The greatest relief there is to this tension is the begetting of children, for here the seeming disproportion between a passion for unity and the failure to make it permanent is compensated for by the child, who becomes a new bond of unity outside father and mother. Husband and wife never feel the emptiness of their relations one with another when it is filled up with a new body and a soul directly infused by God, the Creator. God made man right, and man is unhappy as he tries to defeat those laws which make for his happiness.

The basic reason why erotic experiences outside of marriage create psychological strain is because the void between spirit and flesh is more closely felt. Here is the key to the different mental states following a true conjugal union and an adulterous excitement. The first is what is called the payment of a *debitum*. "He, not she, claims the right over her body, as she, not he, claims the right over his" (1 Cor. 7:4). Because it is a combination of justice involving a debt of love, it satisfies the spirit. The second, because it involves no justice, but only body-surrender without soul-love, never nourishes the spirit, but leaves a sense of void and emptiness and potential hate. The first synthesizes the body-soul relations; the second brutalizes it. While the spirit craves unity, the carnal tends toward separateness through its very promiscuity. Those psychologists who think that the problem of marriage is merely one of sexual adjustment start with the assumption that man and woman are no different than two beasts in the forests. The difference between the animal and the human is to be found in the ontological structure of the human creature, who is in a constant state of conflict because he knows he has wings to fly to the heavens and yet must walk the earth. No shame or remorse attend the marriage act even in the face of this body-soul tension, because the body is used as a channel for the communication of the spirit. Then marriage sanctifies and becomes an occasion of merit. The craving for the infinite is to a great degree satisfied, either because the mutual love of husband and wife reflects the union of Christ and the Church, or because their love ends in bearing the fruit of progeny.

The Three Tensions of Love

The second tension inherent in marriage is between the person and humanity. Married love is personal, unique, and jealous, in the right sense of the word. It implies secrecy, togetherness, and resents intrusion. For that reason, it never speaks of its love in public and never demonstrates it. It is a curious psychological fact that those who make their personal love public, and "dear" one another with saccharine epithets, are very often those who when alone quarrel and fight.

Associated with this personal quality of married love is the fact that by its very nature carnal love is social, in the sense that it is ordained by God for the citizenship of earth and the filiation of the Kingdom of Heaven. Some functions of the human are individual, such as seeing and hearing. Every man must blow his own nose and make his own love. But married love also implies social relationship, namely, the propagation of the species. In other language, love is personal, but sex is social, as the right to property is personal, but the use is social. Love looks to a helpmate who is human; sex to humanity. That the latter looks beyond the personal is evident from its somewhat automatic character. It is not completely subject to personal control. It reaches a point where it goes beyond the person to the continuation of the human species. If sex were given by God solely for the satisfaction of the individual, it would in all instances be subject to the individual control, like eating. But its reflex character suggests that God has a hand in preserving the race, even when the individual would distort the social purpose solely for his individual pleasure.

This tension between person and race is not insoluble. When both love and sex have their normal God-given outlets, the contradiction is resolved in the child. The personal love of husband for wife becomes a social contribution in the child. At the same time, the personal element in their love is recovered, in the fact that they can call the child their own. "My son" or "my daughter" represents the social being personally owned.

As man lost faith in God, he also lost belief in his soul, and this increased the tension. Not only did he reach a point where he became unconcerned as to whether or not he saved his soul, but he even denied that he had a soul to save. Left with only a body, he had to decide which part of the body would be the most important. There were only two possible functions of the body from which a choice could be made: eating, which preserved individual life, and mating, which guaranteed social life. Sacred Scripture records that some ancients made their belly a god; it was left to our day to make sex a god. Thus there was substituted for the body-soul-God relationship, the sex-body tension. Sex then became isolated from soul and God and became only a means to the satisfaction of man, who is now described as a "physiological bag filled with psychological libido."

It must not be thought that the difference between the Christian and the pagan view is the difference between soul and body. The choice is never between body and soul, as if either one could be completely excluded. Rather, it is between giving the regnancy to body or to spirit. To be antibody, or to be against any of its functions, is anti-Christian, just as it is anti-Christian to be anti-soul. The harmonious rhythm of both is the fulfillment of the divine decree: "What God has joined, let not man put asunder" (Mark 10:9). With God the body is ransomed from the isolationism of mere matter, while the soul is transfigured, thanks to the flames of passion which nourish both self-life and begotten life. Without God and the soul, the body has no guarantee of the continuation of its thoughts or the fruits of its passions. With God the body can minister either to the mutual helpfulness of husband and wife, to the rearing of a family, or to the ecstasies of a John of the Cross.

The third tension is that of the finite and the infinite. No human heart wants love for two more minutes or two more years, but forever. There is nothing as timeless as love. In its romantic moments it uses the language of eternity and divinity and Heaven, the better to bespeak its everlasting aspirations. But along with this longing for love without satiety, of ecstasy without end, there is the dull, drab realization that we do not completely possess it. The marriage that started as a masked ball, in which everyone seemed sweet and fair and romantic, soon reached the crisis when the masks were removed and one saw the characters for what they really were. As the poetess wrote:

The Three Tensions of Love

"Yes" I answered you last night.
"No" I say to you today;
Colors seen by candlelight
Do not look the same by day.

The Irish writer Thomas Moore, pursuing the same idea, wrote:

Alas! How light a cause may move
Dissension between hearts that love—
Hearts that the world in vain had tried,
And sorrow but more closely tied;
Which stood the storm when waves were rough,
Yet in a sunny hour fell off;
Like ships that have gone down at sea,
When Heaven was all tranquillity.

The paradox of love is that the human heart, which wants an eternal and ecstatic love, can also reach a moment when it has too much love and wishes to be loved no longer. Francis Thompson in a poem tells how he picked up a child to hold, and held him in his arms, and how the child cried and kicked to get down. On reflecting, he wondered if that is not the way some souls are before God. They are not ready to be loved by Him. Certainly some such moment comes in the human order when there is a tug of war between wanting love and not wanting it. What is this mysterious alchemy inside the human heart which makes it swing between a feeling that it is not loved enough and the feeling that it is loved too much? Torn between longing and satiety, between craving and disgust, between desire and satisfaction, the human heart queries: Why should I be this way? When satiety comes, the thou disappears, in the sense that it is no longer wanted. When longing reappears, the thou becomes a necessity. Loved too much, there is discontent; loved too little, there is an emptiness.

The answer to this tension is evident. The human heart was made for the Sacred Heart of Love, and no one but God can satisfy it. The heart is right in wanting the infinite; the heart is wrong in trying to make its finite companion the substitute for the infinite. The solution of the tension is in seeing that the disappointments which it brings are so many reminders that one is on pilgrimage to Love. Both the being loved too much and the being loved too little can go together when seen in the light of God. When the longing for Infinite Love is envisaged as a yearning for God, then the finiteness of the earthly love is seen as a reminder that "Our hearts were made for Thee, O Lord, and they can be satisfied only in Thee."

The tug between what is immediate and what is interior now vanishes, as the very enjoyment which the immediacy of the flesh gives becomes the occasion for joy in the interiority of the soul, which knows that one is using it for God's purposes and for the salvation of both souls. The synthesis of life is achieved when the instincts are integrated to spirit and made useful to the ideals of the spirit. There is for the Christian no such thing in marriage as choosing between body and soul, or sex and love. He must choose both together. Marriage is a vocation to put God in every detail of love. In this way, the dream of the bride and groom for eternal happiness really comes true, not in themselves alone, but through themselves. Now they love each other not as they dreamed they would, but as God dreamed they would. Such a reconciliation of the tension is possible only to those who know that it takes three to make love.

Only God can give what the heart wants. In true Christian love, the husband and wife see God coming *through* their love. But without God the infinity must be sought in the finitude of the partner, which is to gather figs from thistles. Eternity is in the soul, and all the materialism of the world cannot uproot it. The tragedy of the materialist psychologies of our day comes from trying to make a bodily function satisfy the infinite aspirations of the soul. It is this that creates complexes and unstable minds and divorce courts. It is like trying to put all the words of a book on the cover. Eliminate the Divine Third from human love, and there is left only the substitution of cruel repetition for infinity. The need of God never disappears. Those who deny the existence of water are still thirsty, and those who deny God still want Him in their craving for Beauty and Love and Peace, which He alone is.

The Three Tensions of Love

Man has his feet in the mud of the earth, his wings in the skies. He has sensations like the beasts and ideas like the angels, without being either pure beast or pure spirit. He is a mysterious composite of body and soul, with his body belonging to a soul, and his soul incomplete without the body. The true order is the subjection of body to soul and the whole personality to God. "It is all for you, and you for Christ, and Christ for God" (1 Cor. 3:22–23). Man is the pontiff of the universe, the "bridge builder" between matter and spirit, suspended between one foundation on earth and the other in Heaven. He is also, fundamentally, a being in tension with an anxiety of the kind felt by a sailor halfway up to a crow's nest on a stormy sea. His duty calls him to the nest above; his earth-bound character makes him fear falling from his ladder.

No action of man in all its aspects can be said to be completely animal nor completely spiritual. Though he can generate spiritual thoughts, like "fortitude," yet the raw material for such thinking has to come through his senses. Eating and mating not only imply decision on the part of the spirit, but even delight the spirit. Sleeping is a human act; the will to sleep is the act of a human being.

There is not a single error of history which is not a perversion of this mysterious body-soul unity. Some considered the body impure, such as the Manicheans; some considered the soul a parasite or a myth, such as Freud or Nietzsche. Everyone must decide for himself how this pull of opposites is to be resolved. There are only two answers possible: one is to give primacy to the body, in which case the soul suffers; the other is to give primacy to the soul, in which case the body is disciplined. The Christian answer to this polarity is unmistakable: "How is a man the better for it, if he gains the whole world at the cost of losing his own soul?" (Matt. 16:26). "And there is no need to fear those who kill the body, but have no means of killing the soul; fear him more, who has the power to ruin body and soul in hell" (Matt. 10:28).

This ontological tension inherent in man, because of his composition of dust and living breath, has been accentuated into disorder by Original Sin, and is the basic reason why man suffers temptations. "The impulses of nature and the impulses of the spirit are at war with one another"

(Gal. 5:17). "Watch and pray, that you may not enter into temptation; the spirit is willing enough, but the flesh is weak" (Matt. 26:41).

The word "temptation" is never applied to the body-soul discipline, but it is to the soul-body servitude. No one says, "I was tempted to let him live," but one does say, "I was tempted to kill him." The regency of the soul is order, for herein the lower is subject to the higher, as plants are subject to animals, and animals to man. The granting of the primacy to the sensate against the intellectual is a descent, a loosening of bonds, a "fall." This does not mean that the sensible experience in itself is a "temptation," but only when it is enjoyed at the expense of the soul. The pleasure of seeing a setting sun is not hostile to the spirit, but the sensible experience of drunkenness is adverse to the spirit. Reason, in the first instance, transcends the body and inspires the soul to give glory to God for His creation; in the second instance, the body is a vampire against the spirit and militates against its peace, which is conditioned on the observance of the order of the cosmos, namely, the body-soul-God relationship.

Because of this body-soul, or animal-spirit, tension in humans, it is possible to understand love in either one of two ways: as body-primacy or soul-primacy. In the first instance, love is carnal and identified with what the modern world calls sex. In the second instance, love is both spiritual and physical. The great philosophers have called the first, "the love of concupiscence," or the primacy of the sensate, and the second, the love of *benevolence*, or love for the sake of another. The Greeks, too, had their words for it. In their language, *eros* is a passionate, overwhelming desire to possess and enjoy the affections of another. *Agape* is love founded on reverence for personality, its delight being to promote the well-being of the other; its joy is contemplation rather than possession. The two loves are good when understood. The divine command to love one's neighbor as one's self implies a lawful self-love. Here as elsewhere it takes three to make love. Love of self and love of neighbor both require love of God.

The *libido* of modern psychology is *eros* or carnal love divorced from *agape*, or personal love, the body denying the soul, and the ego affirming itself against God. It was this kind of love which St. Paul condemned:

The Three Tensions of Love

"Because natural wisdom is at enmity with God" (Rom. 8:7). Sex understood in the modern way is *eros*-love severed from responsibility; it is desire without obligation. Because it is lawless desire, it is therefore Godless desire. That is why eroticism and atheism always go together.

As soon as one condemns this limitation of the word *love* to the physiological order, one is immediately accused by the carnalists of saying that the Christian is opposed to sex love. The Christian is not opposed to sex love, otherwise there would be no Sacrament of Marriage. The Christian position can be stated as follows: *Carnal love is a steppingstone to Divine Love. The eros is the vestibule to agape. Purely human love is the embryo of the love of the Divine.* One finds some suggestion of this in Plato, who argues that love is the first step toward religion. He pictures love for beautiful persons being transformed into love for beautiful souls, then into a love of justice, goodness, and God, who is their source. Erotic love is, therefore, a bridge which one crosses, not a buttress where one sits and rests. It is not an airport, but an airplane; it is always going somewhere else, upward and onward. All erotic love presupposes incompleteness, deficiency, yearning for completion, an attraction for enrichment; for all love is a flight toward immortality. There is a suggestion of Divine Love in every form of erotic love, as the lake reflects the moon. Love for other hearts is intended to lead to the love of the Divine Heart. As food is for the body, as body is for the soul, as the material is for the spiritual, so the flesh is for the eternal. Sex is only the self-starter on the motor of the family.

Christianity is full of this transfiguration of carnal love into the Divine. The Savior did not crush or extinguish the erotic flames that burned in Magdalene's heart, but He transfigured them to a new object of affection. The divine commendation that was given to the woman who poured out the ointment on the feet of her Savior reminded her that love which once sought its own pleasure can be transmuted into a love that will die for the beloved. For that reason, our Lord referred to His burial at the very moment of the pouring, when her thoughts were closest to life.

On a higher plane, we find that, thanks to the mysterious alchemy of religion, the noble love that the Blessed Mother had for her own Son in the flesh is expanded to a love so wide that she becomes the mother of all men. In marriage *eros* leads to *agape*, as the children draw the husband and wife out of their mutuality into the love of otherness. As the purpose of the vow of chastity is the crushing of the selfishness of the flesh for the purpose of a larger service in the Kingdom of God, so in a diminished way, the begetting of children enlarges the field of service and loving sacrifice for the sake of the family. In a well-regulated moral heart, as time goes on, the erotic love diminishes and the religious love increases. In marriages that are truly Christian, the love of God increases through the years, not in the sense that husband and wife love one another less, but that they love God more. Love passes from an affection for outer appearances to those inner depths of personality which embody the Divine Spirit. There are few things more beautiful in life than to see that deep passion of man for woman, which begot children, transfigured into that deeper passion for the Spirit of God. It sometimes happens in a Christian marriage that when one of the partners dies, there is no taking of another spouse, lest there be the descent to lower realms from that higher love, from the *agape* to the *eros*.

The evolution of *eros* to *agape* in true love has two moments. In the first, the body leads the soul; in the second, the soul leads the body. At first, the physical dominates the soul to some extent, inasmuch as it is carried along by the winds of passion. In the second moment, the soul predominates, even suggesting that the body play its God-destined role. Love now becomes more spiritual. The moral training of children, the deep concern for their spiritual well-being, become paramount problems of married life. From this interest in souls and salvation, all the physical services flow. Generally this transformation from *eros*-primacy to *agape*-primacy takes place in sacrifice. No love ever mounts to a higher level without a touch of the Cross. Love that remains on a horizontal plane dies.

In family life, this transfiguration of *eros* to *agape* takes place generally at birth, when something lower dies and something nobler is born. In domestic love, the bursting of the bonds of duality through a child's birth creates new loyalties, more self-sacrificing devotion, and psychologically liberates husband and wife from egotism. The *word* "love" is used less, but the *deed* love comes more and more into play as altruism, kindness, and sympathy.

What happens when the divine order is not worked out, and the erotic love is not used as the embryo for the Divine? This question puts the finger on the failure of most modern marriages, which look on love not as opening on the heavens, but as stooping with the flesh. When marriages are devoid of religion, which alone can suggest that the love of the flesh is the preface to the love of the spirit, then the other partner is often made the object of worship in place of God. This is the essence of idolatry, the worship of the image for the reality, the mistaking of the copy for the original, and the frame for the picture.

When love is limited to the satisfaction of egotistic desire, it becomes only a spent force, a fallen star. When it deliberately refuses to use the sparks which God gave it to enkindle other fires; when it digs wells, but never drains the water; when it learns to read, but never knows: then does love turn against itself, and because it desires only to enjoy its own life, it ends in hatred or mutual slaughter.

When the other partner becomes an idol and the object of worship because there is no God to adore, erotic love turns against those who have abused it. Each partner begins to feel the torturous contradiction between the infinite longing for Divine Love which it spurned, and its poor finite realizations and satieties in the human form. Both try to live a moment in which Satan's promise would be realized: "You will be like gods." But when there is no *agape* to bridle *eros*, then the furies are unleashed when the other partner is discovered not to be a God, much less an angel, or even a fallen angel. Because the other partner did not give all he promised to give (but which he was incapable of giving because he was not God) the other feels betrayed, deceived, disappointed, and cheated. No human being is Love, but only lovable. Only God is Love. When the creature takes the place of the Creator and is made to stand for love, then erotic love turns to hate; the other partner is discovered to have feet of clay, to be a woman instead of an angel, or to be a man instead of an Apollo. When the ecstasy does not continue, and the band stops playing, and the champagne of life loses its sparkle, the other partner is called a cheat and a robber, and then finally called to a divorce court on the grounds of incompatibility. And what grounds could be more stupid than incompatibility, for what two persons in the world are perfectly and at all times compatible?

A search for a new partner begins on the assumption that some other human being can supply what only God can give. The new marriages become only the addition of zeros. Instead of seeing that the basic reason for the failure of marriage was the refusal to use married love as the vestibule to the Divine, the divorced think that the second marriage can supply what the first lacked. The very fact that a man or a woman seeks a new partner is a proof that there never was any love at all, for though sex is replaceable, love is not. Cows can graze on other pastures, but there is no substitution for a person. As soon as a person becomes equated with a package to be judged only by its wrappings, it will not be long until the tinsel turns green and the package is discarded.

This arrangement enslaves a woman, because she is much more a creature of time than man, and her security becomes less and less through the years. She is always much more concerned about her age than a man, and thinks more of marriage in terms of time. A man is afraid of dying before he has lived, but a woman is basically afraid of dying before she has begotten life. A woman wants the fulfillment of life more than a man. It is less the experience of life that she craves, than the prolongation of life. Whenever the laws and the customs of a country permit an arrangement whereby a woman can be discarded because she has dishpan hands, she becomes the slave, not of the dishpans, but of man.

So selfish is erotic love alienated from Divine Love that sometimes it will permit no flower to grow except its own. It may even resent the conversion of the partner to God on the foolish grounds that there will be less love for self if God is loved, or that love will be more pure and less Freudian. Opposition to religion is often one of the consequences of erotic love, forgetting as it does that love is widened by contact with the Divinity. The result is that persons become reduced to mere chattels who exist for no other purpose than to be possessed. It makes little difference to weary souls whether that which possesses them is a foreign ideology, a body, a Utopia, a drink, or a pill. The fact is that they are so disgusted with themselves and their goalless living that they surrender themselves to a totalitarian system which will dispense with personal responsibility. Eroticism and communism, Freud and Marx, are not so far apart.

If love remained only in the flesh and were like a bitter weed that would suffer no flowers to bloom except its own, love would be most miserable, for love then would only be a quest and not a communion. Love that is only a search or a quest is incomplete. All incompleteness ends in frustration. The difficulty all who are married must feel is the paradox of the romance and the marriage, the chase and the capture. Each has its joys, but never perfectly are they combined here below. The marriage ends the courtship; the courtship presupposes no marriage. The chase ends with the capture. How is this contradiction met? There is only one way that will not sear the soul, and that is to see that both the marriage and the courtship are incomplete. The courtship was really a quest for the infinite, and a search for an unending, ecstatic, eternal love, while the marriage was the possession of a finite and fragmentary love, however blissful might be its moments. The search was for the garden; it ended in eating the apple. The quest was for the melody; the discovery was only a note.

At this point Christianity suggests: Do not think that life is a snare or an illusion. It would be that only if there were no Infinite to satisfy your yearnings. Rather, husband and wife should say: "We both want a Love that will never die and will have no moments of hate or satiety. That love lies beyond both of us; let us, therefore, use our marital love one for another to bring us to that perfect, blissful love, which is God." At that point, love ceases to be a disillusionment and begins to be a sacrament, a material, carnal channel toward the spiritual and the Divine. Husband and wife then come to see that human love is a spark from the great flame of eternity; that the happiness which comes from the unity of two in one flesh is a prelude to that greater communion of two in one spirit. In this way, marriage becomes a tuning fork to the song of the angels, or a river that runs to the sea. The couple then sees that there is an answer to the elusive mystery of love, and that somewhere there is a reconciliation of the guest and the goal, and that is in final union with God, where the chase and capture, the romance and the marriage, fuse into one. For since God is boundless eternal Love, it will take an ecstatic eternal chase to sound its depths. At one and the same eternal moment, there is a limitless receptivity and a boundless gift. Thus does *eros* climb to *agape*, and both move on to that greatest revelation ever given to the world: GOD IS LOVE.

5

It Takes Three to Make Love

Love is the basic passion of man. Every emotion of the human heart is reducible to it. Without love we would never become better, for love is the impetus to perfection, the fulfillment of what we have not. Love, in the broad sense of the term, is found wherever there is existence. It has the same dimensions as being. Whatever has an inclination, whether it be fire to burn upward, flowers to bloom, animals to beget, or man to wed, has love. Chemical elements love one another through the law of affinity of one element for another, as two atoms of hydrogen and one of oxygen make water. Plants love the earth, the sun, the moisture, through the divinely implanted laws of vegetation; animals love through the divinely infused instincts which guide them to the end for which they were created. But when it comes to man, there is no *determined* instinct, but reason and freedom by which he can freely choose that which will complement and perfect his nature. What instinct is to the animal, that the free will is to man. Choice is without reason in beasts, but it is rational in man.

Animal love is tied down to what can be tasted, seen, touched, and heard, but man's love is as universal as goodness, beauty, and truth. Man can know and love not only a good meal, but Goodness. He may not always love what is best for him but this never destroys his power to love Love, which is God.

Archbishop Sheen's Book of Sacraments

Love is an inclination or a tendency to seek what seems good. The lover seeks union with the good which is loved in order to be perfected by it. The mystery of all love is that it actually precedes every act of choice; one chooses because he loves, he does not love because he chooses. The youth loves the maiden not because he chooses her from among maidens, but rather he elects and selects her as unique because he loves her. As St. Thomas puts it: "All other passions and appetites presuppose love as their first root." All other passions, even those which seem the enemy of love, are related to it, such as fear and hate. Fear rises from a danger of losing what is loved, whether it be wealth, possessions, or friends. Hatred springs from an antipathy against those who would do violence to our loves. Hatefulness, bitterness, envy, and fretfulness are all perverted kinds of love.

Love is very different from knowledge. When the mind is confronted with something above its level—for example, an abstract principle of metaphysics or mathematics—it breaks it down into examples so that it can understand it. The reason why many teachers fail in their profession is because they do not know how to bring down to a lower and concrete level the subject which they teach. Maybe they do not know the subject, for the test of knowing anything is the ability to give an example for it. Theses with footnotes, into which are thrown the knowledge that is not understood, are easier to write than a popularization of that same subject for a beginner. Some are thought to be learned when they are only confusing. The Word incarnate spoke in terms of parables illustrating eternal verities, such as judgment of the good and bad, under the analogy of the separation of sheep and goats. If we understand anything, we can make it clear. If we do not understand it, we can never explain it.

But love acts just the opposite to knowledge. Love goes out to meet the demands of what is loved. The intellect pulls higher things *down* to its level; the will, which is the seat of love, lifts itself up to the level of the good which it loves. If one loves music, one meets the demands of music by submitting to its laws; if one wishes to win the love of a poet, one must cultivate some appreciation of poetry. Because love goes up

204

to meet the beloved, it follows that the nobler the love, the nobler the character. We live on the plane of our loves.

If, then, anyone wishes to judge his character, all he has to do is to answer the question: "What do I love most?" As our Lord put it: "Where your treasure-house is, there your heart is too" (Matt. 6:21). Our favorite topic of conversation is the tell-tale of our deepest love. It would be wrong to judge people solely by the snatches of conversation one overhears on the streets and in dining rooms, for these would make it appear that for many men business is their greatest love, while for women, it is fashion or style. Actually, however, there are two basic loves which everyone has without exception: love of self and love of others. The first is the basis of self-preservation; the second is the root of friendship and community. Love exists not in isolation or suspension, it craves involvement with others because love is essentially a relation. Love of self becomes the love of others, either for the sake of association or for the continuation of humankind.

These two loves of self and neighbor ought to go together, but they often pull in opposite directions. On the one hand, we cannot cling to ourselves and love ourselves apart from all others, because he who is absolutely alone is loveless. On the other hand, we cannot cling entirely to others, for though they offer occasion of love, they also set limits to our love. They do this either because they are not absolutely lovable, or because they are really not worth clinging to at all. Loving self alone has many disadvantages: it forces us to dwell in quarters that are too cramped and squalid for comfort; it confronts self with a self that in some moments is not only unlovable, but even intolerable; and it makes us want to get away from ourselves because we find we are not very deep. Probing into the depths of our ego to find peace is too often like plunging into a pool without water. After a while, our self-centeredness ends in self-disruption, as we discover we have no center at all. No one can love himself properly unless he knows why he is living.

Love is useless when alone, as it is in sleep or death. It is really possessed only by giving it to others. Love is a sign of our creatureliness, the strongest proof that we are not gods and have not all we need within ourselves. If we were God, we would have no need of loving anything else, for love would find its perfection within itself, as in God. We must love others because we are imperfect; it is the mark of our indigence, a reminder that we came from nothingness, and that of and by ourselves love is incomplete and sterile. Yet in giving to others, we are often disappointed; some want to use us, others to possess us. The involvement does not come up to our expectations; the one whom we thought was a good angel turns out to be a fallen one. Some contacts with others are like boomerangs; they throw us back on ourselves poorer than when we left, and therefore embittered. Torn between the independence of their own ego and dependence on other egos, tossed between worship of self and worship of others, many hearts develop a restlessness and a fatigue which keep the rich busy running to psychoanalysts to have their anxiety explained away, and the poor having recourse to the cheaper charlatans of alcoholism and sleeping tablets. It is interesting how a materialistic civilization describes the rich as suffering from an "anxiety neurosis," and the poor as being plain "nuts" or "crackpots." If no true solution of the tension between love of self and love of others is found, legitimate self-love degenerates into egotism, pride, skepticism, and arrogance, while love of others degenerates into lust, cruelty, and hatred of the spiritual. Cynics are disappointed egotists, and revolutionists of violence are disgruntled altruists. Perverted self-love, when it became political, created individualism, or historical liberalism; perverted love of others, when it became political, created totalitarianism.

There is a solution to this problem of tension between love of the ego and love of the non-ego, or the independence of the ego and its dependence on other egos, but it is not to be found either in the ego or the non-ego. *The basic error of mankind has been to assume that only two are needed for love: you and me, or society and me, or humanity and me. Really it takes three: self, other selves, and God; you, and me, and God.* Love of self without love of God is selfishness; love of neighbor without love of God embraces only those who are pleasing to us, not those who are hateful. One cannot tie two sticks together without something outside the sticks; one cannot bind the nations of the world together except by the recognition of a law and a Person outside the nations themselves. Duality in love is extinction through the exhaustion of self-giving. *Love is triune or it dies.* It requires three virtues, faith, hope, and charity, which intertwine, purify, and regenerate each other. To *believe* in God is to throw ourselves into His arms; to hope in Him is to rest in His heart in patience amidst trials and tribulations; to love Him is to be with Him through a participation of His divine nature through grace. If love did not have faith and trust, it would die; if love did not have hope, its sufferings would be torture, and love might seem loveless. Love of self, love of neighbor, and love of God go together and when separated fall apart.

Love of self without love of God is egotism, for if there is no Perfect Love from whom we came and for whom we are destined, then the ego becomes the center. But when self is loved in God, the whole concept of what is self-perfection changes. If the ego is an absolute, its perfection consists in *having* whatever will make it happy, and at all costs; this is the essence of egotism, or selfishness. If union with Perfect Love is the goal of personality, then its perfection consists not in *having* but in *being had*, not in *owning* but in *being owned*, or better still, not in *having* but in *being*.

Union with Perfect Happiness or God is not something extrinsic to us, like a gold medal to a student, but is, rather, intrinsic to our nature, as blooming is to a flower. Without it we are unsatisfied and incomplete. The self actually is always craving for this Divine Love. Its insatiable urges toward happiness, its anticipated ecstasy of pleasures, its constant desire to love without satiety, its reaching for something beyond its grasp, the sadness it feels in attaining any happiness less than the infinite—all these constitute the mating call of God to the soul. As trees in the forest bend through other trees to absorb the light, so every self is striving for the Love which is God. If this Love seems contrary to some people's desires, it is only because it is contrary to their developed egotism but not to their nature. God has not given to self everything it needs for happiness; He kept back one thing which is needed, Himself. On this point, there is a similarity between the temporal unhappiness on earth and the eternal unhappiness in Hell: the soul in each instance lacks something.

There is not a golfer in America who has not heard the story, which is theologically sound, about the golfer who went to Hell and asked to play golf. The devil showed him a 36-hole course with a beautiful clubhouse, long fairways, perfectly placed hazards, rolling hills, and velvety greens. Next the devil gave him a set of clubs so well-balanced that the golfer felt he had been swinging them all his life. Out to the first tee they stepped ready for a game. The golfer said: "What a course! Give me the ball." The devil answered: "Sorry, Comrade [they call one another "Comrade," not "Brother" in Hell], we have no balls. That's the Hell of it." And it is just that which makes Hell: the lack of Perfect Life, Perfect Truth, and Perfect Love, which is God, who is essential for our happiness.

God keeps something back on earth, not as a punishment, but as a solicitation. The poet George Herbert has told us that God poured out wealth, beauty, and pleasure on man, but kept back Himself:

> For if I should (said He)
> Bestow this jewel also on creatures,
> He would adore my gifts instead of me,
> And rest in nature, not the God of nature,
> So both should losers be.
> Yet let him keep the rest
> But keep them with repining restlessness;
> Let him be rich and weary, that at least,
> If goodness lead him not, yet weariness
> May toss him to my Breast.

It takes some effort to grow in this love, for as the art of painting is cultivated by painting, and speaking is learned by speaking, and study is learned by studying, so love is learned by loving. It takes considerable asceticism to banish all unloving thoughts and to make us eventually loving. The *will* to love makes us lovers.

There are four stages the soul passes through in its love of God: (1) the soul which starts with loving self for its own sake soon realizes its own insufficiency, seeing that loving self without God is like loving the ray of sunlight without the sun. Perhaps the soul at this point also

sees that even the self would be quite unlovable unless love-energy or
lovableness had been put into it by God. (2) God is loved not for His
own sake, but for the sake of the self. At this stage, there are prayers of
petition because God is loved because of the favors He gives. This was
the love of Peter when he asked of the Lord: "What do we get out of it?"
(see Matt. 19:27). (3) God is loved for His sake, not ours. The soul cares
more for the Beloved than for what the Beloved gives; in the romantic
order it corresponds to that moment when the beloved no longer loves
the suitor because he sends roses, but because he is lovable. It is like the
love of a mother for a child who seeks no favor in return. (4) The final
stage is one of those rare moments when the love of self is completely
abandoned and emptied and surrendered for the sake of God. This would
correspond to a moment in a mother's life when she ceases to think of
her own life in order to save her child from death. In this kind of Divine
Love, the self is not destroyed but transfigured. This is the "love that
leaves all other love a pain."

As a person uses the scalpel on his soul and analyzes his psyche, he
discovers more and more how unlovable he is. The flights from self, the
plunges into the irresponsibility of artificial unconsciousness, prove that
man cannot bear himself. Pascal rightly described the self without God as
despicable, or the "*moi haissable.*" Fundamentally, it is because God loves
us that we ought to love ourselves. If He sees something worthwhile in
us and died to save us, then we have a motive for loving self rightly. As
a person feels ennobled when a beautiful and gracious friend loves him,
then what shall be the ecstasy of a soul at that moment when it awakes
to the shattering truth: *God loves me!*

It is easy to love those who love us, and our Divine Lord told us that
there was no reward in this. But what about the number of people in the
world whom we regard as unlovable? One of the strongest social arguments
for God is this: there must be a God, otherwise so many people would be
unloved. The love of God makes it possible to love those who are "hard
to love." Why should we love those who hate us, malign us, who trample
on our feet to get to the first seats in a theater? There is only one reason:
for God's sake. We may not *like* them, for liking is emotional, but we can

love them, for love is in the will and is subject to command "But I tell you, Love your enemies, do good to those who hate you, pray for those who persecute and insult you" (Matt. 5:44). Because we love God, we can love anyone for His sake, as a lover will cultivate a love of lobster for the sake of the beloved. When therefore some particularly repulsive individual comes our way, and we are inclined to reject his presence even for a brief span of time, we ought to think of God appearing to us at that moment saying: "Listen, I put up with him for forty years; can't you put up with him for ten minutes?"

The love of God also reminds us that we ought not to judge the neighbor by his appearance. If he had all the graces and opportunities we have had, how much more he might love God. The Pharisee in the front of the Temple who kept the law and gave the amount deductible from income tax to the poor was uncommended by God, while the publican who poured out his soul to God, begging pardon, went back to his own house justified. It was this thought that made St. Philip Neri say, as he saw a condemned man go to the gallows: "There goes Philip except for the grace of God." After a while all these people, who before seemed so unattractive, are actually seen as much better than we; spiritually we get to a point where we feel their sin as our own, and take on their debts in penance, as the Savior took on ours, because we love them in God.

Love of neighbor, in like manner, when suffused by the love of God, never uses the neighbor for one's own pleasure. Nothing has so much contributed to the debasement of human relationships as the idea that friends are won by flattery. True love helps the neighbor to fulfill his vocation in God and thus it coincides with his own. As St. Paul told the Romans: "We who are bold in our confidence ought to bear with the scruples of those who are timorous; not to insist on having our own way. Each of us ought to give way to his neighbor, where it serves a good purpose by building up his faith" (Rom. 15:1–2). In human relationships we limit the horizon of our affection to those whom we love. Few are the Samaritans who love those who hate them. Nothing can extend this horizon as much as recognizing not those alone whom we love, but those whom God loves, and that is everybody. Thus the soul becomes like God, the "creator" of the one we love. In Him we make them lovable. Not only does a love of God prolong God's creation, it even continues His Redemption, at least to the extent that we would recreate or redeem those whom we love.

Imagine a large circle and in the center of it rays of light that spread out to the circumference. The light in the center is God; each of us is a ray. The closer the rays are to the center, the closer the rays are to one another. The closer we live to God, the closer we are bound to our neighbor; the farther we are from God, the farther we are from one another. The more each ray departs from its center, the weaker it becomes; and the closer it gets to the center, the stronger it becomes.

The secret of happiness is for each man to live as close to God as he can, and he will thereby live closer to his neighbor. This is the solution to the riddle of Love. In Him self-love becomes perfected; in Him also we love our neighbor as ourselves and for the same reason. If, therefore, I hate anyone, I hate someone God made; if I love myself to the exclusion of God, I find that I hate myself for not being all I ought to be.

Love at first seems a contradiction: How can one love self without being selfish? How can one love others without losing self? The answer is: By loving both self and neighbor in God. It is His Love that makes us love both self and neighbor rightly. God has first loved us while as yet we were sinners. Love of self avoids egotism by love of self-perfection, which is achieved by loving God. Love of others avoids totalitarianism, or the losing of self by absorption in the mass, through the loving of others in the spiritual brotherhood of "Our Father."

The poor frustrated souls who are locked up inside their own minds keep their little egotistic heads too busy and their selfish hands and feet too idle. If they would begin loving their neighbor for God's sake, they would soon find themselves loving their own moral perfection, which consists not in seeing their self-will but in living according to God's will. This double law of love of self and neighbor in God is the secret of life, for our Savior, after giving the law of love of God and neighbor, said: "Do this, and thou shalt find life" (Luke 10:28).

God never intended that the "I" and the "Thou" should be separated. God is no obstacle to the full enjoyment of self, nor is He a competitor to the love of neighbor. But when love becomes triune, God is installed in the center of the "I" and the "Thou," thus preventing the "I" from being an egotist and the "Thou" from becoming a tool or instrument of pleasure. Such love is God in pilgrimage. But if we would seek the reason why it takes three to make love, we must look into the heart of God Himself.

6

Love Is Triune

The love of husband and wife is perfected as it becomes triune; now there is the lover, the beloved, and love — the love being something distinct from both, and yet in both. If there is only the *mine* and *thine*, there is impenetrability and separateness. Not until there is a third acting element, as the soil in which the two vines intertwine, is there oneness. Then is the impotence of the *I* to completely possess the *Thou* overcome in the realization that there is a bond outside pulling them together, hovering over them as the Holy Spirit overshadowed Mary, turning the *I* and *Thou* into a *We*. It is this that lovers mean when, without knowing it, they speak of "our love" as something distinct from each.

Without a sense of Absolute Love, which is stronger than the independent love of each for the other, there is a false duality which ends in the absorption of the *I* into the *Thou* or the *Thou* into the *I*. In divorce cases, this is called "mental torture" or "domination." Really, it is egocentricity, in which one ego loves itself in the other ego. The *I* is projected into the *Thou* and is loved in the *Thou*. The *Thou* is not really loved as a person; it is only used as a means to the pleasure of the *I*. As soon as the other ceases to exhilarate, the so-called love ceases. There is nothing left to hold such a couple together, because there is no third term. There may be idolatry when there are only two, but after a while the "goddess" or the "god" turns out to be of tin. There is a world of difference between loving self in another self, and giving both self and the other self to the Third who will keep both in undying love. Without the Love of God, there is danger of love dying of its own too-much; but when each loves the Flame of Love—over and above their two individual sparks which have come from the Flame—then there is not absorption but communion. Then the love of the other becomes a proof that he loves God, for the other is seen in God and cannot be loved apart from Him.

The difference between this triune love as the basis of the love of husband and wife, and its modern counterpart, which is duality, with its tension and conflict, is this: in the latter, each loves the other as a god, as an ultimate. But no human can long bear the attribute of divinity; it is like resting a marble statue on the stem of a rose. When the "deity" of the other is deflated, either because it is exhausted or because one becomes accustomed to living with a "god" or a "goddess," there is a terrific sense of ennui and boredom. To the extent that the other is blamed, there begins to be cruelty because of the supposed deceit. How much wiser the Japanese were as regards their Emperor! They made him a god, but they also made him invisible and untouchable; otherwise the hollowness of his divinity would have been detected. A man who makes himself a god must hide; otherwise his false divinity will be unmasked. But God can become a child and talk in parables and never lose His divinity.

In authentic love, the other is accepted not as a god, but as a gift of God. As a gift of God, the other is unique and irreplaceable, a sacred trust, a mission to be fulfilled. As Dante said, speaking of Beatrice: "She looks on Heaven, and I look on her." There are perhaps few more touchingly beautiful spectacles in all the world than that of a husband and wife saying their prayers together. The prayer of a husband and wife, said together, is not the same as two distinct individuals pouring out their hearts to God, for in the first instance, there is an acknowledgment of the Spirit of Love which makes them one. Because both are destined for eternity, it is fitting that all their acts of love have that eternal flavor in which their souls in prayer and their bodies in marriage attest to the universality of admiration not only for God, but also for each other. As Maude Royden says:

Love Is Triune

Not I and thou are significant to one another, but to each of us that Third.... Nameless, it has bound us from the beginning, though still covered by a dazzling light when we met each other, unconscious that the Third is more powerful than are both of us. But now we know it. It has disclosed itself to us between your and my isolation, and our love has become a testimony to our impotence to love, our bond an indication of something over us. Now we know it, we poles eternally separated, eternally drawn to each other, imposed upon each other, we have and hold one another, not for our sake, but that in this event of I and Thou that Third may take form, and with it we two as well.

... He has, to our eternal gratitude, chained together the human elements in us; he has, to our still profounder gratitude, thrown us back upon ourselves and led each one by himself to the trust that the last solitude of any human being is not to be filled by any other human being, even the most beloved. He has blessed us with the knowledge that marriage also, in the idiom of religion, is created "toward God".... He, The Third and One in whom we are united, is henceforth our law and our liberty; in Him and through Him is our bond holy, our solitude relieved, nature freed from its dumb existence in itself, the dualism and the opposition of our souls bound up in the more exalted and relieved from the tragedy of their separation.

Now for the first time can I love thee. Now thou art more than thou alone and my love no longer founders on thee, since it reaches out beyond thee to all that is worth loving, which thou art to me. I love thee; now it means this; I love, I am a lover, because thou existest. Now forever we embrace infinitely more than merely one another; in embracing each other, we give testimony of that by which we are embraced. So thou hast become to me the best that one human being can become to another; the sign and pledge of the lovableness of the ultimate ground whence all things rise. If it is of such that it is said: "What therefore God hath joined together let not man put asunder" (Matt. 19:6); then it does not lie in our power to become divorced—for our bond is knotted and preserved by a third hand. Therein lies at the same time the significance of our divided self—also the sense of our "one for the other."

It takes three to make love. What binds lover and beloved together on earth is an ideal outside both. As it is impossible to have rain without the clouds, so it is impossible to understand love without God. In the Old Testament, God is defined as a Being whose nature it is to exist: "THE GOD WHO IS" (Exod. 3:14). In the New Testament, God is defined as Love: "God is love" (1 John 4:8). That is why the basis of all philosophy is *Existence*, and the basis of all theology is *Charity*, or love.

If we would seek out the mystery of why love has a triune character and implies lover, beloved, and love, we must mount to God Himself. Love is Triune in God because in Him there are three Persons and in the one divine nature! Love has this triple character because it is a reflection of the Love of God, in whom there are three Persons: Father, Son, and Holy Spirit. The Trinity is the answer to the questions of Plato. If there is only one God, what does He think about? He thinks an eternal thought: His Eternal Word, or Son. If there is only one God, whom does He love? He loves His Son, and that mutual love is the Holy Spirit. The great philosopher was fumbling about for the mystery of the Trinity, for his noble mind seemed in some small way to suspect that an infinite being must have relations of thought and love, and that God cannot be conceived without thought and love. But it was not until the Word became incarnate that man knew the secret of those relations and the inner life of God, for it was Jesus Christ, the Son of God, who revealed to us the inmost life of God.

It is that mystery of the Trinity which gives the answer to those who have pictured God as an egotist God sitting in solitary splendor before the world began, for the Trinity is a revelation that before creation God enjoyed the infinite communion with Truth and the embrace of Infinite Love, and hence had no need ever to go outside of Himself in search for happiness. The greatest wonder of all is that, being perfect and enjoying perfect happiness, He ever should have made a world. And if He did make a world, He could only have had one motive for making it. It could not add to His perfection; it could not add to His Truth; it could not increase His Happiness. He made a world only because He loved, and love tends to diffuse itself to others.

Finally, it is the mystery of the Trinity which gives the answer to the quest for happiness and the meaning of Heaven. Heaven is not a place where there is the mere vocal repetition of alleluias or the monotonous fingering of harps. Heaven is a place where we find the fullness of all life's greatest values. It is a state where we find in their plenitude those things which slake the thirst of hearts, satisfy the hunger of starving minds, and give rest to unsolaced loves. Heaven is the communion with Perfect Life, Perfect Truth, and Perfect Love: God the Father, God the Son, and God the Holy Spirit.

Here is the answer to the riddle of love. Love implies relation. If lived in isolation, it becomes selfishness; if absorbed in collectivity, it loses its personality and, therefore, the right to love. The ultimate reason why it takes three to make love is that God is Love, and His Love is Triune. All earthly love worthy of the name is the echo of "This Tremendous Lover," who is not an individual Ego, but a Society of Love. As every sentence implies a subject, predicate, and object, so all love implies a triple relationship of Lover, a Beloved, and the Unifying Love. No example is quite adequate to describe this inner life of God! The wisest of all pagans, Aristotle, once described God as Pure Actuality, which is as far as reason alone can go. He distinguished between two kinds of activity: *transitive*, in which the activity moved from the inside out, like heat from a radiator; and *immanent* activity, which is like thinking and willing within man. All life has some immanent activity, but it is imperfect, since it is bound up with transitive activity. For example, the tree has immanent life, but the fruit it generates falls from the tree; the animal has immanent life, but when it begets its kind, the newborn animal lives an independent existence. The most perfect immanent activity on earth is that of man, who can generate a thought which does not fall from his mind like an apple from a tree. It remains inside his mind to perfect and to enrich it!

God is perfect immanent activity. The best example that we can find on earth for the inner life of God is the study of the human mind! Because it faintly reflects the Trinity, we first study its nature, then use it to exemplify the Triune life of God.

The mind conceives a thought — say, "justice," "faith," or "square-ness." Not one of these thoughts has size, weight, or color. No one ever saw "justice" striding along a country lane or sitting down to a meal. Whence has the idea come? It has been *generated* by the mind, just as the animal generates its kind. For there is generation in the mind, as there is generation in the life of the plant or animal, but here the generation is spiritual. There is fecundity in the mind, just as there is fecundity in the lower types of life, but here the fecundity is spiritual. And because its generation and its fecundity are spiritual, what is begotten remains in the mind; it does not fall off outside it, as the seed from the clover. The embryo of the animal was once a part of its parents, but in due course of nature it was born; that is, separated from the parent. But in intellectual conception, when a thought is born of the mind it always remains *within* the mind and never separates itself from it. The intellect preserves its youth in such a way that the greatest thinkers of all times have called intelligence the highest kind of life on this earth. This is the meaning behind the words of the Psalmist. *Intellectum da mihi et vivam* — "Give me knowledge, and I will live." The more inner life one has, the more knowledge. Since God is perfect immanent activity, without dependence on anything outside Himself, He is Perfect Life.

Now we come to the other faculty of the soul, the will. As the intel-lect thinks and seeks truth, so the will chooses and pursues goodness. Choice comes from within. The stone has no will; its activity is wholly determined by force imposed on it from without. It must, in servile obe-dience to the law of gravitation, fall to the earth when released from the hand. Just as material things are directed to their destinies by laws of nature, so, too, animals are directed to theirs by instinct. There is a hopeless monotony in the working of animal instinct. The bird never improves the building of its nest, never changes its style from the Roman to forked twigs to express the piercing piety of the Gothic. Its activity is an imposed one, not free. But in man there is a choice, and a choice freely determined by the soul itself. Reason sets up one of thousands of possible targets, and the will chooses one of many different projectiles for that target. The simple words "Thank you" will always stand out as a refutation of determinism, for they imply that something which was done could possibly have been left undone.

Not only does the choice come from within, but the will may often seek its goodness or love in the soul itself and find repose there. Love of duty, devotion to virtue, pursuit of truth, and the quest of intellectual ideals are all so many immanent goals which prove that man has an internal activity which far surpasses that of lower creatures and gives him spiritual supremacy over them. That is why man is the master of the universe; that is why it is his right to harness the waterfall, to make the plant his food, to imprison the bird for his song, to serve the venison at his table. There is a hierarchy of life in the universe, and the life of man is higher than any other life — not because he has nutritive powers like a plant, not because he has generative powers like a beast, but because he has thinking and willing powers like God. These constitute his greatest claim to life; and in losing these, he becomes worse than a beast.

The best way to grasp, even faintly, the immanent life of God, we said, is to study man's thought and will, which reflect faintly the thought and the will of God. The immanent activity of God certainly cannot be the activity of nutrition as it is in animals, because God has no body. It can, however, be faintly likened to some spiritual activity, as in our own soul, namely, that of thinking and willing. In describing human thinking, three distinct things may be said of it: it has an idea; this idea is generated or born; and finally, it is personal.

Man thinks. He thinks a spiritual thought, such as "relation." This thought is a word. It is a word even before I speak it, for the vocal word is only the expression of the internal word in the mind. The Greek word for "word" is "idea."

This idea, or thought, or internal word, is generated or born. The spiritual thought, "relation," has no size, weight, or color. No one has ever seen, tasted, or touched it, and yet it is real. It is spiritual, and since it is

219

not wholly in the outside world, it must have been produced, or generated, by the mind itself. There are other ways of begetting life than the physical or carnal. The most chaste way that life is begotten is the way in which thoughts and ideas are born in the mind. It may be called, in a diminished way, the immaculate conception of the mind.

Finally, the idea, or thought, or word of man, is personal. Some thoughts of man are banal and commonplace, trite thoughts which no man remembers; but there are also thoughts which are spirit and life. There are some thoughts of man into which he puts his very soul and his very being, all that he has been and all that he is. These thoughts are so much the thoughts of that thinker as to carry his personality and his spirit with them, so that we can recognize them as his thoughts. Thus we say, that is a thought of Pascal, of Bossuet, of Shakespeare, or of Dante.

Now, apply these three reflections about human thought to God: (1) God thinks a thought, and that thought is a Word; (2) it is generated or born, and is therefore called a Son; and (3) finally, that Word or Son is Personal.

God thinks. He thinks a thought. This thought of God is a Word, as my own thought is called a word, even before or after it is pronounced. It is an internal word. But God's thought is not like ours. It is not multiple. God does not think one Thought, or one Word, one minute and another the next. Thoughts are not born to die and do not die to be reborn in the mind of God. All is present to Him at once. In Him there is only one Word. He has no need of another.

The more clearly a man understands anything, the more readily he can summarize it in a few words. Speakers who have nothing to say are like railroads without terminal facilities. In one single idea, a wise teacher sees things which an ignorant man would require volumes to understand. We often condemn people as having few ideas. It is well to remember that God has one Idea, and that Idea is the totality of all Truth. That Thought, or Word, is infinite and equal to Himself, unique and absolute, first-born of the Spirit of God; a Word which tells what God is; a Word from which all human words have been derived, and of which created things are merely the broken syllables or letters; a Word which is the source of all the science and art in the world. The latest scientific discoveries, the new knowledge of the great expanse of the heavens, the sciences of biology, physics, and chemistry, the more lofty ones of metaphysics, philosophy, and theology, the knowledge of the shepherds, and the knowledge of the wise men — all this knowledge has its Source in the Word or the Wisdom of God.

The Infinite Thought of God is called not only a Word — to indicate that it is the Wisdom of God — but *It is also called a Son, because it has been generated or begotten.* The Thought or the Word of God does not come from the outside world; it is born in His nature in a much more perfect way than the thought of "justice" is generated by my spirit. In the language of Sacred Scripture: "What, says the Lord thy God, shall I, that bring children to the birth, want power to bring them forth: Shall I, that give life to the womb, want strength to open it?" (Isa. 66:9). The ultimate Source of all generation or birth is God, whose Word is born of Him, and therefore the Word is called a Son. Just as in our own human order, the principle of all generation is called the Father, so, too, in the Trinity the principle of spiritual generation is called the Father, and the one generated is called the Son, because He is the perfect image and Resemblance of the Father. If an earthly father can transmit to his son all the nobility of his character and all the fine traits of his life, how much more so can the Heavenly Father communicate to His own Eternal Son all the nobility, the perfection, and the Eternity of His Being! God the Father is related to God the Son as the Eternal Thinker is related to His Eternal Thought.

Finally, this Word or Son, born of the Eternal God, is personal. The thought of God is not commonplace, like ours, but reaches to the abyss of all that is known or can be known. Into this Thought or Word, God puts Himself so entirely that it is as living as Himself, as perfect as Himself, as infinite as Himself. If a human genius can put his whole personality into a thought, in a more perfect way God is able to put so much of Himself into a thought that that Thought or Word or Son is conscious of Himself and is a Divine Person. We humans can know ourselves, but it is first the exterior world that we know. Then we come to know ourselves as a result of knowing the world. We are dependent on whatever is outside us. But God knows Himself without any original assistance from the outside world. God has an idea of Himself, as a face is seen in a mirror, but this idea is so deep and so reflective of His nature as to be a Person.

The Father does not first exist and then think; the Father and Son are co-eternal, for in God all is present and unchanging. An unbelieving father one day said to his son, who had just returned from catechism class: "What did you learn today?" The boy answered: "I learned there are Three Persons in God—Father, Son, and Holy Spirit—and they are all equal." The father retorted: "But that is ridiculous! I am your father; you are my son. We are not equal. I existed a long time before you." To this came the answer: "Oh, no, you didn't; you did not begin to be a father until I began to be a son." The relationship of father and son on earth is contemporaneous; so the relation between Father and Son is co-eternal. Nothing is new, and nothing is lost. Thus it is that the Father, contemplating His Image, His Word, His Son, can say in the ecstasy of the first and real paternity: "Thou art my Son; I have begotten thee this day" (Acts 13:33). "This day"—this day of eternity; that is, the indivisible duration of being without end. "This day" in that act that will never end as it has never begun, this day of the agelessness of eternity—"Thou art my Son."

Go back to the origin of the world, pile century on century, aeon on aeon, age on age—"The Word was with God." Go back before the creation of the angels, before Michael summoned his war hosts to victory and there was a flash of archangelic spears—even then, "The Word was with God." It is that Word which St. John heard in the beginning of his Gospel, when he wrote: "At the beginning of time the Word already was; and God had the Word abiding with him, and the Word was God" (John 1:1). Just as my interior thoughts are not made manifest without a spoken word, so the Word in the language of John, "was made flesh, and came to dwell among us" (John 1:14). And that Word is no other than the Second Person of the Blessed Trinity; the Word who embraces the beginning and end of all things; the Word who existed before creation; the Word who presided at creation as the King of the Universe; the Word made flesh at Bethlehem; the Word made flesh on the Cross;

and the Word made flesh dwelling with divinity and humanity in the Eucharistic Emmanuel.

The Good Friday of twenty centuries ago did not mark the end of Him, as it did not mark the beginning. It is one of the moments of the Eternal Word of God. Jesus Christ has a prehistory that is prehistory—a prehistory not to be studied in the rocks of the earth, nor in the caves of man, nor in the slime and dust of primeval jungles, but in the bosom of an Eternal Father. He alone brought history to history; He alone has dated all the records of human events ever since into two periods—the period before and the period after His coming: so that if we would ever deny that the Word became Flesh and that the Son of God became the Son of Man, we would have to date our denial as over one thousand nine hundred years after His coming.

Every mind and heart in the world is aspiring to this kind of Love which is the very essence of God! We all want wisdom, learning, truth; but we do not want it in books, theorems, or abstractions. Truth never appeals to us unless it is personal. No purely philosophical system can long hold the devotion of men. But as soon as Truth is seen incarnate in a Person, then it is dynamic, magnetic. But nowhere else can we find life and Truth identical except in the Word of God, who became our Lord, Jesus Christ. Every other teacher said: "Follow my code," "Observe my Eightfold Way." But our Lord, the Son of God, and the Son of Man, alone could say: "I am the Truth" (John 14:6). For the first time in history, as from all eternity in God, *Truth is Personal!*

But generation does not tell the full story of the inner life of God, for if God is the source of all life and truth and goodness in the world, He has a Will as well as an Intellect, a Love as well as a Thought. Nothing is loved unless it is known. There is no love for the unknown. Love implies knowledge. The intellect sets up the goal or target; the will is the bow and the arrow combined, directed to that target. Whenever we meet anything good we are drawn to it, and the more good it is, the more desirable it is—whether it be a meal, a vacation, or a human heart. Whenever love is deep and intense, a tremendous transformation is wrought within the soul! This is because love does something to us;

it affects us so profoundly that the only way we have of expressing it is by the lover's sigh, which is expressed in the Latin word *spiritus!* The deeper love is, the more wordless it becomes. Byron spoke of "the sigh suppressed, corroding in the cavern of the heart."

In the divine essence, the Father not only contemplates His Son, who is His Eternal Image. As a result of the mutual love for one another, there is also a *spiration*, or an act of mutual love, which is called the Holy Spirit. Just as to speak means to pronounce a word, and to flower means to produce blossoms, so to love is to breathe love, or sigh, or *spirate*. As we know that a rosebush is in flower by its blossoms, so the Father gives intellectual expression to all knowledge by His Word. Now we know that the Father and Son are in love, both for themselves and even for us, through their Holy Spirit of Love. This mutual love of Father for Son and of Son for Father is not a fleeting love like ours, but so eternal and so rooted in the divine essence as to be personal. For that reason, the Holy Spirit is called a Person. The love of friend for friend is sometimes said to make them *one soul;* but in no sense does it breathe forth a new person. In the family, however, the analogy is better, for the mutual love of husband and wife does "breathe," not wholly in the order of the spirit but in the order of spirit and matter, a new person, who is the bond of their love. But all this is imperfect, for regardless of how much love there is among humans, the good which is loved remains separated and external.

A kiss is a sign of love; but it is a giving of one's breath, or spirit, which is inseparable from life itself. The purpose of all love is to take the beloved into oneself to possess it, to become identified with it. A mother pressing a child to her breast is seeking to make that child one with her in love. "I bear you in my heart" is a romantic expression of the same craving for unity through love — for love, as we shall see, by its nature is unitive.

But despite this desire to be one with the beloved, there must still be distinctness. If the other person were destroyed, there would be no love. Unity must not mean absorption or annihilation or destruction, but the fullness of one in the other. To be one without ceasing to be distinct, that is the paradox of love! This ideal we cannot achieve in this life because we have bodies as well as souls. What is material cannot interpenetrate! After a union in the flesh, one is thrown back on one's own individual self. In Holy Communion there is the closest approximation there can be on earth to this, but even that is a reflection of a higher love. We can never completely give ourselves to others, nor can others entirely become our own. All earthly love suffers from this inability of two lovers to be one, and yet distinct. Love's greatest sufferings come from the exteriority and separateness of the beloved! But in God, the love uniting Father and Son is a living flame, or the Eternal Kiss of the Father, and the Son.

In human love, there is nothing deep enough to make the love for one another personal, but in God, the Spirit of Love uniting both is so personal that it is called the Holy Spirit. It is a fact of nature that every being loves its own perfection. The perfection of the eye is color, and it loves the beauty of the setting sun. The perfection of the ear is sound, and it loves the harmony of an overture by Beethoven or a sonata by Chopin. Love has two terms: he who loves and he who is loved. In love the two are reciprocal: I love and I am loved. Between me and the one I love there is a bond. It is not my love; it is not his love; it is *our* love: the mysterious resultant of two affections, a bond which enchains, and an embrace wherein two hearts leap with but a single joy. The Father loves the Son, the Image of His Perfection; and the Son loves the Father, who generated Him. Love is not only in the Father. Love is not only in the Son. The Father loves the Son, whom He engenders. The Son loves the Father, who engendered Him. They contemplate each other; love each other; unite in a love so powerful, so strong, and so perfect that it forms between them a living bond. They give themselves in a love so infinite that, like the truth which expresses itself only in the giving of a whole personality, their love can express itself in nothing less than a Person, who is Love. Love at such a stage does not speak, does not cry, does not express itself by words, nor by canticles; it expresses itself as we do in some ineffable moments by that which indicates the very exhaustion of our giving, namely, a sigh or a breath, and that is why the Third Person of the Blessed Trinity is called the Holy Spirit, something that lies too deep for words.

As the Son is God eternally expressed to Himself (that is, the Eternal consciousness of whole being), so God the Spirit is God in the act of loving (that is, giving Himself without reservation). The Holy Spirit is the Spirit of the Father, as He is the Spirit of the Son, but the Holy Spirit personifies that which the Father and Son have in common. Love is not a quality in God as it is in us, for there are moments when we do not love! Because the Holy Spirit is the Bond of Love of Father and Son, it follows that it will also be the bond of love between men! That is why our Lord, on the night of the Last Supper, said that as He and the Father were one in the Holy Spirit, so men would be one in His Mystical Body, for He would send His Spirit to make them one.

The Holy Spirit is necessary to the nature of God as its harmony through love! With a feeble reflection men have always recognized love as the unitive, cohesive force of human society, as they saw in hate the occasion of its disintegration and chaos. As God in creating the world put into it a gravitational pull which affects all matter, so He has put into hearts another law of gravitation, which is the law of love by which all hearts are attracted back again to the center and source of Love, which is God. St. Augustine said: "My love is my weight," which means that every soul has a longing desire to return to its Original Source, its Divine Heart or Center. Desire is everything in nature and, with some appositeness, Heaven has been described as "nature filled with divine life attracted by Desire." Love is the soul's last habitation.

That breath of love in God is not a passing one, like ours, but an Eternal Spirit. How all this is done, no one knows, but on the testimony of God's revelation we know that this same Holy Spirit overshadowed the Blessed Virgin Mary, and that He who was born of her was called the Son of God. It was the same Spirit of whom our Lord spoke to Nicodemus, when He told him he must be born again of "water and the Holy Spirit." It was the same Spirit of whom our Lord spoke at the Last Supper: "And he will bring honor to me, because it is from me that he will derive what he makes plain to you. I say that he will derive from me what he makes plain to you, because all that belongs to the Father belongs to me" (John 16:14). In this passage our Lord tells His disciples that the Holy Spirit, who is to come, will in the future reveal divine knowledge which has been communicated to Him in His procession from both the Father and Son. It is that same Spirit, who in fulfillment of the promise "It will be for him, the truth-giving Spirit, when he comes to guide you into all truth" (John 16:13), descended on the Apostles on the day of Pentecost and became the soul of the Church. The continuous, unbroken succession of the truth communicated by Christ to His Church has survived to our own day — not because of the human organization of the Church, for that is carried on by frail vessels, but because of the profusion of the Spirit of Love and Truth over Christ's Vicar, and over all who belong to Christ's Mystical Body, which is His Church.

Divine Life is an endless rhythm of three in oneness: Three Persons in one nature. If God had no Son, He would not be a Father; if He were an individual Unity, He could not love until He had made something less than Himself. No one is good unless He gives. If He did not give to the highest way by generation, He would not be Good, and if He were not Good, He would be Terror. Before the world began, God was Good in Himself, because He eternally begot a Son. There is no act in God which is not God Himself. Thus, God is the eternal vortex of love, which is ever in blissful activity because He is Three, and yet One because proceeding from one nature which is God. Here is the White Source of all love whence comes to us all its straggling rays. Here alone is the Source, the Stream, and the Sea of all love. All fatherhood, motherhood, sonship, espousals, friendship, wedded love, patriotism, instinct, attraction, all interaction, and generation, is in some faint measure a picture of God. Father and mother in their unity constitute a complete principle of generation, and the child born of this principle is attached to the parents by a spirit: the spirit of the family. This spirit does not proceed uniquely from the love of parents for their children, but from the reciprocity of their affection. The spirit of love in parents is at once desire, pity, tenderness, bearing all things, suffering all things for the children. In the children, it is an offering such as the birds make to the branches in the springtime. The spirit of the family is as necessary to the family in generation, as the Holy Spirit is to the love in Father and Son.

Three in One, Father, Son, and Holy Spirit; Three Persons in One God; One in essence with distinction of Persons—such is the Mystery of the Trinity, such is the Inner Life of God. Just as I am, I know, and I love, and yet I am one nature; just as the three angles of a triangle do not make three triangles, but one; just as the power, light, and heat of the sun do not make three suns, but one; as water, air, and steam are all manifestations of the one substance, H_2O; as the form, color, and perfume of the rose do not make three roses, but one; as our life, our intellect, and our will do not make three substances, but one; as 1 times 1 times 1 does not equal 3, but 1; so, too, in some much more mysterious way, there are Three Persons in God yet only one God. William Drummond sang:

> Ineffable, all-pow'rful God, all free,
> Thou only liv'st, and each thing lives by Thee:
> No joy, no, nor perfection To Thee came
> By the contriving of this world's great frame;
> Ere sun, moon, stars, began their restless race,
> Ere paint'd with purple light was heaven's round face,
> Ere air had clouds, ere clouds wept down their showers,
> Ere sea embraced earth, ere earth bare flowers,
> Thou happy liv'd; world nought to Thee supplied,
> All in Thyself, Thy self Thou satisfied.
> Of good no slender shadow doth appear,
> No age-worn track, in Thee which shin'd not clear;
> Perfection's sum, prime cause of every cause,
> Midst, end, beginning, where all good doth pause.
> Hence of Thy substance, differing in nought,
> Thou in eternity, Thy Son forth brought,
> The only birth of Thy unchanging mind,
> Thine image, pattern-like that ever shin'd,
> Light out of light, begotten not by will,
> But nature, all and that same essence still
> Which Thou Thyself; for Thou dost nought possess
> Which He hath not, in aught nor is He less

Love Is Triune

Than Thou His great begetter. Of this light,
Eternal, double, kindled was Thy spirit
Eternally, who is with Thee the same,
All-holy gift, ambassador, knot, flame.
Most sacred Triad! O most holy One!
Unprocreate Father, every procreate Son,
Ghost breath'd from Both, You were, are aye, shall be,
Most blessed, Three in One, and One in Three,
Incomprehensible by reachless height,
And unperceived by excessive light.
So in our souls, three and yet one are still
The understanding, memory, and will:
So, though unlike, the planet of the days,
So soon as he was made, begat his rays,
Which are his offspring, and from both was hurl'd
The rosy light which comfort doth the world,
And none forewent another: so the spring,
The well-head, and the stream which they forth bring,
Are but one self-same essence, nor in aught
Do differ, save in order, and our thought
No chime of time discerns in them to fall,
But three distinctly bide one essence all.
But these express not Thee: who can declare
Thy being: Men and angels dazzled are;
Who force this Eden would with wit or sense,
A cherubim shall find to bar him thence.
And John Donne, in turn, gave us:
Batter my heart, three person'd God; for, you
As yet but knocke, breathe, shine, and seeke to mend;
That I may rise, and stand, o'erthrow mee, and bend
Your force, to breake, blowe, burn and make me new.
I, like an usurpt towne, to 'another due,
Labour to' admit you, but Oh, to no end,
Reason your viceroy in mee, mee should defend,

But is captiv'd, and proves weake or untrue.
Yet dearly 'I love you,' and would be loved faine,
But am betroth'd unto your enemie:
Divorce mee, 'untie, or breake that knot againe,
Take mee to you, imprison mee, for I
Except you' enthrall me, never shall be free,
Nor ever chast, except you ravish mee.

Love is best understood when seen in its perfection, rather than in its broken fragments. Once seen in Heaven, it can be defined on earth. From the above description of the Trinity, we learn the definition of love: *Love is a mutual self-giving which ends in self-recovery.* It must first of all be a gift, for nothing is good unless it gives. Without self-outpouring, there is no love. God is good because He made a world. But before there was this *extrinsic* diffusion of His Goodness, there was the eternal inner generation of the Son, who is "the splendor of the Father's glory, the image of His Substance" (Heb. 1:3). Applied to marriage, love is first mutual self-giving, for love's greatest joy is to gird its loins and serve, to diffuse itself without loss or separation. They who are Two, the Father and the Son, are One in the divine nature; the heavenly pattern of a marriage wherein two are in one flesh.

But if love were only mutual self-giving, it would end in exhaustion, or else become a flame in which both would be consumed. Mutual self-giving also implies self-recovery. The perfect example of this recovery, in which nothing is lost, is the Trinity, wherein Love circles back upon itself in an eternal consummation. Not as two rivers unite as they flow into the sea, do Father, and Son, and Holy Spirit unite in one nature, for this example implies the mingling of two strange unities. In the Eternal Godhead there is what theologians call "circumincession," which means that they "co-inhere" in one another, so that the act of each is the act of God. God-love circles back on itself, so that God is Society, in the sense that in His one divine nature there is an eternal communion of Life, Truth, and Love. God is related to nothing other than Himself, and this triple relation of Life, Truth, and Love is called the Trinity. In the world of matter, there must be a medium between objects. That is why scientists originally posited ether in the universe. In God, the Father and the Son cannot be united one to another by anything outside of God, but by Love alone. Thus, God is a vortex of love, ever complete in an endless action of Being, Wisdom, and Love, and yet ever serene, for nothing outside Divinity is needed to His complete happiness.

Since love means a mutual self-giving which ends in self-recovery, the love of husband and wife, in obedience to the creative command, should "increase and multiply" (Gen. 1:28). Like the love of earth and tree, their marriage should become fruitful in new love. There would be mutual self-giving as they sought to overcome their individual impotence by filling up, at the store of the other, the lacking measure; there would be self-recovery as they begot not the mere sum of themselves, but a new life which would make them an earthly trinity. As the three Divine Persons do not lose their personality in their oneness of essence but remain distinct, so the love of husband and wife leaves their souls distinct. As from the love of the Father and the Son proceeds a third distinct person, the Holy Spirit, so in an imperfect way, from the love of husband and wife, there proceeds the child who is a bond of union which gives love to both in the spirit of the family. The number of children does not alter the basic family trinity, for numerous are the fruits of the Gift of the Most High, He is One. The Sacrament of Marriage, because it is life-giving love and love-giving life, is the image of the Trinity. As the riches of the Holy Spirit of Love are at the disposal of those who live under His impulse, so marriage, lived as God would have it lived, associates partners to the creative joy of the Father, to the self-sacrificing love of the Son, and to the unifying love of the Holy Spirit.

Even those without faith speak of their mutual love in the third person. They say "our love." They speak of love as if love were a third person common to them, belonging to them, and uniting them in a mysterious way. They are paying tribute without knowing it, to the mystery-model of their union. This Third Person, *altissimum donum Dei*, is also given to human beings to unite them in love, in the measure that the couple accepts it as the "spirit" of their union. Marriage is a trinity even when no child proceeds from it through no fault of the parents. But if the child comes, then love is made incarnate.

Love is at first dual, then triune. Duality, or two in love, is the consolation that God has provided for our finitude. "It is not well that man should be without companionship" (Gen. 2:18). But perfect love is triune, either in the sense that it appeals to "our love" as something outside both coming from God, or as the "fruit of our love," which is the child, whose spirit or soul has come from God.

Love that is only giving, ends in exhaustion; love that is only seeking, perishes in its selfishness. Love that is ever seeking to give and is ever defeated by receiving is the shadow of the Trinity on earth, and therefore a foretaste of Heaven. Father, mother, child, three persons in the unity of human nature: such is the Triune law of Love in Heaven and on earth. "No one can love without being born of God, and knowing God" (1 John 4:7). Love is an eternal mutual self-gift; the recovery in the flesh, or in the soul, or in Heaven, of all that was given and surrendered. In love no fragment is lost.

7

Unfolding the Mystery

Those who start with the pagan philosophy of sex must face life as a descent. Associated with a growing old, there is a loss of physical energy, and the horrible perspective of death. The Christian philosophy of love, on the contrary, implies an ascension. The body may grow older, but the spirit grows younger, and love often becomes more intense. With time there is an unfolding of the mystery of love.

The difference between sex and love is like the difference between an education without a philosophy of life and one with such an integrating factor. A system without a philosophy measures progress in terms of *substitution*. Spencer is substituted for Kant, Marx for Spencer, Freud for Marx. There is no continuity in mental development any more than the automobile grew out of the horse and buggy. But in a Christian education, there is a deepening of a mystery. One starts with a simple truth that God exists. Instead of abandoning that idea when one begins to study science, one deepens his knowledge of God with a study of the Trinity and then begins to see the tremendous ramifications of divine power in the universe, of divine providence in history, and of divine mercy in the human heart.

So it is with love. The Christian marriage is the deepening of a mystery in two ways: first in the raising of a family, and secondly in the ascension of love.

There comes a moment in the noblest of human love when one "gets used to" the best. Jewelers lose the thrill of seeing precious stones. There must always be a mystery in life. Once it disappears, life becomes banal. One wonders if the reason for the popularity of murder mysteries today is because they fill up the void created by the loss of the mysteries of faith. The extreme interest in murder mysteries is a sign that people are more interested in *how* a person is killed than in the eternal lot of the one who is killed. So long as there is nothing undisclosed and unrevealed in life, there is no longer a joy in living. The zest of life partly comes from the fact that there is a door that is yet unopened, a veil that has not yet been lifted, a note that has not yet been struck.

No one is ever thirsty at the border of a well. There is little desire for the possessed, and no hope for that which is already ours. Marriage often ends the romance, as if the chase were ended and one had bagged the game. When persons are taken for granted, then is lost all the sensitiveness and delicacy which is the essential condition of friendship and joy. This is particularly true in some marriages where there is possession without desire, a capture without the thrill of the chase.

The Christian way of preserving mystery, and therefore attractiveness, is through the unfolding of love into the next generation, which is what we mean by making it triune. Modern life is geared to the idea that beauty in a woman and strength in a man are permanent possessions. All the mechanics of modern advertising are directed to this lie. If a man eats certain kinds of crunchy, cracky food, he is told that he can take ten strokes off his golf, and that if he swallows a few pills, he will no longer have a fine head of skin. The woman, in her turn, is told that beauty can be a permanent possession, and that her rough laundry hands, her unattractive smile, can all be remedied by a tube of this or that; or she is led to believe that after a few days of diet she will no longer be a victim of circumference, and will not look as if she had turned forty, but as if she had returned twenty.

Despite all this propaganda for the fixity of strength and beauty, it often happens that, a year or two after marriage, the husband no longer seems to be that strong brave Apollo who made end runs on the football team on Saturday afternoons, or who came home from the war with three stars on his breast. One day the wife asks him to help wash the dishes and he retorts: "That's a woman's job, not mine." In her turn, she no longer seems to him as beautiful as the first day of the honeymoon. Her baby talk that once seemed so cute, now begins to get on his nerves. Then it is that some couples feel there is no longer any love, because there is no thrill.

God did not intend that strength in a man and beauty in a woman should endure, but that they should reappear in their children. Here is where God's providence reveals itself. Just at a time when it might seem that beauty is fading in one, and strength in the other, God sends children to protect and revive both. When the first boy is born, the husband reappears in all his strength and promise and, in the language of Virgil, "from high Heaven descends a worthier race of men." When the first girl is born, the wife revives in all her beauty and charm, and even the baby talk becomes cute all over again. He even likes to think that she is the sole source of the daughter's loveliness. Each child that is born begins to be a bead in the great rosary of love, binding the parents together in the rosy chains of a sweet slavery of love.

The transports of a newborn life come to youth and maid with all the sweet and true illusion of an eternal bliss. The moment for which their mutual love had been yearning has at last arrived; the seed they planted is born. The secret of their love has been whispered and understood, in the full consciousness that they who were given heaven's fires passed on the torch aflame to other generations. Their love was made flesh and dwelt amongst them, and that joy no one shall take from them. Eyes that at first could see no vision but the other, now center on a common image which is neither his nor hers, but their joint "creation" under God.

In this kind of life, like the bush Moses saw, the fires of love burn but there is nothing consumed. Love becomes life's champion and answers the challenge of death. Thus is married love saved from disillusionment. Phoenix-like it is always rising from the ashes, as husband and wife draw up reinforcements of their love in the eternal campaign for life. No self-loathing, satiety and fear seize their souls, for they never pluck the fruit of love at its core nor break the lute to snare the music. Love becomes an ascension from the sense-plane through an incarnation and rises back again to God, as they train their children for their native Heaven and its Trinity, whence came their sparks of fire and love. From the time the children learn to bless themselves and say the name of Jesus, through that hour when they learn in little catechisms greater truths than the worldly wise could give, to that day when they themselves start love again on its pilgrimage, the parents have a consciousness of their trusteeship under God.

The children thus become new bonds of love between husband and wife as a new quality appears in marriage, namely, the penetration of a mystery. There is never any love when one hits bottom. Love demands something unrevealed; it flourishes, therefore, only in mystery. No one ever wants to hear a singer hit her highest note, nor an orator "tear a passion to tatters," for once mystery and the infinite are denied, life's urge is stilled and its passion glutted.

In a true marriage, there is an ever-enchanting romance. There are at least four distinct mysteries progressively revealed. First, there is the mystery of the other partner, which is body-mystery. When that mystery is solved and the first child is born, there begins a new mystery. The husband sees something in the wife he never before knew existed, namely, the beautiful mystery of motherhood. She sees a new mystery in him she never before knew existed, namely, the mystery of fatherhood. As other children come to revive their strength and beauty, the husband never seems older to the wife than the day they were married, and the wife never seems older than the day they first met and carved their initials in an oak tree. As the children reach the age of reason, a third mystery unfolds, that of father-craft and mother-craft; the disciplining and training of young minds and hearts in the ways of God. As the children grow into maturity the mystery continues to deepen, new areas of exploration open up, and the father and mother now see themselves as sculptors in the great quarry of humanity, carving living stones and fitting them together in the temple of God, whose Architect is Love.

The fourth mystery is their contribution to the well-being of the nation. Here, too, is the root of democracy, for it is in the family that a person is valued, not for what he is worth, nor for what he can do, but primarily for what he is. His status, his position, is guaranteed by the very fact of being *alive*. The children who are dumb or blind, sons who were maimed in war, are all loved because of themselves and their intrinsic worth as gifts of God, and not because of what they know, or what they earn, or because of the class to which they belong. This reverence for personality in the family is the social principle upon which the wider life of the community depends, for the state exists for the person, not the person for the state.

In the love of friends, in the love of husband and wife, there must be a recognition of a Love beyond both, in which, as in a sea, they bathe for refreshment. As everything the human mind knows is intelligible only because it is in some way related to being, as the eye sees what is colored, so one heart loves another heart in that immense dimension outside of both, which is the Love of God.

When that marital love is fruitful, the children represent in the order of flesh that *third* which is so essential for happiness. They rescue duality from boredom; they prevent life from ever touching bottom; they turn new pages in the book of life; they explore depths beyond body and education and democracy, thereby bringing astonishment and wonder and mystery into love. As friend and friend, husband and wife call on the Third outside themselves to save each from isolation, and to make them a family in the mystery of Giver, Receiver, and Gift.

When there is duality, there is need; where there is Trinity, there is pity. Need is avid to be filled out of the neighbor's basket. Pity is born of a plenitude restless to empty itself. Strip love of its triune quality, and all internal relationships dissolve; and what is left is only the external. For example, the epidemic contacts in man and woman, capital and labor in competition, or the Eastern and Western World at war, hot or cold. A society in which the unifying bond is dismissed, progressively becomes an agglomeration of atoms. Finally, the disorganized cry out for a totalitarian force to "organize" the chaos. Thus is atheistic socialism born. As education, when it loses its philosophy of life, breaks up into departments without any integration or unity except the accidental one of proximity and time, and as a body, when it loses its soul, breaks up into its chemical components, so a family, when it loses the nullifying bond of love, breaks up in the divorce court without the third element outside both, the human is first suppressed, and then compressed, by hostile forces until he is locked inside his mind, solitary, alone, and afraid, a prisoner of his very self. In relation to nothing, what can satisfy him? Rejecting Love outside of his ego, he cannot understand sacrifice except as amputation and self-destruction. How can such a consciously self-deficient and helpless being give, without diminishing his own emptiness? He is ready for self-immolation understood as a suicide, but not the sacrifice of self for others. Nothing exists but his own ego, the other egos outside himself limit his personality and cross his wishes, and therefore are detestable. Not until the wider and deeper Love appears, which is the fulfillment of personality, will the ego ever cease to revolt against sacrifice, whether it be giving way to the partner for the sake of peace, or raising a family to see strength and beauty prolonged even "unto the third and fourth generation" (see Ps. 128:6).

The only really progressive thing in all the universe is love. And yet that which God made to bloom and blossom and flower through time and into eternity is that which is most often nipped in the bud. Perhaps that is the reason why artists always picture love as a little cupid who never grows up. Armed with only a bow and arrow in an atomic universe, the poor little angel has hardly a chance. St. Paul speaks of faith and hope disappearing in Heaven, but love remaining forever. Yet that one thing that mortals want to be eternal is that which they most quickly choke before it has begun to walk. If a man came from Mars and had never heard of the greatest event in history, which was the birth of the Divine Love in the person of Christ, he probably could guess the rest of the story and predict His Crucifixion. All he would need to do would be to look at the way even the best of human loves are divorced, denied, mutilated, bartered, and stunted.

But if love be what the heart wants above all things else, why does it not grow in love? It is because most hearts want love like a serpent, not like a bird. They want love on the same plane as the flesh, and not a love

238

which wings its way from earth to mountain peak and then is lost in the sky. They want a love that, like Cupid, does not grow; not a love which dies in order to ascend, like the Risen Christ, who accepts defeat and conquers it by Love. They want the impossible: repetition without satiety, which no human body can give. The refusal to surrender the horizontal for the vertical, because it demands sacrifice, condemns the heart to mediocrity and staleness. Love is no bargain. It appears so attractive, like a precious violin advertised at a low price, but one discovers that after one has it without much effort it is useless unless one disciplines himself to its use. The cross is a far better picture of what love really is than Cupid. The latter's darts are shot in the dark in a moment when the heart least suspects it; but the cross is something one sees on the roadway of life a long time ahead, and the invitation to carry it to a resurrection of love is frightening, indeed. That is why the Sacred Heart has so few lovers. They want that cross streamlined, without Him, who said: "If any man has a mind to come my way, let him renounce self, and take up his cross daily, and follow me" (Luke 9:23).

The ascension of love in marriage proceeds through three stages, each of which has its transfiguration. These three loves are *eros*, or sex love; personal love; and Christian love.

Sex love is here understood as carnal love outside of marriage, or in marriage with a denial of its social function. There is no direct connection between sex love and personal love. Sex love of another is for the sake of pleasure which the other person gives the ego. The partner is regarded as one of the opposite sex, instead of as a person. The infatuation associated with it is nothing but the boundless desire of self-centeredness to express itself at all costs. Because it cares only for its own rapture and its own fulfillment, such love most quickly turns to hate when no longer satisfied. With promiscuity and divorce so very general, with each one looking for his own pleasure without regard for God's directions about love, it is only natural that our century should be the one to unveil the mystery of sex. Those who believe that there are other loves beyond the carnal are not so anxious to unveil sex as they are to have the higher loves revealed. If, on entering a home with three floors, one deludes himself into believing that there is nothing above the basement where the id lives, then, to have fun, one must explore every nook and corner of that subliminal floor. But to one who knows that there are two other floors above, each one more beautiful than the other, the joy of life will be in having these higher mysteries revealed. Literature throughout the centuries depicted love but never concentrated very much on sex until *this* century, and that is because our times refuse to believe that there is anything beyond. Modern man substitutes prodding for discovery, analysis for ascension, the scalpel for the microscope, and the couch for the *prie-dieu*.

Over and above sex love, there is *personal love*. Personal love includes sex in marriage, but in its essence it is based on the objective value of another person. The other person may be loved for artistic or moral excellence, or because of a common, sympathetic interest. Personal love exists wherever there is reciprocity, duality, and understanding. This kind of love can exist with carnal love in marriage, or quite apart from carnal love, for there is no direct connection between the flesh and love. It is possible to be in love without there being physical attraction, as it is possible to have physical attraction without being in love. Personal love is in the will, not in the body. In personal love, there is no substitution of persons possible; this person is loved, and not another. But in carnal or erotic love, since there is not of necessity a love for another person, but only a love of self, it is possible to find a substitute for the one who gives pleasure. Sex love substitutes one occasion of pleasure for the other, but love knows no substitution. No one can take the place of a mother, or a devoted husband, or a loving wife. Since personal love is directed to a person which it affirms for eternity, it has a wider range than carnal love, for it exists wherever there is a twoness and a sympathy. Sometimes it may become blind, when it overlooks the real needs and requirements of others. Such is the case with parents who spoil their children by interpreting faults as virtues, license as liberty, and anarchy as progressiveness.

Beyond each of these two is *Christian love*, which loves everyone either as a potential or actual child of God, redeemed by Christ; it is a love which loves without even a hope of return. It loves the other, not because of attractiveness, or talents, or sympathy, but because of God.

Unfolding the Mystery

To the Christian, a person is one for whom I must sacrifice myself, not one who must exist for my sake. Sex love demands carnal reciprocity; personal love finds it difficult to survive without it, but Christian love requires no reciprocity. Its inspiration is Christ, who loved us while we were sinners, and therefore unlovable. Nowhere else but in Christian love is the tortuous contradiction between infinite desire and finite being resolved, for here all human limitations become the channels to the spiritual and the eternal. The urge toward the fulfillment of self can never adequately be satisfied by another self on the same level; to attempt this is to become the victim of cynicism and boredom. Christian love alone supplies that deficiency of human love, by loving every other person for God's sake. The very fact that one suffers more in the absence of the one loved than he rejoices in the other's presence reveals that it is something unpossessed that we crave; namely, God's love, which alone can fill the emptiness of the human heart.

As personal love includes sex, so does Christian love include it in a truly Christian marriage. Even though the marriage is an unhappy one, there can still be Christian love, for the other partner is then loved for Christ's sake and for the purpose of prolonging Christ's Redemption. From a natural point of view, some people are quite unlovable. It is only when one begins to see God's love in them that they become first bearable and then lovable. As, in the physical order, it is the sick child in the family who receives the most attention and care, so, in the moral order, it is the unworthy member who becomes the object of the greatest Christian solicitation and prayer. The children who write begging for prayers for their drunken father, or for their unfaithful mother, are already trained in Christian love long before they know the meaning of sex.

No life is happy without mystery, and the greatest of all mysteries is love. Great are the joys in marriage as there is the lifting of progressive veils until one is brought into the blazing lights of the Presence of God. Whether the marriage is happy or unhappy, whether life is sweet or bitter, makes no difference to the heart which aspires to a more and more purified love. It may even be that the waters of life become more purified by running over the jagged mountain streams of suffering.

Love never grows old except to those who put its essence into that which grows old: the body. Like a precious liquid, love shares the lot of the container. If love is put in a vessel of clay, it is quickly absorbed and dried; if, like knowledge, it is placed in the mind, it grows through the years, becoming stronger, even as the body grows weaker. The more it is united with the spirit, the more immortal it becomes. Just as some theologians know about God in an abstract way, so there are some who know love only from afar. As other theologians know God through abandonment to His will, so there are those who know love because they sought it in God's way, and not their own. Once the spirit of Divine Love enters marriage, as it does at the altar, there is no magic faith introduced that the partner is absolutely perfect. But there is introduced the idea that this partner has been given by God until death and, therefore, is worthy of love for Christ's sake, always.

The sanctity of married life is not something which takes place *alongside* of marriage, but *by* and *through* marriage. The vocation to marriage is a vocation to happiness which comes through holiness and sanctity. Unity of two in one flesh is not something that God tolerates, but something that He wills. Because He wills it, He sanctifies the couple through its use. Instead of diminishing in any way the union of their spirits with one another, it contributes to their ascension in love. The union of two in one flesh is the symbol of the union of their souls, and both in turn are a symbol of the union of Christ and His Church.

Looking back on a happy married life, the spouses can see the footprints of the ascension of their love. In the first moments there is the joy of possession, which is the natural reaction of the desire of a body-soul in the face of a body-soul. Next there comes the more personal joy of giving oneself to the other, where one loves to give just to please. Finally, there comes the stage where one self is not given for the sake of the other self, but where *both* together are given to God and to His Holy Designs. It is now *unity* that is offered, and to something outside both; first to the children and through them to God, who is the bond of their unity. "I have other sheep too, which do not belong to this fold; I must bring them in too; they will listen to my voice; so there will be one fold, and one shepherd" (John 10:16). The love which sustained them at every step of the road is the Love that created them and witnessed their union. This vision becomes clearer as life goes on; the flesh has fewer overtones, and the spirit begins to play in a major chord. When the autumn of life comes they suddenly realize that they love one another more now than ever, because they love the Love which authored their love. The Lover, the Beloved, and Love now merge into a beautiful Trinity toward which they aspire.

This elevation of love from one stage to another is inseparable from the crushing of selfishness, which is the enemy of love. A young couple enter marriage with distinct personalities, and each one dreams of *his* and *her* happiness, as if they were in separate vessels. This preoccupation with personal futures soon merges into a common future and common destiny, and there is no doubt that the unity of the flesh had much to do with the unity of their minds and wills and aspirations. *External time* with its daily routines, and *internal time* with its growth in common ideals, fuse into a higher unity. That is why, in moments of physical separation, there is less a sense of being apart. The children who are born to them become successive incarnations of their one-flesh, one-heart bonds. As the economic stress of life, sickness, and habitude lay their heavy hands upon them, it becomes necessary to resign themselves to the other's incompleteness and imperfection. This means "putting up" with the shortcomings which long living together brings out.

At this point, unless there is an ascension through deeper faith, the marriage may fail. But if the other partner, despite all failings, is seen as a trust and a responsibility before God, then He is brought more and more into the picture to heal the wounds. Deceptions in a Christian marriage, instead of causing depression, summon forth a sacrifice in union with the Cross. What God has begun to work in the partners, namely, union with the pleasures of the flesh, He will perfect in the end through the joys of the spirit. Recalling that Christ still loves His Church, though it is made up of so many imperfect members, they resolve to love one another despite imperfections, that the symbol may not fail the reality. As life goes on, they become not two compatible beings who have learned to live together through self-suppression and patience, but one new and richer being, fused in the fires of God's love and tempered of the best of both. One by one, the veils of life's mysteries have been lifted. The flesh, they found, was too precocious to reveal its own mystery; then came the mystery of the other's inner life, disclosed in the raising of young minds and hearts in the ways of God; then came the fuller mystery of how they showed forth the love of Christ and His Spouse, the Church. And now the greatest mystery of all awaits them still, a mystery infinite in its unbodied essence, a mystery about which eternity cannot begin to sound its heavenly voluptuousness, and that is the mystery that made them one: the Lover, the Beloved, and Love; the Father, Son, and Holy Spirit.

8

Purity: Reverence for Mystery

The two words most often abused today are "freedom" and "sex." "Freedom" is often used to mean absence of law, and "sex" is used to justify absence from restraint. Sometimes the two words fuse into the one, "license." Reason, which should be used to justify God's law, is thus invoked to justify human lawlessness and carnality with two spurious arguments. The first is that every person must be self-expressive, that purity is self-negation; therefore, it is destructive of freedom and personality. The second argument is that nature has given to every person certain impulses and instincts, and that principal among them is sex. Therefore, one ought to follow these instincts without the taboos and restrictions which religion and custom impose. Consequently, purity is looked upon as negative and cold, or as a remnant of Puritanism, monasticism, and Victorian strait-lacedness, despite the fact that the Lord of the Universe in the first of the Beatitudes said: "Blessed are the clean of heart; they shall see God" (Matt. 5:8).

Purity is as self-expressive as impurity, though in a different way. There are two ways in which a locomotive can be self-expressive: either by keeping its pressure within the limits imposed by the designer and the engineer, or by blowing up and jumping the tracks. The first self-expression is the perfection of the locomotive; the second is its destruction. In like manner, a person may be self-expressive either by obeying the laws of his nature, or by rebelling against them, which rebellion ends in slavery and frustration. Suppose the same argument of self-expression were used in war as is used to justify carnal license. In that case, a soldier at the front who, on hearing screaming shells, dropped his gun and ran to the rear line, would be greeted by a captain full of modern self-expression and told: "I commend you for throwing off Victorian convention and moral scruples. The trouble with the rest of the army is that they are not self-expressive; they overcome their fear and fight. I shall recommend a medal of honor for asserting your personality."

There is no quarrelling with those who say, "Be yourself." The point is, which is your true self: is it to be a beast, or to be a child of God? Those who get over the wickedness of licentiousness say: "Thank God, I am myself again." This is real self-expression.

It is true that God gave us a nature equipped with certain impulses. It is also true that He expects us to obey nature. But our nature is not animal but rational. Since it is rational, our impulses ought to be used rationally: that is, for the highest purposes, and not the lowest. Many a man has a hunting instinct and so has a fox, but a man ought not to go hunting mothers-in-law. Everyone has an eating impulse, but no one ought to drink sulphuric acid. These basic impulses are used according to reason, and so should one use the impulses of life. Just as dirt is matter in the wrong place, so lust is physical energy in the wrong place.

Purity at times does appear to be negative because it has to resist so many attacks upon it. Too often those who are its greatest defenders present it to the young as if it were wholly repression. Their purity themes strike two notes: "Avoid what is impure" and "Imitate the Blessed Mother." The first makes the young wonder why their instinct of procreation should be so strong, if it has evil associated with it. The second gives no explanation of how the Blessed Mother is to be imitated. The ideal is so high and abstract as to seem impractical to the young. But as pure water is more than the absence of impurities, as a pure diamond is more than the absence of carbon, and as pure food is more than the absence of poison, so purity is more than the absence of voluptuousness. Because one defends the fortress against the enemy it does not follow that the fortress itself contains no treasure.

Purity: Reverence for Mystery

Purity is reverence paid to the mystery of sex. In every mystery, there are two elements; one visible, the other invisible. For example, in Baptism, water is the visible element, the regenerating grace of Christ is the invisible element. Sex is a mystery, too, because it has these two characteristics. Sex is something known to everyone, and yet it is something hidden from everyone. The known element is that everyone is either male or female. The invisible, hidden, mysterious element in sex is its capacity for *creativeness*, a sharing in some way of the creative power by which God made the world and all that is in it. As God's love is the creative principle of the universe, so God willed that the love of man and woman should be the creative principle of the family. This power of human beings to beget one made to their image and likeness is something like God's creative power, inasmuch as it is related to freedom; for God's own creative act was free.

Breathing, digestion, and circulation are to a great extent unconscious and involuntary. These processes go on independently of our wills, but our power to "create" either a poem, a statue, or a child, is free. In that moment when freedom was born, God said: "Creatures, create yourselves." This divine commission to "increase and multiply" new life through love is a communication of the power by which God created all life (Gen. 1:28). Not like wanton children, playing recklessly with the levers of the universe, are man and woman sent into this world. Rather, they are intended to see that the torch of life, which God has put into their hands, is to burn controlled unto the purpose and destiny set by reason and reason's God. Purity is reverence paid to the mystery of sex, and the mystery of sex is creativeness.

The mystery of creativeness is surrounded with awe. A special reverence does envelop the power to be co-creators with God in the making of human life. It is this hidden element which in a special way belongs to God, as does the grace of God in the sacraments. Those who speak of sex alone concentrate on the physical or visible element, forgetting the spiritual or invisible mystery of creativeness. Humans in the sacraments supply the act, the bread, the water, and the words; God supplies the grace, the mystery. In the sacred act of creating life, man and woman supply the unity of the flesh; God supplies the soul and the mystery. Such is the mystery of sex.

In youth, this awesomeness before the mystery manifests itself in a woman's timidity, which makes her shrink from a precocious or too ready surrender of her secret. In a man, the mystery is revealed in chivalry to women, not because he believes that woman is physically weaker, but because of the awe he feels in the presence of mystery. Because, too, of the reverence which envelops this mysterious power which came from God, mankind has always felt that it is to be used only by a special sanction from God and under certain relationships. That is why, traditionally, marriage has been associated with religious rites, to bear witness to the fact that the power of sex, which comes from God, should have its use approved by God because it is destined to fulfill His creative designs.

Certain powers may be used only in certain relationships. What is lawful in one relationship is not lawful in another. A man can kill another man in a just war, but not in his private capacity as a citizen. A policeman can arrest someone as a duly appointed guardian of the law fortified with a warrant, but not outside of that relationship. So, too, the "creativeness" of man and woman is lawful under certain relationships sanctioned by God, but not apart from that mysterious relationship called marriage.

Purity is now seen not as something negative, but positive. Purity is such a reverence for the mystery of creativeness that it will suffer no schism between the use of the power to beget and its divinely ordained purpose. The pure would no more think of isolating the capacity to share in God's creativeness than they would think of using a knife apart from its humanly ordained purpose, for example, to stab a neighbor. Those things which God has joined together, the pure would never separate. Never would they use the material sign to dishonor the holy inner mystery, as they would not use the Bread of the altar, consecrated to God, to nourish the body alone.

Purity, then, is not mere physical intactness. In the woman, it is a firm resolve never to use the power until God shall send her a husband. In the man, it is a steadfast desire to wait upon God's will that he have a wife, for the use of God's purpose. In this sense, true marriages are made in Heaven, for when Heaven makes them, body and soul never pull in opposite directions. The physical aspect, which is known to everybody as sex, is never alienated from the invisible, mysterious aspect which is hidden from everyone except the one willed by God to share in God's creativeness, in God's own good time. The pure in heart shall see God, because they always do His will. Purity does not begin in the body, but in the will. From there it flows outward, cleansing thought, imagination, and, finally, the body. Bodily purity is a repercussion or echo of the will. Life is impure only when the will is impure.

Experience bears out the definition of purity as reverence for mystery. No one is scandalized at seeing people eat in public, or read in buses, or listen to music on the street, but they are shocked at dirty shows, foul books, or undue manifestations of affection in public. It is not because we are prudes, nor because we were educated in Catholic schools, nor because we have not yet come under the liberating influence of a Freud, but because these things involve aspects of a mystery so deep, so personal, so incommunicable, that we do not want to see it vulgarized or made common. We like to see the American flag flying over a neighbor's head, but we do not want to see it under his feet. There is a mystery in that flag; it is more than cloth; it stands for the unseen, the spiritual, for love and devotion to country. The pure are shocked at the impure because of the prostitution of the sacred; it makes the reverent irreverent. The essence of obscenity is the turning of the inner mystery into a jest. Given a hidden presence of a God-gift in every person, as there is a hidden Divine Presence in the Bread of the altar, each person becomes a kind of unconsecrated host. As one discerns the Bread of Angels under the sign of bread, so one discerns a soul and potential co-partnership with God's creativeness under a body. As the Catholic craves the embrace of Christ in the Blessed Sacrament because he first learned to love Him as a Person, so he reveres the body because he first learned to revere the soul. This is adoration in the first instance, and purity in the second.

Educators who hope to make sex "nice and natural" will end in confusion worse confounded because, while sex is natural, it is yet a mystery. It is not body wholeness but body holiness, and to be holy means to live in correspondence with God's creative purpose. Educators who assume that purity is ignorance of life are like those who think that temperance is ignorance of drunkenness.

On the positive side, purity is the sacristan of love, the reverence paid to the sanctity of personality, the tribute paid to a mystery. It is not the abjuration of desire, it is the culture of the desire to love; it refuses to allow material signs and symbols to be prostituted of the holy content and meaning with which God had endowed them. Purity is a vision, the seeing of the soul in the body, a holy purpose in the flesh. Virginity among pagans meant a bodily condition, a physical intactness, a preserved isolation, to which there was nothing corresponding in the man. Hence, pagans never glorified the virgin man, but only the virgin maid. But with Christianity, virginity ceased to mean physical intactness, but unity. It meant not separation but relationship, not with the will of another person alone, but also with the will of God.

The Holy Word of God tells us: "It is not well that man should be without companionship" (Gen. 2:18). Happiness was born a twin. There can be no love without otherness. Purity, too, has its relationship, namely, to the will of God, whence flows the sacredness of personality. Not even the most pure ever understood purity as isolation, negation, or detachment. And here we touch on the way the Blessed Mother is the example of purity. The Blessed Mother consecrated her virginity to God, for she was in love not with the lovable, but with Love. Her first love was the last love, which is the Love of God. When the Angel announced to her that she was to become the Mother of God through the power of the Holy Spirit, her purity of intention remained absolutely unchanged, for by the will of God, a virgin could now be a mother. Whatever the will of God decreed, would be to her a loving command. Her virginity was finding a new expression, namely, in bearing a Son, rather than in bearing none.

What the modern world calls "sex" has two sides: it is personal, and it is social. God has associated personal pleasure with the two acts essential for life: eating and procreation. The first is necessary for individual existence; the second is necessary for society. Now, God never intended that the personal pleasure of either should be differentiated from its purpose.

Purity: Reverence for Mystery

It would be wrong to eat, and then tickle one's throat in order to disgorge what one had eaten, because eating has an individual function, the preservation of life. In like manner, it would be wrong to say that "sex" is purely personal, when it is primarily social. Its function is obviously social, unless distorted by the perverse will of man. Personal pleasure of husband and wife is the "sweet snare" of God to complete His creation.

In the case of Mary, the personal element of pleasure was absent, the social was present. She asked of motherhood none of its enticements, allurements, or pleasures. The only love she wished was the love of God. It is not uncommon to find generous souls who willingly surrender all personal advantages for the sake of the betterment of their fellowman. Mary is the supreme instance of one assuming the social responsibilities of marriage without asking God for the recompense of personal love.

Because she is both Virgin and Mother, she becomes the model of purity, not only for consecrated virgins but also for those whose love is sacramentalized in marriage. What makes her purity imitable to all, in varying degrees, is the fact that she kept her purity for God's will. At first, she thought it would always be serving God in the Temple, but after the visit of the angel, she learned it would be by bearing the Messiah. So the watchword of her purity was: "Be it done unto me according to thy word" (Luke 1:38). Purity is the guardian of love until God's will manifests itself. Mary's purity to man and maid means that each will keep his or her mystery sacred, until God's holy will determines the one to whom it is to be revealed. The preservation of innocence is not due to prudery, to fear, to love of isolation, but to a passionate desire to preserve a secret until God gives the one to whom it can be whispered.

There is, therefore, no such thing as an "old maid" or a "bachelor" from the Christian point of view. These terms apply only to those unhappy ones who have found no will to share, no purpose to fulfill either in Heaven or earth. To find no ear in Heaven or on earth to listen to "I love you," or "I surrender," or "Be it done unto me according to thy word" (Luke 1:38), must indeed be of all human existences, the most tragic. But to keep the secret for God, until God calls to another in time, is the greatest happiness given to hearts in this vale of tears.

It may very well be that, with God's special grace, the secret in some will be kept forever, because of the desire that no other shall know it but God Himself. Such is in brief the religious life of consecrated souls: the pursuit of God through purity. Although many minds are willing to concede that the real goal of the human heart is God, they are not willing to admit that one should seek it directly. Hence, they raise a protest against the young men and women who, in the full bloom and blossom of life, embrace the cross. They can understand why a human heart should weave the tendrils of its affection around a passing love, but they cannot understand why those tendrils should twine about a Cross on which hangs Eternal Love. They can understand why youth should love the lovely, but they cannot understand why it should love Love. They quickly comprehend why affection should be directed toward an object which age corrodes and death separates, but they cannot grasp the meaning of an affection which death makes more intimate and present.

Despite the failure of many to understand the call of God's love, there are always some hearts, like Saint Agnes, who could say before her martyrdom, when an earthly love was presented to her: "The kingdom of the world and every ornament thereof have I scorned for the love of Jesus Christ, my Lord, whom I have seen and loved, in whom I have believed, and who is my Love's choice"! Young men and women are constantly putting their whole selves at the disposal of God, knowing that the value of every gift is enhanced when it exists solely for the one to whom it is given, fulfills no other purpose, and remains unshared. It is only natural that hearts which are so much in love with God should build walls around themselves—not to keep themselves in, but to keep the world out.

To those awaiting marriage, purity is the same in essence: the keeping of the seed in the granary until God sends the springtime. No one would plant flowers in a wintry December. He would wait on God's will for the season, however great his impatience. Purity is love awaiting fecundation, understood as the overshadowing of the Holy Spirit of Love. The Blessed Mother at the Annunciation is a perfect picture of purity awaiting God's time for fecundation, although to her surprise it was to be done not through man, but through the overshadowing of the Holy Spirit.

Purity: Reverence for Mystery

Purity is not something which is peculiar to the unmarried alone but to the married, in the sense that both hold themselves in readiness to do God's will and to fulfill His mystery. The purity in each differs to the extent that the will of God is fulfilled either directly or indirectly through the intermediary of another human. Purity is the merging of a great desire and passion into a cosmology. It never isolates the passion from the divine plan for the entire universe. Purity in the young destined for marriage begins by being universal, and develops by being particular. It is first on the periphery of the circle, and then at the center. It begins by awaiting God's will in general, and then through acquaintance and courtship sees that will focused on one individual. Once it is brought to great centrality in the union of two in the one flesh, it then pays back creation by expanding from the center to the circumference, from the particular to the universal, by the begetting of the family. But in souls consecrated to God, purity is never focused on a particular person but is a constant tendency to universality, by loving and praying for all men as children of God.

Impurity is the concentration on the individual without regard for the universal. It is the isolation of love from otherness; the utilization of tenderness for selfish ends; the turning in upon oneself of that which by its nature was meant to be outgoing. Impurity is introversion, as the miser is an introvert when he hoards his gold; it is the use of pleasure for the sake of excitation alone, and not as an exhilaration to reach the summits of life; it is the man seeing love as male, and the woman seeing love as female, in the sense that love is directed only to self-enjoyment. Impurity is a distraction from the cosmic and the universal, the affirmation of the non-eternal, the isolation of one part of self from the totality of life, and hence it is a deformation of life.

Sang Shakespeare:

> Such an act
> That blurs the grace and blush of modesty,
> Calls virtue hypocrite, takes off the rose
> From the fair forehead of an innocent love

And sets a blister there, makes marriage vows
As false as dicers' oaths; O! such a deed
As from the body of contraction plucks
The very soul, and sweet religion makes
A rhapsody of words.

Purity is first psychical before it is physical. It is first in the mind and heart, and then overflows to the body. In this it differs from hygiene. Hygiene is concerned with a *fait accompli*; purity, with an attitude before the act. Our Lord said: "But I tell you that he who casts his eyes on a woman so as to lust after her has already committed adultery with her in his heart" (Matt. 5:28). Our Savior did not wait until the thought became the deed but entered into a conscience to brand even a thought impure. If the rivers that pour into the sea are clean, the sea itself will be clean. If it is wrong to do a certain thing, it is wrong to think about that thing. Purity is reverent inwardness, not biological intactness. It is not something private, but rather something secret which is not to be "told" until it is God-approved.

Purity is a consciousness that each possesses a gift which can be *given* only once, and can be *received* only once. In the unity of flesh he makes her a woman; she makes him a man. They may enjoy the gift many times, but once given it can never be taken back, either in man or in woman. It is not just a physiological experience, but the unraveling of a mystery. As one can pass just once from ignorance to knowledge of a given point, for example, the principle of contradiction, so one can pass just once from incompleteness to the full knowledge of self which the partner brings. Once that border line is crossed, neither belongs wholly to self. Their reciprocity has created dependence; the riddle has been solved, the mystery has been revealed; the dual have become a unity, either sanctioned by God or in defiance of His will.

Those who say that purity is ignorance of "the facts of life" are like those who think that knowledge is ignorance of illiteracy. Our Blessed Mother was not ignorant of the mystery of life's begetting, for when the angel appeared to her, she asked: "How can that be, since I have no knowledge of man?" (Luke 1:34). She had consecrated her virginity to God, hence, her problem was how to fulfill that consecration with God's presently revealed will for her to become a mother. But she was not ignorant of life or its purposes. The very vow she had taken implied that she knew what she was giving up. What followed reveals that purity is not something negative, or coldness, but basically a desire, a love for God's intent in relation to a mystery. It is passionless only to those who think that love is bodily passion, and if this were so, how could God be love? If purity were absence of love, how could the Blessed Virgin have become the Mother of our Lord? It is absolutely impossible to have creativeness without love. God could not beget an Eternal Son without Love; God could not make the earth and the fullness thereof without Love; Mary could not conceive in her womb without Love. She did conceive without human love, but not without Divine Love. Though fragmentary human passion was lacking, Divine Love was not, for the angel said to her: "The Holy Spirit will come upon thee, and the power of the most High will overshadow thee" (Luke 1:35). Since purity is reverence for the mystery of creativeness, who was more pure than the woman who bore the Creator of Creativeness and who in the ecstasy of that love could say to the world in the language of G. K. Chesterton: "In thy house lust without love shall die. In my house love without lust shall live"?

Because purity is reverence for the mystery of creativeness, it has its range from the child to the youth, from the altar to the home, from the widowed to the consecrated, differing in degrees but not in the sublime consciousness that there must be a divine permission to lift the veil of the mystery. Because purity is the guardian of love, the Church bids all her children look to Mary as their protectress and model. Mary is the abstraction of love from Love; the soft halo of the love of Jesus; the hearth of His Flame; the Ark of His Life. Because she kept her secret until the fullness of her time had come with the Angel's announcement, she became the hope of those who are tempted to premature exploitation of the mystery. There is no class or condition of souls she does not teach that bodily purity is the echo of the will.

From a purely human point of view, there is something incomplete about virginity, something unshared, and something kept back. On the other hand, there is something lost in motherhood, something surrendered, something irrevocable. But in Mary alone, the Virgin and Mother, there is nothing incomplete, nothing lost. She is a kind of springtime harvest, an October in May, wherein the incompleteness of virginity is complemented by the fullness of her motherhood, and where the surrender of her motherhood is forestalled by the preservation of her innocence. Virgin and Mother, she is the common denominator of all because of her sovereign surrender to divine will. She is a Virgin because she sought God's will directly; she is a Mother for exactly the same reason. To man and maid who marry to do God's will through one another, to man and maid who do God's will directly, she is their helper, their guide, their virgin, their mother. She reveals that it is possible to have love without lust, or what Thompson calls "a passionless passion. a wild tranquillity." To those who have surrendered the mystery of life without reference to its creative purpose, Mary is still the hope, for it was she who chose as a companion beneath the Cross that wounded thing the world knows as Magdalen. When Mary stoops down to the broken flowers of humanity in the dark swamps of eroticism, she puts them not in the vase of humanity but bears them upward, as she did Magdalen, to the very altar of God.

To the married, too, Mary is the model, for Sacred Scripture mentions her before her Son as being present at the marriage feast of Cana. In no better way could she reveal the necessity of sacrifice for happy married love than by gently provoking her Son to work His first miracle and thus prepare His hour of sacrifice on the Cross. By implication the married couple were to love by sacrificing themselves for one another, as she surrendered her Son for the love of the world.

A tremendous impetus to purity is given by the Church in holding up the example of our Blessed Mother as a model for the young. There is hardly a young man or woman who has not, at one time, heard from his own mother these words, "Never do anything of which your mother would be ashamed." She means that the basic reason for being good is the consecration of self to something higher than self. When a mother

makes her appeal to a higher love than love of the child, she is trying to
make her children see that they should aim to care for another person
rather than having the other person care for them. But to do this, they
must have a love higher than their own will and pleasure. Since there is
another life beyond the natural, and higher love than the human, what
was more natural than for our Blessed Lord to say to us all from the Cross:
"Behold thy Mother!" (John 19:27). It was the divine way of saying:
"Never do anything of which your Heavenly Mother would be ashamed."

Francis Thompson wrote:

> But Thou, who knowest the hidden thing
> Thou hast instructed me to sing,
> Teach Love the way to be
> A new Virginity.

> Do Thou with Thy protecting hand
> Shelter the flame Thy breath has fanned;
> Let my heart's reddened glow
> Be but as sun flushed snow.

> And if they say that snow is cold,
> O Chastity, must they be told
> The hand that's chafed with snow
> Takes a redoubled glow?—

> That extreme cold like heat doth sear?
> O to the heart of love draw near,
> And feel how scorching rise
> Its white cold purities.

> But Thou, sweet Lady Chastity,
> Thou, and Thy brother Love with Thee,
> Upon her lap may'st still
> Sustain me, if you will.

9

The Dignity of the Body

Sex is a function of the whole personality and not of the body alone, much less of the sex organs alone. Plato and his followers bequeathed the false idea to history that man is primarily spirit, or a rational being who, unfortunately, has a body. The soul, according to him, is in the body as a man rowing is in the boat. As there is no intrinsic connection between the two, so neither is there an intrinsic bond between body and soul. For later and wiser philosophers, body and soul are not two distinct things but two irreducible and implied aspects of the one sole being, which is man. It is not, therefore, the sex organs which have sexual desires, it is the self, or human personality. Hence, their use or abuse is fundamentally a moral problem, because it is the act of a free being. The very impetuosity of carnal desires, the urgency of their impulses, are an indication that not a biological organ but the needs of personality are clamoring for satisfaction. Even the most materialistic, who deny that man has a soul, agree with the Christian position in affirming that sex does affect the ego and the spheres of mental life. If sex were only a physiological phenomenon restricted to a certain area, it would not have much repercussion on the psychic life of individuals. Precisely because it is essentially bound up with the body-soul unity of a human, it affects him mentally, morally, and socially.

Our Divine Lord, in warning personality to keep itself integrated by refusing to allow carnal explosions to disturb right reason, said: "If thy right eye is the occasion of thy falling into sin, pluck it out and cast it away from thee; better to lose one of thy limbs than to have thy whole body cast into hell. And if thy right hand is an occasion of falling, cut it off and cast it away from thee; better to lose one of thy limbs than to have thy whole body cast into hell" (Matt. 5:29–30). Since the body affects the soul for good or evil, it is better to do violence to the body than to violate purity of soul. Our Lord did not mean here a physical plucking of an eye or an amputation of an arm but a self-denial in their use, rather than permitting them to be an occasion of sin. In the same vein our Lord warns: "There is no need to fear those who kill the body, but have no means of killing the soul; fear him more, who has the power to ruin body and soul in hell " (Matt. 10:28). The Divine Savior would never have made such a demand if the exercise of one organ of the body did not affect the harmony of life as a whole.

The disciplining of the errant impulses of the body when they initiate against the soul and its destiny in no way implies a disrespect for the body, any more than putting a bridle in a horse's mouth means a disrespect for the horse. It is merely a means of bringing out the best that is in it for the sake of the master. The bridling of passions in like manner is for the sake of bringing out the best that is in man for the sake of the Divine Master! If there had been no disharmony in man because of the original rebellion against God, there would be no need of taming the body. It now revolts against the spirit, because the spirit revolted against God. Because so many identify asceticism of the body with being anti-body, as they might identify housebreaking a dog with being anti-dog, it is necessary to recall some Christian truths about the dignity of the human body.

The body supplies the raw material for thinking. Our minds at birth are like blank sheets of paper; our eyes, ears, sense of touch, write their impressions on the infant's mind. Later on, the mind working on this sensible data develops them into abstract thoughts, the sciences and the arts. As it is not sex but man who mates, so it is not intelligence but man who thinks. Since the body is the tool of one's knowing, as well as the instrument by which one becomes conscious of himself, it is honorable in the sight of God who made it, and ought to be honorable in the sight of men who were made by God.

The body is also the means by which we enter into communion with one another: *verbally*, through words, which are broken fragments of the Eternal Word; *physically*, by the assistance of our neighbor in the common tasks of daily life, culture, and civilization; *artistically*, in the dance, the theater, and the arts; *sexually*, by reducing duality to unity, which is the mission of love; *religiously*, by adding force to prayer in outward symbols, such as by kneeling to express the humble attitude of the soul before God.

The body is also a constant reminder of some basic tension, pull, and dichotomy, existing inside of personality. Ovid, noting it, said: "I see and approve the better things of life, and the worse things of life I follow." The ideals our mind conceives the body does not always attain, and then only with the greatest of effort. The inner antagonism of body and soul, this conflict of the ego and the id, this consciousness of the body and mind having different landing fields for their respective pleasures, suggests that the *complete solution* is not to be found within the soul-body unity itself, for that is the seat of the conflict. As the teacher is outside the mind, and the physician outside the body, so the body and soul, in their moments of opposition, recognize the need of a Teacher and a Physician who is more than human, to pacify the civil war within.

From the Christian point of view, the body is noble, because the Son of God took a body, or human nature, like ours in all things save sin. God descended to the body and so assumed it that of Christ, we say: "In Christ the whole plenitude of Deity is embodied, and dwells in him" (Col. 2:9). Our Lord called His body a temple, because a temple is a place where God dwells. The carnal-minded could not pierce the depth of His thought when He said to them: "Destroy this temple, and in three days I will raise it up again" (John 2:19). He here referred to the lapse of time between Good Friday, when His body would be delivered to His enemies, and the Resurrection, when His body would be glorified for all eternity.

The body is noble because the Son of God, in assuming flesh, did not do so by appearing in the full bloom and blossom of manhood. He thought so much of it, that He took His body from the body of a woman:

"He took birth from a woman" (Gal. 4:4). Like every body that He made, His, too, drew nourishment from her body and blood; like all the children of men, He was nursed at her breasts and remained with her for thirty years in obedience. It is thanks to a body that the world could see God in the form of a man; it is thanks to a body that this God-Man could utter the sweetest word that has rung down the corridors of history: "Mother."

The body is again noble because through it the fruits of Christ's Redemption are communicated to the soul. In *Baptism* the ears are touched to open them to the hearing of God's truth; the nostrils are touched to make them avenues for the odor of sanctity; the tongue is touched with salt to preserve the spiritual truths into fearless confession; the head is touched with water to wash away the guilt of Original Sin, and to make the body the temple of the Living God. In the *Holy Eucharist*, the tongue is the medium by which the Body of Christ comes to our body and soul to tame the fires of the libidos, to nourish the divine life within, and to bind us to His Mystical Body the Church. In *Confirmation* the body is touched by a blow on the cheek to remind the future soldier of Christ that he must be ready to suffer anything for Christ's cause. In the Sacrament of *Penance*, the body humbles itself by kneeling and makes the tongue declare the secrets of the soul, that the soul being cleansed, the body may once more be the temple of God. Then, in expiating its faults, the body is used either for penitential prayers, or is subjugated by fasting, or is deprived of its comforts by alms. In the Sacrament of *Holy Orders*, the body surrenders the right to be two in one flesh in order to be two in one spirit with Christ; it receives the breath of another body to symbolize the conferring of the powers of the Holy Spirit, and has the thumb and forefinger anointed with oil, because these two members will touch the Body of Christ in the Consecration of the Mass. In the Sacrament of *Matrimony*, the man and woman administer the sacrament to themselves, the priest being a witness to the deliverance of their bodies one to another until death do them part. Finally, in the Sacrament of *Extreme Unction*, the ears, the nose, the hands, the feet, and the lips, which could have been the five channels of sins, are now purged of sin or trace of sin, as the soul for the moment leaves the body, to appear before God in judgment.

The Dignity of the Body

From another point of view, the body is noble because of all the blessings which the Church gives to it in its various vocations and duties through life. Limiting this observation solely to marriage, it may come as a surprise to some to learn that the Church has a blessing for the marriage bed. With her eyes and heart full of eternity she says in solemn tones:

> Bless, O Lord, this bed, in order that those who are to lie thereon may be re-established in Thy peace, and may persevere in Thy will, may grow old and multiply for many years, and attain to the Kingdom of Heaven.

The wedding ring has its blessing, so that even that which the finger of the body wears shall not be without its prayer:

> Bless Thou O Lord, this ring which we bless in Thy name, that she who is to wear it may render to her husband unbroken fidelity. Let her abide in Thy peace, and be obedient to Thy will, and may they live together in constant mutual love.

Then there is the blessing for an expectant mother, in which in addition to Psalm 66, the following prayer is said:

> O Lord God, Author of the universe, strong and awesome, just and forgiving, who alone art good and kind; who didst deliver Israel from every evil, making our forefathers pleasing unto Thee, and sanctifying them by the hand of Thy Holy Spirit; who didst by the cooperation of the Holy Spirit prepare the body and soul of the glorious Virgin Mary that she might merit to be made a worthy tabernacle for Thy Son; who didst fill John the Baptist with the Holy Spirit, and didst cause him to exult in his mother's womb—accept the offering of a contrite heart and the fervent prayer of Thy handmaid (N), as she humbly pleads for the life of her offspring whom she has conceived by Thy will. Guard her lying-in, and defend her from all assault and injury of the unfeeling enemy. By the obstetric hand of Thy mercy may her infant

happily see the light of day, and being reborn in holy baptism, forever seek Thy ways and come to everlasting life. Through the same Lord, Jesus Christ, Thy Son, who liveth and reigneth with Thee in unity of the Holy Spirit, God, eternally. Amen.

There is also a long ceremony of blessing for a mother after childbirth, which concludes with this prayer:

Almighty, everlasting God, who through the delivery of the Blessed Virgin Mary has turned into joy the pains of the faithful at childbirth, look kindly upon this Thy handmaid who comes rejoicing into Thy holy temple to make her thanksgiving. Grant that after this life she together with her offspring may merit the joys of everlasting bliss, by the merits and intercession of the same Blessed Mary. Through Christ our Lord. Amen.

The home in which the married live out their heaven-appointed destiny is also the object of prayer:

Thee, God the Father Almighty, we fervently implore for the sake of this home, and its occupants and possessions, that Thou wouldst bless and sanctify it, enriching it with every good. Pour out on them, O Lord, heavenly dew in good measure, as well as the fatness of earthly needs. Mercifully hear and grant the fulfillment of their prayers. And at our lowly coming, deign to bless and sanctify this home, as Thou didst bless the homes of Abraham, Isaac, and Jacob. Within these walls let Thine angels of light preside and stand watch over them that dwell here. Through Christ our Lord. Amen.

When the children are sick, the Church comes to them and prays:

O God, for whom all creatures grow in years and upon whom all depend for continued existence, extend Thy right hand upon this boy (girl) who is afflicted at this tender age, and being restored to health, may he (she) reach maturity, and ceaselessly render Thee a service of gratitude and fidelity all the days of his (her) life. Through our Lord, Jesus Christ, Thy Son, who liveth and reigneth with Thee in the unity of the Holy Spirit, God, for ever and ever. Amen.

Father of mercy, and God of all consolation, who having the interests of Thy creatures at heart, dost graciously heal both soul and body, deign kindly to raise up this sick child from his (her) bed of suffering, and return him (her) unscathed to Thy holy Church and to his (her) parents. And throughout the days of prolonged life, as he (she) advances in grace and wisdom in Thy sight and man's, may he (she) serve Thee in righteousness and holiness, and return Thee due thanks for Thy goodness. Through Christ our Lord. Amen.

O God, who in a marvellous way dost dispense the ministries of angels and of men, mercifully grant that the life on earth of this child may be protected by those who minister to Thee in Heaven. Through Christ our Lord. Amen.

And when there is a sick adult in a home, the Church prays:

Consider, O Lord, Thy faithful one suffering from bodily affliction, and refresh the life which Thou hast created, that being bettered by chastisement, he (she) may ever be conscious of Thy merciful salvation. Through Christ our Lord. Amen.

O Lord of pity, Thou the Consoler of all who trust in Thee, we pray that of Thy boundless love Thou wouldst at our humble coming visit this Thy servant (handmaid) lying on his (her) bed of pain, as Thou didst visit the mother-in-law of Simon Peter. Let him (her) be the recipient of Thy loving consideration, so that restored to former good-health, he (she) may return thanksgiving to Thee in Thy Church. Thou who livest and reignest, God, forevermore. Amen.

May the Lord, Jesus Christ, be with thee to guard thee within thee to preserve thee, before thee to lead thee, behind thee to watch thee, above thee to bless thee. Who liveth and reigneth with the Father and Holy Spirit, forever. Amen.

From an entirely different point of view, the body is noble because one day it will rise from the dead. The soul can exist without the body after death, but it always retains its disposition for the body and is destined one day to be reunited with it. Since the body contributed to the spiritual condition of the soul, it is fitting that it share in its glory if the soul is saved, and share in its shame if the soul is lost.

The bodies of the wicked shall be immortal and incorruptible, and their very incorruptibility shall be one of continuous corruption. The bodies of the just shall be immortal and incorruptible, too, but glorified after the pattern of the Risen Savior. The bodies will not be given over to the activities of generation and nutrition. Even the defects of the body in this life will disappear in the clarity of the glorified body. The natural body of the just will rise a spiritual body. The risen bodies will vary in degrees of merit, depending on the merits acquired by the soul. The glory of each soul will shine through the body as a glass reveals the color of the liquid poured into it. "The sun has its own beauty, the moon has hers, the stars have theirs, one star even differs from another in its beauty" (1 Cor. 15:41).

Man will in the afterlife remain a being of soul and body. The immortality will be not only of soul, but of body and soul, since both are necessary for the full and perfect man. The body is not a prison house, nor a tomb in which the soul is confined for a time and from which it gladly makes its escape. The loss of bodily life is a tragedy to human nature, since it is not natural for the soul to be without the body.

"I believe in the resurrection of the body," says the Apostles' Creed. This resurrection will not be due to natural causes, but will be accomplished through the power of God as its only and sufficient cause. "Why should it be beyond the belief of men such as thou art, that God should raise the dead?" (Acts 26:8). The Resurrection of Christ is the example and model of our resurrection. "Then, when this corruptible nature wears its incorruptible garment, this mortal nature its immortality, the saying

The Dignity of the Body

of Scripture will come true: 'Death is swallowed up in victory.' 'Where then, death, is thy victory; where, death, is thy sting?'" (1 Cor. 15:54–55).

This separation of body and soul at death, quite apart from any superficial explanations in the biological order, is due, fundamentally, to sin. "It was through one man that guilt came into the world; and, since death came owing to guilt, death was handed on to all mankind by one man" (Rom. 5:12). Death, though natural to the plants and animals, has the peculiar added quality of being penal in the case of man. It was the rejection of this gift of immortality by man that made death a punishment: "Except the tree which brings knowledge of good and evil; if ever thou eatest of this, thy doom is death" (Gen. 2:17).

Death as a penalty for sin could be adequately overcome only by God becoming man and taking upon Himself the punishment which our sins deserved. This could not be accomplished by a martyrdom understood as death inflicted for a noble cause. It could be done, not by death coming to take Him, but by His going out to meet death. "This my Father loves in me, that I am laying down my life, to take it up again afterward. Nobody can rob me of it; I lay it down of my own accord" (John 10:17–18). This is the reason why Christians pray to be delivered from a "sudden and unprovided death," in order that they, like their Master, may submit deliberately, as much as it lies in their power, to the penalty of death. By rising from the dead through the power of God, He overcame death. "None of us lives as his own master, and none of us dies as his own master. While we live, we live as our Lord's servants, when we die, we die as our Lord's servants; in life and in death, we belong to the Lord" (Rom. 14:7–8). By mortification and penance and "daily dying," we show forth the death of the Lord. The Christian in this world may never forget that the Risen Christ, to whom he is incorporated by Baptism, is not a white Christ but a Christ slain, and risen, and bearing in His risen body not wounds, but scars of the Crucifixion, to prove that love is stronger than death.

The Church reminds poor mortals with their weak bodies to keep their eyes on Heaven, for there are two human bodies there: the body of our Lord through His Ascension, and the body of the Blessed Mother through her Assumption. On the fifteenth of August, each year, the

Church commemorates the taking up of the holy body and soul of Mary into Paradise, where she was crowned as Queen of Angels and Saints. The Church does not teach that Mary did not die, but only that her body did not suffer corruption. If our Lord did not disdain to take on the sufferings of life to purify them, and the pang of death in order to conquer it, He would not dispense His own Mother from them. If He, the New Adam, would drink the chalice of sufferings, she, the New Eve, must have a share in them. But though she died, her body was not corrupted but assumed into Heaven. The primal penalty of sin was the dissolution of the body: "Dust thou art, and unto dust shalt thou return" (Gen. 3:19). But if corruption was the penal consequence of Original Sin, it follows that she who was preserved from Original Sin should also be preserved from its penalty, namely, corruption. Quite apart from the ancient Christian tradition concerning her Assumption, it hardly seems fitting that she, who gave to the world Him who conquered death, should herself be completely under its heel. Should not He who, by His own divine power, rose from the dead, use that same power to preserve His Mother from the grave, so that His Resurrection and Ascension should have their counterpart in a lower level in the Assumption of His Blessed Mother?

She was the flesh-girt garden of the New Adam, and it is unthinkable that the Heavenly Gardener, once He had gathered His human life from her as a garden, should suffer it to be overrun by dust. The chalice which contains the Blood of Christ does not become a profane cup when once the Wine of Life is drunk. Only holy hands may touch it. There is no reason to believe that, once He conquered sin by His Resurrection and ascended to the glory at the right hand of the Father, He could forget the one who had given Him a human nature. A son remembers his mother even more in triumph than in battle. He spoke to her in the battle of Calvary; then He should not forget to call her to Himself in the triumph of His Ascension. He who received the hospitality of this spiritual Bethlehem would not be an ungrateful Host. As the homes in which great men were born are preserved for posterity, so His home (which she is) would be preserved for eternity. If the innkeeper had only given shelter to that maid on Christmas night, history would never have forgotten his name.

The Dignity of the Body

It is incredible then that she who housed Him should not have immortality, not of name only, but of body and soul. If He who conquered death ascended into Heaven to be a Mediator between God and man, then should not she, who received the high summons to share in His Redemption, be near Him now in Heaven, to mediate between His power and our needs, as she did at Cana? Certainly she who begot Him, who empties all sepulchers, should not herself be one of its first inhabitants. Corruption ought not touch her who begot our incorruptibility, nor should she whose virginity He preserved in motherhood be now a virgin body despoiled and ravished by death. Eve, our first mother, lent her ear to the tempting Satan and justly was returned again to dust, but Mary, our new Mother, who lent her ear to the Holy Spirit, could not be the prey of the selfsame dust.

A Church once consecrated may not be delivered over to profane use, nor shall the temple of the Living God be profaned by the dust. Die indeed she ought, for she should have no other law than that to which her Son was subject; but corrupted she should not be, for she gave birth to Him who broke the jaws of death. As a member of the human race, death was normal. Clothed with the power of God, dissolution would be abnormal. There are only two empty tombs in all the world: the tomb where the Resurrection and the Life was buried for three days, and the tomb where the Mother of the Resurrection and the Life was laid when she fell asleep in the love of the Lord. Mary's empty tomb was to woman what Christ's empty tomb was to man, with this difference: that only through His power was her tomb made empty.

The Resurrection of our Lord, the Assumption of our Lady, and the glorious resurrection of the just on the last day are all varying aspects of the Christian cult of the body. Mary's Assumption in a special way proclaims this cult, for while Christ's Resurrection was by His own power, Mary's was by His special privilege. It was a kind of a stamp and seal He put upon the cult of the body, which regards it as the tabernacle of the soul and the temple of God. So long as the soul is preserved in its unity with God, one need not fear what happens to the body, for the sanctity of the soul will reassure its integrity on the day of resurrection. "There is no need to fear those who kill the body, but have no means of killing the soul; fear him more who has the power to ruin body and soul in hell" (Matt. 10:28).

The Christian idea of the body is based on the sanctity of the soul which vivifies it. The body is holy because the soul is holy. Our Blessed Lord commended the woman for "pouring this ointment over my body" (Matt. 26:12). St. Paul wrote to the Corinthians: "Have you never been told that your bodies belong to the body of Christ?... Surely you know that your bodies are the shrines of the Holy Spirit, who dwells in you. And he is God's gift to you, so that you are no longer your own masters. A great price was paid to ransom you; glorify God by making your bodies the shrines of his presence" (1 Cor. 6:15, 19, 20). The body is precious because it is vivified by a soul; the body is holy because God dwells in it, as in a temple. The more the soul is united with God, the more sacred the body becomes.

Beauty of body attracts the eyes; beauty of soul attracts God. Man sees the face; God sees the soul. Mary's beautiful purity must have been such that it attracted less the eyes than the souls of men. No one would have loved her mind or soul because of the beauty of her body, but they would have so loved her beauty of soul as almost to forget she even had a body. It is very likely that a human eye, looking on Mary, would scarcely have been conscious that she was beautiful to the eye. Just as corrupt men are made pure in thought by the sight of an innocent child, so all fleshly thoughts would have been left behind, by one vision of the Immaculate Mother. As one listens to a consummate artist playing the piano, one forgets that he has hands; so, in the ravishing melodies of Mary's Immaculateness, one would have hardly adverted to that fleshly keyboard from which they came. When one is overjoyed by the beauty of a picture, he does not pay much attention to the frame.

Lest our admiration for Mary's purity of soul make us forget the flesh-encircled Eden wherein the Heavenly Father housed His Divine Son, the Church on the feast of the Assumption proclaims the holiness of Mary's body; not the body alone in isolation from the soul, for the Church knows not body alone or soul alone, but the person. Her Assumption

The Dignity of the Body

is inseparable from her Immaculate Conception. Her escape from dust is one with her motherhood of divine life. Since Heaven had already descended to her, so, when Heaven went back to Heaven, she should be assumed to it.

The cult of the body can be understood in two ways: one after the fashion of the world, and one in the light of Mary's Assumption. Both are agreed that the body should be beautiful. The one beautifies it from without; the other beautifies it from within. One adorns the body that it may be attractive through what it has; the other adorns the body with the reflections of the virtues within. It was only after our first parents sinned that they perceived they were naked. When the soul lost its raiment of grace, the body lost its attractiveness. The less beauty the soul has, the more it needs to decorate the body. Excessive luxury of dress and vain display of external beauty are signs of the nakedness of the soul. "The beauty of the King's daughter is from within."

The blind always have kindly faces, probably because they are less materialized by the things which the rest of men see. An inner radiance seems to shine through them. Those who are naturally ugly, such as St. Vincent de Paul, become very attractive once they become saintly, as he did. The only ones who are truly beautiful are those who look beautiful when they come in out of the rain. That kind of beauty comes from the inside out, not from the outside in. It is the product of virtue, not rouge; it is not skin-deep, but soul-deep.

The cult of the body is best served by the cult of the soul. It is a by-product, not a goal; it is a fruit, not a root. That is why no one ever becomes truly beautiful until he stops trying to make himself beautiful and begins making himself good. Mary was not "full of grace" because she was beautiful; she was beautiful because she was full of grace.

Francis Thompson wrote:

> Mortals, that behold a Woman
> Rising 'twixt the Moon and Sun;
> Who am I the heavens assume: an
> All am I, and I am one.

Multitudinous ascend I,
Dreadful as a battle arrayed,
For I bear you whither tend I;
Ye are I: be undismayed!
I, the Ark that for the graven
Tables of the Law was made;
Man's own heart was one; one, Heaven;
Both within my womb were laid....

I, the flesh-girt Paradises
Gardenered by the Adam new,
Daintied o'er with dear devices
Which He loveth, for He grew.

I, the boundless strict Savannah
Which God's leaping feet go through;
I, the Heaven whence the Manna,
Weary Israel, slid on you!

10

Marriage and the Spirit

There is a law running through human nature, that he who does not spiritualize the flesh will carnalize his spirit. Sex and spirituality do not walk hand in hand; rather, one leads the other. Sex can dominate the spiritual simply through nonresistance, but for the spiritual to rule over the flesh requires discipline and effort. Just as, to discover the secrets of history, one must learn to see eternity in time, so, in order to understand marriage, one must learn to see the spirit in the flesh. When someone complained to St. Catherine of Siena that she was too much obsessed with temporal affairs to think of God, the Saint answered: "It is we who make things temporal; everything that comes from the Eternal God is good."

This is the alternative presented to every bride and groom: whether to eroticize marriage or eternalize it; whether to base it on sex or on spirit. There is a tension between the two which has its historical origins in Original Sin. But even apart from the Fall of man, there still would have been some tension because of the difference between body and soul. St. Thomas speaks of this natural tension as being due to the "necessity of matter," as opposed to the freedom of the spirit.

This does not mean that marriage must choose between sex and spirit (for without either marriage is incomplete) but rather that it must choose between giving the primacy to one or the other. It cannot be repeated too often that the human sexual desire is never simply an animal instinct and nothing more. The desire is at every moment informed and activated by the soul. Those who say the Church is opposed to sex are talking nonsense, because they refuse to understand the soul-body unity of the human person. There is no such thing as a choice between the flesh and the soul, because there is never flesh without the spirit, and never spirit without the flesh. Christianity is not against anything (except evil, and that is not a thing, but a privation), whether it be body, or soul, flesh, or sex, or mind.

There are two symbols for marriage: one is the pyramid, the other is the cellar. The Church sees each aspect of marriage as the reflection, the echo, or the shadow cast by some great Divine Truth. At the top of the pyramid is the Trinity. From this Triune Love there floods down on the sides of the pyramid (which represents time and history) the richness of this Love in Creation, revelation, the Incarnation, the Mystical Body, the Eucharist, grace, and the sacraments, one of which is marriage. Everything noble and beautiful about it is a descent from above, a shadowing forth in the flesh of that Divine Love on which it lives and feeds and grows.

The other symbol of marriage is the cellar. This cellar, or cave, is filled with some cast-off fears and fixations of rational life which have been thrown into it, as so much rubbish, by the conscious mind, either because suppressed, or repressed, or feared. In this cellar, too, are to be found the bones of animals and the memory of the animal origin of man. Marriage, in this view, is an ascent from the beast, or a push from below. The Christian view is that marriage is a descent from God, or a gift from above.

From these two views of marriage, there have developed two distinct psychological attitudes toward sex. One group talks about it as they would about eating, drinking, or politics; their jokes are seasoned with it; their reading, advertising, interests, all center about it, as if sex were the basic energy of man. The other group treats the subject with reverence and mentions it only under certain conditions, resenting what is personal being made public. The reason for this sensitiveness is not due to prudery, but to piety before the *tremendum*. It no more comes into their heads to joke about the relations of man and woman in marriage, than to joke about the relations of the soul and our Lord in Holy Communion, and for identically the same reason; they are face to face with the sacred, aye! the Divine. As a man will take off his hat on passing a Church with the Eucharistic presence of our Lord, so he will show a becoming delicacy in the face of this mystery, which makes for unity of the flesh, as Communion does for unity in the spirit.

Because spirit impregnates marriage, there is first seen in it the reflection of the Mystery of the Trinity. As the Father knows Himself in His Wisdom, or Word, or Son, who is distinct but not separate, so the husband discovers opposite to himself one in flesh with him. As the Father knows Himself in His Son, so man knows himself through the person opposite. He is present to himself in her for, thanks to sex, two persons are merged and revealed, one to the other. As the Father and Son are one in nature through the Spirit of Love which binds them, so the husband and wife find unity of sex, despite their differences, through the bond of love which makes them one. The Descent of the Holy Spirit upon the Apostles not only made them one, but also apostolic and fruitful in the development of the Mystical Body of Christ. So, too, husband and wife, through the deepening of their unifying love, become fruitful unto new life, thanks to an earthly Pentecost which begets raw material for the Kingdom of God.

The differences in the characters of man and woman have their roots in creation. "Man and woman both, he created them" (Gen. 5:2). Man is made by God; woman is made by God from man. As God is present at the creation of the world, so man is present, though in ecstasy, at the creation of woman. The immediacy and the mediacy of the origin of the two sexes are mirrored forth in their differences. Man, coming directly from God, has initiative, power, and origin. Woman, coming from God through the ecstasy of man, has intuition, response, acceptance, submission, and cooperation. Man lives more in the external world, because made from the earth and closest to it. It is his mission to rule over it and subject it. Woman lives more in the internal world, because she was created from an inner, human life. Man is more interested in the outer world; woman in the inner world. Man talks about things; woman more about persons. Man fashions the products of the earth; woman fashions life, having come from life, both divine and human. Man, more related to the earth, makes sacrifices for things which are in the future and which are abstract; woman, more related to the human, is more inclined to make sacrifices for persons and for that which is immediate. Because more objective, man is inclined to give reasons for what he loves and for what he does; woman, being more subjective and having issued from the human, is more inclined to love just for love's sake. Man's reasons for loving are because of the qualities and attributes of the beloved. Man builds, invents, conquers; woman tends, devotes, interiorizes. The man gives; the woman is a gift. Even after the Fall and the disruption of the harmony of man and woman, man, despite all disappointments, never fails to possess the image of an Ideal Woman, and woman never ceases to love the image of the Ideal Man. The Golden Age may be in the past for those who know not Redemption, but among those who see the Fall as the *felix culpa*, all humanity knows the name of the Ideal Woman, the New Eve, and everyone knows the name of the Ideal Man, the New Adam, Christ.

God creates a woman for man, to be his helpmate. "It is not well that man should be without companionship; I will give him a mate of his own kind" (Gen. 2:18). The divine creation of the two sexes is here suggested as essential from the point of view of fellowship. A helpmate does not mean servile inferiority, but rather that through differences, like a bow and violin, they would complement each other. Sex is not only the divinely willed manner in which mankind will increase and multiply; it is also to be the basis of mutual helpfulness. Not to every husband and wife is given the privilege of having a Pentecost of the flesh through the birth of a new physical body, but to every one is given the companionship which God wills should be his lot on earth.

Mutual helpfulness implies an interpretation of ideals. Nietzsche once said that before a man married, he should ask himself: "Would I be willing to talk to this woman all the days of my life?" This brings up the question of the merging of personalities. There are only two genders, but there are millions of different personalities. The body by its very physical nature is incommunicable. Two bodies cannot occupy the same space at the same time. Animals never get inside of one another's mind by mating, for there is no mind to penetrate. But there is something in a human which is communicable, and which can get inside of another personality, and that is his mind, his attitudes, his ideals, and his moods. A mere physical content can throw personalities back into their solitude and isolation in a way which never happens after a conversation.

God ordained that the unity in the flesh be not transitory, or spasmodic, but enduring until death. The body symbolizes and intensifies the union of souls. Because there is unity in spirit, in love, and in ideals, the bodies concretize and intensify that union. The happiness of marriage depends upon common denominators, and the most common denominator of all is the love of God expressed in a common liturgy, a common faith, wherein husband and wife receive the same Bread and are made one Body in Christ. When this is lacking, the love of humans lacks the best inspiration. They are like two of Leibnitz's atoms, which bump and hit one another but have no windows through which one can look out on the other. Man and woman marry to make one another happy, but they never can do this until they have agreed on *what is happiness.*

There is no solitude worse than the solitude of the one who is bound to live a dual life, or of those whose epidermal unities drive them back to themselves in greater loneliness than before. But God intends that there should be a growing-together. What started as a *passion* of love becomes an act of love and then a *habit* of love. The body of each moves the soul of each; then the soul of each moves the body of each; and finally, at the height of mutual togetherness, God moves the body and soul of each to Himself, and therefore closer to each other. The growth they know, even if God has not blessed them with children, is a growth in God. A marriage need not have children to be a divinely blessed marriage, for children depend on the will of God, cooperating with husband and wife.

Marriage exists for the sake of intimacy, and, as such, is ordained to intimacy. Feuerbach said: "A man is what he eats." In a higher order, a person becomes that with which he communes. The food which is taken into his body becomes unified with that body. In like manner, the person who has this mysterious marital communication with another body becomes "personalized" to some extent by that body, and also with that personality. The sentiments and the affections of one become the sentiments and the affections of the other in a great moment of identification. As people are united by speaking a common language, and as people are united through sharing the same ideals, so in marriage people are united in a more binding way by this new *knowledge of sex*. From this point of view, quite apart from the fruit of love in the child, this knowledge which one has of the other is not discursive, like that which comes from reason. It is rather more intuitional, in the sense of being more immediate. Marriage, by its very nature, tends to this unity, through a communication of the flesh with flesh. The very fact that God made woman as the helpmate of man means that He intended that spiritual impregnation be closely associated with physical impregnation; one without the other is contrary to His divine purpose. To use the physical basis of unity, while deliberately rejecting the mental unity which it implies, is to poison that mysterious food which came clean, from the hand of God.

Spirit impregnating sex finds its next inspiration in the Incarnation. Here is the model nuptials of all, for on the altar of Mary's flesh was celebrated the nuptials of the divine and human nature in the unity of the Person of our Lord and Savior, Jesus Christ. The great mystery of "the Word is made flesh and dwelt amongst us" (John 1:14), which was verified through her, now becomes reflected in the father and the mother, leaning over their newborn infant and saying, "Our love became flesh and dwelt amongst us." No wonder some young fathers and mothers say their prayers before the crib of their infant; in their little world, their child is God amongst them.

Pregnancy, too, becomes illumined by mystery, as the prospective mother hears the chant of the liturgy: *Non horruisti Virginis uterum.* "Thou has not despised the womb of a woman." Every descent of new life into the body of a woman is possible only because God infused the soul into the child by a creative act. The child is not the Person of God, as it was within the womb of the Virgin, but it is nevertheless the act of God, which is present within her. Nowhere within creation does God more intimately cooperate with a human than in the generation of life. The liturgy, speaking of Mary's pregnancy, says: "He whom the heavens could not contain, thou didst contain within thyself." So the mother whose model is the Mother of Mothers sees herself as bearing within her the creative act of God, which not even the universe can limit.

When, as a bride, she went to the altar, the Church said to her and her husband: "You will be two in one flesh." Looking to the Incarnation, she perceives in a dim way that such must have been Mary's thought as she bore within herself the Word incarnate. She and her Son were two in one flesh, the symbol of Matrimony. In Mary, the sexes were reconciled, and a woman and a man were one. Now, bearing the child, the mother sees how the unity of two in one flesh, which existed between her and her husband, passes into a new unity of two in one flesh: herself and her unborn child.

Mothers who know not the spirit in sex can see themselves only as higher developed animals, bearing within a new biological content. But the Catholic mother finds a model of pregnancy in the Mother who began the bringing of God to man. Physical trials become more bearable when she sees herself a co-worker with God in the making of life. A dying man in a country region of France, unable to receive the Eucharist, asked that a poor person be brought to him so that he might at least have Christ in a lesser way. The woman with the child may sometimes be unable to receive Holy Communion, but she can, with an act of faith, see that she already is bearing a lesser host within the tabernacle of her body.

The papal encyclical related Holy Orders to Matrimony, in the sense that both are the bearers of life. Mary, bearing Divine Life, the mother bearing human life, and the priest or the apostle begetting divine life through grace, are all united in a concept of pregnancy. Sex then is just a shadow cast by the spirit on the walls of the flesh.

No new life comes into being without labor. Now there is a double life to which humans can be introduced: the physical life which incorporates them to the old Adam, and the spiritual life of grace which incorporates them to the New Adam, Christ. The first is done through pregnancy;

the second through instruction of converts, teaching, missionary, and apostolic endeavor. St. Paul, taking the analogy of the mother unto himself, wrote to the Galatians: "My little children, I am in travail over you afresh, until I can see Christ's image formed in you" (Gal. 4:19). St. Paul is here saying that it takes sacrifice, prayer, and labor to bring forth a new life in Christ. Physical life is born of the womb of the flesh; spiritual life, of the womb of the baptismal font. Great as is the joy of a mother in bringing a new life into the world, greater still is the joy of an apostle in bringing a convert with new life unto Christ. The mother, too, shares this joy in seeing her child made a child of God. There are some mothers who confess that they loved their children more after Baptism than before, for the child, sharing the divine nature, became more lovable than before.

This analogy is carried further by St. Paul. Since God is goodness, and goodness tends to diffuse itself, God hates voluntary barrenness and sterility. Those who refuse to bring new life into the world will not be blessed by God. The priest who goes before the judgment seat of God without having brought souls to Christ, either through active ministry in which he saves them directly, or through a contemplative ministry in which he saves them indirectly, will be frowned upon by God. God will ask each person on Judgment Day: "Where are your children?"

Generation there must be, either physical or spiritual. There is a close connection between saving our souls and begetting life. In the spiritual order, St. James tells us that if we save a soul, we save our own. In the physical order, St. Paul tells mothers: "Woman will find her salvation in child-bearing, if she will but remain true to faith and love and holy living" (1 Tim. 2:15).

Sex and apostolate are God's twin plans for fulfilling the plan of His Redemption. The pains which a woman bears in labor help to expiate the sins of mankind, and draw their meaning from the Agony of Christ on the Cross. Mothers are, therefore, not only co-creators with God; they are co-redeemers with Christ in the flesh, as the apostle is a co-redeemer in both the flesh and the spirit. And the greatest mystery of spirit to illumine sex is that of the Mystical Body of Christ, to which we now turn.

11

The Great Mystery

God does not have one law for Holy Rollers and another for Holy Romans. Even in the natural order the lover's language is never temporal nor promiscuous. There are only two words in the vocabulary of love: "you" and "always." "You," because love is unique; "always," because love is enduring. No one ever said: "I will love you for two years and six months." All love songs have the ring of eternity about them. Love, too, has its sign language. Lovers often carve their names inside of two interlocked hearts on an oak tree to express the fixity and permanence of their love. True love "alters not when it alteration finds." Each person has only one heart, and as he cannot eat his cake and have it, so he cannot give his heart away and keep it. Jealousy, which has been instinctively inseparable from the beginnings of love, is a denial of promiscuity and an affirmation of unity. Jealousy is nature's vanguard to monogamy.

In the natural order, too, every child has a fundamental right to a real mother and father. The flesh and blood originators of life alone can put into play those spiritual forces which are essential for the development of the child. Social culture also demands a permanent bond between man and woman, for no civilization can endure without responsibility and loyalty to one's trust. When 50 percent of married couples feel that they can throw overboard pledged loyalty in order to suit their own pleasure or convenience, then the hour has struck when citizens will no longer feel a need to keep their pledges to America as citizens. Once a citizenry does not feel bound to the most natural and democratic of all self-governing commonwealths, the home, it will not be long until it ceases to feel bound to a nation. When a Mrs. White is ready to call herself Mrs. Brown, then it will only be a short time before Americans will be calling themselves Soviets. The traitors to the home today are the traitors to the nation tomorrow. A people who are not loyal to a home will not be loyal to a flag.

The permanence of the bond is necessary also for sacrifice. So long as a nation of families learns to renounce the "mine" in the "ours" of their offspring, there is strength. The family then becomes a training school in self-discipline; it crushes egotism for the sake of the group, as all members learn the supreme lesson of living with others for the sake of others. But if there is the slightest disagreement resulting from the eating of crackers in bed, or if the other party fails to give pleasure, or if the desire of greener pastures makes the present grazing less appealing; if every emotion, whim, appetite, and fancy has a right to be satisfied even at the cost of another person; then what shall happen to the sacrifice so necessary for a nation in time of crisis and conflict? The fewer sacrifices a man is required to make, the more loath he will be to make those few. His luxuries soon become necessities, children a burden, and the ego a god. Whence will come our heroes in a crisis, if we no longer have heroes in the home? If a man will not put up with the trials of a household, will he put up with the trials of a national emergency? Once the need of sacrifice for maintenance of the home is uprooted, there is simultaneously uprooted the need of sacrifice for the maintenance of a nation. Only a nation that recognizes sweat, toil, hardship, and sacrifice as normal aspects of life can save itself, and these virtues are first learned in the home.

The decline in the permanence of family life is, therefore, intrinsically bound up with the decline in democracy. Here democracy is understood, in its philosophical sense, as a system of government which recognizes the sovereign worth of a man. From this flows the notion of the equality of all men, and the repudiation of all inequalities based on race, color, and class. Nowhere is the dogma of the worth of a man better preserved and practiced than in the family. Everywhere else man may be reverenced and respected for what he can do, for his wealth, his power, his influence, or his charm; but in the family a person is valued because he *is*. Existence is *worth* in the home. That is why the crippled, the sick, and those who are of no economic value to the family are given more affection than those who normally provide for its subsistence. The family is the training school and the novitiate for democracy. Free and promiscuous marital relationships are the training ground for treating humans, first flippantly, then cruelly. The protection of the weaker members of society, the socially disinherited, and the economically dispossessed depends upon a sense of responsibility to those handicapped, which is best fostered in the home. As persons lose a sense of loyalty and obligation, the state picks it up, and then begins the tyranny of the weak. State socialism, understood as state control not only of the means of production but also of life itself, is the political expression of psychological laziness and irresponsibility first manifested in the family.

Within the broad field of culture, too, the indissoluble family tie is one of the best forces for the sublimation of awakening sex feelings. From the beginning, a boy or girl in a good family has been associated with a permanent institution whose function is the prolongation of life. Sex relationships thus become inseparably bound up with the moral and spiritual side of life. They are sublimated, not by a false self-expression which "makes hungry where most it satisfies," but, rather, by integration into a lifelong bond instead of a momentary self-indulgence. The most stable youths, from a moral point of view, come from those families where the creative instinct is inseparable from an unbroken and perpetuating love. In Dante's *Inferno* the slaves of *eros* are depicted as being whirled helplessly through the air by one gigantic, erotic whirlwind. But such aberration and uneasiness never come to those who, in a family, learned that sex and service are inseparable.

The marriage of pagans, primitives, and non-Christians in general is still a *res sacra*, because the use of the flesh of man and woman is not something completely at their disposal; it is *God's way* of preserving and continuing mankind. Their act is incomplete and insufficient to attain this end without divine cooperation, for it is God who breathes a soul into the life of a child.

Marriage is a mystery, St. Paul tells us. Its meaning becomes clear only in relation to another world of spiritual reality. It is an index and symbol of a higher world which alone gives it significance, just as the countless sacrifices throughout the centuries have meaning only in the Cross and the Atonement of our Lord. An equally important idea is that of nuptials, which has always been in Christian Revelation an earthly symbol of a Divine Reality. Throughout the Old Testament, the union of God and Israel is described as nuptials. God is pictured as the Husband; Israel as the bride; and their union is consummated in sacrifice. "Husband she calls me noe.... Everlastingly I will betroth thee to myself; by the keeping of his troth thou shalt learn to know the Lord" (Hos. 2:16–20).

As time goes on, we see a gradual evolution of the nuptial idea. The Bridegroom changes from the Lord to the One whom He sends, namely, His Divine Son. When Christ was born, this idea of nuptials was so familiar to the people that John the Baptist, with a certain casualness, says that "he was not the Christ." A moment later he implies that he is a friend of the Bridegroom, but not the Bridegroom. "He it is, who, though he comes after me, takes rank before me" (John 1:27 [30]).

Our Lord implied that He had come for His Marriage to His Spouse, the Church. Negatively, He did this by calling Israel an "unfaithful and wicked generation" (Mark 8:38). Positively, our Lord did it in His answer to the Pharisees who wanted to know why His disciples did not fast: "Can you expect the men of the bridegroom's company to go fasting, while the bridegroom is still with them? As long as they have the bridegroom with them, they cannot be expected to fast; but the days will come when the bridegroom is taken away from them; then they will fast, when that day comes" (Mark 2:19–20).

It is highly significant, too, that "Jesus began his miracles" (John 2:11) at a marriage feast. At that moment, He addressed His mother for the first time as "woman" (John 2:4), the formal title of a Bride in the spiritual sense, and as it later appears in the book of the Apocalypse. At the Last Supper, or Passover, our Lord made a new Covenant. The Passover was a sign of the nuptials of God and Israel. In this new Covenant, He was actually solemnizing a Spiritual Marriage between Himself and His Church. As a pledge of that eternal union, He gave His Body and His Blood to His Spiritual Spouse. Speaking of that unity in the analogy of the vine, He said, "You have only to live on in me, and I will live on in you. The branch that does not live on in the vine can yield no fruit of itself; no more can you, if you do not live on in me. I am the vine, you are its branches; if a man lives on in me, and I in him, then he will yield abundant fruit; separated from me, you have no power to do anything" (John 15:4–5).

When St. Paul had received his revelation directly from the Lord and began to teach, he wrote to the Corinthians: "I have betrothed you to Christ, so that no other but he should claim you, his bride without spot" (2 Cor. 11:2, 3). As Eve was a continuation or a projection of Adam's body, "bone of his bone, flesh of his flesh" (Gen. 2:23), so the Church is the continuation of Christ's Incarnation. "Each of us has one body, with many different parts, and not all of these parts have the same function; just so we, though many in number, form one body in Christ, and each acts as the counterpart of another" (Rom. 12:4–5).

The abundant references in the Scriptures to the Church as the Body of Christ have, as their basis, the idea that the Church is the Mystical Bride of Christ. The Church is His Body, because it is His Spouse. In developing the analogy, St. Paul speaks of Christ as the invincible Head of the Body, and this is because: "The head to which a wife is united is her husband" (1 Cor. 11:3). It is very likely that the divine prohibition against women appearing in church with their heads uncovered is related to this idea. As the Church can have no Divine Head other than Christ, so the woman should have no head except her husband; therefore, her natural head should be covered.

St. Paul was not saying that the union of Christ and His Church is like a human marriage, but rather that the human marriage is like the union of Christ and His Church. The realities are eternal; what happens in time is its shadow. For example, earthly fatherhood is a reflection of Heavenly Fatherhood. "Father of our Lord Jesus Christ, that Father from whom all fatherhood in heaven and on earth takes its title" (Eph. 3:14-15). Because human marriage is an imperfect reflection of a divine-human unity, it follows that sex does not enter at all into the analogy. "No more male and female; you are all one person in Christ" (Gal. 3:28). A worm's-eye view of marriage from the pasture or the stable makes it seem as if its substance were sex. A heavenly view makes marriage seem precisely what Paul calls it: "a great mystery" (Eph. 5:32).

To the Christian, however, there is added an additional sanction for the perpetual bond of husband and wife to love one another until death do them part. Every true marriage is lasting because God so ordered: "What God, then, has joined, let not man put asunder" (Matt. 19:6). But in the supernatural order of baptized souls, the marriage between Christians recalls the union of Christ and His Church. "Yes, those words are a high mystery, and I am applying them here to Christ and His Church" (Eph. 5:32). As Christ took His human nature not for three years, nor for thirty-three, but for all eternity, so do husband and wife take one another not for a time, but until death do them part. This is the basic reason why the marriage of two baptized persons is absolutely unbreakable, because it is the symbol of the unbreakable union of Christ and His Spouse. As Christ has only one Church for His Spouse, otherwise He would be guilty of spiritual adultery, so a husband may have only one wife, and a wife only one husband. As Christ would never leave His Spouse, so neither may one spouse leave the other.

In the marriage ceremony it is not simply the exchange of consent by bride and groom which constitutes the symbol of the union of Christ and the Church, but rather the *will* in that consent to make such a union a reality. The Church teaches that the Sacrament of Matrimony brings married love to its perfection. But this elevation is not due to man's efforts nor to anything human in the Church. The Council of Trent expressly stated: "It is Christ who by the merit of His Passion has obtained this grace." St. Thomas Aquinas reflects: "Although there is no likeness between marriage and that part of the Passion which is suffering, there is likeness between marriage and that part of the Passion which is love,

for Christ suffered for the Church when He became its Spouse." Thus
marriage which, in the natural order, is already a unity in love, is here
pictured as possessing a deeper unity and love through the merits of Christ
dispersed through the sacrament.

Because divinely strengthened, marriage takes on a deeper significance.
As Christ gives His Body and Blood to the Church, so now the personal
physical giving of husband and wife to each other is no longer seen as
an act in common with the animals, but as an echo of the Divine. The
gift in both instances proceeds from Love. St. Thomas Aquinas suggests
that, just as the fulfillment of the marriage of Christ and His Church
was reached through the Glorious Ascension, so in the lower order, the
fulfillment of the marriage of man and woman is reached in the consummation of the marriage. The ecstatic moment when two are in one flesh
is, to the greatest of the world's thinkers, the symbol of Ascension into
Heaven. Did the young married couple but know it, their description of
their happiness as "heavenly" is not far from the Divine Reality it was
meant to convey. It is a pity that they ever have to come down to earth,
but the shadow must not expect to be as enduring as the Substance,
which is Divine.

This same brilliant Aquinas also tells us that a marriage, before it is
consummated, represents the union of *Christ with the soul through grace*.
But once the physical union has taken place, then marriage symbolizes
the union of *Christ and the Church*. In the first instance, it is a symbol
of the individual nature of man; in the second, his social nature. The
spiritual repercussions of this doctrine are considerable. The union of
the individual with Christ can be broken by sin; but the union of Christ
and His Church is unbreakable and eternal. Canon law, reflecting this
idea, concedes that a marriage *ratum non consummatum*, or a marriage
in which the husband and wife never lived together, is breakable under
certain conditions; but the marriage bond of baptized husband and wife
which has been consummated is absolutely unbreakable.

Sacred Scripture, in developing this Mystery, never tells wives that
they must love their husbands, although husbands are bidden to love their
wives. Rather, the wives are to be subject to their husbands. This implies

no servility, for there is this parallel: Christ loves the Church, but it is for the Church to submit to Christ. Once again, St. Paul is arguing from the divine to the human nuptials, and not from the human to the divine.

Symbol	Reality
Wives must obey their husbands.	As they would obey the Lord.
The man is the head to which the woman's body is united.	Just as Christ is the head of the Church, He, the Savior, on whom the safety of His body depends.
And women must owe obedience at all points to their husbands.	As the Church does to Christ.
You who are husbands must show love to your wives.	As Christ showed love to the Church when He gave Himself up on its behalf.
And that is how husband ought to love wife, as if she were his own body; in loving his wife, a man is but loving himself.	He [Christ] would hallow it [the Church], purify it by bathing it in the water to which His word gave life. He would summon it into His own presence, the Church in all its beauty, no stain, no wrinkle, no such disfigurement: it was to be holy, it was to be spotless.
It is unheard of that a man should bear ill will to his own flesh and blood: no, he keeps it fed and warmed.	And so it is with Christ and His Church; we are limbs of His body: flesh and blood, we belong to Him.

The Great Mystery

Symbol	Reality
That is why a man will leave his father and mother and will cling to his wife, and the two will become one flesh.	Yes, these words are a high mystery, and I am applying them here to Christ and His Church.

Meanwhile, each of you is to love
his wife as he would love himself,
and the wife is to pay reverence
to her husband.

Not in these words, but with this idea, the Church asks the bride and groom: "What guarantee will you give that you will love one another until death do you part?" If they say: "We give the pledge of our word," the Church will answer: "Words and pacts can be broken, as the history of our world too well proves." If they say: "We give the pledge of a ring," the Church will again answer: "Rings can be broken and lost, and with them the memory of a promise. Only when you stake your eternal salvation as a guarantee of your fidelity to represent the union of Christ and the Church will the Church consent to unite you as man and wife." Their lives thus become bonded at the altar, sealed with the seal of the Cross, and signed with the sign of the Eucharist which they both receive into their souls as a pledge of the unity in the Spirit, which is the foundation of their unity in the flesh.

When husband and wife live their married lives as reflections of the Divine Prototype, their relations one with another become a source of merit. They save their souls through union with one another. Sacramental grace is communicated in the marriage act. If the act is nothing more than another form of the copulation of the beasts in the field, then it is bound to sicken with its own "too much," for it leaves out the soul, whose needs have to be satisfied, as well as the body. As a man labors differently when a tyrant stands over him than when he freely creates for his beloved, so husband and wife react differently to their mutual relations when they see them mirroring forth the great truths of their faith.

As each soul in the state of grace is a spouse of Christ, and as that union thrives by love which is the Spirit, so in the external order of the flesh, husband and wife ought to love one another with such abiding and sacrificial affection and mutual helpfulness as to manifest the union of Christ and His Mystical Body, the Church. Man represents the Word made flesh; woman represents humanity, toward which God bends and which is purified and united to Himself in a union so personal that it is forever His Spouse. Woman thus represents the religious vocation of humanity in the face of God. When conjugal love is understood as symbolizing this love of Christ and His Spouse, then the charity that one spouse has for the other will aid their complete spiritual development until Christ be formed in them. The avidity to possess the other in love is superseded by the interest in seeing the other grow in love of God. Everything is done for love.

The great tragedy of life is to go to the limits of love, to become a spent force, to see the élan evaporate and vanish. But this exhaustion is impossible when conjugal love is seen as the means to a deeper love. The partner cannot give the infinity which love demands, but he or she can point the way to it. Then the creature gives what it has not, as it points to love of Christ, who is now in their midst, to unite the couple more than ever in soul as well as in body. The husband or wife who has never climbed to the love of Christ has never fully understood the mystery of a spouse. As the encyclical on marriage expresses it: "This mutual inward moulding of husband and wife, this determined effort to perfect each other, can in a very real sense be said to be the chief reason and purpose of matrimony, provided matrimony be looked at not in the restricted sense as instituted for the proper conception and education of the child, but more widely as the blending of life as a whole and the mutual interchange and sharing thereof."

This beautiful prayer read in the Nuptial Mass summarizes the "Great Mystery":

O God, who by Thy mighty power didst make all things out of nothing; who having set in order the elements of the universe and made man to God's image, didst appoint woman to be his inseparable helpmate, in such wise that the woman's body took its beginning out of the flesh of man, thereby teaching that what Thou hadst been pleased to institute from one principle might never lawfully be put asunder; O God, who hast hallowed wedlock by a mystery so excellent that in the marriage bond Thou didst foreshow the union of Christ with the Church; O God, by whom woman is joined to man, and that union which Thou didst ordain from the beginning is endowed with a blessing which alone was not taken away, either by the punishment for Original Sin or by the sentence of the flood; look in Thy mercy upon this Thy handmaid, who is to be joined in wedlock and entreats protection and strength from Thee. May the yoke of love and of peace be upon her. True and chaste may she wed in Christ; and may she ever follow the pattern of holy women; and may she be dear to her husband like Rachel; wise like Rebecca; long-lived and faithful like Sara. May the author of deceit work none of his evil deeds within her. May she ever be knit to the Faith and to the commandments. May she be true to one husband, and fly from forbidden approaches. May she fortify her weakness by strong discipline. May she be grave in demeanor and honored for her modesty. May she be well-taught in heavenly lore. May she be fruitful in offspring. May her life be good and sinless. May she win the rest of the blessed and the Kingdom of Heaven. May they both see their children's children unto the third and fourth generation, and may they reach the old age which they desire. Through the same Christ, our Lord.

May the God of Abraham the God of Isaac, and the God of Jacob be with you, and may He fulfill His blessing in you, that you may see your children's children even to the third and fourth generation, and thereafter may you have life everlasting, by the grace of our Lord Jesus Christ; who with the Father and the Holy Ghost liveth and reigneth God for ever and ever. Amen.

12

The Unbreakable Bond

If the basis of marriage were sex, then it would be as promiscuous as the mating of beasts. If it is based on love, it is unbreakable. Marriage based on sex alone is like establishing a lifelong association on a love of Ping-Pong. There will come days when we cannot play, other days when we will get tired of playing, and still other days when we would like to play something else, or to play with somebody else. Identification of marriage with the pleasure which marriage brings is a misunderstanding. Then, when the first thrill is gone after a couple of years, it is felt that the bond no longer endures. We say we no longer love one another, when we mean that the exchange of selfish pleasure is no longer satisfying. Remarriage while the true partner is living is a vain attempt to give respectability to dishonor by invoking a human law which overthrows God's law: "And so they are no longer two, they are one flesh; what God, then, has joined, let not man put asunder" (Matt. 19:6). The very fact that a first marriage, born in love, can be broken for a second marriage, desired in love, proves that the most beautiful word in our language has been distorted by the lie of Satan. What is called "love" today is often nothing more than a confused mixture of sentimental pathos, disguised egotism, Freudian complexes, frustrated living, and weakness of character.

The basis of unity is the fact that in this bond two persons are joined together so as to become "one flesh" (Gen. 2:24). This inviolable bond, according to our Divine Savior, excludes not only desiring another partner but also entering into another union while the partner lives. Our Lord even forbade unlawful desires: "But I tell you that he who casts his eyes on a woman so as to lust after her has already committed adultery with her in his heart" (Matt. 5:28). These words cannot be annulled even by consent of one of the partners, for they express a law of God and nature which no one can break. He directly forbade any remarriage while one bond endured. Even though there might be a legitimate reason for the partners separating, this would not give either one the right to marry again.

"Then the Pharisees came and put him to the test by asking him, whether it is right for a man to put away his wife. He answered them, What command did Moses give you? And they said, Moses left a man free to put his wife away, if he gave her a writ of separation. Jesus answered them, It was to suit your hard hearts that Moses wrote such a command as that; God, from the first days of creation, made them man and woman. A man, therefore, shall leave his father and mother and will cling to his wife, and the two will become one flesh. Why then, since they are no longer two, but one flesh, what God has joined, let not man put asunder. And when they were in the house, his disciples asked him further about the same question. Whereupon he told them, If a man puts away his wife and marries another, he behaves adulterously towards her; and if a woman puts away her husband and marries another, she is an adulteress" (Mark 10:2–12). St. Paul confirmed our Lord's words: "For those who have married already, the precept holds which is the Lord's precept, not mine; the wife is not to leave her husband (if she has left him, she must either remain unmarried, or go back to her own husband again), and the husband is not to put away his wife" (1 Cor. 7:10, 11).

This unity of two in one flesh is not just biological, as it is in animals. Rather, it has a spiritual and psychic quality understood by few. Nowhere does Sacred Scripture speak of marriage in terms of sex. Instead, it speaks of it in terms of *knowledge*. "And now Adam had knowledge of his wife, Eve, and she conceived. She called her child Cain, as if she would say, I have been enriched by the Lord with a man-child" (Gen. 4:1). And when the Angel Gabriel announced to the Blessed Virgin that she was chosen to be the mother of God, Mary asked: "How can that be, since I have no knowledge of man?" (Luke 1:34). There was no question here of ignorance of conception but of some deeper mystery. Marriage is here related to knowledge. The closest union that exists between anything in the universe and man himself is through knowledge. When the mind knows *flower* and *tree*, man possesses these objects within his intellect. They are not identified with his intellect, but are distinct from it. These objects exist inside the mind in a new manner of being. Philosophy speaks of man, for example, not only as really and physically existing in his natural being, or *esse naturali*, but also as perceptually and mentally repeated in consciousness, or as existing in *esse intentionali*. An object outside the mind thus exists inside the mind as well and without ceasing to be itself. This union of the object and the mind, or the thing known and the knower, is one of the closest unions possible in the natural order. In the psychological order, this unity is akin to sympathy, by which one enters into another's anxiety because, in some way, his anxiety has entered into the other.

Sacred Scripture speaks of marriage as knowledge, because it represents a union much more profound and lasting, much more bound up with our psychic structure, than the mere biological unity that comes from the mating of animals. Marriage involves a soul, a mind, a heart, and a will as much as it involves reproductive organs. Because the union of man and woman is something more than a union of diverse biological functions, it has repercussions on the mind which are totally absent in the animal order. The union, therefore, may be described as psychosomatic, in the sense that it affects the whole person, body and soul, and not merely the lower part alone.

Because marriage is knowledge, it follows that its unity is one which demands fidelity. Suppose a student never knew, until he entered college, the soliloquy of Hamlet. Once he had come *to know* that, which he never knew before, he would always be *dependent* on the college which had given him that knowledge. That is why he calls that college his "beloved mother," his *alma mater*. It caused something to happen to him which was unique. He could go on enjoying the soliloquy all the days of his life, but he could never reacquire it. So, too, when man and woman come to the knowledge of another person, when they, as rational creatures, establish a unity in the flesh which before they never knew; they can go on enjoying that knowledge, but they never can reacquire it. So long as time endures, he gave to her the knowledge of man, and she gave to him the knowledge of woman. And they gave knowledge because they gave unity, not of object and mind, but of flesh and flesh. Others can repeat the knowledge, even unlawfully, but there was always someone who was the first to unfold the mystery of life.

Thus, the union between husband and wife is not an experience that may be forgotten. It is a knowledge or an identity that has permanence about it. They are "two in one flesh." From this point of view, there is nothing that happens to a woman that does not happen to man; the accidents of the union are only a symbol of a real change that has occurred in both. Neither can live again as if nothing had ever happened. There is a kind of ontological bond established between the two which is related, though not in the same order, as the bond between a mother and her child. By the very nature of things, only one person can bring this knowledge to another. This already suggests a union that is more personal than carnal. No one minds eating in public, because there is not a personal union of the food and the stomach. But making love in public is vulgar because, by its very nature, it is personal. It exists between two persons, and only two, and therefore resents intrusion or vulgarity. Their love is spoiled when others know it, and so marriage is spoiled when a third knows its secret. As the mind and its object are made one in knowledge, so man and woman are made one in flesh, even outside Matrimony, as St. Paul suggests: "Or did you never hear that the man who unites himself to a harlot becomes one body with her?" (1 Cor. 6:16).

The unification from the duality of flesh of husband and wife is one of the reasons why the Savior forbade the breaking of the bond. Both men and women, in the moment of the *knowing*, receive a gift which neither ever knew before, and which they can never know again except by repetition. The resulting psychic changes are as great as the somatic.

The woman can never return again to virginity; the man can never return again to ignorance. Something has happened to make them one, and from that oneness comes fidelity, so long as either has a body.

The second quality of faithfulness is charity, in the sense that husband and wife love one another not with adulterous love, where there is a giving of a body without a soul, but as Christ loves the Church. Here marriage is revealed not only as the symbol of knowledge, but as the symbol of His marriage with the Church, which is His Spouse. Hence St. Paul enjoins: "You who are husbands must show love to your wives, as Christ showed love to the Church when he gave himself up on its behalf" (Eph. 5:25). The encyclical of Pope Pius XI on marriage explains the effect of this symbolism:

> The love, then, of which We are speaking is not that based on the passing lust of the moment nor does it consist in pleasing words only, but in the deep attachment of the heart which is expressed in action, since love is proved by deeds. This outward expression of love in the home demands not only mutual help but must go further; it must have as its primary purpose that man and wife help each other day by day in forming and perfecting themselves in the interior life, so that through their partnership in life they may advance ever more and more in virtue, and above all that they may grow in true love towards God and their neighbor, on which indeed "dependeth the whole law and the prophets" (Matt. 22:40). For all men of every condition, in whatever honorable walk of life they may be, can and ought to imitate that most perfect example of holiness placed before man by God, namely, Christ our Lord, and by God's grace to arrive at the summit of perfection, as is proved by the example set us of many saints.

The great advantage of the vow, which binds until death, is that it guards the couple against allowing the moods of time to override reason, and thus protects the general interests from canceling the particular. There is no other way to control capricious solicitation except by a vow. It may be hard to keep, but it is worth keeping because of what it does to exalt the characters of those who make it. Once its inviolable character is recognized before God, an impulse is given to self-examination, the probing of one's faults and new efforts at charity. It is too terrible to contemplate what would happen to the world if our pledged words were no longer bonds. No nation could extend credit to another nation if the compact of repayment was signed with reservations. International order vanishes as domestic society perishes through the breaking of vows. To say, two years after marriage: "I gave my oath at the altar, yes, but since I am in love with someone else, God would not want me to keep my oath," is like saying: "I promised not to steal my neighbor's chickens, but since I fell in love with that handsome Plymouth Rock, God would not want me to keep my promise." Once we decide, in any matter, that passion takes precedence over truth, and erotic impulse over honor, then how shall we prevent the stealing of anything, once it becomes "vital" to someone else? As Chesterton put it:

> Numbers of normal people are getting married, thinking already that they may be divorced. The sincere and innocent Victorian would never have married a woman reflecting that he could divorce her. He would as soon have married a woman reflecting that he could murder her. The psychological substance of the whole thing has altered; the marble has turned to ice, and the ice has melted with most amazing rapidity. The Church was right to refuse even the exception. The world has admitted that exception, and the exception became the rule.... They ought surely to know that the foe now on the frontiers offers no terms of compromise; but threatens a complete destruction. And they have sold the pass.

When fidelity to spouse is the echo of the fidelity of Christ and His Church, then the couple is bound together not in a collective egotism, but in true charity. As our Lord loves His Church and the Church loves Him, so married love is not an exchange of services but a living fellowship. Each takes all the other has or is, and uses it for the benefit of the other and for the love of God. Fidelity is related to obedience, and obedience implies order. Nothing is so much inclined to provoke the unthinking as the assertion that there is a hierarchy in love. This order includes the primacy of the husband in regard to the wife and children, and the obedience of the wife and children to the husband. Such is the divine command: "Let women be subject to their husbands" (Eph. 5:24). Those who have no understanding of function regard this order in love as the servile subjection of the wife to the husband, which it is not.

The relation between husband and wife is the relation, again, of Christ and the Church. "Wives must obey their husbands as they would obey the Lord; the man is the head to which the woman's body is united, just as Christ is the head of the Church, he, the Savior, on whom the safety of his body depends" (Eph. 5:22–23). As Christ does not deprive His Church of liberty, but gives to all the members of His Body the "glorious liberty of the children of God" (Rom. 8:21), so neither does the primacy of the husband take away any freedom that belongs to the dignity of a human person. It does not imply a servile obedience to the husband's wishes if contrary either to right reason or the dignity of the wife, nor does it place the wife on the level of the children, for children are subject to both father and mother. But the order of love does forbid to the wife a license which would destroy the good of the family.

In the words of the papal encyclical on marriage: "It forbids that in this body which is the family, the heart be separated from the head to the detriment of the whole body.... For if the man is the head, the woman is the heart, and as he occupies the chief place in ruling, so she may and ought to claim for herself the chief place in love." If the husband should be recreant in his duty, then the double empire of ruling and loving would fall to the wife. In no sense then is the wife the servant, but rather the companion of man, their relations always being governed by Divine Charity "both in him who rules and in her who obeys, since each bears the image, the one of Christ, the other of the Church." The notions of despotism, tyranny on the part of the husband, and a sense of inferiority and subjection on the wife's, vanish when the relationship is seen as modeled upon the union of Christ and His Spouse, the Church. Christian perfection, which consists in the self-donation of the soul to Christ, finds its symbol in the ordering of wife to husband, from which the husband learns the necessary indigence of the creature in the face of the Creator.

St. Peter, developing this theme, wrote: "You, too, who are wives must be submissive to your husbands. Some of these still refuse credence to the word; it is for their wives to win them over, not by word but by example; by the modesty and reverence they observe in your demeanour" (1 Pet. 3:1–2).

The mission of the woman is a reflection of the mission of Mary, who defined herself as "the handmaid of the Lord" (Luke 1:38). Mary renders captive the heart of man to deliver him over to her Divine Son. The woman who rules by love manifests this dependence on her husband, so that the flesh might tell, in feeble babblings, what the Spirit speaketh in the Word. This is the hidden meaning of the words of St. Paul: "The man is the head to which the woman's body is united, just as Christ is the head of the Church" (Eph. 5:23). The woman by nature seeks to found her love on another; but, lest the husband should trample on that which is confided and even surrendered to him, he must in turn be subject to Christ. As, in the spiritual order, Christ, the God-Man, came to us through a woman, Mary, the New Eve; so souls return to God through the woman, Mary, the Mediator's grace. In the dimension of flesh, this order is suggested in a woman saying to a man: "Be it done to me according to thy word" (see Luke 1:38), and the man saying to God: "All things that are pleasing to Him, that I do" (see John 8:29). But since the two are in one flesh, they go to God, not in tandem fashion, but together. As Christ is one body with His Church, so husband and wife are one flesh. Since "it is unheard of, that a man should bear ill-will to his own flesh and blood" (Eph. 5:29), the symbolic primacy of the husband in ruling will never be detached from the primacy of love, where the woman is queen.

The woman is man's sister-soul. Her man is hers; she is his. From this, it follows: "And that is how husband ought to love wife, as if she were his own body; in loving his wife, a man is but loving himself" (Eph. 5:28). Man loves because he needs to love, and woman loves because she sees that she is needed. Mutual need does not have to be equal need; the need will differ with function and with nature. In a certain sense, there is no equality in love; the lover always sees the beloved as "way up there" on a pedestal, transcendent to others and beyond comparison. The beloved always sees the lover as "without an equal."

This sense of inequality is seen in its brighter light in Communion, when the soul says to God: "O Lord, I am not worthy." All love is humble. But when love leaves, equality in the strict sense takes its place. In the happy home there is no such thing as saying: "This is my chair; this is yours." But when love leaves, then comes the lawyer, the division of property, and an equality which kills all love. Genuine love excludes all servility but includes a surrender to the other of the peculiar advantages of each.

The emptiness of one calls for the fullness of the other. The relation of husband and wife is not to be understood in a mathematical or naturalistic sense, which would degenerate into whether a feminine intellect has more power than a masculine intellect. Such narrow rules assume the primacy of sex, and not the bond of love, which is really the heart of the matter. From this point of view, the man is not an overlord but a companion who labors for the happy response of his spouse. Each seeks to dignify self, not by possessing the other in lust but winning the other by honor and sanctification. "Each of you must learn to control his own body, as something holy and held in honor, not yielding to the promptings of passion, as the heathen do in their ignorance of God" (1 Thess. 4:4–5).

Fidelity in marriage implies much more than abstention from adultery. All religious ideals are positive, not negative. Husband and wife are pledges of eternal love. Their union in the flesh has a grace which prepares and qualifies both souls for the union with God. Salvation is nothing but wedlock with God. All those who have taken hold of Christ in marriage wear a "yoke that is sweet and a burden that is light" (Matt. 11:30). As yoke-mates of love, they pull together in the tilling of the field of the flesh, until there is finally revealed to them the full splendor of harvest in eternal union with God. Marital fidelity is not something added to love; it is the form and expression of that love. It is not a giving way to the domination of the other party, for love is not a fusion but a communion. Marriage brings into play not two biological functions, but two personalities. The dialogue is of the spirit; the kiss is that of the souls; to intensify that spirit and echo the flesh itself has its echo. Even their word is made flesh. The momentary harmony can be spoiled by one false note. But the total surrender in love, revealing the union of Christ and His Bride the Church, never is interrupted and never wears out. When all else fails in the world, God is still left. When in the lower order all else is gone, there is one who symbolizes Christ in the Church, on whom one can always rely, always trust.

The passing of time wears out bodies, but nothing can make a soul vanish or can diminish its eternal value. Nothing on earth is stronger than the fidelity of a heart fortified by the sacrament, which becomes like the unshakable columns of the Roman Forum against which the ravages of time are powerless. Pleasure is the play of the now-moment. Fidelity is an engagement with the future. When the future is eternity, and when the soul knows that it cannot be saved unless it is faithful to the spouse, it remains faithful even when faced with infidelity. As God's love is never withdrawn, so the fleshy counterpart of that love is also incorruptible in its unity. He who changes love would also change the love of Christ and His Church. The indifferent or "broadminded," in the false sense of the term, who deny Truth in the order of knowledge, are like the promiscuous and the unfaithful in the order of love. Fidelity is strength, for it is unity in plurality. Such fidelity is not discovered; it is made. It is not automatic in marriage but requires renewed efforts at mutual understanding, in order that there may finally result an alliance of mind and soul and destiny.

Union in the flesh can cement this accord of the spirit, and for that reason St. Paul forbids a separation of husband and wife to the point where fidelity might be endangered. "Do not starve one another, unless perhaps you do so for a time, by mutual consent, to have more freedom for prayer; come together again, or Satan will tempt you, weak as you are" (1 Cor. 7:5). Those wholly absorbed by their own emotions or their selfishness make themselves impervious to others. They even become a mystery to others, for emotions are incommunicable. No one can communicate a toothache, but love is communicable. The interior world of the other, in true love, is pierced by the body and soul. If the body alone is used, then the other soon becomes a weaker and weaker echo of its own egotism.

Everyone believes in the eternity of love, and eternal love is found only in God. To just the extent that the sparks of earthly love are stolen from the great heart and hearth of God, does earthly love remain abiding. They who possess this *fides* every now and then are cast into the ecstasy of love and are lifted to a higher dimension of ravishing affection, but knowing its Source and Origin, they whisper to themselves in sweet anticipation of heaven: "If the spark is so great, oh, *what must be the flame!*"

13

Generation

If our eyes could see into nature deeply, we would see in it a reflection of spiritual and eternal verities. As an echo is not the original sound but its distant reverberation, so all the laws of physics, chemistry, biology, psychology, and the like are feeble echoes and dim reflections of Divine Truth. Long before Newton lived, St. Thomas spoke of the law of gravitation, not in the mathematical language of an object and its distance from the earth, but in terms of the increased motion as a body approaches the end of purpose for which it was made. He saw in this a reflection of spiritual gravitation, by which a soul increases its virtue as it gets closer to God.

One of the great joys of eternity will be seeing the correlation between all branches of knowledge, arts and sciences, and the Word and Wisdom of God. But even now the dim glimpses we catch of that order make us see all human generation as the reflection of the eternal generation of the Word in the bosom of the Father. Our entire outlook on life, conception, and birth changes once these things are seen not as an evolution from slime, but as a gift from the Divine. Human generation is not a push upward from the beast, but rather a gift downward from the Trinity. The begetting of children is not an imitation of the beasts of the field, but a feeble reflection of the eternal generation of the second Person in the bosom of the Father.

God made the universe fecund. The understanding of this mystery will throw a new light on the family. It is the very nature of life to be enthusiastic, for all life tends to diffuse and communicate itself and even to overflow its perfections in order that others may share its joy of living. The Greeks and Scholastic philosophers used to express this truth in the principle: "Everything that is good tends to diffuse itself." In biological language, this truth is expressed in these words: "All life is fecund."

The fountainhead of all generation, the source of all artistic creation, the prototype of the birth of children, the archetype of every mind that generates a thought, if carried back to its ultimate source is the Goodness of God, who diffuses Himself internally by the eternal generation of the Son, and externally in creation. Whether we think of the earth's first family, when the Father sent the Spirit to a maiden as a Spouse, begetting in her soul-garden and "flesh-girt Paradise" the Son of Man, who is the Son of God, or whether we think of the last birth in the world, here is the pattern of all generation: the Triune God in whom self-giving is self-receiving.

This brings us to the first law of Love: *All love ends in an Incarnation, even God's.* Love would not be love if it did not escape the limitations of individual existence by perpetuating itself, nor if it did not achieve a kind of immortality in progeny, wherein death is defeated by life. Behind the urge to procreate is the hidden desire of every human to participate in the eternal. Since man cannot do this in himself, he compensates for it by continuing life in another. Our inability to externalize ourselves is overcome by giving, with God's help, something immortal to the human race. As St. Thomas tells us: "The intention of nature is directed toward that which is always and perpetual. Since in corruptible things, there is nothing which is always and perpetual except the species, the good of the species belongs to the chief intention of nature and natural generation is directed to the conservation of species."

Human generation is related in a special way to eternity. Sex love is not meant for death: rather, *eros* is for bios; love is for life. But once the Divine Source of Love is denied, then *eros* becomes death. The denial of the immortality of the soul, and the parents' attempt to deliberately frustrate new life, go together. If the soul has no relation to eternity, then why should the body seek to overcome death by begetting new life? *Eros* does lead to death. As Rom Landau put it: "If the ultimate aim of sex is not new life, what else can it be? There is one alternative and one alone: Death. Sexual life that has become chaotic implies both spiritually and physically a nationwide waste (killing) of the procreative potential (which means unborn children). Such a waste is identical with death."

The cell division of the amoeba, the generation of plants and animals, and the begetting of human kind are the mirrorings of a generation in the heart of God. The fecundity of God is the source of all fecundity on earth. St. Thomas, speaking of generation, writes: "Those things which in carnal generation belong separately to a father and mother are all attributed in Holy Scripture to God the Father in the generation of the Word, for the Father is said to give life to His Son, to conceive Him and give Him birth." Not only does the child reflect the eternal generation of the Word but, from another point of view, it faintly echoes the Incarnation. All love tends to become like the one loved. God loved man and He freely became man and appeared as Jesus Christ, the Son of the Living God. Man loves woman and woman loves man, and their loves, too, tend to an incarnation of love in the flesh of their offspring. With perfect justice, then, did the Word, who was made flesh through the Spirit of Love, call all children who were born of love unto Himself: "Let the children come to me, he said, do not keep them back; the kingdom of God belongs to such as these" (Mark 10:14).

Thus is physical desire transmuted into something nobler than the instinct that moves the animal world, as parents see themselves called to be co-creators with God Himself. Such was the meaning of marriage that the angel gave to Tobias: "Take the maid to thyself with the fear of the Lord upon thee, moved rather by the hope of begetting children than by any lust of thine. So, in the true line of Abraham, thou shalt have joy of thy fatherhood" (Tob. 6:22). "We come of holy stock, you and I, and God has life waiting for us if we will but keep faith with Him" (Tob. 2:18). It was this same insight into the eternal purposes of God that caused a woman in the crowd, on seeing our Blessed Lord, to exclaim:

"Blessed is the womb that bore thee, the breast which thou hast sucked" (Luke 11:27).

"Two in one flesh" which is the condition of producing offspring is to be seen as the poorly lighted symbol of the union of two natures, the divine and the human, in the Person of the Word of God. The yearning of lovers to be one in marriage is born of a oneness in soul, which is translated into oneness of body. Souls fall in love first, and then they are united in mind, and then there is a union in flesh. It was said of the Blessed Mother that "she had already conceived in her heart that which the Spirit now conceived in her womb." This means she was already so identified with God through love, and she so possessed God through grace, spiritually, that the physical presence was a corollary through a distinct act of God's Omnipotence. But in a lesser degree, the "being in love" naturally tends to unity and therefore "two in one flesh." As Browning expressed it:

> Because of our souls' yearning that we meet
> And mix in soul through flesh, which yours and mine
> Wear and impress, and make their visible selves,
> —All which means, for the love of you and me,
> Let us become one flesh, being one soul.

The act of generation, when seen as the gift of God and performed in the state of grace or love of God, merits for husband and wife further graces and helps them to save their souls. As St. Thomas puts it: "If one is led to perform the marriage act either by virtue of justice, in order to render the debt to the partner, or by virtue of religion, that children may be procreated for the worship of God, the act is meritorious."

Every Catholic mother whose increase of grace is rewarded with increase of life sees herself as feebly imitating Mary, who for nine months bore within herself her Guest, who was destined to become the Host of the Word. As the priest in the Mass offers bread and wine which has been harvested and rescued from an unredeemed nature, so the wheat that Mary ate, the wine that Mary drank, the light that entered into her chaste body, the images her eyes saw, and the song of the birds her

Generation

ears heard, all became her Offertory to Him who was to be the Body and Blood of Christ. Motherhood is sacred because Jesus had a mother. Birth is sacred because Mary threw open the portals of her flesh to the "first-born of all creation" (Col. 1:15).

Maternity is a natural eucharist. To every child at her breast, the mother says: "Take ye and eat; this is my body; this is my blood. Unless you eat my flesh and drink my blood you shall not have life in you." Our Divine Lord said: "As I live because of the Father, the living Father who has sent me, so he who eats me will live, in his turn, because of me" (John 6:58 [57]). The mother says to her child: "As I live because of Christ, so you will live because of me." As under the species of bread, day by day, Christ nourishes the Christian, so drop by drop, the mother nourishes the child. As the Divine Eucharist gives immortality ("The man who eats this bread will live eternally": John 6:59 [58]), so this human eucharist of motherhood is the guarantee of temporal life. The angel that once stood at the gates of paradise to prevent man from eating the tree of life now sheathes the sword, as life communes both at an altar rail and at a breast. That which in motherhood was first a nourishment of a body, with the passage of time becomes the nourishment of the mind and soul, as now not drop by drop, but word by word, the child is brought closer to the Word, his Savior, and Love.

The creative act of God is necessary to the human act of generation. Just as two men in business, or two artists in cooperation, produce results beyond the sum of their individual contribution or inspiration, so does the touch of the finger of God upon man and woman awaken something to immortal life. Neither mother or father really know what strength they have until the child comes to prove it. Two animals can unite and out of their parental powers form an animal soul, because the animal soul has no operations apart from the biological and chemical constituents of its organism. But the human soul has two operations independent of matter, such as thinking and loving. Because the greater cannot come from the less, because we cannot gather figs from thistles, it follows that the human soul must, in Aristotle's language, "come from without"; or in our language, be created by God.

309

Nothing is more binding than a child, who is the symbol of the survival of man, the pledge of the resurrection of the body. As God took a rib from Adam and gave him a helpmate so, in marriage, the husband again loses something to gain a richer inheritance, as the farmer who sows his seed reaps his harvest. Nothing is more religious in nature than procreation; it is the sign both of unity and continuity. The disjointed, separated, and egotistical have no use for the child. The men and women who think of their lives as bounded by the time limits of a cow cannot wait for the future; the craving for immediate pleasure and repose kills the willingness to plant a flower and wait for its maturity. Only those who have immortality in their hearts really yearn to prolong that immortality through the child. An impoverished heart has nothing to contribute to another but its emptiness and, therefore, nothing to transmit to posterity. No one can transmit what he has not got. The will not to prolong life is a confession that one lacks life. When the spirit has become sterile, then even human life seems worthless. And if one cannot bear the ennui and boredom of his own life, there is no urge to give life to others. The denial of the offspring is a sign of the deadening of the spirit.

But the begetting of new life is a sign that the heart is so full of happiness and love that it will die unless it overflows. The choked and dammed river collects scum and dirt, but the quick mountain streams that hurry over sacrificial rocks are purified in their flight to bedew newer and richer fields. Man is not made for isolation, neither is he made for collectivity; but he is made for the living group, the family, the community, the nation, and the Church. To live in it, however, he must contribute to it: husband and wife by physical birth, the priest by spiritual birth or conversion. For body and soul, therefore, generation is the condition of wholeness, sanity, and order. The priest who begets no new life in Christ, either through his preaching, his sacrifices, his mortifications, or his actual conversions, is condemning himself to the same penalties of sterility as do the husband and wife who rebel against the law of life.

The human body has little or no power of renewal. The old cannot, like a crab, go backward, nor can an aged Faust ever return to youth outside of legend. But the soul can be renewed. Dead to divine life, it can be reborn. The soul may be described as the faculty for both enjoyment and renewal: to just the extent that the spirit or soul is recognized in marriage, do the partners feel an urge for renewal in procreation. As humans lose the consciousness of the divine image within them, and as the body becomes the sole existent, the instinct for renewal is lost. The consciousness of the soul and the desire for procreation go hand in hand, as do materialism and sterility.

The boredom written on the faces of humans who deny the soul is the harbinger announcing death. Their agony is that they have no mystery. Lacking the secret of eternity, they have no passion to tell it to other generations. They who bear the mystery of eternity in their hearts cannot bear the thought of time killing that mystery. As the power of keys is passed on from Peter to Peter "until the consummation of the world," so the mystery of generation that God has given to espoused lovers is whispered from generation to generation. No wonder, then, that the Woman who was conscious of her fecundity through the Spirit should exclaim in her song, the *Magnificat*: "All generations shall call me blessed" (Luke 1:48). The secret of God's goodness is too good to keep!

There is no disgust in a life that is fecund, because there is a mystery. As time goes on, the river of rapture of husband and wife broadens. The eddies of passion may remain in the shallows, but their current never stops flowing. The companionship that began in ecstasies of flesh now widens into the sharing of bread, the communion of mind, and heart, and will, as they taste the sweet delirium of simply being together. Love is soon discovered to be oneness, more than the mere assimilation at which new lovers strain. The glamour passes, but the mystery deepens until they are made one through the deep sharing of life's meaning in the Mystery of an Eternal Love that gave only to receive.

Every dawning motherhood has received the sweet visit of the Holy Spirit. The *Fiat* of the Annunciation is repeated by every woman accepting in herself the incarnation of love. The veneration surrounding motherhood is due to the fact that a woman becomes the mother not only of a body but of a soul. The majesty of the Creator descends upon her marriage, as she becomes the guardian and priestess of a life given by God. Something of the imperfect priestly character of the Mother of God is given to each woman as she brings down to earth a soul by her consent, and as she offers it to God, as the Mother of God offered up her Son. Each new child with Baptism becomes a brother or sister by adoption of Christ, co-heir of Heaven.

As the whole of the divinity abides within each Divine Person in the Trinity, so the Blessed Trinity abides, through the quality of grace, within the spotless soul of the newly baptized child. In the baptized child, the Father is well-pleased and sees Himself as in a mirror untarnished by sin, unhampered in His action by a perverted will. In him dwells the Holy Ghost, and in him also the soul of Christ offers Himself to His Father in adoration.

God gives to each man the divine life of grace, if he desires it. But He also wants man to be the channel of that divine life. If man refuses to give human life, God cannot give divine life. But whereas man can refuse to give human life, and therefore limits the creation of more souls, God Himself can never refuse to give the body of a child a soul. God obeys man and woman in their union, just as He obeys the priest at the moment of Consecration. Even though the priest who consecrates be unworthy, God nevertheless descends onto the altar. However unworthy and illegal the union of man and woman, God does not refuse to give to the fruit of this union an immortal soul.

In the marriages where the fruit of love is deliberately refused, not only is the incarnation of love denied but love itself is killed. There happens then in that trinity of human love a rupture, caused by the rejection of the living seal to their love. The love they now may profess to have for each other is only love of self in the other, a self-centered, self-feeding, self-destroying, and death-giving love, which is worse than hatred. Both partners in crime are cut off from each other through the death of love. In their separation, they become two isolated beings, a duality instead of a trinity.

The more a marriage union is based on the divine, the more the husband and wife are in harmony with God, the more they find in each other that eternal fascination and satisfaction which transcends earthly frailties and disappointments. Such love reaches to the soul itself, invisible and immaterial, whose beauty can only augment with age, even while the beauty of the body fades. Love is then the love of the Spirit itself, powerful as only spiritual love can be. These bodies later on will win immortality in the resurrection, for nothing that has been found worthy of housing the incarnate Word will perish. Resurrection will come to the bodies of the adopted brothers of Christ, even as it comes to the body of Christ Himself. Lovers always speak of the immortality of their love, and cynics scoff at them, but the lovers are right. Their love can become immortal. It is sufficient to steep it in God, and it becomes impervious to time and space. God is unending Life and Eternal Love, and the lovers united to Him are caught up in the ceaseless current of love which flows between the persons of the Blessed Trinity. Poor indeed would love be if it were only two flames within closed lanterns! Nowhere on earth is the satisfaction for the yearning for eternity to be found. Not here is the last veil lifted for the final revelation of love, not here the Paradise of love without satiety, but beyond the "pillars of death, the corridors of the grave," where finally the companionship of days and years will be summed up, not in an hour of ecstasy where words and looks fail, but where the consummation of love is lost in the ecstasy of eternal union with the Heartbeat of God's Everlasting Love!

14

Paternity

The burden of these chapters is that love is not an evolution from the sex of the animal kingdom, but that sex is a physiological expression of Love, issuing from the Kingdom of God. Love is not an ascent from the beast, but a descent from the Divinity. In like manner, fatherhood is not a complex expression in the human order of what is common to the horse, the bull, the cock, or the stag, but a reflection of the Fatherhood that is eternally in God. "I fall on my knees to the Father of our Lord Jesus Christ, that Father from whom all fatherhood in heaven and on earth takes its title" (Eph. 3:14–15).

Not only does the Father possess the Perfect Life, but He has the power to communicate it. He is Eternal and Divine Fecundity. The Father, in our poor language, is necessarily altruistic, not just because He is Good, but because He is Father. Generosity in God is not what it is in a philanthropist or a hero, a disposition of the soul or a virtue; rather, He is the Personification of Generosity. The Son is generated not by a part of Himself, nor by a division of Himself, nor by a power issuing from Himself, but by the plenitude of all that He is personally. If we can speak of the one thing that He does not give in the unique way He possesses it, it is that of being a Father. That uncommunicable relation is His for eternity. All humans possess, in a relative and diminished way, this quality of personality. The "I" of John can never be communicated to the "I" of Paul. There is an impenetrability which makes each person what he is and different from every other. What makes the Person of the Heavenly Father distinct from the Son or the Holy Spirit is not love, nor power, nor divinity, for the Three Persons share the divine nature. Rather, the secret of the Father is that of being Origin without Origin, Source without Source, Father without Father. Not even the generation of His Son destroys the perfect distinction which exists between Him who gives and Him who receives. The power to give His Divine Splendor belongs to the Father alone; to receive that Image belongs to the Son alone; and never are the two confounded or confused. The Father has and can have only one Son, for the generation is so perfect as to create the Perfect Image. Herein is the mystery of why God gave the command "increase and multiply," in order that the eternal fecundity of God might have its repercussions in time.

As the Son is the Eternal Image of what the Father knows Himself to be, so, in the human order, God wills that an earthly father should know himself in a new way in his son, which explains the pride of a father in his son. Whatever glory the son has, is the father's glory. "That is *my boy*." "My child did this."

The initiative which is given earthly fathers to beget new fountains of life is not only a participation in Divine Fatherhood; there is a further likeness in that the good father will so educate his children that they will go back again to God, from whom they came. As the Eternal Son is distinct but never separated in nature from the Father, so the children will never be separated in education and destiny from their Heavenly Father. Multitudinous, "like an army in battle array," are the "Associations of Christian Mothers," but the poor Christian Fathers are forgotten. Our Lord, the night of the Last Supper, held up the beautiful ideal of His Love for His Heavenly Father as the basis of the unity to be found among men: "I am in the Father, and the Father is in me" (John 14:10).

There are no great physiological changes in the father at birth as in the mother, but he undergoes profound psychological changes. Maternity hospitals find it more difficult, at times, to deal with the peripatetic fathers than with the laboring mothers. The fact is that the consciousness of fatherhood does something to one's mental vision of the world, as a priest, hearing himself called "Father" after his ordination, summons in his soul a world of souls to whom his spiritual responsibility is committed.

The thrill of the farmer in the springtime, as he sees the grains of a wheat which he planted come up through the dead earth, little green swords pledging defense of human life; the joy at seeing a geranium bud in a tin full of earth on a tenement window sill; the ecstasy of the saint at seeing a sinner, dead in sin, responding to a word or a prayer and beginning to live in Christ: all these are earth's witnesses to the inherent happiness that comes to anyone who sees life springing, sprouting, or a-borning. Love does not mean merely the joy to possess; it means also the will to see a new life born out of that love. The realization that he has passed on the torch of life, and can see it flowering before his eyes in "his own image and likeness," is the basic reason why a man when he has become a father is no longer just a man. His is the supreme moment of self-recovery, the resigning of a lease on life; it is time's best moment, when a man feels, within himself, the shimmering refraction of the Eternal Joy of an Eternal Father begetting an Eternal Son, and saying to Him in the noontide of Paternity: "Thou art my Son; I have begotten thee this day" (Ps. 2:7). As the Son is the *Lumen de Lumine*, the Light of the Light, so in the newborn infant is "flesh of his flesh, bone of his bone" (see Gen. 2:23).

This psychic revolution at the instant of paternity has also a further effect. Not only is it a bond with a child, but it is also a new bond with the mother. The newborn child not only unveiled fatherhood in the husband, but also motherhood in the wife. From that moment on, she appears before him in a relationship which never before existed. Not only did he "make" a son; he also made a "mother." He pays back to his own mother her gift of himself by dignifying another woman with that most glorious of titles. Our Lord thought of His own Mother before the world was made; then He created His Mother, in a way no creature could ever do. In His Goodness, He communicated to a husband the power to make his greatest love a mother, not his mother but the mother of his son. The unmarried women who long for a child of their own to love are in their heart of hearts glorifying the power of fatherhood. Which of the wonders of fatherhood strikes him most, the father has probably never decided for himself: that of generating a son, or that of making a mother for his son. But since the two are inseparable aspects of his sacrament of paternity, he will never again be the same in the face of that double mystery.

Our Lord changed His relation with His Blessed Mother at the Cross by making her His Spouse, from whom would be begotten the members of His Mystical Body. In marriage, the mystery is reversed; the bride is first the spouse, and then the mother. In Christ, Mary is first the Mother of Christ, and then the Mother of all the children of men, and, therefore, the Spouse, or the New Eve of the New Adam.

The "Our Father," which expresses the attitude that creatures should have to their heavenly Father, must also be, analogically, a compendium of the attitude children should have to their earthly father. The prayer has seven petitions. There is one central petition which ties the first three petitions, which take us to Heaven, to the last three, which picture us struggling on earth. In the first three, we raise the soul to God; the last three lift the soul from the thralldom of evil. The middle petition is the only one that has to do directly with the body.

After an address, "Our Father who art in Heaven," there follow three petitions, which center on:

1. Worship of God	"Hallowed be Thy name."
2. The spreading of God's Kingdom	"Thy kingdom come."
3. Doing of God's will	"Thy will be done."
4. *Middle petition*, which unites both Heaven and earth and is the condition of the union	"Give us this day our daily bread."

Paternity

Then follow the three prayers that do not deal with the purposes of God, but with the combat of man:

5. Forgiveness for past sins	"Forgive us our trespasses, as we forgive them that trespass against us."
6. Preservation from future sins	"And lead us not into temptation."
7. Preservation from all trials	"But deliver us from evil."

These may be applied to the earthly father:

"Hallowed be Thy name."	"Children must be obedient to their parents in every way; it is a gracious sign of serving the Lord" (Col. 3:20).
	"Honour thy father and thy mother" (Exod. 20:12).
	"For a father's good repute or ill, a son must go proudly, or hang his head" (Sir. 3:13).
"Thy kingdom come."	His kingdom is the family.
	"I never understood the meaning of 'Thy kingdom come' until I looked up into the face of my child" (Léon Bloy).
	"It was not you that chose me; it was I that chose you. The task I have appointed you is to go out and bear fruit, fruit which will endure" (John 15:16).

"Thy will be done, on earth as in Heaven."	"Heed well, my son, thy father's warnings" (Prov. 1:8).
	"Do you, sons, give good heed, and follow these counsels, if thrive you would" (Sir. 3:2).
	"You who are children must show obedience in the Lord to your parents" (Eph. 6:1).
"Give us this day our daily bread."	The father is the provider of the family.
	"Whatever gifts are worth having, whatever endowments are perfect of their kind, these come to us from above; they are sent down by the Father" (James 1:17).
	"It is for thy children to ask thee for what they need, not to have thyself for their pensioner" (Sir. 33:22).
"Forgive us our trespasses."	"You who are fathers, do not rouse your children to resentment; the training, the discipline in which you bring them up must come from the Lord" (Eph. 6:4).
"And lead us not into temptation."	"How bitter their complaints against the father who is the author of their ill fame" (Sir. 41:10).
"But deliver us from evil."	"Was there ever a son whom his father did not correct? No, correction is the common lot of all; you must be bastards, not true sons, if you are left without it" (Heb. 12:8).

15

Motherhood

As Fatherhood has its prototype in the Eternal Father, who generated a Son to His Eternal Image, so Motherhood has its prototype in the Woman who, from all eternity, was given the high summons to be the Mother of God incarnate. Since St. Paul describes our Lord as "the first-born" of all creatures (Col. 1:15), Mary must therefore be the first Mother, after whom all mothers are patterned.

The essence of motherhood is twofold: (1) The *begetting of life*, which is a biological process, with its reflections in the animal kingdom. Birth establishes a mother-child relationship. As the tree has its fruit, and the mother hen hatches her eggs, so of every mother who creates dependence may it be said: "Blessed is the fruit of thy womb" (see Luke 1:42). (2) But human motherhood is not like animal motherhood, for the soul of the child is not an emanation from its mother's body but a direct creation by God Himself, who infuses it into the body of the child. As the priest prepares the bread of sacrifice, so the mother prepares the material of birth. But as the power of God changes the bread into the Body of Christ, so the power of God infuses life into a body and makes it a human person. This adds to physiological birth, which is in common with animals, the note of cooperation with God. There is something given to her by God which she clothes with flesh. Something is here added to the first notion of motherhood, namely, the bringing into being, not of a flesh, but of a man made to the image and likeness of God. In the case of Mary, we add to the words "Blessed is the fruit of thy womb" (Luke 1:42), the personal name of Jesus.

Human motherhood has two sides: the bringing of life into the world, which involves the cooperation of the father; and the bringing of a person or an "I" into the world, which demands the cooperation of God. The mother-child relationship creates dependence of the offspring on the mother; the mother-person relationship, which is expressed in the personal name given to the child, creates independence of its parents and the right of the child eventually to lead his own life, and even to leave his father and mother and cling to his wife.

This distinction is made clear in the prophecy of our Lord, who would be born to Mary: "For our sakes a child is born, to our race a son is given" (Isa 9:6). St. Luke takes up the same refrain: "Thus this holy offspring of thine shall be known for the Son of God" (Luke 1:35).

As Mary had something that was her own, namely, her Divine Child, and something that was not her own, namely, Emmanuel, God with us, or our Savior, so every mother has something which is uniquely her own, and yet something not her own. Being a person, her child must live as a person, with his own rights and liberties, and must work out his own salvation. "You must work to earn your salvation, in anxious fear" (Phil. 2:12). Mothers who abandon their children deny the first aspect of motherhood. Mothers who refuse to give up their sons or daughters, either in marriage or in religious vocations, deny the second aspect of motherhood. "Honor thy father and thy mother" (Matt. 19:19) is the tribute the children must pay to those who gave them life, but "He is not worthy of me, that loves father or mother more" (Matt. 10:37), is the declaration of independence a soul must make when God calls it to be His spouse.

In both her roles, as a mother who brings life into the world and as a cooperator with God, she assures her own salvation. Maternity in its mere physical aspects has a quality of salvation about it, for Scripture says a woman will find her salvation in child-bearing (1 Tim. 2:15). But a mother is also glorified in her children, who mirror forth the grace of

Christ in their lives. Mothers are made famous by their children; at the sight of noble sons, there will always be someone in the multitude to cry out, as a woman did to our Lord: "Blessed is the womb that bore thee, the breast which thou has sucked" (Luke 11:27).

A mother is a double benefactor to humanity: its physical preserver, and its moral provider. Through life, and through the high personal qualities of her children, she is the universe's constant challenge to death, the messenger of cosmic plenitude and the bearer of eternal realities. May it not be true that many women today are loath to create new life because they see motherhood only in its first degree as progenitor, and not in the second degree as cooperator with God in the increase of His Kingdom and the enrichment of His Mystical Body? Motherhood loses half its beauty at least, when it sees birth only from the point of view of biology and ignores the point of view of theology. If birth is only an affair of a man and woman, and not a cooperation between man, woman, and God, then, indeed, it has lost much of its beauty. St. Thomas says: "It is greater and better to be joined to that which is superior, than to supply the defect of what is inferior." Woman primarily is not a restorer of ruins; she is first a cooperator with the Divine. Adding to her cooperation with man the cooperation with God, she once more affirms the secret of marriage: it takes three to make love; man and woman as a generative principle, and God who infuses an immortal soul.

Planned unparenthood is the deliberate and willful decision on the part of a husband and wife to exclude from God the opportunity to create another to His image and likeness. It is the human will freely frustrating divine will, as certain agricultural policies deliberately control the productivity of the earth for the sake of a higher economic price. The *non-serviam* of Lucifer has had its catastrophic effect throughout creation, and particularly in those who say: "I refuse to accept from God that which is His holy will, the increase and multiplication of life." The refusing to be a cooperator with God is to spoil and maim oneself, for of the unused talents, our Lord said: "Take the talent away" (Matt. 25:28).

Medical opinion today is that the increasing psychoses and neuroses in women are due to a flight from motherhood. A wife who had a young tree planted in her garden would not go out each night with a scissors and cut off each new branch that might grow upon the root. She knows it is normal for a tree to sprout branches; she knows, too, that a Planned-Trunkhood, which could bear only one branch in the fifth year, would injure both the trunk and the branch. Branch-control could ultimately spoil the trunk. In statistical language, it does! Five out of every six cases of divorce, or 83.5 percent, stem from marriages having no children!

Returning to the positive, not only is motherhood cosmic through cooperation with a man and cooperation with God for the sake of salvation, it also illustrates the beauty of the world of the supernatural. Man by his nature is dedicated to "making"; woman by her nature is consecrated to "becoming" or "generation." We make what is unlike us in nature; for example, a carpenter makes a table. But we beget what is like us; for example, a mother begets a child. Man's creation is, therefore, a symbol of Creation. God made the world, and the world is unlike Him by nature. Man himself, inasmuch as he is made by God, has no strict right to call God "Father," for he is only the handiwork of the Creator. Woman's role, as generator of life, is a symbol of divine grace, which makes us "children of God" (John 1:12) and gives us the right to call Him "Father," and our Lord "Brother."

We are constantly invited in Scripture to become what we are not, namely, to convert creaturehood into Christianity, to "become the children of God" (John 1:12). But entrance into the realm of the supernatural order is accomplished only by the death of the old Adam, by sacrifice, and penance; there is a foreshadowing of this in the sacrifices of motherhood in bringing a new life into the world. There is not as much pain in creation as there is in generation, as it is easier to remain a natural man than it is to be born again as a "child of God." If mothers but realize it, they are prolonging the Passion of Christ through the centuries and, at each birth in the flesh, telling mankind that only through labor and self-effacement does one become a child of grace under the Fatherhood of God amidst the brotherhood of man.

Our Lord Himself told the aged Nicodemus that, to be saved, he would have to be born again. The carnal-minded old man could see no spiritual significance in birth, and so he asked our Lord: "Can he enter a second time into his mother's womb?" (John 3:4). Our Lord then affirmed that motherhood and conversion to Him are related, as symbol and reality; that the womb of a mother is to new physical life what the womb of baptismal waters is to spiritual life. "Believe me, no man can enter into the kingdom of God unless birth comes to him from water, and from the Holy Spirit" (John 3:5).

In our individual Christian lives, most of us cultivate the body and the soul separately. There are many days given to physical betterment; there are very few minutes given to the spiritual. Motherhood recalls that the best lives are those in which the physical and the spiritual development are never separated, as in the mother and in her child's education; both grow together. Precisely because of the soul, there is body development at each instant. The Christian mother is like Simeon, who took the forty-day-old Divine Child in his arms. But the true picture is not that he bore the Child, but the Child bore him. The mother, too, will see herself not merely *physically* bearing a child, but the child, composed of body and soul inseparably, bearing her. The new life in her womb comes from God, as grace in the soul comes from God. This spiritual truth at each moment is inseparable from the physical development of the life within. As God Himself stirred within Mary, so the image of God stirs within the mother. Mary bore the Consecrated Host, which is Christ Himself; the mother bears the bread of the sacristy, which is destined for the altar. When finally her child is born, if she is truly Christian she will see that body and soul both grow together, and that the healthy body, at each moment, is vivified by a spiritual-mindedness which will once more declare unto men that sanctification is of body and soul together.

Good and holy thoughts in the mother while bearing the child will affect the child, as fears and shock will affect it in the opposite way. The psychological effects of love on others are tremendous. The mother who bears her child in love and who is conscious that she is fulfilling a divine command and a holy Messiahship, must see verified in her life the words of our Lord: "If a man has any love for me, he will be true to my word; and then he will win my Father's love, and we will both come to Him and make our continual abode with Him" (John 14:23). Then the Child will bear her, for it is God's latest act of love to her. "The soul became flesh and dwelt within me" (see John 1:14). What she is, that her child will be. A mother is like the earth in which the seed of youth develops.

The Gospel tells us that there are four kinds of mothers: "There were grains that fell beside the path, so that all the birds came and ate them up. And others fell on rocky land, where the soil was shallow; they sprang up all at once, because they had not sunk deep in the ground; but as soon as the sun rose they were parched; they had taken no root, and so they withered away. Some fell among briers, so that the briers grew up and smothered them. But others fell where the soil was good, and these yielded a harvest, some a hundredfold, some sixtyfold, some thirtyfold. Listen you that have ears to hear with" (Matt. 13:4-9). As the bearer of seed, she throws herself completely on God, saying with Mary: *Ecce ancilla Domini.* "Behold the handmaid of the Lord" (Luke 1:38).

The submission of the earth to seed is passive, although the earth must now undergo the sacrifice of digging and harrowing. But in woman the submission is sacrificial. A woman is capable of more sustained sacrifice than man. Man is more apt to be the hero in one great, passionate outburst of courage. But a woman is heroic through the years, months, and even seconds of daily life, the very repetition of her toils giving them the semblance of the commonplace. Not only her days but her nights, not only her mind, but her body, must share in the Calvary of Mothering. She, therefore, has a greater understanding of redemption than man, for she comes closer to death in bringing forth life.

The two great spiritual laws which, in others, are extrinsic and separated, are united in her: love of neighbor and love of sacrifice. The non-mothers show love of neighbor to a non-self. But a mother's neighbor during pregnancy is one with herself and one whom she must love. Sacrifice is usually understood as a thing accomplished outside one's flesh, but the mother's sacrifice is within her flesh. Not a priest, and priesthood, she, too brings God to man and man to God. She brings God to man by preparing the flesh into which God's power is already present in the soul; she brings man to God in the second birth of Baptism, by offering her

Motherhood

child to Christ the Savior. As earth's beautiful reflection of the Motherhood of Mary; she, too, can be saluted in an earthly Hail Mary!

Hail Mary	Hail! Mother
Full of grace!	Full of human life; a body formed of the love of husband and wife; a soul born of love of God.
The Lord is with thee!	God is with all mothers! "What you have done to the least of these… you have done unto me" (Matt. 25:40).
Blessed art thou among women.	Every woman is called to be a mother; either physically or spiritually. A woman is most a woman when she is a Christian. A wife is most a spouse when she is a mother.
And blessed is the fruit of thy womb, Jesus.	And blessed is the fruit of thy womb—John, Peter, Mary, Ann. "Blessed is he who comes in the name of the Lord."

16

The Role of Children

The royal destiny of marriage, which is a community of love as in the Trinity, is to beget something outside itself. The nuptial chalice is too small for the love it contains and therefore it must overflow. Since God is in all love, love cannot be limited. It must go on even unto infinity. The temporal continuity of parents in their children thus becomes the fleshly symbol of the eternal continuity of God. God communicates His power of creativity to His subjects. This does not mean that people marry in order to have children; they have children because they are truly in love. The less the triune element enters into that love, the less is the desire for children. There is, indeed, in a selfish world such a thing as an "unwanted child" or a "child by accident." It means that despite their best attempts to stifle love, it overflowed through the very impetus that God gave His creation. Where there is love, there is no calculation. Hence our Lord, when asked by Peter how many times he should forgive, answered: "Seventy times seven." That did not mean 490, but rather that there must be no mathematical exactness in love. Nothing is as cold as mathematics, wherein people limit the expression of their love. Love is outside of law. Without it, all the rhythm of daily exchanges becomes an unsupportable banality.

Love between two who deliberately exclude the triune element would, in a desert, bore more quickly than anything else in the world. Very soon the two become juxtaposed. This does not mean that, in those cases where God does not bless a union with children, there is failure. As we pointed out, there is trinity here, too, when husband and wife understand love not as looking at one another, but as looking to God. The child is the physical expression of that divine counterpart of love. For childless couples, where there is no frustration of love's overflow, the law of marriage still holds true; it takes three to make love, and that third is God seen not in children, but through resignation to His will.

The first direct, human limitation of infant life in the history of Christianity took place in the village of Bethlehem through an Infant-Controller whose name was Herod. The prevention of infant life was simultaneously an attack upon divinity in the person of God made man, Jesus Christ, our Lord. No one strikes at birth who does not simultaneously strike at God, for birth is earth's reflection of the Son's eternal generation. To those who conspire against life in Herod's way or more scientifically, there will one day come the haunting conscience described by John Davidson:

> Your cruellest pain is when you think of all
> The honied treasure of your bodies spent
> And no new life to show. O, then you feel
> How people lift their hands against themselves,
> And taste the bitterest of the punishment
> Of those whom pleasure isolates. Sometimes
> When darkness, silence, and the sleeping world
> Give vision scope, you lie awake and see
> The pale sad faces of the little ones
> Who should have been your children, as they press
> Their cheeks against your windows, looking in
> With piteous wonder, homeless, famished babes,
> Denied your wombs and bosoms.

From the day when the Son of God became a child, there has been an intimate bond between Christianity and the family. Bethlehem was a kind of earthly trinity. It placed primacy at a point never before seen in history.

The Role of Children

Up until that first Christmas, the hierarchy had been father, mother, and child. Now it was turned backward and became Child, Mother, and father. For centuries humans looked up to the heavens and said: "God is away up there." But when the Mother held the Child in her arms, it could be truly said that she looked *down* to Heaven. Now God was "way down here" in the dust of human lives. Did Mary have other children than our Lord? No! Not of the flesh. The word "brethren" (Matt. 13:55), applied to our Lord in Scripture, refers to all kinds of relatives. It no more implies that He had blood brothers than a preacher, addressing his congregation as "My Dear Brethren," implies that he and the congregation have the same parents. But our Blessed Mother did have other children according to the spirit. Our Lord was her "first-born"; what St. Paul calls "the first-born of creatures" (Col. 1:15). As in the stable she became the Mother of God, so at the Cross she became the Mother of men. When her Divine Son spoke to her calling her the Universal Mother, or "Woman" (John 19:26), and telling her that John was her new "son" (John 19:26), she entered into a new relation with mankind. Our Lord did not here call John by name. If He had, John would have been only the son of Zebedee and no one else. In virtue of his anonymity, he stood for all of us to whom our Lord was saying: "Behold thy mother." It was a poor exchange for Mary. She was giving up the Son of God to get the children of men, but really, it was to gain a larger family in her Son. At that moment, Mary suffered the pangs of childbirth for all the children who would be born to her until the angel of doom comes. She brought forth Jesus in joy; us in labor, and in such agony that the Church has called her "Queen of Martyrs."

In Mary's Child all children are found; in her motherhood all women are mothers; and through her, as Gate of Heaven, all men see the Ancient of the Days grown young. Of that beautiful relationship of Mother and Child, Chesterton writes:

> Or risen from play at your pale raiment's hem
> God, grown adventurous from all times repose,
> Of your tall body climbed the Ivory Tower
> And kissed upon your mouth the Mystic Rose.

Since in her Child through the flesh at Bethlehem Mary had many children through the spirit, at Calvary the word *child* has a collective meaning and refers here not to a unique offspring, but to the fruit of love as God bestows it.

One of the greatest mistakes that couples make is to think that their love will endure because it is strong. Rather, love continues not because of its strength, but because it is related to the power of self-renewal. The love of husband and wife is less a continuing thing than it is, like Calvary and the Resurrection, the finding of new life at a moment when it was believed that satiety was the master. The Church is not a continuous phenomenon through history. Rather, it is something that has been through a thousand resurrections after a thousand crucifixions. The bell is always sounding for its execution which, by some great power of God, is everlastingly postponed. The world is ready to chant a requiem over its grave, and it rises to chant a requiem over their graves. In family life, in like manner, two hearts do not move on a roadway to a happier love; rather, every now and then they seem on the brink of losing their love, only to find it on a higher level. The child is not just a birth; the child is a resurrection and perhaps even an ascension. The seed that is dropped into the field in the springtime is not the same seed that is gathered in the harvest, but rather its effect, multiplied in quantity, renewed and vivified in quality. The child is not the proof that the love of father and mother continues to endure; it is the sign and symbol that, phoenix-like, their love has found its spring and its renewal.

The newly married often describe their love as "out of this world." In a certain sense it is true, for they are called upon to create a new world. In the Incarnation, "The Word became flesh and dwelt amongst us" (John 1:14). In the family, "Our love became flesh and dwelt amongst us." As the Christ-Love left a Memorial of His Sacrificial Love in the Eucharist, so the father and mother leave a memorial of their love in their children. As witnesses through history, they will testify to the parents who once walked the earth! Standing before the feeble creature who prolongs their life, the parents experience both an *attachment* and a *detachment*. They feel an attachment because the child is their love, their body and blood;

The Role of Children

a detachment because the child is someone else. Creation and birth are both solemn separations. Because he is born of them, the child is also born from them and has a destiny all his own. Love means not only to captivate a free soul, which is conjugal love, but also to liberate a captive soul, which is birth. Anyone who gives freedom to another takes a risk. God took a risk when He made man free; parents take a risk when they open the prison doors of their flesh to beget a child. Each child has his own soul to save, but the child will not know it until he has already been formed for some seven years by the parents. Their child is therefore a trust. His target is fixed, and as the poet has said, the parents must realize that they take the place of God in the beginning of the soul's salvation. Kahlil Gibran wrote:

> And a woman who held a babe against her bosom said,
> Speak to us of Children.
> And he said:
> Your children are not your children,
> They are the sons and daughters of Life's longing for
>   itself.
> They come through you but are not from you,
> And though they are with you yet they belong not to you.
> You may give them your love but not your thoughts,
> For they have their own thoughts.
> You may house their bodies but not their souls,
> For their souls dwell in the house of tomorrow, which
>   you cannot visit, not even in your dreams.
> You may strive to be like them, but seek not to make
>   them like you.
> For life goes not backward nor tarries with yesterday.
> You are the bows from which your children as living
>   arrows are sent forth.
> The archer sees the mark upon the path of the infinite,
>   and He bends you with His might that His arrows
>   may go swift and far.

Let your bending in the archer's hand be for gladness;
For even as He loves the arrow that flies, So he loves
also the bow that is stable.

Children have a messianic character in the family. First of all, they represent the conquest of Love over the insatiable ego; they symbolize defeat of selfishness and the victory of charity. Each child begets disinterestedness, inspires a sacrifice. As all love tends toward an incarnation, even God's, so does all love move toward a cross, even Christ's. So long as love has a body, there will never be any other way to prove love than by sacrifice. Possessed of soul and body, man always has a choice. He can give supremacy to the flesh or to the spirit, but one must "suffer" at the cost of the other. Love's greatest luxury is to spend itself on others. Until the child is born, the little sacrifices are for one another, made in the form of gifts and, above all, the gift of self. Then the sacrifices are made for the sake of the crushed-out sweetness of their two hearts. Because a child is born of a mother's pain, it brings a certain redemption into the world. Wrote Victor Hugo:

When she cried, "My Father"
My heart cried out "My God."

Children also take away any shame that may have been attached to the mutual act of love. Sowing seed, or planting a garden, would indeed be tedious if there were no fruit. The union of two in one flesh is the overflow of the cup of love. Even in the childless marriage, the body becomes the gesture of the soul and thus a reflection of God's increasing revelation of His Love through history. Even without children, love answers love with a perfect reciprocity, so that an ideal love spirates and breathes forth from both. In their union of irreversible and indissoluble love is proclaimed that unity of Christ and His Bride, the Church, which is the model of their union. Though childless, they are to be likened to the contemplatives who glorify God without making converts; while the husband and wife who are blessed with children are like the active clergy, whose mission it is to increase and multiply the Kingdom of God.

The Role of Children

In the child the parents have a feeling that their soul-love which expresses itself in the flesh-unity, has had a function. Love now has no more shadows. Satieties disappear as the fatigue after work vanishes in seeing the product of labor. The more love is spiritualized, the more quickly *eros* passes into *agape*. The more the union ceases to be the possession of the other and becomes a gift, the more harmonious is its orchestration. The psychic and the spiritual, dominating the physical and the sexual, have their own peculiar melody, which is sweetest when the two who listen to it hear, as well, the voice of the child of love. A wise father once said to his son, about to be married: "Try to make it last for only ten years. After those ten years, your heart will be full of memories and your house full of children and you will never want it to end."

The child is also the sign and promise of human liberty, because he is a new act of freedom added to the world. The increase of marital introversion through the prevention of buds on the tree of life goes hand in hand with the increase of totalitarianism and suffocation of personal liberty. The furnace of Dachau was only one of the scientific ways modern man has found to snuff out the candles of freedom. There are other ways, too, all performed to "benefit" humanity. Herod said: "Go, and enquire carefully for the child, and when you have found him, bring me back word, so that I, too, may come and worship him" (Matt. 2:8). But the gift he gave was the sword meant to bleed infant freedom white.

The frontiers of freedom today are not on the political and economic front, but in the home. Not they who prattle about freedom, but they who create new areas of freedom through birth, are the true defenders of real democracy. Children are conceived despite the exact calculations of man. Their sex cannot be absolutely determined, nor the exact time of their coming. There is something beautifully undetermined, something free about their advent. Like the love from which they issued, they are as free at creation as a poem. All things else are slavery compared to this new act of freedom and the promise of a better world. It is, indeed, curious that those who would shirk the responsibility of life defend their egotism, on the ground that they want to be "free." If freedom is egotism, the plea is justified. Freedom belongs to pioneers who bring new choices and revolutions and decisions into a weary and old world. Here is novelty at its best; thanks to the child, all covenants with death are abrogated.

Love exists only where there is freedom. To be forced to love is Hell; to be free in love is Heaven. Where love is, there is freedom. Since the child is the flower of love, it is earth's sacrament of freedom. As the cradles come back into the world, freedom will come back. This freedom will consist not in throwing off restraint, which is license, but in the increase of new centers of freedom. In each child God whispers a new secret to the world; adds a new dimension of immortality to creation; and makes the clinging hearts of husband and wife feel a little freer, as they look into that strange and mutual hope which has come to them from God.

Children also beget humility. Before an infant, the big feel little, and the proud so insignificant. As an elephant before a mouse, so is the egotist before the child. There is something about a baby that disarms, attracts, and makes even the evil want to appear as good. Everyone unconsciously puts himself on the level of a child; even the scholars descend to baby-talk. It may be that all love makes us little; or perhaps it is our littleness that makes us love. There was something staggering to the wise men about that Child, whose Hands were not quite long enough to reach the huge heads of the cattle. Somehow they felt that they were Hands that steered the sun, moon, and stars in their courses. Before that Infant, the wise men discovered Wisdom and the shepherds discovered their Shepherd. Every child in talking us back to the source of life, takes us back to God who is the Fount of Life. Only two classes of people found that Littleness who is Greatness: the shepherds and the wise men; those who knew they did not know anything, and those who knew they did not know everything, never the man with one book, or the man who thinks that he knows.

The intelligentsia, who are educated beyond their intelligence, stay away from children for the same reason that they stay away from God. They cannot bear the vision of the source of life. But the humble, who live in communion with the life of all living, like to get as close to it as possible, and from this flows the family. There is something awesome about a child, for it is the unveiling of love. A great secret has been let out and one stands in filial fear of it.

The child makes men humble as the thought of God makes men humble. There is little difference between the two, for the child is, in a certain sense, "Emmanuel," or God with us. Great depths of true wisdom are hidden in the heart of those parents who always say their night prayers before the crib of the last-born child. In that as yet wordless word they see not the increase of their image, but the very image and likeness of God. With the crib seen as a tabernacle and the child as a kind of host, then the home becomes a living temple of God. The sacristan of that sanctuary is the mother, who never permits the tabernacle lamp of faith to go out.

17

Mary, Motherhood, and the Home

The perfection of all motherhood is Mary the Mother of Jesus, because she is the only mother in all the world who was "made to order" by her Divine Son. No creature can create his own mother. He can paint a picture of his own mother, for in the field of art, the artist preexists his product; he is a symbol of God the Creator preexisting His creatures. All art is an imitation of the Divine Artist who, from all eternity, possessed in His Divine Mind the archetypal ideas according to which He made the world in time. The most famous painting of a mother is probably that by Whistler. Once, when complimented on its beauty, he answered: "You know how it is; one tries to make one's mother as nice as possible."

Our Divine Lord preexisted His own Mother existentially, as Whistler preexisted his mother artistically. Every bird, every flower, every tree, has been made according to an idea existing in the mind of God from all eternity. When He came into the world at Bethlehem, He was unlike anyone ever born; creation was no stranger to Him. He was like a bird that might have made the nest in which He was hatched. He came into the universe as a Master into His own house, or as an Artist into his own studio. The universe was His, and the fullness thereof.

In a particular way He created His own Mother. He thought of her before she was born, as the poet thinks of his poem before it is written. He conceived her in His eternal mind before she was conceived in the womb of her mother, St. Ann. In an improper sense, when she was conceived eternally in the Pure mind of God, that was her first "Immaculate Conception." In the Mass of that Feast, the Church puts into her mouth the words from the book of Proverbs, saying from all eternity God had thought of her; even before the mountains were raised and the valleys were leveled.

> The Lord made me his when first he went about his work, at the birth of time, before his creation began. Long, long ago, before earth was fashioned, I held my course. Already I lay in the womb, when the depths were not yet in being, when no springs of water had yet broken; when I was born, the mountains had not yet sunk on their firm foundations, and there were no hills; not yet had he made the earth, or the rivers, or the solid framework of the world. I was there when he built the heavens, when he fenced in the waters with a vault inviolable, when he fixed the sky overhead, and leveled the fountain-springs of the deep. I was there when he enclosed the sea within its confines, forbidding the waters to transgress their assigned limits, when he poised the foundations of the world. I was at his side, a master workman, my delight increasing with each day, as I made play before him all the while; made play in this world of dust, with the sons of Adam for my play-fellows. Listen to me, then, you that are my sons, that follow, to your happiness, in the paths I show you; listen to the teaching that will make you wise, instead of turning away from it. Blessed are they who listen to me, keep vigil, day by day, at my threshold, watching till I open my doors. The man who wins me, wins life, drinks deep of the Lord's favour; who fails, fails at his own bitter cost; to be my enemy is to be in love with death. (Prov. 8:22–36)

But God not only "thought" about Mary. He actually created her soul and infused it into a body, co-created by her parents. It was through her portals as the Gate of Heaven, that He would come into the world. If God labored six days in preparing a paradise for man, He would spend a longer time preparing a paradise for His Divine Son. As no weeds grew

Mary, Motherhood, and the Home

in Eden, so no sin would arise in Mary, the paradise of the Incarnation. Most unbecoming it would be for the sinless Lord to come into the world through a woman afflicted with sin. A barn door cannot fittingly serve as an entrance to a castle.

God in His Mercy remits Original Sin after our birth in the Sacrament of Baptism; it is only natural that He should grant a special privilege to His Mother and remit her Original Sin before she was born. This is what is meant by the Immaculate Conception: namely that, by the special grace and privilege of Almighty God, and in virtue of the merits of Jesus Christ, Savior of the human race, the Blessed Virgin Mary was preserved from every stain of Original Sin at the first moment of her conception. She was, in the improper sense, "Immaculately conceived" in the Mind of God from all eternity. But in the proper sense of the word, she was Immaculately conceived in the womb of her mother in time. Mary, therefore, is no afterthought in the Mind of God. As Eden was the paradise of perfect delight for man, so Mary became the Eden of innocence for the Son of Man. For the simple reason that the Son of God chose her from among all women to be His Mother, it follows that she above all women is the model mother of the world.

No mother was ever favorably known to the world except through her children; No one ever heard of the mother of Judas, but all know Mary through Jesus. The painting of Whistler's mother bears on the back of its canvas the portrait of Whistler himself as a boy. Even in art, the child and mother are inseparable. As one cannot go to a statue of a mother holding a child and cut away the mother without destroying the child, so neither can one have Jesus without His Mother. Could you claim as a friend one who, every time he came into your home, refused to speak to your mother, or treated her with cold indifference? Jesus cannot feel pleased with those who never give recognition to or show respect for His Mother. Coldness to His Mother is certainly not the best way to keep warm a friendship with Him. The unkindest cut of all would be to say that she, who is the Mother of our Lord, is unworthy of being *our* Mother.

To show her veneration is not to adore her. Only God may be adored. Mary is an abstraction of love from Love. All the myth-creations of the upward struggling of men, and far-off yearnings for a mother of mothers in such crudities as Penelope, Isis, Astarte, and Diana, were unconscious, prophetic witnesses to a fulfillment in Mary, whom Francis Thompson has called:

> Sweet stem of that Rose, Christ, which from the earth
> Sucks our poor prayers, conveying them to Him.

Love for Mary no more derogates from Christ's divinity than the setting robs the jewel, or the hearth the flame, or the horizon the sun. She exists but to magnify the Lord, and that was the song of her life. Knowing her as the Tower of Ivory, He climbs up the stairs of her encircling virtues, to "kiss upon her lips a mystic rose." Acknowledging her as the Gate of Heaven, through her portals He comes to us. He who slams the gate in the face of the Queen bars the entrance of the King. As His Mother, she must be ours for, as our Lord said: I will not leave you orphans."

Mary holds an important place in Christianity — not because men put her there, but because her own Son put her there. He needed body and blood to be a man. He who is God created the Mother to make Him a man. He needed lips with which to teach, hands to bless, feet to search for wandering sheep, a side whereon John might lean; He needed eyes that He might read hearts, fingers that would mould clay to open blind eyes to the light of God's sunshine, ears to hear the plaintive plea of ragged beggars; He needed a human will by which He might give an example of obedience; hands and feet to nail upon a Cross in propitiation for the sins of man; so He made Mary. He who is Joy asked her to give Him tears. He who is rich asked her to make Him poor, that through His poverty we might be rich. He who is Wisdom asked her to give Him the gift to grow in wisdom by learning through suffering. He who is the Shepherd bade her make Him a lamb, that He might be the Sacrifice for our sins. He who is Spirit begged her for Flesh and Blood, that He might give us the Eucharist. So devoted was He to her that when a woman in the crowd lifted up her voice in praise of His Mother, "Blessed is the womb that bore thee, the breast which thou hast sucked" (Luke 11:27), He reminded that woman that His Mother's glory was greater still: "Shall we not say, Blessed are those who hear the word of God, and keep it?" (Luke 11:28). He was harkening back then to Mary's humble answer to God's Word as announced by the Angel: "Let it be unto me according to thy word" (Luke 1:38). Finally, at the Cross, He proclaimed that she who is His Mother is also ours: "This is thy mother" (John 19:27).

Devotion to the Mother of our Lord in no way detracts from the adoration of her Divine Son. The brightness of the moon does not detract from the brilliance of the sun, but rather bespeaks its brilliance. The baptismal water does not detract from Christ's power of regeneration. The preaching of men does not diminish the glory of God. Never has it been known that anyone who loved Mary denied the divinity of her Son. But it very often happens that those who show no love for Mary have no regard for the divinity of her Son. Every objection against devotion to Mary grows in the soil of an imperfect belief in the Son. It is an historical fact that, as the world lost the Mother, it also lost the Son. It may well be that, as the world returns to love of Mary, it will also return to a belief in the divinity of Christ. The reason why Mary should be honored above all mothers was given by her cousin: "How have I deserved to be thus visited by the mother of my Lord?" (Luke 1:43). The Angel Gabriel also gave the answer when he saluted her as "full of grace" (Luke 1:28). But her Son gave the best and perfect answer when He willed her to us from the Cross.

Mary is, first of all, the model of the family. In the Annunciation story, there appears the action of the Three Persons of the Blessed Trinity: Father, Son, and the Holy Spirit. God the Father sends the angel to announce that He will send His Son to be conceived in her, and that this will take place through the Holy Spirit. When Mary accepts, a new society begins; a human family among human families, which is at one and the same time an ideal and an earthly trinity. In all other families there is father, mother, and child. In this family there is Child, Mother, and father. It is the Child who makes the family; it is the Child who created the parents. Next to Him comes the Mother, for she alone, through the Holy Spirit, conceived the Son in her virgin womb. Finally comes Joseph, the foster father chosen by God to be protector of the group and, for that reason, protector of the Church, which is the expansion of that original family. All through the preceding ages, from the crudest wigwam where spouse lighted fire for spouse, to the castle of the prince and princess wherein the two looked down on heirs of earthly kingdoms, mankind has been either looking forward or backward to that Holy Family, in which God veiled the glory of His divinity and became Flesh through the selfless love of Mary under the strong and reverent wardship of Joseph.

That home of Nazareth, wherein the earthly trinity lived its round of mutual love and obedience, was indeed different from any other home. It had to be; otherwise it could not have been the prototype. The pattern cannot be the cloth, nor the original, the copy, nor the example the thing exemplified. The Child was God's Son. Eternally generated in the bosom of the Heavenly Father, He had no earthly father, but only a kindly carpenter who acted as a foster sire. Mary, the Mother, was different from all mothers, for she conceived that Son with a passionless passion of a soul, as the love of her Creator supplied the passion of a soul in the place of the passion of a creature. Passion is love in bondage; it is the spirit in us straining at the leash of the flesh; it is like an eagle made for the flights over mountaintops, yet caged within a canary's range. For this one time in history, love, by being emptied of passion, is permitted to spread its wings and fall in love with Love. "For it is by the power of the Holy Ghost that she has conceived this child" (Matt. 1:20).

Because Nazareth was so different, it is since then so imitable. Because it is the light, we can see our way. Once that earthly trinity stood revealed, the family could never again be the result of a lease or a contract alone; it would be a union, a fellowship, as indissoluble as the Trinity of which it was the reflection. Nazareth tells us the kind of love that makes a home, namely, Divine Love on a pilgrimage into time from eternity.

There is but one life, because there is but one Source of Life. The life in flower and plant, and the life in man and woman, is but the slowly smoldering spark caught up in a clay-kindled flame from the Eternal Fires of God. Man could not call God "Father" unless He had a Son; and we could not be sons of the Father, unless from all eternity the Heavenly Father had made us "to be moulded into the image of His Son" (Rom. 8:29).

Mary, Motherhood, and the Home

Because images become blurred, the Father sent His Son to this earth to teach us the manner of beings He had eternally meant us to be. Human generation had thus become ennobled, because it is the reflection of that eternal generation in which life flows from Life, and then goes marching, in created forms, through all the kingdoms of earth, and with such force and vitality that death alone can conquer it. Here is the pattern of all fatherhood, all generation, and all life-giving processes, for in it love overflows into love! This is the beginning of the earthly family: the original of Nazareth.

Because Divine Love as a Messiah came to earth, it became natural that husband and wife should not only give themselves to one another in mutual sacrifice but also should recover themselves in the love of their children, who tie them together as father and mother as the Holy Spirit is the bond of unity between Father and Son. If human love fails, it is because it is short-circuited, not directed to a mutual incarnation of love but rather turned back upon itself, where it dies of its own too-much. Without the child as the bond of mutuality, or at least the desire for the child, passion can end in mutual slaughter. But with the child, love discovers itself to be immortal. By giving its flesh and blood as a kind of earthly Eucharist, it lives on what it feeds.

Marriage must end in the family, at least in intention if not in act; for only through the family does life escape exhaustion and weariness by discovering its duality to be trinity, by seeing its love continually reborn and re-known, by having its mutual self-giving transformed into receiving. Love thus defeats death, as it defeats exhaustion. It achieves a kind of immortality as self-renewal becomes self-preservation. God is eternal society; Three Persons in one divine nature. The family is human society; mutual self-giving which ends in self-perfection.

Deep mystery is hidden in the fact that Mary was "conceived by the Holy Spirit" (see Luke 1:35). It meant that the love which begot her child was not human love. A child is the fruit of love. But in this one instance, the love which begot was the love of God, which is the Third Person of the Trinity. Under the sun one needs no candle. When conception takes place through Spirit love, there is no need of human love. The Virgin

Birth did not imply that Mary conceived without love; it only meant that she conceived without passion. Birth is impossible without love. Human husband love is unnecessary if God sends His Spirit of Love. Where there is no love, there is no family.

To Mary alone was given the gift of bearing a child directly through God. But in a lesser way, every child is born of God. The parents cannot create the soul of the child; that must come from God. Flesh cannot beget spirit. At the very beginning of the human race, Eve, in the ecstasy of the firstborn in the world, cried out: "I have been enriched by the Lord with a man-child" (Gen. 4:1), "by the Lord," but using the intermediary of man. Mary, the New Eve, in the ecstasy of her "first-born" (Col. 1:15), could cry: "I have been enriched by the Lord with a man-child," without the intermediary of man; because she was begetting the New Adam, the new head of the human race. As in the Trinity there are Three Persons in one divine nature, as in Adam there are millions of human persons in one fallen human nature, so in Christ there are millions of human persons in one regenerated human nature. "In Adam," man with his heritage of sin can become "in Christ" with a heritage of grace.

The Trinity as the ideal family is the model not only for the human family, but also the model for the family of nations and the human race. The Giver, the Receiver, the Gift were first reflected in Adam, Eve, and their offspring, and later at Bethlehem in Child, Mother, and father. "Beloved, let us love one another; love springs from God; no one can love without being born of God, and knowing God" (1 John 4:7). Mary also reveals the beautiful relationship that ought to exist between mother and children.

There really is such a thing in the world as two hearts with but a single thought. Hearts are like vines; they intertwine and grow together. One can give his heart away, but since there is no life without a heart, one must receive another in return, or die. Deep love does not so much exist between two hearts as between one heart in two bodies. A community of interests, thoughts, desires, develop as if from two mountain currents a single river flowed.

What makes parting and death so tragic to lovers is that it is not two hearts which are separating, but one heart which is being broken in two.

Mary, Motherhood, and the Home

A broken heart is not the fracture of a single heart, but the rupture of two hearts once united in the rapture of a single love. In fear, one's heart can be in one's mouth; but in love, one's heart is in the beloved. And since each of us has only one heart, it can be given away only once.

No two hearts in the world ever grew together like the hearts of a Mother and a Son: Jesus and Mary. "Where your treasure-house is, there your heart is, too" (Matt. 6:21). His treasure was His Mother, her Treasure was her Son. These two hearts, the Immaculate Heart of Mary and the Sacred Heart of Jesus, kept their treasures in each other and in the sovereign will of the Father. In a certain sense, there were not two hearts but one, so deep was the love for each, so at one were their wills, so united were their minds.

These two hearts, the Immaculate Heart of Mary and the Sacred Heart of Jesus, threw defiance to the world's warning not to wear your heart upon your sleeve, for they wooed the world openly. Shakespeare wrote: "I will not wear my heart upon my sleeve for daws to peck at." But the Savior, wearing His heart upon His sleeve, said: "Come to me, all you that labour and are burdened; I will give you rest" (Matt. 11:28). The love of Jesus and Mary for mankind was so open, they left their hearts exposed to every errant dart from the bow of sinful man. Standing at the portals of every heart in the world, each could say: "Behold, I stand at the door and knock" (Rev. 3:20). They would break down no doors; the latches are on the inside; only we can open them. Because they have wooed, they can be wounded.

The Sacred Heart gave an example to children by allowing His incarnate Life to be formed by the Immaculate Heart of His Mother. No other human being in the world contributed to His Sacred Heart. She was the anvil on which the Holy Spirit, amidst the flames of love, hammered out the human nature with which the Eternal Word of God was one. From her own body and blood, as a human eucharist, He was nourished for life in the world. As the vineyard of His Wine, as the wheat field of His Bread, she supplied the materials for that Divine Eucharist which, if a man eat, he will live forever. As friends and relatives crowded about to seek resemblances, they found them double. He resembled His Heavenly

Father, for He was indeed "the splendor of His Glory; the image of His Substance." But He resembled His Mother, too, for, reversing Eden, man now comes from a woman, and not woman from a man. "He was bone of her bone, flesh of her flesh" (see Gen. 2:23).

So submissive was He to her care, that the door that slammed in her face in Bethlehem, also slammed on Him. If there was no room for her in the inn, then there was no room for Him. As she was the ciborium before He was born, so she was His monstrance after Bethlehem. To her fell the happy lot of exposing, in the chapel of a stable, the "Blessed Sacrament," the body, blood, soul, and divinity of Jesus Christ. She enthroned Him for adoration before wise men and shepherds, before the very simple and the very learned. Through her hands He received His first gifts, which as all mothers do, she would keep until He "grew up." None of them were toys. One of these gifts was gold, because He was King; another was frankincense, because He was Teacher; but the third gift was bitter myrrh for His burial, because He was Priest and Redeemer. Myrrh, signifying death, was accepted by her as a sign that, even at the crib, she would help fashion Him for the Cross and the Redemption, for that was why He came.

Through her arms He goes out into other arms. Men do not receive Jesus except through Mary. Simeon "also took him in his arms" (Luke 2:28). But in no other arms is He really safe, not even in the arms of a saintly old man. For Simeon, too, brought myrrh, when he said to Mary: "Behold, this child is destined to bring about the fall of many and the rise of many in Israel; to be a sign which men will refuse to recognize; and so the thoughts of many hearts shall be made manifest; as for thy own soul, it shall have a sword to pierce it" (Luke 2:34–35).

"A sign which men will refuse to recognize," means the Cross: one bar in contradiction with another bar, man's will in opposition to God's will. Nowhere in all the world is He safe from contradiction except with His Mother; for, being conceived without sin, she was immune from the original contradiction of sin. But with others this was not true. When a wise man first saw Him, he gave myrrh for His death. When another old, wise man first touched Him, he spoke of a Cross. "As for thy own soul, it shall have a sword to pierce it" (Luke 2:35). Her own Immaculate Heart and His Sacred Heart would be as one in love through life, that the spear to be driven through His Heart would also pierce her Heart. As the innkeeper's words to Mary pierced His Heart, too, so the sword of Calvary would also pierce her Heart, as if the heart cord of Mother and Son had never been broken at birth. For nine months she bore Him in her womb, but for thirty-three years she bore Him in her Heart. One stone sometimes can kill two birds, and one sword sometimes can pierce two hearts. As He received His human life from her, so He would not give it up without her. He does not wait until maturity before announcing that the reason for His coming is to take up the sign of contradiction. He makes the offering when He is only forty days old, but He does it *through His Mother*.

As He was formed by her body and given to mankind by her arms, so He was formed by her mind. The world received only three years of His life, but Mary had thirty years of His obedience. Down to Nazareth He went to be subject to her. He, the Divine Word, for three long decades responded to a human word. Nazareth was the first university in the history of Christianity, and in it all humanity, in the Person of Christ, was trained in obedience under the tutelage of a Woman. It was no wonder that, when He was graduated, men marveled at His learning: "No man ever spoke as this man" (John 7:46). Nazareth was the school for Golgotha.

Her Divine Son could not submit His divine will to a human mortal, but He could submit His human will, which He received by becoming man. Just as in the unity of His Divine Person He is immortal in virtue of His divine nature but mortal through His human nature, so He is beyond submission as God, and yet freely within submission, except in those things which bear directly on the mission of His Heavenly Father: "Know you not that I must be about my Father's business" (Luke 2:49). As He depended on her answer to the angel, before turning back eternity and becoming flesh, as He depended on her for His birth, as He depended on her to present Him at the Temple for the prediction of the Cross, so He depended on her for the announcement of His public life at the marriage feast of Cana. "The Mother of Jesus was there. And Jesus also was invited" (John 2:1–2). She is mentioned before He is in the Gospel story of Cana. She enters; He follows. He is at a marriage feast because she is there. Because she asks for it, He works His first miracle. Perhaps it would be truer to say that she did not ask for it, but insinuated it. Her words were merely the affirmation of fact: "They have no wine" (John 2:3). But though she expressed a wish to her Divine Son, she nevertheless uttered a command to men: "Do whatever He tells you" (John 2:5). Her Son fulfilled her wish; men obeyed her command. Mary was not a spectator at Cana's miracle. She was His inspiration. The Mother is as conscious of her power over her Son, as He is conscious of His power over creatures. She suggests; He grants.

All through His life, we find a loving dependence of the Sacred Heart on her Immaculate Heart. The blood that flowed in His veins came from her; His body that was later delivered for sin was first delivered by her. The divine fires which kindled the earth were housed in her heart. The waters of Everlasting Life, which are dipped to those that thirst, came through her as a fountain.

This love which the Sacred Heart had for His Mother, was reciprocated by the love of Mother for Son. The life of Jesus speaks to us and says: "I gave Myself to my Mother. My Body was fashioned by her; my will was subject to her; my miracles were begun through her; my Crucifixion was announced through her; my Redemption was perfected with her at the foot of the Cross. Unlike other men, I did not leave her to start a family, for as I told my Mother, there are other bonds than those of the flesh. 'If anyone does the will of my Father who is in heaven, he is my brother, and sister, and mother' (Matt. 12:50). My family, the family of all who live by my Spirit, started with her. I was the first-born of the flesh; John was the second-born of the spirit at the foot of the Cross. No one, therefore, can be an adopted son of my Heavenly Father without being, at the same time, my brother; but no one can be my brother who does not depend on our Mother. To each of you on the Cross I said: 'This is thy mother' (John 19:27). A Christian means another Christ. You must therefore be formed as I was. I ask that she be your mother, not that you rest in her, for a creature can never be the end of a creature. Her mission is to transform you into me, so that you put on my mind, think my thoughts, desire my will, and live by my life. But how shall you put on me except through her who is clothed with me as the sun? Easier it would be to separate light from the sun, and heat from the fire, than to separate growth in me from devotion to her. I came to you through her; through her, you come to me. 'What God, then, has joined, let not man put asunder'" (see Matt. 19:6).

When any other mother loves her child, she loves a creature. In the case of Mary, she loved her Creator, too, for it was not a nature she loved but a Person, and the Person is the Son of God. In the Transfiguration, the Heavenly Father said: "This my beloved Son, in whom I am well pleased" (Matt. 17:5). The Father here spoke of Jesus Christ, true God, true man, appearing in glory before His Apostles, with His face shining as the sun and His garments white as snow. When the Eternal Father willed to associate the Virgin Mary in some way to His generation of the Son by sending Him into her body as a temple, there must have arisen in Mary's heart some spark of that Infinite Love which the Father has for His Son. Thus, the love of Mary for Jesus comes from the same Source as Her Son in God, the prototype of the love of a mother for children as gifts of God and of children for mothers as prolongers of the Incarnation. Some idea of this love is suggested in the simple lines of the Gospel, when her Son went down to Nazareth: "While his mother kept in her heart the memory of all this" (Luke 2:51). And the words were the words of the Word. In this reciprocal love of the Sacred Heart and the Immaculate Heart, there is suggested the conclusion that if the Sacred Heart willed to have His body, His mind, His will, and His mission formed by the Immaculate Heart of His Mother, then shall not earthly mothers form Christ-life in their children through the inspiration of that same Immaculate Mother? In a broader way, all grown children, adults in the Mystical Body, have their love for Christ formed by His Mother.

As Mary and Jesus are the model-love of mother and children and of Christians and Christ, so she is the inspiration of a home. The principal difference between a house and a home is a child. In a house individuals dwell; in a home the family lives. There are more persons in a boarding house or hotel than in a home, but since there is no deep unifying bond of love, the group never makes the family. The two principal virtues of a home are consecration on the part of parents and obedience on the part of the children. The first of these lessons is revealed in the Presentation, the second in the life at Nazareth.

St. Luke begins the story of the Presentation in these words: "And when the time had come for purification according to the law of Moses, they brought him up to Jerusalem, to present him before the Lord there. It is written in God's law, that whatever male offspring opens the womb is to be reckoned sacred to the Lord; and so they must offer in sacrifice for him, as God's law commanded, a pair of turtledoves, or two young pigeons" (Luke 2:22–24).

All the women of Israel who had brought forth a child were obliged, at the end of forty days, to present it to the Temple, and, if it were a firstborn, to ransom it. The ransom imposed was in memory of God's ransoming the firstborn of the Jews while they were in captivity in Egypt. Jesus was "the first-born," not only of Mary (and the only born) but was also "the first-born" of creatures: "His is that first birth which precedes every act of creation" (Col. 1:15). In the name of all humanity, Mary offers her Son as a ransom for the world's Redemption. Her act of dedicating her Son was a continuation of the *Fiat* she pronounced at the Annunciation. Mary was not a priest, but she was the Mother of the High Priest, and as such offered in her heart her Child for the salvation of the world. She was not an altar, but the Mother of the Living Temple of God, which if men destroyed, He would rebuild in three days. As a kind of paten, she holds in her hands Him who is "the Lamb slain from the beginning of the world" (Rev. 13:8).

When Mary Magdalen poured out the precious perfume on the feet of her Savior, the Lord said she was doing it in preparation for the day of His burial. When our Lady presented her Child in the Temple, she was offering Him, too, for the day of His burial, for the Redemption of the world. Not to other mothers comes the high summons to offer their sons in reparation for the world; but to every mother does come the summons to consecrate her child to the service of God. I know a mother who, when her firstborn was baptized, immediately placed him on the altar of the Blessed Mother and there consecrated him to God. He is now in the service of God.

The right to educate the children does not belong primarily to the state, but to the parents. The state may instruct, but only the parents can consecrate. Since they hold the right from God, they will be held responsible for the proper exercise of the right. Like Mary, they must consecrate their children to the love and service of God. Unlike Mary, they are not called to consecrate unto a Crucifixion, for there will never be another Redeemer. Mary here is imitable in the consecration, not in the one who is offered. The consecration of Mary's Child was in a Temple; the consecration of every mother's child must also be in the House of God. Without religious education, there is no consecration, and without consecration a child is like an errant arrow, knowing neither the power which gave him motion, nor the goal toward which he tends. But the child trained in sacrifice because Jesus Christ died for his sins, trained in truth because of a belief in Him who is Truth, trained in purity because his body is the temple of God, becomes the redeemer of the parents, as their love pays back the spark of Heaven with the flames of faith.

As parents would not think of stealing a neighbor's child, so neither would they ever dream of cheating God of His heritage. They are the trustees of that carnal wealth, not its creator. They have been sent out "two by two" not to picnic on the way, but to reinforce the ranks of earth. Mary has taught the mother the first step in the founding of a home by offering it to God, then taking the child back in her arms full of God's purpose.

Correlative to consecration of the part of the parents, is obedience on the part of the children. St. Luke tells us, after the finding of the Divine Child in the Temple: "But he went down with them on their journey to Nazareth, and lived there in subjection to them, while his mother kept in her heart the memory of all this. And so Jesus advanced in wisdom with the years, and in favour both with God and with men" (Luke 2:51–52). A triple humiliation is here revealed. "He went down" was a miniature of the Incarnation when God *came down* from Heaven and became man. Physically, Nazareth was below Jerusalem in the topography of the country. Spiritually it was lower too, for the Creator now goes down to His creatures. "To Nazareth." "Can anything that is good come from Nazareth?" (John 1:46) was asked by one of the Apostles on hearing that the Messiah came from that tiny little village. He was born in "the least of the cities of Israel"; now He would live in a scorned town, but the ignominy of His death and His apparent defeat He would proclaim in the great city of Jerusalem. "And He was subject to them." Here the sculptor obeys his chisel, the painter is subject to his brush, the winds obey the dictates of the leaves. Two decades later men will see Him washing the feet of His disciples. "So it is that the Son of Man did not come to have service done him; he came to serve others, and to give his life as a ransom for the lives of many" (Mark 10:45).

What makes the obedience of this Child all the more impressive is that He is the Son of God. He who is the General of humanity becomes a soldier in the ranks; the King steps from His throne and plays the role of a peasant. If He who is the Son of God makes Himself subject to His Mother and foster father in reparation for the sins of pride, then how shall children escape the sweet necessity of obedience to those who are their lawfully constituted superiors? The Fourth Commandment, "Thou shalt honor thy father and thy mother" (Exod. 20:12), has been broken by every generation since the dawn of man. At Nazareth children would be taught obedience by Him who really is the Commandment. In this particular instance, where the Child is divine, one might think that at least He would have reserved for Himself the right of "self-expression." Mary and Joseph, it seems, could have with great propriety opened the first "progressive school" in the history of Christianity, in which the Child could do whatever He pleased; for here the Child could never have displeased. "And he who sent me is with me; he has not left me all alone, since what I do is always what pleases him" (John 8:29).

But there is no evidence that He gave to Mary and Joseph just the nominal right to command. "And lived there in subjection to them" (Luke 2:51). God subject to man! God before whom the angels, principalities, and powers tremble, is subject to Mary, and to Joseph for Mary's sake. Two great miracles of humility and exaltation: God obeying a woman; and a woman commanding God. The very fact that He makes Himself subject endows her with power. And this obedience lasted for thirty years. Three hours He spent in Redemption; three years in teaching; thirty years in obedience. By this long span of voluntary obedience, He revealed that the Fourth Commandment is the bedrock of family life. In a larger way, how else could the primal sin of disobedience against God be undone except by the obedience in the flesh of the very God who was defied? The first revolt in God's universe of peace was the thunderbolt of Lucifer: "I will not obey!" Eden caught up the echo, and down the ages its inflection traveled, worming its way into the nooks and crevices of every family where there gathered a father, mother, and child.

By making Himself subject to Mary and Joseph, the Divine Child proclaims authority in home and in public life to be a power granted by God Himself. From this disclosure follows the duty of obedience for the sake of God and one's conscience. As, later on, He would tell Pilate that the civil authorities exercise no power except that given them from above, so now by His obedience He bears witness to the solemn truth that parents exercise their authority in the name of God. The parents have the most sacred claim on their children, because their first responsibility is toward God. "Every soul must be submissive to its lawful superiors; authority comes from God only, and all authorities that hold sway are of his ordinance" (Rom. 13:1).

If the parents surrender their legitimate authority and primary responsibility to the children, the state takes up the slack. When obedience in conscience in the home vanishes, it will be supplanted by obedience by the force of the state. The divine glory of the ego, which characterized the nineteenth and twentieth centuries, is so much social nonsense. The divine glory of the state, which is now taking the ego's place, is a social nuisance. Believers in ego-consciousness and collective-consciousness may regard humility and obedience as a vice, but it is the stuff of which homes are made. When in the one family of the world where one might legitimately excuse "child-worship," for here the child is God, one finds on the contrary child-obedience; then let no one deny that obedience is the cornerstone of the home. Obedience in the home is the foundation of obedience in the commonwealth, for in each instance, conscience submits to a trustee of God's authority. If it be true that the world has lost its respect for authority, it is only because it lost it first in the home. It is a peculiar paradox that as the home loses its authority, the authority of the state becomes tyrannical. Some moderns would swell their egos to infinity, but at Nazareth infinity stoops down to earth to shrink into the obedience of a child. There is a bond established. Democracy put "man" on a pedestal; feminism put "woman" on a pedestal; but neither democracy nor feminism could live a generation unless a "Child" was first put on a pedestal, and such is the significance of Nazareth!

18

The Dark Night of the Body

One of the greatest mistakes the human heart can make is to seek pleasure as a goal of life. Pleasure is a by-product of the fulfillment of duty; it is a bridesmaid, not a bride; it is something which attends and waits on man when he does that which he *ought*. To go through life with the idea of always having a good time is not to have a good time. A boy does not eat ice cream to have pleasure; he has a pleasure because he eats ice cream. The satisfaction of the appetite of hunger gives pleasure, but one does not eat just to have pleasure. One does not marry to enjoy pleasures of the flesh; one enjoys the pleasures of marriage because one fulfills to the utmost the functions and obligations of the married state. A good husband wants to love and to have a happy life; a wicked husband wants to be loved and to enjoy himself. The good man seeks a woman to complement his imperfection and to work toward mutual enrichment. The evil man wants to immolate a woman in order to enjoy himself. The happiness of marriage is in a certain sense a prepayment of God for its trials. Because its burdens are many, its pleasures are meant to be many. The honeymoon precedes the labors of birth, and is a credit God extends in advance because of the responsibilities involved.

The greatest joys of life are purchased at the cost of some sacrifice. No one ever enjoys good reading, good music, or good art without a certain amount of study and effort. Neither can one enjoy love without a certain amount of self-denial. It is not that love by its nature demands suffering, for there is no suffering in Divine Love. But whenever love is imperfect, or whenever a body is associated with a soul, there must be suffering, for such is the cost of love's purification. One cannot grow from ignorance to love of poetry without discipline. Neither can one mount from one level of love to another without a certain amount of purification. The Blessed Virgin passed from one level of love, which was for her Divine Son, to the higher level of a love for all whom He would redeem, by willing His Passion and Death at the Marriage Feast of Cana.

All love craves a cross by the very fact that love is forgetful of self for others. But even in the midst of sacrifice, it can say: "Suffering is in me, but I am not in it." The joy which is seen forthcoming as the result of the trial makes one in some way independent of it. A marriage which is entered into solely for the sake of pleasure lacks this essential element of love. Seeking pleasure alone, husband and wife live on the surface of life instead of in its depths; there is sex, but no love; there is an epidermal contact, but no communion of spirit. A family without the spirit of sacrifice is only an agglomeration of separate atoms; they sit in a common refectory, sleep in a common dormitory, but lack all internal relations which are the condition of family love. The husband and wife and children are held together like a business organization. Each member of the family feels himself imprisoned by the collectivity, as the citizens of a totalitarian state do on a larger scale. Crushed by hostile forces, external to himself, each one wonders why the yearning of love within him cannot be satisfied. Each tries to compensate for this desire of unity through love, by some external activity which amounts to busybody-ism. The wife forms a bridge club or a "Society for the Elimination of Theater Queues," and the husband becomes a "go-getter." The value of life is judged not in terms of being, but in terms of not-being, or having. Instead of being drawn toward self-perfection and fulfillment, they are full rather of emptiness and frustration. They are always wanting something, but what that something is, they know not. They think that by increasing activity, they will fill up the void; whereas happiness lies in the discipline of the ego and not in its satisfaction. John the Baptist, on seeing our Lord, said: "He must become more and more, I must become less and less" (John 3:30). Their motto is: "I must become more and more; He must become less and less."

One of the most insidious influences in modern society comes from those who develop a social conscience without an individual conscience, or who separate love of neighbor from love of God, or who feel that by transferring their inner sense of guilt to others whom their social conscience derides, they can thereby escape the inner sense of guilt to which their personal consciences bears witness. By reforming others, they acknowledge the need of regeneration, but not in their own hearts. Many disillusioned married people practice escapism in their mature lives to avoid the need of the reformation of their own family. Because their egotism has become social, they think that they have become loving; when really the last thing they want to do is to immolate their egotism. They give themselves to others, but in the way *they have chosen* to give themselves, and not in the way their human nature, under God, dictates. They are actually increasing their egotism at the moment when they feel least selfish. But this expansive feeling is really only an excrescence, like a boil on the neck of their egotism.

What is really at the bottom of such a peculiar type of social interest is a hatred of self, which others might overcome and try to forget in alcoholism, but which they try to forget in a kind of altruism. The escapes are means of overcoming a sense of absolute sterility and futility. Their egotism is concealed under the language of humanitarianism and philanthropy, but there is no love, because there is no sacrifice of the ego. There is ceaseless activity, but no joy; there is philanthropy, but no inner peace; there is a social conscience, but no individual conscience. There is communism in the social order because there is first atheism in the human heart. The great natural necessities of the soul, the deepest aspirations of the human heart, are abolished for the sake of the triumphant ego. The result is that there is a terrific inner dislocation of self, for as life ceases to be unified, it becomes like a body devoid of a soul; it disintegrates into its component elements. An ego without sacrifice is closed to itself and impenetrable to others. Hence the impression that selfish couples give, that they are living in another world; each has his or her own planet; they hardly ever come in contact except to collide and quarrel. They may be two in one flesh, but they are not two in one mind, or heart, or ideal. Like the modern atom, such partners are so fissioned and rent as to make a Hiroshima of a home and a marriage.

There are many egotists who boast of the sacrifice that they have made toward a person or a cause, and indeed the communist can point to "sacrifices" which he made for world revolution. From the point of view of quantity alone, his "sacrifice" surpasses that of an individual Christian. But there is a world of difference between the "sacrifice" of a communist for revolution, and that of a devoted husband for a sick wife, or of a wife for an alcoholic husband. *In the egotist, the object of the sacrifice is what his ego has chosen for itself; in love the sacrifice is for what God has chosen.* The sacrifices of a husband for his second wife, while his first wife is living, are not to be put in the same category as the sacrifices of a husband for even an unfaithful first wife. In the first instance, there is the freedom of license; in the second there is freedom within the law. The second wife is a self-gratification the ego chose in violation of God's law. The difficult wife is the one whom God *imposes* on the man after his initial act of freedom: "I choose thee until death do us part." The sacrifices of the egotist have no eternal value; they have value only for him. The sacrifices of the lover under God are directed to the absolute, to a loyalty and devotion greater than and beyond self.

True love has its infallible watermark: the immolation of self in the face of the Eternal. Of those who sacrifice to satisfy their ego in contradiction to the law of God, our Lord said: "They have their reward already" (Matt. 6:2). You did it to please yourself, and you got exactly what you wanted. But the other group did not make the sacrifices to please themselves; they made them for the sake of the Absolute Love, i.e., for the Divine Thou which binds two hearts together. Sacrifice is not made for the sake of self but for the expropriation of self through an act of freedom, in order that nothing may keep one back from union with Love Divine.

Love at the beginning is a paradise. Its foundation is a dream that each one has found to be something unique and a happiness which is eternal. That is why all love songs of the theater sing of "how happy we shall be." Love songs treat what is in prospect, not what is in retrospect. This is because there is a kind of infinity about imagining what will happen, while there is only reality about what has already happened. The young still dream dreams of the future; the old, like Horace, look back to the "glorious past." This is not in any way to minimize the value of paradisal future, but merely to place love in its ontological setting. Every great thing begins with a dream, whether it be that of the engineer who plans a bridge, or of the heart that plans a home. The soul draws upon its infinity and colors it with the gold of Paradise. No one ever climbs to the heavens without passing through the clouds, and at the beginning every lover has his head in the clouds. This foretaste of Heaven is good, and even heaven-sent. It is the advance agent of Heaven, telling the heart of that real happiness which lies ahead. Actually, it is a bait, a blueprint, a John the Baptist, an announcer telling of the program yet to come. If God did not permit this preview of joy, who would venture in beyond the vestibule?

But such primitive love does not continue with the same ecstasy. Because flesh is the medium of married love, it suffers the penalty of the flesh: it becomes used to affection. As life goes on, a greater stimulus is required to produce an equal reaction to sensation. The eye can soon become used to beauty, and the fingers to the touch of a friend. The intimacy which at first was so desirable, now becomes at times a burden. The "I-want-to-be-alone feeling," and the "I-think-I-will-go-home-to-mother feeling" strip the eye of its rose-colored glasses. Bills coming into the kitchen make love fly out of the parlor. The very habit of love becomes boring, because it is a habit and not an adventure. Perhaps the yearning for a new partner accompanies a disgust with the old partner. The care of children, with their multiplying accidents and diseases, tends to bring love down from its vision in the clouds to periodical, realistic visitations to the nursery.

Sooner or later those living the affective life are brought face to face with this problem: Is love a snare and a delusion? Does it promise what it cannot give? I thought this would be complete and total happiness, and yet it has settled down to a routine sprinkled with an occasional faint recalling of what love was in the beginning. At this point, those who think that love is an evolution from the beasts and not a devolution from God, falsely believe that if they had another partner, he or she could supply what the other lacks. The fallacy here is that they forget that the indigence and emptiness comes not from the other partner, but from the very nature of life itself. The heart was made for the infinite, and only the infinite can satisfy it. That first ecstasy of love was given to remind the couple that their love came from Heaven, and that only by working for Heaven would they ever find the love they wanted in its infinity. Our Lord gave bread at Capharnaum to lead the souls of His listeners to the Eucharist, or the Bread of Everlasting Life, which is His very Self. The love of marriage is given in the same way, as a divine "come-on," until one has learned to save his soul.

Those who think that by breaking the marriage vow and taking another partner they can satisfy the infinite, forget that they are now off the road and into a rut. Instead of following the ray of light to the sun, they will become like eccentric planets that run out of their orbit and burn in space. They try to satisfy the infinite craving for love, not by a vertical line to God but by a horizontal line through a succession of finite stimulations. By the addition of zeros, they hope to make their infinite, only to find that they are most hungry where most they are satisfied.

As the violin needs tuning, as the block of marble needs cutting before it can make a statue, so the love of husband and wife needs purification before it can rise to new heights. The satiety and emptiness which come to the flesh are reminders that one has hit bottom; therefore, one must rise to new heights. But this is not done without a certain abnegation of the ego. The very fact that a certain satiety and fed-upness result from the first love is a proof that there was some egotism hidden in it. What one loved was the pleasure the other gave; what caused the disillusion was the misplaced Infinite, the error of expecting from a creature that which only the Creator can give.

There comes to every human, at one period or another, the discovery of his nothingness. The man who wanted a certain position eventually

The Dark Night of the Body

becomes dissatisfied with it, and wants something higher; he who has wealth does not have enough, not even with the first million. So in married love, there comes the crisis of not completely realizing the ideal. But this crisis of nothingness which comes to everyone, whether he is married or not, does not mean that life is to be mocked. *One has not hit the bottom of life, but only the bottom of one's ego.* One has not hit the bottom of his soul, but only of his instinct; not the bottom of his mind, but of his passions; not the bottom of his spirit, but of his sex. The aforementioned trials are merely so many contacts with reality which Almighty God sends into every life, for what we are describing here is common to every life. If life went on as dream without the shock of disillusionment, who would ever attain his final goal with God and perfect happiness? The majority of men would rest in mediocrity; acorns would be content to be saplings; some children would never grow up and nothing would mature.

Therefore, God had to keep something back, namely, Himself in eternity, otherwise we would never push forward. So He makes everyone run up against a stone wall every now and then in life; on such occasions they feel the crisis of nonentity and have an overwhelming sense of nothingness and loneliness, in order that they may see life not as a city but as a bridge to eternity. The crisis of nothingness is caused by the meeting of a fancied ideal and reality; of love as the ego thinks it is, and of love as it really is. These are the moments when adults burn their fingers on the matches of love, that they might realize the fires of love have divinely ordained purposes, and one of them is not to play.

During this crisis of nothingness, the thing that hearts are kicking and complaining against is not their destiny, nor their nature, but their limits, their weaknesses, their insufficiency. The human heart is not wrong in wanting love; it is wrong only in thinking that a human can completely supply it. What the soul yearns for in the crisis is the Light of love, which is God, and not the shadow. The crisis of nothingness is a summons to the Everything which is God. The abyss of one's own poverty cries out to the abyss of the infinite richness of Divine Love. Instead of thinking that the other partner is to blame for this emptiness, which is so common today, one ought to peer into his own soul. He wants the

363

ocean, and he is drinking from a cup. If there is a thorn in the flesh at this moment of life, as our Lord gave a thorn to the flesh of Paul for the purpose of purification (2 Cor. 12:7–10), the thorn is a summons to climb to the Flame of Love which is God.

Purification of love saves love. It saves it by not blaming the partner as the cause of the crisis; it also saves faith in love itself by pursuing it to a higher level. Neither the lover nor the love are at fault in this dark night of the body. Those who do not purify their love generally resort at this moment to one of five false solutions: (a) They seek a new partner to satisfy their egotisms; (b) they decide to live apart; (c) the husband absorbs himself in business and the wife in bridge clubs; (d) they resort to alcohol in an attempt to drive the conscious problem into unconsciousness; (e) they consult a Freudian psychoanalyst, who tells them to divorce and remarry, or to repeat the problem all over again.

It must not be thought that the crisis of nothingness is peculiar to marriage. It can happen in the spiritual life, too. Those who have dedicated themselves to religion, as priests and nuns and contemplatives, reach a crisis in Divine Love Their prayers become dry, arid, and formal; they are now used to the spiritual realities which they touch. The priest no longer has the thrill of the ineffable presence of God on opening the tabernacle door, or in carrying the Blessed Sacrament to the sick. The nun, who regarded the children in her classroom as potential saints, now is apt to look upon her task as the fulfillment of a duty. Self-examination becomes irksome; there is a decreasing consciousness of the Presence of God; humility is harder to practice; it becomes more difficult to get up for meditation; and thanksgiving to God becomes shorter and shorter.

The problem created in this hour of mediocrity and tedium is often expressed as: "How can I pray better? Why do I not feel greater union with God? Why are sacrifices irksome now, which once were so pleasant? Why is my breviary read with distraction?" There is one answer to these questions. One is in a spiritual rut because one has not practiced mortification. In order to lift the love of the soul to new heights, one must begin to do some works of penance which have not been done before; there must be a rebirth of sacrifice; a fresh taming of the ego; a

The Dark Night of the Body

disciplining of the flesh; more fasting, almsgiving; and more self-denial for the sake of one's neighbor.

What the Dark Night of the Soul is to the spiritual life, the Dark Night of the Body is to marriage. Neither are permanent; both are occasions of purification for fresher insights into Love. If the fig tree of love is to bear fruit, it must be purged and dunged. Dryness in the spiritual life and in marriage are really actual graces. God's finger is stirring the waters of the soul, creating discontent, that new efforts may be put forth. As the mother eagle throws its young out of the nest, in order that they may fly, so now God is giving love its wings in place of its clay feet. This dryness, in either the spiritual or married life, can be either salvation or damnation, depending on how it is used or not used. There are two kinds of dryness: there is one which rots, which is the dryness of love without God; and there is also a dryness which ripens, and that is won when one grows through the fires and heat of sacrifice.

Aridity in love is not the defeat of love, but rather its challenge. If there were no love above the human, or if life were only sex, there is no reason to suppose that love would ever become dull. The major tragedies of life come from believing that love is like a child in a progressive school, and that if left to itself without any discipline, it will grow to perfection. Dryness, mediocrity, and tedium are danger signals! Love, too, has its price, and no one ever became a saint, or made a marriage a joy, without a fresh struggle against the ego.

The modern solution in marriage is to find a new love; the Christian solution is to recapture an old love. Divorce with remarriage is a sign that one never loved a person in the first place, but only the pleasure which that person gave. The Christian attitude is that one must now love the same person, but on a higher level. To seek to overcome the depression by finding a new love is to intensify egotism, and make the other the victim of that egotism under the appearance of devotion and love. The Christian solution is to conquer egotism. Instead of discovering a new love, it discovers the same love. The modern solution is to chase new prey; the Christian solution is to bind up the wounds of the divinely sanctioned marriage.

Those who leave one thrill for another never really love, for no one loves who cannot love through disenchantment, disillusion, and deception. It is sex which seeks a new stimulus; but Christian love seeks a *higher* stimulus. Sex ignores eternity for the sake of passing experience; love tries to bring eternity more into love, and thus make it more lovable. Love, at the beginning, speaks the language of eternity. It says, "I will love you always." In the Crisis of Nothingness the idea of eternity cries to be reintroduced. There is this difference, however. In the days of romance, the eternal emphasis was on the ego's durability in love; in the Crisis of Nothingness, the eternal element is God, not the ego. Love now says, "I will love you always, for you are lovable through eternity for God's sake." He who courts and promises eternal love is actually appropriating to himself an attribute of God. During the Dark Night of the Body, he puts eternity where it rightly belongs, namely, in God.

Once purified, love returns. The partner is loved beyond all sensation, all desire, all concupiscence. The husband who began by loving the other for his own sake, and then for her sake, now begins to love for God's sake. He has touched the depths of a body, but now he discovers the soul of the other person. This is the new infinite taking the place of the body; this is the new "always," and it is closer to the true infinite because the soul is infinite and spiritual, whereas the body is not. The other partner ceases to be opaque and begins to be transparent, the glass through which God and His purposes are revealed. Less conscious of his own power to beget love in others, he sees his poverty and begins to depend on God to complement that poverty. Good Friday now passes into Easter Sunday with the Resurrection of Love.

Love, which once meant pleasure and self-satisfaction, changes into love for God's sake. The other person becomes less the necessary condition of passion and more the partner of the soul. Our Blessed Lord said that unless the seed fall to the ground and die, it will not spring forth into life. Nothing is reborn to a higher life without a death in the lower. The heart has its cycles as well as the planets, but the movement of the heart is an upward spiral, and not a circle which turns upon itself. The planetary circles are repetitious, the eternal return to a beginning.

The Dark Night of the Body

There are some who say that their love lives on memories, but they know in their hearts that the memories are unsatisfying. The body that has lost an arm or a leg is not consoled by recalling the departed member. Life is progressive rather than reminiscent. If love does not grow, it becomes sterile and flat. The living on memories assumes that the heart, like the planets, travels in a circle and not in a spiral. He who loses his arm, and then utilizes the loss to incorporate himself more closely to the will of God, has spiraled upward in his love. He who takes the aridities and the ordinariness of love, and utilizes them to lift self and partner to new horizons, has proven that he belongs to the realm of life rather than to that of planets.

Progress begins with a dream, and progresses through the death of that dream. Marriage would never begin, if there were no dream of happiness. When finally the dream comes true, there will be no progress in joy unless one is prepared to die to that old dream and begin to dream new dreams. To live on the memory of a love is as unsatisfying as to live on the memory of food. The Crisis of Nothingness, which follows a dream come true, needs its purification and its cross. The cross is not a roadblock on the way to happiness; it is a ladder up which one climbs to a Heaven of love.

Another name for the purification of love is transfiguration, which means the use of a loss, or a pain, or a mediocrity, or a disillusionment, as a steppingstone to a new anointing of joy. When Peter saw the face of our Lord, as bright as the sun and with His robes white as snow, he wanted to capture that ephemeral glory in a permanent form. But all the while, our Lord was talking to Moses and Elias of His death. He was reminding Peter that there is no true glory without a Cross. This momentary glory is only an anticipation and a preshadowing of a glory that comes after a crucifixion. Transfiguration in marriage comes through an intensive retraining of the ego. The more one gives up the self, the more one possesses self. It is the ego that stands in the way of all fine social relationships. The egotist has no friends in the social order, and the egotistic spouse precludes the possession in joy of the other.

Transfiguration is based on the idea that love resides in the will, and not in the emotions. The emotions lose their thrill, but the will can become stronger with the years. Those who identify love and the glands feel their love decreasing as time goes on, despite the injection of hormones. Those who identify love and the will and admit the third which makes love, find that age never affects love. The will really can grow stronger as the body becomes weaker. One therefore always has it in his or her power to lift himself to new heights through a willed and deliberate sacrifice of the ego, even when the body-love has begun its decline.

George Bernard Shaw once said that it is a pity that youth has been wasted on the young. On the contrary, this is one of life's greatest blessings. If youth were not wasted on the young, if the tendency to equate love and sensation had not finally been overcome in youth through disillusionment, how few would find the love of God which they are really seeking. Only when some exhaust the substitutes and find them unworthy, do they ever begin to think of reality. It is possible to come to God through a series of disgusts, which the excesses of youth beget. The Psalmist asked God not to remember the sins of his youth. The maturity which age brings associates regret with the abuse of the wellsprings of life. Sublimation is the condition of sound thinking. God in His Mercy has made it easier for the young to make fools of themselves than for the old. The old fools who try to live as if human love had no Dark Night are, however, the greatest fools of all.

The divine law which forbids divorce and remarriage has also a sound psychological basis. The permission to alter one love for another, while the first partner is living, is to permit the suicide of character. Those who violate God's law run away whenever they encounter a difficulty. They are like an army that refuses to fight the opposition and win a victory. When they come to that moment in human love when they are given an opportunity to perfect their love in God and save their souls, they run to another human love and thus miss the chance of salvation. They are like flowers that identify love with blossom; just as soon as the strong winds or a storm come, they refuse to bear fruit and begin to wither and die. The world is full of people who "give up" instead of going forward in a marriage. Instead of being loyal and faithful to a word, they break their trust and substitute sensation for ideals and mediocrity for sacrifice. The very expressions that are used to justify such capitulation to dishonor, as "I must live my own life," and "I have a right to my happiness," indicate that their standard is the ego. The ego must be satisfied at all costs, even though it means trampling on another soul for the sake of a new thrill. The Christian doctrine on the unbreakable quality of marriage is aimed at character-making. It wants captains to stay on the deck during a storm and not to jump overboard. Too many now are deserting their ships. As the French proverb puts it: "Divorce is the sacrament of adultery."

There can be no happiness in the home without the sacrifice which transfigures love. No wound caused by quarrels can fester when the ego is willing to humble itself. The commonest events of daily life and the vulgarity of the smallest minute are made sacred through the delicate attention to the partner which sacrificial love engenders. No one should ever enter into marriage without promising to de-egotize, for marriage is communion! To read some modern books, one would think the biggest problem in marriage was that of being sexually adjusted. It is not sex that needs adjustment, it is the egotism, selfishness, and animality which want their own pleasure without regard to the other's.

The best physical adjustments science can make possible will go for naught unless there is a spiritual adjustment which sacrifice alone makes possible. It is in the interior world of the partner in which happiness lies, and not on the surface of the skin. What is pleasantness in the last analysis but a profound abrogation of one's own likes and tastes and preferences and fatigues, for the sake of being attentive to others? The real happiness of life begins to leave at the moment when the ego experiences its greatest pleasure, for no egotistical satisfaction is ever attained except at someone else's expense. Love without sacrifice diminishes the love. To demand pleasure without loving revolts the partner. To demand without patience, discourages. During the Dark Night of the Body one is closest to capturing the prize. One step beyond mediocrity, and we are saved.

19

For Better or for Worse

In erotic or selfish love, the burdens of others are regarded as impeding one's own happiness. But in Christian love, burdens become opportunities to serve. That is why the symbol of Christian love is not the circle circumscribed by self, but the cross with its arms outstretched to infinity to embrace all humanity within its grasp. But despite love's best effort, there is no control over a partner. What if the husband becomes an alcoholic, or unfaithful, or beats his wife and children? What if the wife becomes nagging or unfaithful, or neglects her children? Should there not be a separation? Yes, under certain circumstances there may be a separation but this does not give the offended party the right to contract a new marriage. "What God, then, has joined, let not man put asunder" (Matt. 19:6).

Another problem is resolving the trials and sorrows, the disillusionments and tears, which sometimes come to married life. Certainly not by allowing a man or woman, who has got some other woman or man into a hole, to be free to get other people into other holes; for if society will not let a man live as he pleases, why should it let him love as he pleases? Neither is the solution to be found in claiming that another person is "vital" for happiness. If desire takes precedence over right and honor, then how prevent future rapes of Poland, or the stealing of a bicycle? How circumvent any passion becoming the basis of usurpation, which is the ethics of barbarism?

Suppose the promise of marriage "for better or for worse" turns out for the worse; suppose either husband or wife becomes a chronic invalid, or develops antisocial characteristics. In such cases, no carnal love can save it. It is even difficult for a personal love to save it, particularly if the other party becomes undeserving. But when these lower loves break down, Christian love steps in to suggest that the other person is to be regarded as a *gift* of God. Most of God's gifts are sweet; a few of them, however, are bitter. But whether that other person be bitter or sweet, sick or well, young or old, he or she is still a gift of God, for whom the other partner must sacrifice himself or herself. Selfish love would seek to get rid of the other person because he is a burden. Christian love takes on the burden, in obedience to the divine command: "Bear the burden of one another's failings; then you will be fulfilling the law of Christ" (Gal. 6:2).

And if it be objected that God never intended that anyone should live under such difficulties, the answer very flatly is that He does: "If any man has a mind to come my way, let him renounce self, and take up his cross, and follow me. The man who tries to save his life shall lose it; it is the man who loses his life for my sake that will secure it" (Matt. 16:24–25). What sickness is to an individual, an unhappy marriage may be to a couple: a trial sent by God in order to perfect them spiritually. Without some of the bitter gifts of God, many of our spiritual capacities would be undeveloped. As the Holy Word of God tells us: "We are confident even over our afflictions, knowing well that affliction gives rise to endurance, and endurance gives proof of our faith, and a proved faith gives ground for hope. Nor does this hope delude us the love of God has been poured out in our hearts by the Holy Spirit, whom we have received" (Rom. 5:3–5).

Such a marriage may be a kind of martyrdom, but at least the one who practices Christian love can be sure that he is not robbing another soul of its peace, nor his own life of honor. This acceptance of the trials of marriage is not a sentence to death, as some believe. The soldier is not sentenced to death because he takes the oath to his country, but he admits that he is ready to face death rather than lose honor. An unhappy marriage is not a condemnation to unhappiness; it is a noble tragedy in which one bears the "slings and arrows of outrageous fortune," rather than deny a vow made to the Living God. Being wounded for the country we love is noble; but being wounded for the God we love is nobler still.

Christian love, on the part of one spouse, will help redeem the other partner. God must have His saints not where all is pleasant, but most of all where saints are least appreciated and hated. St. Paul wrote to the Philippians: "The brethren who are with me send you their greetings; greeting, too, from all the saints, especially those who belong to the Emperor's household" (Phil. 4:22). What these saintly souls were to the entrenched evil of Nero's household, namely, its cleansing atmosphere and its redeeming heart, the Christian spouse will be toward the other; the good influence in an environment that might be as evil as Caesar's palace. If a father will pay his son's debts to keep him out of prison, if a man will give a blood transfusion to save his friend's life, then it is possible in marriage for a spouse to redeem a spouse.

As the Scriptures tell us: "The unbelieving husband is sanctified by the believing wife; and the unbelieving wife is sanctified by the believing husband" (1 Cor. 7:14). This is one of the most forgotten texts on the subject of marriage. It applies to the spiritual order the common experiences of the physical. If a husband is ill, the wife will nurse him back to health. In the spiritual order, the one who has faith and love of God will take on the burdens of the unbeliever, such as drunkenness, infidelity, and mental cruelty, for the sake of his soul. What a blood transfusion is to the body, reparation for the sins of another is to the spirit. Instead of separating when there are difficulties and trials, the Christian solution is to bear the other as a cross for the sake of his sanctification. The wife can redeem the husband, and the husband the wife.

This transferability of sanctification from a good wife to a bad husband, or from a good husband to a bad wife, follows from the fact that they are two in one flesh. As skin can be grafted from the back to the face, so merit can be applied from spouse to spouse. This spiritual communication may not have the romantic satisfaction in it that carnal communication has, but its returns are eternal. Many a husband and wife after infidelities and excesses will find themselves saved on Judgment Day, as the faithful partner never ceased to pour out prayers for his or her salvation. St. Peter confirms this idea: "You, too, who are wives must be submissive to your husbands. Some of these still refuse credence to the word; it is for their wives to win them over, not by word but by example; by the modesty and reverence they observe in your demeanour. Your beauty must lie, not in braided hair, not in gold trinkets, not in the dress you wear, but in the hidden features of your hearts, in a possession you can never lose, that of a calm and tranquil spirit; to God's eyes, beyond price. It was thus that the holy women of old time adorned themselves, those women who had such trust in God, and paid their husbands such respect. Think how obedient Sara was to Abraham, how she called him her lord; if you would prove yourselves her children, live honestly, and let no anxious thoughts disturb you. You, too, who are husbands must use marriage considerately, paying homage to woman's sex as weaker than your own. The grace of eternal life belongs to both, and your prayers must not suffer interruption" (1 Pet. 3:1–7).

Most marriages fail not because of infidelity or because of selfishness, but because of the refusal to make sacrifices when needed, or through expecting the other party will always enter into one's moods with reciprocity and simultaneity. Sometimes moods cannot be reciprocated. Then it is that Christian love climbs to the peak, counting its sweet sorrow a cheap price to pay for the blissful monopoly of loving while yet unloved, desiring, like Paul, to spend itself and to be spent for others, feigning all faults as its own, being dismissed if the other's contentment is isolation, putting love in the one who is apparently not lovable, and thus finding him lovable, as God finds us lovable because He first put His love in us.

The Christian answer in trial is to love one another for Christ's sake. Peace would reign if neither became angry at the same time, if they never retired without prayers together, nor met without a warm welcome, nor parted without reluctance, nor failed to see in the other an opportunity to manifest that love that came from the Cross. "This is the greatest love a man can show, that he should lay down his life for his friends" (John 15:13).

For Better or for Worse

Love on pilgrimage would then march with winged feet back again to the great flame of God, ever realizing this profound truth that the greatest mistake in life is in seeking to be loved. May it not be true after all, that only in the degree that we love, shall we be loved? Given this Christian love which puts love where it does not find it, then in any marriage, bitter or sweet, there will be at least one of the partners who can say with Elizabeth Barrett Browning:

> How do I love thee? Let me count the ways.
> I love thee to the depth and breadth and height
> My soul can reach, when feeling out of sight
> For the ends of Being and Ideal grace.
> I love thee to the level of everyday's
> Most quiet need, by sun and candle-light.
> I love thee freely, as men strive for Right;
> I love thee purely, as they turn from Praise.
> I love thee with the passion put to use
> In my old griefs, and with my childhood's faith.
> I love thee with a love I seemed to lose
> With my lost saints, — I love thee with the breath,
> Smiles, tears, of all my life! — and, if God choose,
> I shall but love thee better after death.

Since the blessings and happiness of married life need no elaboration, but the trials and crosses of life do, it is necessary to penetrate more deeply into the spirit of sacrifice. Here we assume at the beginning not only the "worse" mentioned in the formula "for better or for worse," but even the worst. Whether it be a wife struck down with illness the day after marriage, or a ruined home full of children after twenty years of married life, makes little difference. The important question is: "How interpret and accept these trials in a truly Christian spirit?" No human being has a choice of whether he will go through life with or without suffering, because this is to a great extent beyond his control. But each one has this choice: Will the suffering open on a cross and therefore see the joy beyond, or will it be closed to the cross and therefore be the beginning of Hell on earth?

The great difference between a Christian and a pagan in suffering is that for the Christian all suffering is from the *outside*; that is, it is a trial permitted by God for self-purification and sanctification. For the pagan, suffering is on the *inside*; it is in his soul, in his mind, in his consciousness, in his unconsciousness; it is so much a part of him that it is a Hell, though that Hell often goes by the name of "anxiety" or "frustration." The Christian *receives suffering*, and he even speaks of it as coming from the hands of the Crucified; the pagan *creates suffering*. Because he cannot see its place in the universe, because it negates his egotism, and because it cancels his love of pleasure, he begets an inferno within himself. The crosses from the outside are bearable; the double-crosses inside are insoluble. In the latter case, even where there is a nominal belief in God, the sufferer will unconsciously betray his egotism with the query: "Why does God do this to me?"

Pure suffering is what is seen as coming from the Crucified Hands. Impure suffering is what the mind sees when it is in rebellion against itself. In this sense, the Oriental philosophers were right in regarding suffering as a kind of an illusion. They are illusions to the extent that they are of the non-soul given for the sake of the soul. Being extraneous to the soul which possesses the joy of union with God, they are "only the shade of His Hand outstretched caressingly." When our Divine Lord stretches out His Arms in wide embrace, with the sun behind Him, what falls upon earth is the shadow of His Cross. The more the sun is behind Him, the greater is the length and breadth of the Cross. To just the extent that we turn our backs to Him who is the Light of the World, the greater becomes the cross. The farther we walk away from Him, the more the cross lengthens, until we reach a point where we may begin to identify ourselves with our shadow. This is sometimes called "psychoneurosis," though it is nothing but the pursuit of the superficial self, in which the personality possessed with a soul made for God becomes confused with the shadow of self caused by an externalization of oneself through an undue concern with things outside. When the point is reached where wealth, pleasure, power, sex, and publicity, which are only the shadows of real values, become identified

For Better or for Worse

with personality, then begins that series of queer mental states which end in despair on a psychoanalytic couch.

But as the soul turns around to the Light of the World, the illusions vanish. Eventually, a moment is reached when there is no longer a shadow on love, but an identity with Christ best expressed by Paul: "And yet I am alive; or rather, not I; it is Christ that lives in me" (Gal. 2:20).

The key to the solution of crosses of married life, if they come, is not in the breaking of the bond, for that is unbreakable. Rather, it is the utilization of its sufferings for self, for children, and for the spouse, who for the present at least is the cause of the suffering. Christian love not only can make such suffering bearable; it can even make it sweet. The love of God voluntarily ended in a Cross; but it did not conquer Him, because it came from without: "He suffered under Pontius Pilate." The Christian, in like manner, sees that if Innocence did not spurn the Cross, then somehow or other it must fit into his life which is far from innocent. Eternal Love has no cross. But once it takes on a human nature and enters into a spatio-temporal environment, it exposes itself to a Cross. A cross is nothing else but want of love, or better still, it is anti-love. The refusal to love Love is Crucifixion. The noblest love of a spouse can be exposed to the negation of love, because if love is not returned by the other spouse, it is no reason for abandoning love altogether. When a husband gives up an unloving wife, or an unloving wife gives up an unloving husband, there is a denunciation of love in the universe, a betrayal of the Love of God who loved us even while we were sinners. Granted that fidelity to the bond would not make such love revive in time, it must not be forgotten that there is an eternity, and faithful love can redeem unfaithful love.

As God does not coerce our free soul, but woos it, so there is a warm prayer-wooing in marriage, even when the heart-wooing has long since grown cold. All over this earth, even in little apartments, houses, and tiny hovels, there are free wills that make themselves little gods. Christ felt their rebellion in Gethsemane and feels their *non-serviam* now in His Mystical Body, but He does not let go His love for such souls. Magdalens and penitent thieves will still return, so long as the door of love is left open. If, then, husband and wife reflect the love of Christ by continuing

377

to love, even in disaster, sickness, or trial, it will be as redemptive as His Love. In the end, they will count their sufferings nothing but a feeble payment of their debt to Him.

Love is the expansion of being. Want of love, even when one is un-loved, is a decrease of being. If suffering enters love, it is to be accepted as a purification of both husband and wife. When accepted as redemp-tive, a great joy takes possession of the soul. This joy is rather difficult to explain, but its secret probably is this: suffering enters into me, but I do not enter into suffering. If I entered into suffering, there would be an externalization of personality. Just as a person loses something of himself by being absorbed in alcohol or sex, so the soul loses something in be-ing possessed by suffering. The spirit is impoverished through a loss of immanent or self-contained activity, which is the attribute of life. But when suffering enters into me, it becomes an enrichment of the spirit, as knowledge is the ennoblement of the mind. What comes into a man is mastered by man. And as the mind changes the nature of a flower by knowing it, giving it a mental existence instead of a plant existence, so suffering assimilated by the soul in union with Christ changes its nature and actually becomes joy.

But only Christ-conscious souls have the power to effect this trans-formation. An animal cannot know "goodness" as such, but only this good water, or that good thing; but man can, because he has the power of abstracting the universal from the particular. The pagan, seeing the gold mixed with dross, throws away the treasure because he has no knowledge of how to refine it. The Christian, however, can extract the divine gold from the dross of suffering and thus add to the wealth of his Christian character. Suffering then becomes assimilable to the soul through the power of the Cross. But to the worldling, it becomes a double-cross; *inside* as an intellectual complexity incapable of solution, and *outside* as a violent intrusion and disturbance of one's egotism. The man without faith is no more immune from a cross than the man with faith. The difference is that the Christian has only one cross, which is so understandable, while the egotist has two crosses, whose names are Rebellion and Suffering. A moment can actually be reached by the Christian when his suffering is felt less and less as coming from the outside, or as being imposed on him, and more and more as a failure to accomplish perfectly within himself the will of God.

The cross that was given from the outside can be now offered from the inside by the Christian as part of his very self, as something so vital to his self-development in Christ that he would feel the poorer without it. To the onlooker, it seems like suffering; to the Christ-lover, it is joy; just as to the unmarried, an infant is the sum of economic expense, confinement, tears, baby sitters, measles, and worry, but to the father and mother it is a joy and a benediction. The child, viewed as an *object* external to self, is a burden; but seen as a *subject*, it is a prolongation of personality and the fleshly symbol of their love.

No believer in an abstract deity or a vague power behind the universe can comprehend this mystery of joy in suffering, for such a god reigns but does not govern. He asks no sacrifice, and therefore he does not dignify man, who wants to love by giving. On the lower levels of reason, without faith in the Redemptive Cross, man is unarmed to live and understand his life. What he calls "fate," or "bad luck," or "misfortune," or "incompatibility," is looked upon as a resistance to his ego. To the Christ-dominated soul, these seeming contradictions are seen in relation to the totality of God's plan, or as invisible rays of light putting man in touch with the sound and video of Heaven's eternal purposes. Life then becomes a conquest of unity, a progressive triumph over distraction and digression. In marriage, the union of husband and wife is seen first as cooperation; with the birth of children, it becomes corporation. If joys come, then it is con-corporation with Christ in His Glory, but if sorrow comes, it is as incorporation to His Cross. But the husband and wife who would set *limits* to their creative love, and determine exactly the minimum number of concrete living objects to which their love will extend, necessarily incapacitate themselves to embrace a cross. Nothing so untrains a soul as the limitation of creative goodness. Such rationalization of love, or perhaps better its atomization, can never grasp those suprarational joys which come from accepting everything from God's Hands, whether it be a child, childlessness, or a cross.

Trials and misfortunes endured with Christ-love diminish the suffering of others. It prevents them from multiplying like a pestilence. Any dissolution of the marriage bond wrecks another home and spoils another heart. Not only does the faithful spouse perfect his own soul, but he absorbs the agony of another, as Christ took on the sins and infidelities of mankind. Life is made less rough for others by localizing marital infections, and thus preventing them from becoming epidemics.

Those who understand not the Cross call on others to help them make their boredom less boring. What these unspirited lives seek on the *outside*, the Christian through the Holy Spirit of Love finds on the *inside*. God gives a curing without destroying, an illumination without burning, a making tender without touchiness. Even in the midst of little crosses, the Spirit makes life be seen not as a "road out," but simply "closed for repairs." An officer in the last World War, after being wounded, made the offering of the wounds to Christ, and then said to his friend: "A piece of the Infinite is under construction!"

What makes life tragic is not so much *what* happens, but rather how we *react* to what happens. No one can prevent suffering and infidelity, but he can prevent himself from being soured by them. Our Lord never promised that His followers would be without a cross. Rather did He promise they would have one. He did guarantee, however, that we would never be overcome by it. Love of Christ will not kill pain, but it will diminish it.

All suffering becomes bearable if there is someone we love. Sacrifice is pain with love; pain is sacrifice without love. The mother suffers for her children, but it is sweet because she loves. Battlefields, hospitals, and homes are filled with thousands and thousands of cases of wasted pain. It is wasted because those who sweat and groan under life's crosses have no one to love, or for whom they can bear the pain. The Christ love on the Cross can make even the worst of marriages bearable, and certainly extinguish any desire to contract a second while the first spouse is living. Religions without a cross will satisfy when romance blooms, but when life becomes sordid and dull and hard, it takes faith with a cross in it to salvage the mind and bring peace.

For Better or for Worse

Because the Christian marriage is the fleshly symbol of the Divine Espousals of Christ and His Bride the Church, no infidelity or unworthiness can justify the breaking of the bond for the sake of contracting a new marriage. Separation may be allowed; but, even then, the faithful one must be redemptive of the other. Faithfulness to the bond is here not to be interpreted as a passive resignation to a duty. It is not the nature of love ever to abandon the one in moral need, any more than it is the nature of a mother's love to abandon a child with polio. There may be a case here and there of a mother leaving her sick child at another's doorstep, but this is only because there is a failing of love. Likewise in marriage, the wife who contracts a new marriage because her husband "ran off with another woman" does so only because love in her heart became contaminated. The soldiers who desert their country's cause in the heat of battle do not display patriotism, but a diseased cowardice.

The "believing wife" or the "believing husband" (1 Cor. 7:14), whichever the case may be, refuses entreaties to another marriage (while the spouse is living) not for the negative reason, "The Church will not allow me," but for the positive reason, because "I love in a Christian way." Each refusal is a deepening of the first love! Fidelity in crisis is therefore not something one "puts up with" or "makes the best of"; it is something that is ardently chosen for love's sake. Homer had a better understanding of this than the modern pagans. Penelope, during the absence of her husband, was courted by many admirers. Each day she worked on a tapestry to keep her hands busy, while her heart awaited his return from the wars. The years rolled on, and though she was told her husband would never return, she still believed he would. Her faith was not based on his charm, but on the original gift of her love and his. She told her suitors she would marry when she finished her tapestry, but each night she would undo the stitches she knitted during the day, until Ulysses returned.

It is a false idea of liberty to think that it promises a release from love in order to please oneself. No person in all the world is made happier by the breaking of a pledged love. There are certain things that once accepted are never to be surrendered. Food is one of them in the lower order. What is forcibly ejected from the stomach has a mark of vileness and impurity. But it is pure compared to a love that is vomited from the heart. Hell is full of hearts which took back their love. As breathing in the same air the lungs exhaled is slow poison, so the lover who draws back into his heart the love he gave in marriage suffers a spiritual thrombosis, which is eternally disastrous.

Since marital love is the shadow cast on earth by the love of Christ for His Church, then it must have Christ's redemptive quality. As Christ delivered Himself up for His Spouse, so there will be some wives and some husbands who will deliver themselves up to Golgotha for the sake of their spouses. The young suitor does not abandon his beloved because she falls in the mud. Why then, when there is moral dirt into which she tumbles, should the husband claim that love does not demand the rescue? There is not a child who was ever born who did not introduce suffering into love. The coming into being of a new love is heralded by the labor of the mother, but the pain soon passes into joy. Our Lord uses this analogy to suggest that every pain nobly borne can bring joy into the soul, even the spiritual "labor" of a husband bringing forth a wife unto conversion, or a wife bringing forth a husband to sobriety after a long period of spiritual parturition. "A woman in childbirth feels distress, because now her time has come; but when she has borne her child, she does not remember the distress any longer, so glad is she that a man has been born into the world. So it is with you, you are distressed now; but one day I will see you again, and then your hearts will be glad; and your gladness will be one which nobody can take away from you" (John 16:21–22).

This mystery of the Cross before the crown, the egotist cannot understand, and for that reason did St. Paul call it "the folly of the cross " (1 Cor. 1:18). But those who have sounded its depths know that God gives the strength to carry it! As one non-Catholic woman wrote to the other: "I decided to get a divorce from my alcoholic husband. Then, suddenly, I realized that by doing so, I was making a contribution to the disintegration of civilization. So I resolved to stay with him and be faithful to him. But I cannot do it alone, nor without the Faith. How can I get it?" Her sorrow was turned into joy. At her First Communion she said: "I feel as if I presided at the Creation of the world, before the mountains and the hills were made, and only this morning I caught up with my Lover." Her husband gave up drinking, and the two of them now meet the Love in Communion which makes their twain a trinity. How the love of Christ works miracles with human love is best told by those in whom the miracles were worked. Some stories of those who have spiritualized love to assure its perpetuity are told in the next chapter.

20

Love's Reaction to Loss

Inasmuch as psychoneurosis has become such a characteristic of our modern civilization, it is fitting that there be mirrored forth for the example of Christians the story of how one husband lived through its Golgothas and kept his faith in God.

Sophie-Charlotte Wittelsbach (1847-1897), at the age of nineteen was betrothed to the King of Bavaria, who was already beginning to show signs of incipient insanity. The hopes of the young bride for an early marriage were wrecked, time and time again, as her prospective husband put off the marriage, and then, finally, told her that his only love in the world was for Wagnerian music. Her mind, somewhat shattered by this blow, found a temporary release when she met an exiled French Orléans, Ferdinand Philip, the Duke of Alençon, whom she married. It was his first love, and his last love as he told her one day: "I have loved you with the most tender affections on this earth, for I love you with an eternal love because it is a Christian love." This declaration of his love was made in the midst of a growing consciousness of her defects. Melancholia, which was one of the family traits, soon began to appear in her, manifesting itself in undue sensitiveness, impulsiveness, capriciousness and morbidity. The young husband, with a prophetic intuition of her needs, began a passionate and pathetic fight to tear his wife away from the clutches of mental instability and her repeated relapses into disturbing psychoses and neuroses. The struggle which he faced was one which he confessed would require not only a husband much in love with his wife but also a guardian angel. He tried to introduce her to the realities of religion but without much success until he brought her to Rome for a visit, where he saw on an ancient tomb the inscription: "Sophronia may you live." Hundreds of times a day he recited the prayer for his wife, "Sophie may you live." Later on he changed it to an assertion: "Sophie, you *shall live.*"

After many years of suffering he said to his wife, in one of her rare moments of lucidity, "I have told you nothing in order not to trouble you, but I have been watching over you in silence. On the day of our marriage God gave you to me, body and soul. If, by chance, you happen to fall I would be the guilty one, for I answer for you and if I had remained not true it would have proven that I did not know how to preserve you." Despite her impossible conduct, her anti-religious outbursts, he never left her side except to visit their children in school.

Finally, when his wife had reached the age of thirty-six, through his patience and his prayers she emerged from her last and terrible crisis, transformed and transfigured. He joined the Third Order of St. Dominic and she joined the Third Order of St. Francis and both united in works of charity. Many people began coming to her seeking her advice; the poor she visited on foot for many hours during the day and night; her former melancholia had given place to a joy which nothing could quench, and with that joy there came an amazing moral strength. On the fourth of May in her fiftieth year she left her home to preside over the Bazaar of Charity which was then being held in Paris. The Bazaar was a monstrous affair in a huge tent sheltering an array of tables and counters. The center of attraction was a recent invention, a motion picture machine which was installed behind an arbor of flowers. Her husband had come to the Bazaar in order to see his wife preside. Suddenly the motion picture apparatus caught fire and the two exits became jammed with escaping people. Because she presided, some people came to save her, but as she directed the women and children she said: "I shall go out last, save the others first." A Dominican nun who stood by her, seeing the flames coming closer, said: "My God, what an awful death." "Yes," smiled the Duchess quietly, "but think of it, we shall see God in a few minutes."

Her husband, who tried to remain with her, was pushed by the crowd and left in a bedlam of smoke and fire and madness. The last that was seen of her was when she was kneeling by a young and fair girl, turning the latter's head toward her own bosom in order to hide from the young face the horrors of death. A few days later her husband, recovering consciousness in a hospital, was informed of his wife's death. His first words were: "Oh God, of course I know that I must not ask you why." Then a smile came over his lips, and resuming the prayer he learned at the ancient tomb in Rome, he now added a new invocation: the "Sophie may you live," which later on became "Sophie, you shall live" now became: "Sophie, you live!"

There are many instances of a husband or a wife offering himself or herself in order that the other may gain the gift of faith. Inasmuch as the diaries and letters of this couple have been preserved, it is easy to follow the ascension and transfiguration of their souls. The woman was Alexandrine d'Alopeus of St. Petersburg who, though not a member of the Church, was very fond of visiting the churches when she was in Rome. In the year 1832, she saw a young man, a French diplomat by the name of Albert de la Ferronnays, praying at the Communion rail. She said she felt such a strong urge to pray alongside of him that she actually would have done it if her sisters had not been with her. On coming out of the church, she was introduced to him. They made a visit to the four great basilicas of Rome and when finally they finished the visit, Albert knelt before the main altar and offered to our Lord the sacrifice of his life if He would give to this beautiful young girl the gift of faith.

Later on, while courting, she wrote to Albert: "When I am near you and when I feel that you love me, my happiness would sadden me if there were no God whom I could thank. Do you think that those who have no faith really love? Do they have deep emotions? Can they be truly devoted?" When Albert received the letter, he wrote in his diary: "Oh, my God, enkindle again in my heart the fire of your most Divine Love. Purify this sentiment which is today my whole life, that I may respect her more than anything else in all the world, and that I may become worthy to love her." Then, answering her letter, he said to her: "No, I do not believe that anyone can love with innocence and with depth, I do not believe that anyone can love at all, without being penetrated by a deep sense of God and immortality." Married on April 17, 1834, in Naples, they spent for the next ten years a life so beautifully ecstatic that she asked her husband if this love was not a foretaste of the manner in which they would be allowed to love God and one another eternally in Heaven.

This confession of the triune quality of love soon began to pass through the phases of Divine Love when God came to this earth and took upon Himself a Cross. Her husband fell seriously ill with consumption, but still their love did not diminish amidst suffering, for every night they read together the *Imitation of Christ*. Their dear friend, de Montalembert, was then writing a life of St. Elizabeth. Having learned that the saint and her husband used to call each other "brother" and "sister," they adopted the practice. She wrote in her diary: "He called me 'sister' and I remember the angelic tenderness on his face when he said that word."

But still Alexandrine did not have the gift of faith, and Albert's greatest sorrow was that his wife could not kneel alongside of him at the Communion rail and receive the Savior's greatest gift of love. One night as the husband's illness became worse, he said to her: "And if God were to take me, dear?" She wrote to de Montalembert saying: "I would be more happy a widow and a Catholic, than always the wife of Albert and not a Catholic." On the fourth of June, 1836, in the presence of her husband, she heard Mass in their bedroom and there received her First Communion. Making an act of resignation to God's will, she wrote in her diary: "Blessed be God, that after having shared most of His pleasures, I now also must share His Agony and if I had to choose between the two I would always choose the latter." Albert called for a paper and then wrote the last words: "Lord, formerly I told you night and day: 'Allow that she be mine in faith; grant me this happiness, even if it is a duration of only one day.' Now that you have heard me, Oh Lord, why should I now complain? My happiness is brief, is unspeakable. Now that the remaining part of my prayer is to be fulfilled that I give you my life, give me the assurance to see her again there where we shall lose ourselves in the immensity of your Love." As Albert died and received the last blessing of the Church, Alexandrine, kneeling at his side, said: "And, now Jesus, Heaven for him." A few minutes later, she added: "Jesus, I have given you my happiness; give me your Faith."

Her widowhood was given over to constant works of charity, for which she despoiled herself completely that she might be like those whom she served. When friends complained that she was making too many sacrifices, she answered in the words of the famous convert Jew, Ratisbonne: "One cannot give to God less than everything." Just before she died, at the age of forty, she wrote to her sister Pauline: "When I think that after having so loved and desired earthly happiness, having had it and lost it, and having reached the depths of despair and then to have had my soul transformed by joy because of it, I realize that nothing that I ever had or imagined is comparable to that joy." "Peace is my bequest to you, and the peace which I give you is mine to give; I do not give peace as the world gives it" (John 14:27).

When one reads of the tremendous transformation of souls in the Sacrament of Matrimony, one realizes that through them, as well as in a life specifically ascetic and detached, such as in the monastery and the cloister, there can be born a fiery and ardent love of God. There is a story to this effect told about St. Macarius, the Egyptian hermit, who one day in his meditations wondered to what degree of holiness and union with God his solitude and years of fasting and prayer had lifted him. Falling asleep, he was told by an angel that he had not reached the level of holiness of two women who lived in a nearby town of whom he should learn. Greatly interested, St. Macarius went to the town and there found the women, and to his great astonishment found that they were married. He entreated them to tell the secret of their sanctity, but the two women, greatly confused, assured him that there was nothing remarkable about them: "We are but poor wives amidst constant worldly cares." But Macarius pressed his question and asked them how they came to be so holy in the eyes of God. Their answer was that for fifteen years they had been married to two brothers and had lived together under the same roof, never once quarreling nor permitting a single unpleasant word to pass between them. Thus did St. Macarius learn that peaceful co-habitation can be even more praiseworthy in the eyes of God than solitary fasting and prayer.

Because of our deep affection for the Russian people who have been much maligned because the world judges their depths by the crust of communism, we here seek within the history of the Russian people some exemplary married lives which witness to the eternal Truth that it takes three to make love. Sacred to the memory of the Russian people are David and Eufrosnia of Nurom. Before David, Prince of Nurom, ascended the throne following the death of his elder brother, he had for a long time suffered from sores that covered his whole body. The daughter of a simple woodman, a girl renowned alike for her wit and goodness, cured him with ointment and constant care. Impressed with the high quality of her mind and heart, David fell in love with her and gave his word that he would marry her. Once recovered from his illness and restored again to the splendors of the court, he felt ashamed to take for his wife a girl as simple as Eufrosnia, so he broke the promise of marriage.

But he fell ill again with the same disease and for the second time Eufrosnia cured him. This time the grateful prince hastened to keep his word and married her. Once on the throne, the nobility of Nurom, urged on by his younger brother and nephew, declared that it was an offense to the land to see a peasant-born woman on the throne. He was, therefore, ordered either to abdicate or repudiate his wife. Calling to his mind the words of our Lord, "What God hath joined together let no man put asunder," he refused to put away his wife, preferring rather to leave the kingdom. His beautiful young wife consoled him with the words, "Do not sorrow, Prince, the merciful God will not leave us in destitution for long."

In Nurom, meanwhile, incessant and irreconcilable quarrels had started, the seekers of power taking to the sword and creating such a chaos that the people recalled David and Eufrosnia to the throne. Their reign was conspicuous for charity (both seeking occasions to give shelter to the poor and to the afflicted), and also for a deep faith in God and religion. One day while the two were in company with a married courtier while sailing on the Oka River, the courtier began to make improper suggestions to the beautiful Eufrosnia, who said to him: "Take some water from the river on this side of the boat and taste it." The man complied with her demand. Then she said: "Now go to the other side of the ship and take some water there and taste it." When he had done so she asked: "Do you find any difference between this water, and that water?" "None," the courtier replied. Then the princess remarked: "And thus also is the essence of woman similar, and in vain do you, forgetting your wife, think of another."

When David and Eufrosnia were old, he entered a monastery and she entered a convent, he taking the name of Peter and she the name of Fevronia. The Russian Church has a feast to this holy couple in which this prayer is offered: "From your youth working for Christ you have recognized the only One in the world in it who is worthy of glory, therefore you pleased Him with alms and prayers and after your death you bring health to all who venerate you, our beloved Peter and Fevronia."

How a love which is made strong in Christ can overcome obstacles is revealed in the love of Princess Maria Volkonskaya, who at the age of eighteen was married to a distinguished officer and nobleman many years her senior, whom she learned to love only after her marriage. Her husband, for a political crime, was condemned to work in the mines of Siberia. She went to see her husband on the eve of his departure for that dreaded land, and though he entreated her to forget him, she swore that she would join him in Siberia. After many difficulties, she finally obtained, from Czar Nicholas II, permission to leave for Siberia. Selling all of her jewels to pay for the expenses because her father would give her no assistance for an enterprise of such folly, she made the hard journey on her own resources. She wrote: "I cannot stay. If I remain here, I shall always hear the quiet reproachful voice of my husband, and in the faces of my friends I will read the truth concerning my behavior. In their whispers, I shall get a sentence, in their smiles my reproach. My place is not at a ball but in a distant and savage land where a woeful prisoner, a prey to gloomy thoughts, suffers alone without help. I must share his disgrace and banishment. It is the will of Heaven that has joined us, and we shall remain together. I would rather leave my baby here with my family than be unfaithful to my husband, for how will my son judge me one day—when he knows that his mother deserted his father in the hour of need? If I stay I might be tempted, God forbid, to forget my husband."

On her way to Siberia she stopped off at Moscow, where her sister gave an impromptu ball in her honor. Among the throngs of guests that filled the palace to see the young girl abandon her life of luxury for exile was the celebrated Pushkin, who had known Maria as a child. He forsook, for once, the bitterness he had adopted in public and talked to her with great tenderness and admiration and foretold that some day poets would sing of her heroism. After many weeks of the terrible journey, she reached the mines beyond Nertchinsk where her husband worked. By some miracle of kindness on the part of the people, she received permission to surprise her husband while he was at work in the mine. She went down into the depths of the earth and, when finally she saw him coming toward her in the gloom, she flung herself before the dazed, unbelieving man and kissed his chains.

Some years later, the exile ended and they spent the rest of their days giving example of love made stronger by adversity and disgrace. Later on, too, the prophecy of Pushkin came true as Nekrassof, the poet of the people, in a beautiful poem called "Russian Women," makes Maria speak to her father:

> Father, you do not know how dear he is to me; . . .
> at first I eagerly listened to tales of his courage in battle,
> And the hero in him I love with all my soul. . . .
> Later I loved in him the father of my baby. . . .
> But the last and best love my heart could give
> Was the one I gave him in prison.
> And then I lost him like another Christ
> Garbed in the clothes of a convict
> He shines now forever in the eyes of my soul
> Shining with a peaceful greatness.
> A crown of thorns is encircling his brow
> Unearthly love shines from his eyes. . . .

Father, I must see you again
I shall die with longing for him....
Yourself or your duty never spared anything
And have taught us to do ever the same.
Your own sons you sent to battle
At the places thought most dangerous.
You cannot quite truly condemn what I do
For I am only your daughter in doing it.

Another beautiful story of fidelity is that of Princess Katerina Trou-betskaya who, after many difficulties, finally received permission from the czar to join her husband in Siberia. Her father arranged for every detail of comfort on her departure to assure her of his approval. But during the voyage, he secretly arranged to have obstacles put in her way in order to force her to return. He begged one of his friends, the general commander of a town in Siberia, to resort to every harshness to discourage her from making the journey. The general received her very coldly and made her wait for several days for a supposedly needed change of carriages and horses. The time having passed, he argued the validity of the imperial passport; then he questioned her health; finally, he started threats of imprisonment for allegedly disobeying the czar, but Katerina said she did not mind prison if only she could be allowed to visit her husband. The general, in lurid terms, began to speak of the mining region beyond Nertchinsk where she was bound, and of the vicious people who lived there, and of the moral degradation awaiting a young and delicately raised cultured woman, of the death that would come to her in that cruel climate and the despair that would take possession of her soul in the midst of the guard of brutal soldiers.

Katerina answered that she was not afraid of death, as her death caused by love would only open Heaven. Furthermore, she said that her gentle-ness was more needed in a place where it was unknown, and as for moral degradation, there was a moral elevation given by God to those who chose to be the least in the eyes of the world.

The discussion having lasted for several days, the general finally con-sented, saying however that she would have to proceed as an ordinary

393

convict and go in the company of a band of unfortunates who were then passing through the town. The rest of the journey would have to be made on foot and in chains. To which Katerina answered: "Where is this convict band which I am to join, and why could you not have told me the truth at once? Of course, I will go with them. I do not care how I arrive, or with whom, if only I arrive." On hearing this, the General could play his part no longer and confessed to her with a broken heart: "I have only obeyed, now I can torture you no longer. Your carriage will be ready in a few minutes. Please forgive me and God be with you."

G. K. Chesterton, in one of his ballads, wrote:

> And so I bring the rhymes to you
> Who brought the Cross to me.

These words fittingly could be applied to a young French girl by the name of Mireille de la Nenardiere, who fell in love with a distinguished, courageous and cultured man by the name of Pierre Dupouey. He had given up the Faith in his early youth, and from that time on until he met his future wife, never seemed to be able to find a substitute for it.

André Gide, whose disciple he was for a time, wrote: "Gradually there deepened in his soul a void which only the Eucharistic Presence could fill." In 1910 Pierre Dupouey wrote to Gide: "I am engaged to a rare and radiant maiden. I will not tell you what the angels call her, but among men she is called Mireille de la Nenardiere. Despite my astonishment to see something wise bend toward me, I must admit that this time wisdom has a face of love." When Mireille proposed to him she said that she wanted marriage in order to increase her love of God. Brought back again to the Faith through her inspiration and prayers, he married her in 1911 at which time Mireille wrote in her diary: "The light of our home never again will be put out. We have lit you at the new fire: Christ-light that will never cease to sing of hope even in the crumbling of war for the home founded on the union of hearts cannot perish." The very first night of the marriage, Pierre proposed to establish, in memory of that day, a rite of love to be accomplished faithfully every day of their married life. He suggested that it consist of kissing each other's wedding ring before going to sleep, in order to ask God's blessing on their love, which was consecrated to His name. Pierre Dupouey later on became so zealous for the Faith that he converted Henri Ghéon, who later wrote of him: "I cannot tire of the look in his eyes—a just man, a free man who understands everything, even the good."

A son was born, and was baptized Pierre. Then came the First World War; during which Pierre wrote to his wife in a letter of August 21, 1914: "How I appreciate the joyous feeling that our hearts remain united despite the days and weeks of separation! They are united by a delightful and mighty chain of common thoughts and common prayers." A few months later she wrote to him, telling him that she was visiting the poor, to which he answered: "I thank you for helping the poor. Do it in my name. Give for both of us, and do not worry over anything that happens around you. Listen to God, who speaks to your heart, and despise the petty prudences which put life out of the shelter of love. Apart from duty and divine things, I only need you, or rather I need you because you are a part of a divine thing of my life, because it is God who made you enter into it, because you are His living and efficacious blessing to me. Since I have received you from God, I have learned to know what providence means."

A few months later, he wrote to his wife, saying: "Your letters are the bread of my heart. I do not know if I am mistaken, but it seems to me that, even now, we receive the rewards of the effort that we've always made to consider everything in the light of eternity. How much these common thoughts of God, which have become so natural to us, have helped us pass these days and weeks, and how we must thank Him for all the Light that He has put into our hands." Then, as if anticipating death, he said: "If I come to disappear, it would only be to surround you from above more unceasingly. Do not be too preoccupied with the morrow. And remember that a little uncertainty as to the future is the best means to augment our confidence and abandonment to God."

Finally, on the eve of his death, he wrote: "At the end of all, the greatest prayer to make for each of us is included in the magnificent cry of Claudel: 'Lord, deliver me from myself.'" On Holy Saturday, at nine o'clock in the evening, he was struck by a bullet and never regained consciousness. The chaplain who attended him said that he had gone to Heaven to celebrate his Easter.

Having been informed of his death, she wrote to the chaplain of her husband's regiment: "Both of us have made the sacrifice. Some will think me mad, but I can tell it to you: since he is no more I have not ceased my thanksgiving to God. He sees God. I envy him. I shall nevermore be separated from him. As to our little boy, he no longer has a father on earth, but I shall put him in the hands of the Eternal Father."

One of the most remarkable men of contemporary times was Léon Bloy, who called himself the "Pilgrim of the Absolute." To the married, his life bears a twofold lesson: one, the sacrificial love of a mother saving the soul of her son, and the other, how a marriage can be spiritualized, even in the midst of poverty. Mothers who have the great sorrow of seeing their children abandon the Faith can understand the deep mystery in the life of the mother of Léon Bloy. Describing his mother's sacrifices in relationship to himself, he wrote:

> In 1869 I had reached the highest point of my evil life. My mother, a Christian woman and heroine, wrote to me in 1870: "My dear son, you are one of my five sons at the front [in the Franco-Prussian War], and yet I would be more easily consoled of your death than of what is now happening." My dearly beloved mother prayed for me since my childhood. When at first indifference and then hate replaced faith in my heart, she redoubled her prayers, making them more fervent and longer, and more intense; she lighted on the altar of her heart a burning desire which perpetually ascended to God, like the flame of an unextinguishable sacrifice. As for me, I doubled my iniquities. Prayers did nothing for me, and grace found me always rebellious, impervious and inflexible. One day my mother, while meditating on the sorrowful Passion of the Divine Saviour, came to see that because our Lord redeemed men by suffering without measure and without consolation, we who are His own members can prolong this marvelous Redemption through our imperfect sufferings. What Jesus has done absolutely by His perfect

oblation of life, Christian hearts could do relatively through their sufferings. She then offered herself to suffer for her children, and to bear their penances. In a counsel of mysterious and ineffable sublimity, she made a pact with God that she would make the absolute sacrifice of her health, and the complete surrender of all human joy and consolation, if He, in return, would grant the entire and perfect conversion of her children. This prodigious bargain, concluded in the presence and through the mediation of the Most Holy Virgin, received its immediate accomplishment. She lost suddenly and irreparably her excellent health in a manner as complete as was possible without actually depriving her of life. Her life became a torment twenty-four hours a day and, in order that this torment be actually complete, her infirmity assumed a character of physical humiliation and abasement that demanded exacting heroism. As for me, I knew these things very much later, and when I had already become a Catholic. Then only, did I know that my mother had given me birth a second time in pain.... Before I came into this world, she said that she did not want me as a child. But through an extraordinary effort of will and of love, which can be understood only by superior souls, she abdicated completely her maternal rights into the hands of our Lady, rendering the Holy Virgin responsible for all my destiny. As long as she lived, she never ceased telling me with a sublime obstinateness, that Mary was my true mother in a very special and very absolute manner.

Léon Bloy himself was destined to show in his life how even a voluntary poverty could still produce joy in marriage. While yet in his forties, in the year 1889, he met at the home of François Coppe a tall blonde girl, the daughter of the Danish poet Christian Molvech, who was visiting there. Bloy was presented to her and they spoke for a while. After his departure Jeanne Molvech asked her friend Anne Coppe who this strange man was? "A beggar," she said.

Later on, Jeanne Molvech wrote concerning him: "The answer was thundering, inexorable in its absoluteness, forcing me to take sides immediately. I had the feeling that this was an enormous injustice, and immediately my heart flew out to that defenseless man who was talked of in such a way to one who had met him but once. But I had no idea of his real worth. I thank God for having hidden it from me." Jeanne did not share the Faith of Bloy and, with a prejudiced mind, wondered how a man as superior as he was could be a Catholic. A short time after their correspondence started, Jeanne embraced the Catholic Faith. Writing concerning this change of heart, Bloy said: "I am profoundly moved by the idea that you are about to enter the Church, that you are going to become, effectively, a daughter of the Holy Spirit, and that it is partly my doing—in the sense that you are receiving this magnificent reward for your compassionate love of this poor and desperate man.... When we receive a Divine Favour, we must be persuaded that somebody has paid for it; such is the law."

After their marriage not only to one another but to a voluntary poverty, they were to change residence some eighteen times in the space of twenty years, Bloy saying that this was a prefigurement of the fact that their home only would be in Heaven. Every morning, the two of them went to the earliest Mass and received Holy Communion. At breakfast, they talked to each other of God. They lived through atrocious hours of mental, moral, and spiritual anguish, but beneath the surface, their lives possessed an incredible beauty and bliss. Jeanne, describing it, said: "There is a lamp lighted for us that does not burn for others."

21

Love Endureth Forever

Modern psychology speaks much of "sublimation," or the finding of outlets in a lower realm for certain basic urges and instincts. Sublimation
indeed has its place particularly in resisting temptation. As J. A. Had-
field has said: "Temptation is the voice of repressed evil; conscience is
the voice of repressed good." One must therefore look to the positive
side of love and its true nature. Marriage is not a sublimation of the sex
instinct; it is the consecration of Divine Love. All love is an initiation
into the Eternal, the reflection of the Divine in the human. Those who
have entered into it and not understood how it prolongs the Incarnation,
or the union of the Divine and the human, have a suffering like to the
moment of our Lord on the Cross, when He spoke the fourth Word of
Abandonment. The *eros*, through a transfiguration, should lead to the
agape, but those who know not Christ are harassed by an infinite nostalgia
for something beyond what they have. Earth and Heaven, love and God,
were not meant to be in a state of suspension and irreconcilability. But to
redeem those who feel abandoned by the love they wanted, and frustrated
by the love they possess, our Lord had to suffer to show them that the
Cross alone with its Transfiguration can tie the two extremes together.

It is so easy to describe the modern concept of married love based on
sex because, being carnal and having its own specific instruments, it can
be analyzed by the Freuds, reported on by the Kinseys, and statistized by

Metropolitan Life. But once a spiritual principle is introduced, then marriage becomes much more difficult to describe. A man is easy to describe if he has only the material components of a matchstick, but it requires more wisdom to define him if he has human freedom and infinite aspirations. If love is mere animal-mating, then any physiologist is its master; if it be a spark from the Divine Flame, then one must pray in order to understand its mystery.

The essence of married love is not *sex*, but *consent*; not animality, but freedom; not a libido, but a choice. If marriage is a love of "the opposite sex," it is selfishness disguised as love. If marriage is love of a person, it is eternity in the garments of time. The instinctive hatred of a woman for a man who violated her comes because he destroyed her freedom. She was *forced* to that which should have been her own election. The reason a man scorns a woman who "throws herself" at him is that she spoils by her overtures his right to choose. Freedom is the condition of all love, and not mere physical attraction. The latter is far wider than love. The *free choice* of another person, against the idea of attraction for one of the opposite sex, is the difference between a true marriage and an unhappy one. But because freedom is the mark of the human spirit which comes from God, a marriage based on *consent* partakes of divinity at its very beginning. More than that, it proves that he who freely chooses is also ready for sacrifice. Every consent is not only an affirmation of freedom, but also a restriction of all that would destroy the original choice. The man who chooses the woman, and the woman who accepts, both reject any attachment to others of the opposite sex. Sex becomes personalized, and therefore human and divine. As Frederick Ozanam in his *History of Civilization in the Fifth Century* wrote:

> Marriage is something greater than a contract, for it involves also a sacrifice. The woman sacrifices an irreparable gift, which was the gift of God and was the object of her mother's anxious care: her fresh young beauty, frequently her health, and that faculty of loving which women have but once. The man, in his turn, sacrifices the liberty of his youth, those incomparable years which never

return, the power of devoting himself to her whom he loves, which is vigorous only in his early years, and the ambition — inspired by love — to create a happy and glorious future. All this is possible but once in a man's life — perhaps never. Therefore Christian marriage is a double oblation, offered in two chalices, one filled with virtue, purity, and innocence; the other with unblemished self-devotion, the immortal consecration of a man to her who is weaker than himself, who was unknown to him yesterday, and with whom today he is content to spend the remainder of his life. These two cups must be both filled to the brim in order that the union may be holy and that Heaven may bless it.

Every person carries within his heart a kind of blueprint of what he loves. Plato may not have been far wrong when he described knowledge as a memory. The blueprint or the ideal is not a memory from another life, but is, rather, made up of the millions of thoughts, actions, and desires which have fused together in the making of character. One hears a melody for the first time and loves it; that is because that kind of music was already within the heart. So it is with love! A person is met and suddenly one "falls in love." May it not be that the particular person is the incarnation of an ideal? "The Word became flesh" (see John 1:14). The ideal became personal. What was dreamed became historical and real. As a French author put it: "To know a woman at the hour of desire, one must first respect her at the exquisite hour of dream." Love then is an act of faith; a declaration of the unseen as the real.

If ideals are not high, if the blueprints of love are not beautiful, then the marriage itself will not be beautiful. As some minds can listen to the barbaric tom-toms of anti-music, so there are hearts that can be satisfied with a body without a soul. Hence the need of a moral preparation for marriage. St. Francis de Sales once said that: "In marriage, one takes a vow. But it is the only instance where a vow is taken without a novitiate. If it had a year of novitiate, how few would enter into it." The novitiate of marriage must necessarily embrace two elements: the spiritualization of personal lives, in order that the sublime architectural blueprint of life's partner be formed within; and a constant prayer that God Himself will dispose historical conditions to make the dreams come true.

With marriage and its ripening with the fruit of love, there will dawn a new understanding that everyone carries with him a blueprint of the one he loves, and that One is God. The other partner then is seen as the Lord's John the Baptist, preparing the way and making straight His paths. God was just half-seen through the flesh, but thanks to life's companionship, one becomes more and more attuned to the Divine Fork that gave the original melody on the wedding day!

Love which began as passion, then became an act, and now in the autumn of life becomes once again a desire born of memory; the new "passionless passion" strains at the leash of life to be one with Life, and Truth, and Love. The words of our Lord now repeatedly come to their minds: "Those who are found worthy to attain that other world, and resurrection from the dead, take neither wife nor husband" (Luke 20:35). That means that sex, which reflected the animal kingdom, will not exist in eternity, but love, which is a reflection of God's unbodied essence, will remain their eternal ecstasy! There will be no faith in Heaven, for we will already see; there will be no hope in Heaven, for we will already possess; but there will always be love. God is Love!

Archbishop Fulton J. Sheen:
Author, Orator, and Missionary

by Fr. John A. Hardon, S.J.

During the *Tre Ore* sermon that he preached on Good Friday some years ago, Fulton J. Sheen asked his audience: "If Jesus Christ thirsted for souls, must not a Christian also thirst? If He came to cast fire on the earth, must not a Christian be enkindled? Has he not called us to be His apostles and His ambassadors, in order that His Incarnation might be prolonged through the continued dispensation of the divine through the human?" He answered his own question by declaring that, "A Catholic who does not strive to spread his Faith is a parasite on the life of the Church."[7]

This apostrophe on the duty and dignity of the Christian apostolate is a faithful description of Bishop Sheen himself, whose zeal in advancing the Kingdom of Christ in America made him "the most widely publicized 'converter' in the Church, perhaps the most famous preacher in the United States, and certainly America's best known Catholic priest."[8]

---

[7] Fulton J. Sheen, *The Rainbow of Sorrow* (New York: P.J. Kenedy and Sons, 1938), 69–70.

[8] *Pageant*, June 1950, and *Time*, April 14, 1952.

Archbishop Sheen's Book of Sacraments

Born in the small country town of El Paso, Illinois, on May 6, 1895, Fulton Sheen was ordained to the priesthood at the age of 24. After receiving a doctorate in philosophy from the University of Louvain in Belgium, and in theology from the Angelicum in Rome, he returned to the United States in 1925, and two years later began teaching philosophy at the Catholic University of America in Washington, D.C. In 1950, he was appointed national director of the Society for the Propagation of the Faith, and shortly after, went to Rome, where he was consecrated titular Bishop of Caesariana and made auxiliary to His Eminence Francis Cardinal Spellman, Archbishop of New York.

Opponent of Modern Atheism and Communism

Fulton Sheen realized from the outset that the apostolate in our times, before everything else, means to expose the errors and tactics of the enemies of Christ. Unless the evils which surround them are understood, he argued, how can faithful Christians protect themselves from contagion; and unless their disease is made known to them, how can those who now hate and revile Christ be finally converted to love Him?

The first of his sixty-six published volumes, therefore, was a carefully documented analysis of the godlessness of modern civilization, especially in the United States. "Modern philosophy," it began, "has seen the birth of a new nation of God. It is God in evolution. God *is* not; He *becomes*. In the beginning was not the Lord, but in the beginning was *Movement*. From this movement God is born by successive creations. As the world progresses, He progresses; as the world acquires perfection, He acquires perfection. (Moreover) man is a necessary step in the evolution of God. Just as man came from the beast, God will come from man.... It is the purpose of this work to examine this new notion of God," which he did, through three hundred pages of quotations from American and English pragmatists like James, atheists like Dewey, naturalists like Sellars, and agnostics like Hume, Huxley, and Hocking. His conclusion, which might serve as a thesis for all his future writings, was that: "The wisdom of the ages and the epitome of our experience is given in the simple truth

404

understood by the simple and forgotten by many a philosopher, that we are not 'God-makers but God-made.'"⁹

Between 1925 and 1937, three other books dealt with the same general theme, the decadence of western society as the result of its estrangement from God.¹⁰ By 1937, however, it became sufficiently clear to Sheen that modern atheism was not only an esoteric philosophy preached by learned professors at Harvard and Yale;¹¹ it was a new messianism emanating from Moscow and threatening to cover the face of the earth. So in the same year that Pope Pius XI issued his encyclical *On Atheistic Communism*, Msgr. Sheen published three books entitled, in sequence: *Communism, Communism and Religion,* and *Liberty Under Communism.* All through the war years, when others were silent on the subject because of our alliance with Russia, Sheen was unsparing in his denunciation of the "Red Terror."

Finally in 1948 he published *Communism and the Conscience of the West,* which competent critics have justly described as "a prerequisite for an intelligent understanding of communist thought and development."¹²

Regarding the origin of communism, Sheen is convinced that this "apocalypse of violence" is the price of our sins:

Communism is both an effect and a judgment on our Western world; an effect because it was born of our unfulfilled Christian duties, our abandonment of the Father's House in favor of

⁹ Fulton J. Sheen, *God and Intelligence* (London: Longmans Green, 1925) 1, 2, 287. The full title of this first published work was *God and Intelligence in Modern Philosophy; A Critical Study in the Light of the Philosophy of Saint Thomas.*

¹⁰ Fulton J. Sheen, *Religion without God* (London: Longmans Green, 1928); *Old Errors and New Labels* (New York: Century, 1931); *Moods and Truths* (New York: Century, 1932).

¹¹ William James, the father of American pragmatism, was professor of philosophy at Harvard until his death in 1910; and John Dewey's clearest exposition of atheistic naturalism was given in a series of lectures at Yale University in 1934.

¹² *America,* March 10, 1948.

materialism; a judgment because it reveals how wrong has been our thinking, how evil have been our deeds.[13]

Where, he asks, did the philosophy of communism begin? Not in Russia, but in the Western world of the last century. It is western in origin: its philosophy is German, its sociology French, its economics English. Karl Marx, its founder, patched the dialectics of Hegel on to the materialism of Feuerbach, to the sociology of Proudhon, to the economic problems born of liberalism, and out of it came the new gospel which has now turned upon its creators to torment them for the past.[14]

Since our generation is responsible, we must humbly acknowledge our guilt before God, sincerely repent, and do penance for the errors of the past. But even this is not enough. For "unless there is a moral revival in our Western world (especially) a rebirth of family life, communism may be the instrument for the liquidation of a bourgeois civilization that has forgotten God."[15] We are afraid of communism, and with justice; but our fears should be rational. "Communism," he says, "is not to be feared just because it is anti-God, but because we are Godless; not because it is strong but because we are weak, for if we are under God, then who can conquer us?"[16]

Christian Psychology Versus Freudianism

In 1946, Dr. Joshua Liebman, rabbi of Temple Israel, Boston, and one of the leading radio preachers in the United States, published a best seller on Freudianism called *Peace of Mind*. The first issue of twenty thousand was sold out in a month. By the end of 1947, over 475,000 copies had been

---

[13] Fulton J. Sheen, *Communism and the Conscience of the West* (Indianapolis: Bobbs-Merrill, 1948), 57.
[14] Ibid., 52.
[15] Ibid., 54.
[16] Ibid., 55.

bought by anxiety-ridden Americans who desired the peace of mind which the author promised them. But the price of this peace was high. Under the title of "Conscience doth make cowards of us all," in one chapter Rabbi Liebman disposed of sin, guilt, penance, and the commandments of God, as relics of "the early stages of mankind," from which it is high time that our scientific age should be delivered.

Liebman died not long after publishing his book, but this was too widely read and imitated by others to be left unchallenged. Fulton Sheen answered Liebman in the *Peace of Soul*, which attained a popularity not incomparable to Liebman's. Besides appearing in book form, it was also published serially in the secular newspapers, whose editors recognized that true peace is possible only with a Christian solution of the problems that are torturing men's souls.

"Unless souls are saved," Sheen began, "nothing is saved. There can be no world peace unless there is soul peace. During World War II, [Pope] Pius XII said that postwar man would be more changed than the map of postwar Europe. It is this postwar, frustrated man, or the modern soul, who interests us in this volume."[17] Fourteen chapters then follow in the order of Liebman's panegyric on Freud. He begins by "debunking" the assertion that psychoanalysis has something "new and better" to offer for the care of men's souls than the wisdom of the Church and her saints. "In the whole gamut of modern psychology there is nothing written on frustration, fears, and anxieties which can even faintly compare in depth or breadth with St. Thomas's treatise on the Passions, St. Augustine's *Confessions*, or Bossuet's treatise on Concupiscence."[18]

In answer to the rabbi, who described religion as "a fossil in an age that has turned to Marx and Freud and Einstein for salvation,"[19] Sheen logically reduced the various tensions which psychology studies to a

[17] Fulton J. Sheen, *Peace of Soul* (New York: Whittlesey House, 1949), 1.
[18] Ibid., 7.
[19] Joshua Loth Liebman, *Peace of Mind* (New York: Simon and Schuster, 1946), 179. Liebman's book was translated into Italian, with the title *Pace dello Spirito* (Milano: Bompiani, 1948). A review of the Italian translation may be found in *La Civiltà Cattolica* 3, (1949): 164–165.

reflection of the "deeper metaphysical tension, inherent in every human being, between his contingent and limited being and the Infinite and Absolute Being" of God.[20]

And instead of surrendering to one's feelings, which Liebman recommended as the condition for peace of mind, Sheen explains and proves that "anxiety cannot be cured by a surrender to passions and instincts; the basic cause of our anxiety is a restlessness within time, which comes because we are made for eternity. If there were anywhere on earth a resting place other than God, we may be very sure that the human soul in its long history would have found it before this."[21]

Speaking for the Freudians, Liebman had scoffed at the idea of guilt and sin. But sin, says Sheen, is relentless. "If we remain in sin through the denial of sin, despair takes possession of our souls." And then follows a terrible indictment of those who, under cover of science, would destroy the foundation of the moral order. "The condition of despair induced by unrepented sin often reaches a point where there is a positive fanaticism against religion and morality. He who has fallen away from the spiritual order will hate it, because religion is the reminder of his guilt."[22]

It is to the credit of the American people that *Peace of Soul* was so favorably received. It is a further tribute to their faith in God and His revealed truth that Bishop Sheen's television broadcasts every week over a national network has been officially rated as "the outstanding television contribution to American culture in 1952." These programs, called *Life Is Worth Living,* were a dramatic exposition of the principles outlined in the *Peace of Soul.* On Tuesday evenings, an estimated audience of two to five million heard and saw a Roman Catholic bishop, chalk in hand and in front of a blackboard, explain the purpose of man's life in this world; how because of the fall of Adam, sin and concupiscence have entered into our lives; how through the help of God's grace and the use of our reason, we may resist the drag of concupiscence and avoid the pitfalls

[20] *Peace of Soul,* 32.
[21] Ibid., 33.
[22] Ibid., 74.

of sin; and how if we are faithful in resisting temptation until death, we shall be happy with God for all eternity.

The DuMont Television Network, which presented the show, got no money for it, and gave the Bishop what in radio parlance is called an "obituary spot," i.e., conflicting with two very popular shows on other networks. Against this formidable competition, the Bishop made a spectacular showing. DuMont was deluged by mail response (8,500 letters a week).[23] And the popularity rating of his program is regarded as "unequalled by any other 'inspirational' or intellectual show" in American television. One TV commentator at the time remarked, "It is quite possible that he is the finest Catholic orator since Peter the Hermit."[24]

Maker of Converts

Fulton Sheen's interest in converting non-Catholics and bringing lapsed Catholics back to the Church dates from his earliest years in the priesthood. With his increased popularity as a speaker and writer, requests for instruction multiplied from prospective converts — with remarkable success. Senator Robert F. Wagner, the champion of labor; Heywood Broun, columnist and freethinker; Gretta Palmer, the writer; Fritz Kreisler, violinist; Elizabeth Bentley, communist underground worker; Henry Ford II, the motor industrialist, are some of the "notables" whom Bishop (as Fr. and Msgr.) Sheen brought to the Catholic Faith. But there have been hundreds of obscure converts too: the English actress who later became a contemplative nun; the French woman on the verge of suicide whom

[23] Bishop Sheen was the regular speaker on the Sunday afternoon broadcasts of *The Catholic Hour* from 1930 to 1950. Sponsored by the National Council of Catholic Men and the National Broadcasting Company, the program was carried by 102 radio stations in 1950. In February 1941, Msgr. Sheen had received his one hundred thousandth letter of response from the radio audience; one-third of the letters were from Protestants. As a result of one broadcast, requests for his *Prayer Book for Our Times* totaled over fifty thousand.

[24] Quoted from the *World-Telegram and Sun* in *Time*, April 14, 1952.

he saved and turned into a daily communicant; the Jewish girl, cast off by her family for becoming a Catholic, whom he set up in a beauty shop; the bigot who approached him to abuse him, and who ended as a zealous lay apostle for the Faith.

The Bishop gives three reasons why non-Catholics turn to the Church: (1) a moral crisis, especially the consciousness of sin and the desire of forgiveness, which the sacraments of the Church assure them; (2) an intellectual crisis, when people who have wandered for years in the desert of agnosticism suddenly realize that in the Catholic Faith are to be found that conviction of mind and peace of soul which they had been looking for elsewhere in vain; (3) a physical crisis such as illness, an accident, or the loss of a loved one by desertion or death, when they realize that only in the teachings of the Church can they find that courage and strength of will which they need to carry their cross in conformity to the will of God.

Before instructions are possible, a likely convert must first be disposed to wish to become a Catholic or, if lapsed, to return to the Church. Sheen went out in search of the sheep, not hesitating to call on them personally, or to call them by phone and invite them to pay him a visit.

Louis Budenz had left the Church to join the Communist Party, and eventually became managing editor of the Communist *Daily Worker*. In 1937 he publicly invited Catholics to join forces with communism in the interest of world peace. Fulton Sheen answered him in a pamphlet in which he said: "I am convinced that the greatest propagandists of communism know practically nothing factual about it. They talk of Russia either in general terms or in the stereotyped language of its propaganda. That is why I believe many communists are in good faith, and here I include you, Mr. Budenz."

Not satisfied with this, the Monsignor arranged to meet Budenz personally in a New York hotel. At dinner together, Budenz started to argue in favor of the democratic merits of the new Soviet Constitution. But, as he later confessed, "Msgr. Sheen knows the secret of dealing with people who have broken with the Church. Pushing aside the remaining cutlery on the table as though to waive any argumentation, Monsignor bent forward and exclaimed: 'Let us now talk of the Blessed Virgin!'"

Archbishop Fulton J. Sheen

This was the beginning of the end. Budenz continues: "Immediately, I was conscious of the senselessness and sinfulness of my life as I then lived it. The peace that flows from Mary, and which had been mine in the early days, flashed back to me with an overwhelming vividness. There rang in my ears for a moment the prayer which comes from the salutation of Gabriel: 'Ave Maria, gratia plena.' How often, I thought, has that supplication gone up from thousands in distress and brought them peace—and I, who know better, reject it!"[25] It took six more years of persistent effort, patient correspondence, and prayer, but finally Budenz returned to the Church and has since become one of the star witnesses before the American Congress in its fight against communism in the States.

Clare Boothe Luce, congresswoman and ambassador to Italy, described her conversion to the Faith in *McCall's* magazine (circulation 4,150,347) in a series of articles called *The True Reason*. Speaking of the man whose instructions saved her from "the godless and atavistic underbrush of Freudianism" and brought her into the peace of God's truth, she says:

Many people are curious about Msgr. Fulton J. Sheen. I would like to satisfy their curiosity, because it always pleases me to talk about him. He was so great a friend, being so great a friend of God's, when I needed such a friend so greatly. I can tell you that it is true when it is said that in his apostolic zeal he generates both heat and light. I never knew a teacher who could be at once so patient and yet so unyielding, so poetic and so practical, so inventive and so orthodox. But rumor to the contrary, there is nothing particularly hypnotic about Fr. Sheen. What 'hypnotizes' his converts is the sudden and unfamiliar sight of Truth and Love and Life eternal, which his instructions open up to them. This 'hypnotism' soon wears off as Fr. Sheen hopes it will, when you come to realize that the sight of these things which all men seek is in reality the sight

[25] Louis F. Budenz, *This Is My Story* (New York: McGraw-Hill, 1947), 162–163.

of Home; and Home is a place where you may move easily and freely and need not strike attitudes or talk in whispers.

For this brilliant teacher, this good and gifted professor of Catholic philosophy, I thank God. I have often been asked, 'Would you have become a Catholic if you had not had Fr. Sheen to give you instructions?' My answer is, 'Of course.' God intended me to be a Catholic or He would not have sent me to Fr. Sheen, the one best equipped to rid my mind of nonsense and fill it with the sense of our Lord Jesus.[26]

National Director of the Propagation of the Faith

In 1950, Msgr. Sheen took over the direction of the Society for the Propagation of the Faith in the United States. With this new appointment, he resigned as teacher of philosophy and subsequently produced results that were truly amazing.

To make the Missions better known, he began a "revolutionary streamlining of Catholic money-raising methods." Checking over the new trends in the secular publishing field, he found that small, pocket-sized magazines are becoming most popular. The first step then was to change the large rotogravure *Catholic Missions* into the 14x10-centimeter *Mission* booklet, which came out every two months and ran to forty-eight pages. Pointed epigrams: "Most people are unhappy because they make no sacrifice for others"; urgent appeals like the picture of a starving Chinese baby, subtitled: "Hunger: two-thirds of the people of the world go to bed hungry every night"; striking quotations like the one from Pascal: "Mohammed chose the way of human success, Jesus Christ the way of human defeat"; statistics on the Missions, like: "In St. Peter's Parish, Bombay, a total of 55,000 Holy Communions were distributed in two months"—were integrated with a running commentary on the sufferings of the pagans and the work of the missionaries, contrasted with the prosperity in the States and the need for self-sacrifice if the wish of Christ "that they all may be one" (John 17:21) is ever to be fulfilled.

---

[26] *McCall's*, April 1947.

Archbishop Fulton J. Sheen

Besides the little *Mission* for popular appeal, Bishop Sheen started a new quarterly, *World Mission*, a scholarly magazine which received contributions from experts in the mission field. For example, the Spring 1953 issue had an article on "The Catholic Church and Indian Culture," another on "Federation in British Central Africa," also "Craftsmen of Ranchi," "Opportunities in Viet Nam," etc. — all carefully documented with cross-references and footnotes. There follow a dozen pages on "Current Trends," dealing with subjects like "Christian Art Trends in Asia," "Catholic Textbooks for Japan," and "Polygamy, West African Plague." The last twenty pages were given to short reviews of books which treat of the Missions or mission lands.

Finally, to keep a constant reminder before the people of their obligation to the Missions, the Bishop wrote a syndicated column, *God Love You* — a mixture of mission news and ten-word ferverinos — which ran in all the Catholic weeklies throughout the country. It was made strikingly personal by the Bishop's acknowledgment of gifts received for the Missions. Thus: "God love you to J. F. G. 'Please accept this donation of $10 for the Missions. I was going to buy a book with it, but maybe the Missions could use some books in my name,... God love you to Mrs. J. K. who sacrificed going to the movies to send $5 to the Holy Father's Missions.... God love you to A.D. 'My mother just got *Mission*, and I feel very sorry for that hungry little girl, and this $1 of my savings is to feed her. I am 8.' ... God love you to T. L. 'Enclosed please find a money order for $15.65. This is my first job and I want my first week's pay to go to the Holy Father's Missions.'" Always the weekly column stressed the need to pray for the Missions, pointing out that, "The most worthy of causes is to pray for the 1.1 billion pagans in the world who know neither the Sacred Heart, nor the Immaculate Heart."

Apostle of the Mother of God

No account of his prodigious achievement would be complete without reference to Bishop Sheen's personal devotion to the Mother of God and the efforts he made to extend this devotion in the United States.

All of his published books are formally dedicated to the Blessed Virgin Mary, with each dedication different and each a declaration of its author's own great love for the Mother of Christ.

Thus: *"Reginae sine labe originali conceptae.... Mule beneficiorum memor Ejusdem Virginis patrocinio.... Dedicat auctor indignus."*

Again: "Dedicated to Mary, Gracious Mother-Heart of the World's Savior, In prayerful hope of the Conversion of Russia."

And again: "Dedicated to the Woman I love, The Woman whom even God dreamed of before the world was made; The Woman of whom I was born, at cost of pain and labor at a Cross. The Woman who, though no priest, could yet on Calvary's Hill breathe: 'This is my Body; this is my Blood.' For none save her gave Him human life. The Woman who guides my pen, which falters so with words, in telling of the Word. The Woman who, in a world of Reds, shows forth the blue of hope."[27]

At least three entire volumes deal expressly with the subject of Mary.[28] And in most of the others she figures so largely that, without her, the books would lose their organic unity. However, it is in *The World's First Love*, that something of the secret of Bishop Sheen's inspiration and a reason for his success in the apostolate are best revealed. Commenting on the divine paradox which makes Mary at once the Virgin of virgins and the Spiritual Mother of all men, Bishop Sheen wrote:

As virginity is not the opposite of love, neither is it the opposite of generation. The Christian blessing on virginity did not abrogate

---

[27] The three selected dedications are taken, in sequence, from the following books: *God and Intelligence, Communism and the Conscience of the West,* and *The World's First Love.*

[28] Best known are the children's book *The Queen of the Seven Swords* (Fort Wayne, IN: Our Sunday Visitor Press, 1934); *Seven Words of Jesus and Mary* (New York: P. J. Kenedy and Sons, 1945); and the children's book *Jesus, Son of Mary,* 1947.

the order of Genesis to 'increase and multiply,' for virginity, also, has its generation. Mary's consecration of virginity was unique in that it resulted in a physical generation—the Word made flesh. But it also set the pattern for spiritual generation, for she begot the Christ-life. In like manner, virgin love must not be barren but, like Paul, must say: 'I have begotten you as most dear children in Christ.'

God who hated the man who buried his talent in the ground, will certainly despise those who pledge themselves to be in love with Him, and yet show no new life—converts or souls saved through contemplation. Birth control, whether undertaken by husband and wife, or by a virgin dedicated to Christ, is reprehensible. On Judgment Day, God will ask all the married and all virgins the same question: 'Where are your children?' Virginity is meant for generation as much as married love is, otherwise the Model-Virgin would not have been the Mother of Christ, giving an example to others to be the fathers and mothers of Christians.[29]

Bishop Sheen strived to live up to this ideal. In imitation of Mary, he was cooperating with God in bringing the life of Christ to thousands of souls who never knew Him or who, having known, forgot Him. And God blessed these efforts with an abundance of grace.

---

[29] Fulton J. Sheen, *The World's First Love* (New York: McGraw-Hill, 1952), 170–171.

Acknowledgments

I want to thank Almighty God for the health of mind, body, and spirit to put together these reflections.

To my good wife, Isabel, my children, and my grandchildren, who keep me young at heart and are truly a blessing from God. Thank you for sharing in my joy.

I wish to express my gratitude to members of the Archbishop Fulton John Sheen Foundation in Peoria, Illinois — in particular, to the Most Rev. Daniel R. Jenky, C.S.C., Bishop of Peoria, for your leadership and fidelity to the cause of Sheen's canonization and the creation of this book.

To Julie Enzenberger, O.C.V., who repeated to me time and time again Sheen's words: "Believe the incredible, and you can do the impossible."

To the staff of Inter Mirifica, who have given permission to use extensive quotes from some of the writings of the Servant of God Fr. John Hardon, S.J., in the introduction of this book. For more information about Fr. Hardon's books and articles, please visit www.intermirifica.org. And for details regarding his cause for beatification and canonization, please visit https://hardonsj.org.

To Thomas J. Nash, who brought his thirty-plus years of editing experience to this endeavor. Tom's grasp and appreciation of both Sacred Scripture and the *Catechism of the Catholic Church* provided the necessary bridge for making Archbishop Sheen's writings relatable to today's reader.

Archbishop Sheen's Book of Sacraments

To my good friend and radio mentor, Terry Barber. Your passion for bringing souls to Christ through the teachings of Archbishop Fulton J. Sheen is infectious. Your cassette tape ministry that began in the 1980s to help share the recordings and writings of Archbishop Fulton J. Sheen has enriched the lives of countless souls. Thank you for telling everyone who would listen, "Your life is worth living." Full Sheen ahead my friend! Full Sheen ahead!

To the many seminarians, priests, religious, bishops, and cardinals I have met during this journey. Always remember the words of Archbishop Sheen that "The priest is not his own."

To the tens of thousands of people I have met in my travels, giving presentations about Archbishop Fulton J. Sheen at parishes, conferences, universities, high schools, church groups, and even pubs: thank you for sharing with me your many "Sheen Stories." I truly cherish each one of them.

And lastly, to Archbishop Fulton J. Sheen, whose teachings on prayer, the sacraments, our Lord's Passion, and His Seven Last Words continue to inspire me to love God more and to appreciate the gift of the Church. His teachings and his encouragement to make a holy hour each day has been a true gift in my life. May I be so blessed as to imitate Archbishop Sheen's love for the saints, the sacraments, the Eucharist, and for the Mother of God. May the Good Lord grant him a very high place in Heaven!

— Al Smith

Works Used in This Book

Fulton J. Sheen
(1895–1979)

Fulton John Sheen was born in El Paso, Illinois, in 1895. In high school, he won a three-year university scholarship, but he turned it down to pursue a vocation to the priesthood. He attended St. Viator College Seminary in Illinois and St. Paul Seminary in Minnesota. In 1919, he was ordained a priest for the Diocese of Peoria, Illinois. He earned a licentiate in sacred theology and a bachelor of canon law at the Catholic University of America and a doctorate at the Catholic University of Louvain, Belgium.

Sheen received numerous teaching offers but declined them in obedience to his bishop and became an assistant pastor in a rural parish. Having thus tested his obedience, the bishop later permitted him to teach at the Catholic University of America and at St. Edmund's College in Ware, England, where he met G. K. Chesterton, whose weekly BBC radio broadcast inspired Sheen's later NBC broadcast, *The Catholic Hour* (1930–1952).

In 1952, Sheen began appearing on ABC in his own series, *Life Is Worth Living*. Despite being given a time slot that forced him to compete with Milton Berle and Frank Sinatra, the dynamic Sheen enjoyed enormous success and in 1954 reached tens of millions of viewers, non-Catholics as well as Catholics.

When asked by Pope Pius XII how many converts he had made, Sheen responded, "Your Holiness, I have never counted them. I am always afraid if I did count them, I might think I made them, instead of the Lord."

Sheen gave annual Good Friday homilies at New York's St. Patrick's Cathedral, led numerous retreats for priests and religious, and preached at summer conferences in England.

"If you want people to stay as they are," he said, "tell them what they want to hear. If you want to improve them, tell them what they should know." This he did, not only in his preaching but also in the more than ninety books he wrote. His *Peace of Soul* was sixth on the *New York Times* best-seller list.

Sheen served as auxiliary bishop of New York (1951–1966) and as bishop of Rochester (1966–1969).

His two great loves were for the Blessed Mother and the Eucharist. He made a daily holy hour before the Blessed Sacrament, from which he drew strength and inspiration to preach the gospel and in the presence of which he prepared his homilies. "I beg [Christ] every day to keep me strong physically and alert mentally in order to preach His gospel and proclaim His Cross and Resurrection," he said. "I am so happy doing this that I sometimes feel that when I come to the good Lord in Heaven, I will take a few days' rest and then ask Him to allow me to come back again to this earth to do some more work."

The good Lord called Fulton Sheen home in 1979. His television broadcasts, now on recordings, and his books continue his earthly work of winning souls for Christ. Sheen's cause for canonization was opened in 2002, and in 2012 Pope Benedict XVI declared him "Venerable."

Sophia Institute

Sophia Institute is a nonprofit institution that seeks to nurture the spiritual, moral, and cultural life of souls and to spread the Gospel of Christ in conformity with the authentic teachings of the Roman Catholic Church.

Sophia Institute Press fulfills this mission by offering translations, reprints, and new publications that afford readers a rich source of the enduring wisdom of mankind.

Sophia Institute also operates the popular online resource CatholicExchange.com. *Catholic Exchange* provides world news from a Catholic perspective as well as daily devotionals and articles that will help readers to grow in holiness and live a life consistent with the teachings of the Church.

In 2013, Sophia Institute launched Sophia Institute for Teachers to renew and rebuild Catholic culture through service to Catholic education. With the goal of nurturing the spiritual, moral, and cultural life of souls, and an abiding respect for the role and work of teachers, we strive to provide materials and programs that are at once enlightening to the mind and ennobling to the heart; faithful and complete, as well as useful and practical.

Sophia Institute gratefully recognizes the Solidarity Association for preserving and encouraging the growth of our apostolate over the course of many years. Without their generous and timely support, this book would not be in your hands.

www.SophiaInstitute.com
www.CatholicExchange.com
www.SophiaInstituteforTeachers.org

Sophia Institute Press® is a registered trademark of Sophia Institute.
Sophia Institute is a tax-exempt institution as defined by the
Internal Revenue Code, Section 501(c)(3). Tax ID 22-2548708.